Soldiers of a Different Cloth

SOLDIERS
of a
DIFFERENT CLOTH

Notre Dame Chaplains in World War II

JOHN F. WUKOVITS

University of Notre Dame Press • *Notre Dame, Indiana*

Published by the University of Notre Dame Press
Notre Dame, Indiana 46556
undpress.nd.edu
All Rights Reserved

Published in the United States of America

Library of Congress Cataloging-in-Publication Data

Names: Wukovits, John F., 1944– author. | Jenkins, John I., writer of foreword. | Hesburgh, Theodore M. (Theodore Martin), 1917–2015, writer of introduction.
Title: Soldiers of a Different Cloth : Notre Dame Chaplains in World War II / John F. Wukovits ; foreword by Fr. John I. Jenkins, C.S.C. ; introduction by Rev. Theodore M. Hesburgh, C.S.C.
Description: Notre Dame, Indiana : University of Notre Dame Press, [2018] | Includes bibliographical references and index. |
Identifiers: LCCN 2018021925 (print) | LCCN 2018025343 (ebook) | ISBN 9780268103958 (pdf) | ISBN 9780268103965 (epub) | ISBN 9780268103934 (cloth : alk. paper) | ISBN 0268103933 (cloth : alk. paper)
Subjects: LCSH: World War, 1939–1945—Chaplains—United States. | Military chaplains—United States—Biography. | University of Notre Dame—Biography.
Classification: LCC D810.C36 (ebook) | LCC D810.C36 U68   2018 (print) | DDC 940.54/78092273—dc23
LC record available at https://lccn.loc.gov/2018021925

∞ *The paper in this book meets the guidelines for permanence and durability of the Committee on Production Guidelines for Book Longevity of the Council on Library Resources*

To my father, Tom, ND '38, and my mother, Grace
Their spirituality was matched by
their love for Notre Dame.
A starting guard on the
1936 National Championship basketball team,
Tom married Grace in the
university's Log Chapel.
They never lost their love for each other
or for Notre Dame.

CONTENTS

PART I

THE CHAPLAINS HEAD TO WAR
1920s to December 1943

FOREWORD

Moments before they were to engage in the Battle of Gettysburg, the Civil War's bloodiest battle with 51,000 casualties, the mostly Catholic Irish Brigade knelt to receive absolution from Father William Corby, C.S.C., a Holy Cross priest from the University of Notre Dame and the brigade's chaplain. Although absolution was common on the fighting fields of Europe, this was the first time it had been given on an American battlefield.

Union Colonel St. Clair Mulholland, attached to the Irish Brigade, gave this eyewitness account:

> The brigade was standing at "order arms," and as he [Corby] closed his address, every man fell on his knees, with head bowed down. Then, stretching his right hand towards the brigade, Father Corby pronounced the words of absolution. The scene was more than impressive, it was awe-inspiring.
>
> Near by, stood General Hancock, surrounded by a brilliant throng of officers, who had gathered to witness this very unusual occurrence and while there was profound silence in the ranks of the Second Corps, yet over to the left, out by the peach orchard and Little Round Top, where Weed, and Vincent, and Haslett were dying, the roar of the battle rose and swelled and echoed through the woods.

The act seemed to be in harmony with all the surroundings. I do not think there was a man in the brigade who did not offer up a heartfelt prayer. For some it was their last; they knelt there in their grave-clothes—in less than half an hour many of them were numbered with the dead of July 2.

Fr. Corby would later recall, "That general absolution was intended for all—in quantum possum—not only for our brigade, but for all, North or South, who were susceptible of it and who were about to appear before their Judge."

Of the hundreds of monuments erected at Gettysburg to commemorate leaders of the South and North, only one is dedicated to a chaplain, Father Corby. However, he would not be the last of his Holy Cross brethren to leave the classroom to answer God's call in war. I recently had the privilege to recognize Father William Dorwart, C.S.C., who served as a navy chaplain in Korea, the Philippines, and Operations Desert Shield and Desert Storm in Iraq, as well as on the U.S.S. *Ronald Reagan* and finally at Arlington National Cemetery.

Holy Cross priests have served God in many ways during peacetime and war. Considering Notre Dame's historic links with the military, it is of no surprise that members of its founding order would volunteer as chaplains, especially during World War II.

The writer, John Wukovits (ND '67), a renowned military author, has in these pages revealed remarkable contributions of thirty-five C.S.C. religious—mostly priests, but brothers and sisters too—in chaplaincies during World War II. None carried weapons, yet they still parachuted into Normandy on D-Day, walked shoulder-to-shoulder with American GIs on the horrific Philippine Death March, survived the bloody combat at Anzio, and prayed for and with the liberators of Dachau and its tortured victims and survivors.

The stories of these heroic members of the Holy Cross order have never been told before. John Wukovits dug deeply into the Notre Dame archives and elsewhere to bring them to light. He does it adroitly, with a historian's care and a writer's heart. We are in his debt.

—Fr. John I. Jenkins, C.S.C.,
President, University of Notre Dame

PREFACE

The genesis of this book came from an unexpected place. As a World War II historian, I am usually digging around in archives or scouring books and reports searching for dramatic story lines, but this emerged from a book unrelated, I thought, to that conflict. While reading a history of my alma mater, Notre Dame, written in the 1950s, I came across a paragraph mentioning that a group of priests from the university had served as chaplains during the war. The author expressed the hope that one day, someone would write their story. I agreed that a potential story existed, but only if these chaplains had experiences beyond the typical stateside posts.

I was astounded as I conducted my initial research. Far from remaining in the United States, these men served in both theaters and in many conflicts. Two struggled to survive the Bataan Death March, and others worked amid shell bursts and bullets in Italy, France, Germany, Belgium, the Philippines, Iwo Jima, Saipan, and dozens of other locales. Better yet, when I first visited one of the four valuable archives at the University of Notre Dame—one for the university itself and one each for the priests, brothers, and nuns of the Congregation of Holy Cross, the religious order that founded Notre Dame—I found a vast collection of letters, papers, records, and photographs relating to their wartime service. The chaplains corresponded with their superior, Father Thomas A. Steiner, explaining their duties and recounting what they had observed. Some, such as the powerful letters Father Joseph

Barry wrote to Father Steiner, moved me with their descriptions of battle and of the painful letters all had to write to the parents of slain young soldiers. It did not take me long to conclude that I would have more than enough material to proceed.

I started with the first of numerous visits to the four archives at Notre Dame and its sister institutions, Saint Mary's College and Holy Cross College, both directly across the street from Notre Dame. I spent hours scanning and reading the letters of Father Barry and the other Holy Cross chaplains held at the Congregation of Holy Cross's U.S. Province Archives Center, where Father Christopher Kuhn, C.S.C., and his assistant Deb Buzzard—two of the most skilled and cooperative archivists a historian will ever meet—went out of their way to locate pertinent records and photographs. Sister Catherine Osimo, C.S.C., at the Congregational Archives and Records, Sisters of the Holy Cross, and Brother Larry Stewart, C.S.C., at the Archives, Brothers of Holy Cross, directed me to valuable material pertaining to the stories of the six religious from Notre Dame—two priests, two brothers, and two nuns—trapped in the Philippines with the onset of war, while Sister Mary Nadine Mathias, Diocese of Toledo, Ohio Archives, opened the vast collection of material relating to Father John E. Duffy. I obtained additional material from archivist Corey Stewart at the National Archives and Records Administration in St. Louis, Missouri; curator Michael Gonzales of the 45th Infantry Division Museum in Oklahoma City, Oklahoma; and from the U.S. Army Chaplain Corps Museum in Fort Jackson, South Carolina.

Other people offered immense help. The late Father Theodore Hesburgh, former president of the University of Notre Dame, provided his insights about the chaplains during our interviews and lent his encouragement to what he deemed a valuable project. My history adviser at Notre Dame, the late Dr. Bernard Norling, and the late Thomas Buell, biographer extraordinaire, provided encouragement and advice to a novice writer when he most needed it. My agent, Jim Hornfischer, who has penned fascinating World War II books of his own, lent his expert comments at every stage of the process. I will never forget their wisdom and patience.

As always, the love and support offered by my family has been invaluable. My brother, Tom, also a graduate of Notre Dame; the memory of my late brother, Fred; and my three daughters, Amy, Julie, and Karen, boosted me during those difficult times during the writing process. I breathed easier knowing that Terri Faitel, my companion of more than two decades, would scrutinize every paragraph of my manuscript with the same skill and professionalism she exhibits in her work as an unparalleled mathematics coordinator in Michigan. The exuberance and joy of my grandchildren, Matthew, Megan, Emma, and Kaitlyn, add an extra bounce to my step (or else I'd never keep pace with them!).

Finally, the unquestioned love of my parents, Tom (ND '38) and Grace, who were married in the Log Chapel adjoining the beautiful Saint Mary's Lake on Notre Dame's campus, have been with me all my life. Although they passed on long ago, I think of them every day. It is only fitting that I dedicate this book to two people who so deeply cared for the university.

John F. Wukovits
Trenton, Michigan
January 12, 2018

INTRODUCTION

Of the many blessings that have come my way during the course of my half-century association with the University of Notre Dame, including serving as its president from 1952 to 1987, one of the most rewarding has been the friendships formed with the people with whom I have come into contact. Prime ministers, presidents, civil rights leaders, educators, and financiers have crossed my path, most of whom have amassed sterling public reputations.

I am especially proud of my association with the individuals historian John F. Wukovits features in this book. In powerful detail he relates the stirring feats of thirty-five individuals who, while garnering little acclaim, performed deeds worthy of the highest praise. They did not carve out fortunes or build nations. Instead, as chaplains during World War II, they aided young men who, because they faced death on a daily basis, turned to chaplains for strength and courage. Because of my acquaintances with these thirty-five, each has left an indelible impression that daily reminds me to perform to the best of my ability while retaining the humility with which these men labored.

They served wherever duty sent them and wherever the war dictated. These chaplains experienced the horrors of the Death March in the Philippines and in the filthy holds of the infamous Hell Ships. They dangled from a parachute while descending toward German fire at Normandy and shivered in Belgium's frigid snows during the Battle of the Bulge. They languished in German and Japanese prison camps, and stood speechless at Dachau, a symbol of all that was wrong with the world.

They were present at Anzio and Iwo Jima, at Monte Cassino and Okinawa. Their service took them from the beauties of South Seas islands to the dangers of flying the Hump in Burma, from celebrating Mass aboard the decks of massive aircraft carriers to makeshift altars set up on the front hoods of tiny jeeps. They served in almost every major campaign in both Europe and the Pacific.

While soldiers and marines battled the Germans or Japanese with rifles and grenades, these chaplains dodged bullets and shells to aid the wounded and bring comfort to the dying. They volunteered for duty not to hurt, as marines, soldiers, and sailors must do, but to help their fellow man. They brought to the battlefield a sense of sacrifice, the love of their fellow man, and a devotion to assisting others that helped offset the impact of bullets and bombs. They were, in effect, soldiers, but instead of inflicting harm they attempted to bring comfort and solace to scared young men.

Making their stories more poignant is that though these chaplains were involved in separate war theaters thousands of miles apart, they were hardly strangers. Each had either graduated from or taught at the University of Notre Dame in South Bend, Indiana, and most belonged to the Congregation of Holy Cross (C.S.C.), the religious organization that founded and, to this day, operates the university. Not only did these men share an attachment from their association with Notre Dame—a place that appears frequently in their correspondence with family and friends—they also drew inspiration from their brother chaplains and strength from their days at Notre Dame that helped them endure the challenges they encountered.

On Notre Dame's campus, where I first met many of these priests, each day the students pass a saying that adorns an arch at the university's Sacred Heart Basilica. "God, Country, Notre Dame" reads the inscription. Honoring Notre Dame men who lost their lives in World War I, the words refer to the duty each Notre Dame graduate has to his Creator, his country, and his school. These chaplains not only read those words; they lived them. As such, these men inspired me and countless others throughout their lives.

They provided decency in an indecent universe and spiritual peace on a stage of turmoil. They offered a touch of home, sanity, and calmness in a world that threatened to demolish all three. They learned that there were no Catholics or Baptists in foxholes, just scared young boys who wanted sanctuary from violence and a shoulder upon which to lean.

A group of men devoted to peace, they stepped into the most violent arena imaginable, the opposite of that love and brotherhood about which they so frequently preached. The university's fabled teams under Knute Rockne and Frank Leahy were called the Fighting Irish for their prowess on the football field, but this group earned their accolades on violent battlefields by declining to fight and without resorting to violence. Instead, they defended their nation by serving their fellow man in his hour of supreme need and helping those in peril on brutal battlefields, many of whom would soon die or suffer from hideous wounds.

Ranging in age from twenty-two to fifty-three, they were counselor, friend, parent, and older brother to the boys they served. They included the soft-spoken Father Joseph D. Barry, C.S.C., who said Mass in abandoned buildings and fields and gained every soldier's admiration for his dashes through gunfire to aid a stricken infantryman, earning a Silver Star in the process. They counted among their numbers the ebullient Father Francis L. Sampson, who jumped into Normandy and became known as the "Parachute Padre" for his willingness to endure the same hardships as his men. They and the other chaplains worked with soldiers who were daily at death's threshold, and in doing so they without hesitation placed themselves in the same peril.

Their motives for entering the chaplaincy varied. Some asked how they could possibly minister to young men after the war if they had not shared the sacrifices faced by those young men during the war. Others could not stand on the sidelines while millions of soldiers suffered and sacrificed. For most, it simply came down to patriotism: their country was at war, and they had to do their part in making the world a safer place. Though they detested war, they could be nowhere else, for on the battlefield was where men most needed spiritual comfort.

John Wukovits's professional background in World War II history—over a thirty-year career he has authored ten books and served as on-air commentator and adviser for television documentaries—as well as his own association with the university as a 1967 graduate, lend credence to his research and writing. His knowledge of World War II history, combined with his ties to the university, make him ideal to tell this story of men who comprised one of Notre Dame's greatest teams.

Because of their service, they were changed individuals by war's end. Some later assessed those years as the most vibrant times in their careers because, unlike teaching school or preaching Sunday sermons, they brought succor to individuals placed in the direst of situations. While in the seminary these men hoped to make a difference in people's lives and become involved with something truly significant. World War II provided that chance.

Besides having a front-row seat to major World War II campaigns, these Notre Dame chaplains left a mark on the young men they served. Their stories offer a unique glimpse of a war that is usually viewed through the prism of military leaders and battle strategies. Enjoy their feats and, as I was, be inspired by them.

Rev. Theodore M. Hesburgh, C.S.C.
University of Notre Dame

CHRONOLOGY

1934

May 1: Diocesan priest Father John E. Duffy arrives in the Philippines for three years of duty as an army chaplain.

1939

September 1: World War II begins when Adolf Hitler's German forces invade Poland.

December: Bishop John F. O'Hara, C.S.C., Notre Dame's president, is appointed military delegate in the Military Ordinariate to manage the increasing numbers of Catholic priests entering service to become chaplains.

1940

April: Father Duffy returns to the Philippines.

1941

April: Father Joseph D. Barry, C.S.C., is posted to the U.S. Army's 157th Regiment of the 45th Infantry Division.

November 9: Six Holy Cross missionaries—Father Jerome Lawyer, Father Robert McKee, Brother Rex Hennel, Brother Theodore Kapes, Sister Mary Olivette, and Sister Mary Caecilius—board the ocean liner *President Grant* for a six-week voyage across the Pacific to their new mission posts in India.

December 4: The six missionaries arrive in Manila, intent on remaining only a few days before continuing their voyage to India.

December 7 (December 8 in the Philippines): The Japanese attack the U.S. naval base at Pearl Harbor and begin a war with the United States.

1942

January 1: In the Philippines, General Douglas MacArthur's forces complete their withdrawal into the Bataan Peninsula. Diocesan priests Father Richard E. Carberry and Father John Duffy work among those beleaguered forces as chaplains.

January 2: The Japanese enter the city of Manila, trapping the six missionaries in that city. The two priests and brothers are confined at the Ateneo de Manila, a Jesuit College in Manila, while the two nuns are ordered to Manila's Convent of the Assumption. The six remain there until July 1944.

March 11: General MacArthur leaves the Philippines after being ordered by President Franklin D. Roosevelt to do so.

April 3: Major General Edward P. King Jr. surrenders the forces on Bataan. Fathers Duffy and Carberry now face uncertain futures as prisoners of war.

April 9: The infamous Death March, in which thousands of American and Filipino forces, including Fathers Duffy and Carberry, were brutally forced to walk to prison camps miles away, begins.

April 22: On the Death March, Father Duffy is bayoneted by a cruel guard nicknamed the Shadow and left for dead. Friendly Filipino civilians drag the badly wounded priest to a jungle hideout and nurse him to health.

April 23 (or later): Father Carberry is incarcerated at Camp O'Donnell, northwest of Manila.

May: Diocesan priest Father Francis L. Sampson arrives at Fort Benning, Georgia, to begin training for eventual posting with the U.S. Army's 501st Parachute Regiment.

May 6: General Jonathan M. Wainwright surrenders all forces in the Philippines to the Japanese.

June: After recovering from his bayonet wounds, Father Duffy joins and helps organize guerrilla forces in the Bataan region; traveling from unit to unit, he also ministers to different groups of American and Filipino guerrillas. The Japanese move Father Carberry to the prison camp at Cabanatuan.

November 7: Father Carberry is transferred to Davao Penal Colony in Mindanao.

1943

January: The Japanese apprehend Father Duffy and incarcerate him in Bilibid Prison in Manila, where he would remain until December 1944.

April 4: Father Carberry, believing his duty rested with the incarcerated and not with his own desire for freedom, chooses not to join ten other inmates in what would turn out to be a successful attempt to escape from Davao Penal Colony.

June 3: Father Barry and the 157th Regiment board transports for the journey across the Atlantic.

July 10: Father Barry and the 157th Regiment land at Sicily and begin combat with German forces.

September 9: Father Barry and the 157th Regiment land at Salerno on the Italian peninsula.

1944

January 22: Father Barry and the 157th Regiment land at Anzio and become involved in a bloody, months-long battle with German defenders.

February 1: Father John M. Dupuis, C.S.C., lands on Roi in the Marshall Islands with his Fourth Marine Division.

June 5: Father Barry and the 157th Regiment enter Rome, thereby concluding nine months of near-constant combat.

June 6: Father Sampson parachutes into Normandy with the 501st Parachute Infantry Regiment; the Japanese move Father Carberry back to Cabanatuan.

June 15: The battleship aboard which Father John J. Burke, C.S.C., works, U.S.S. *Pennsylvania* (BB-38), blasts targets on Saipan in the Mariana Islands. Father Dupuis lands on Saipan with the Fourth Marine Division.

July 8: The Japanese move the six Notre Dame missionaries to Los Baños Internment Camp, southeast of Manila.

August: Father Edmund J. Murray, C.S.C., arrives in Europe with the U.S. Army's 104th Infantry Division and enters combat in France. Over the coming months he also sees action in Belgium and Germany.

August 1: A Japanese document outlines the steps that prisoner-of-war camp commandants are to take if their camps are about to fall to approaching American forces. The chilling document ordered the immediate massacre of all inmates by any means.

August 15: Aboard the escort carrier U.S.S. *Tulagi* (CVE-72) as a navy chaplain, Father Henry Heintskill, C.S.C., participates in the invasion of southern France; the carrier then departs for the Pacific. Father Barry lands in southern France with his 157th Regiment, which embarks on a drive northward toward the German border.

September 17: Father Sampson parachutes into Holland with the 501st Parachute Infantry Regiment, his second jump into enemy-held territory with the airborne troops.

September 21: The people confined at Los Baños, including the six Notre Dame missionaries, spot U.S. aircraft for the first time since early 1942. The indications that American military forces would soon invade the Philippines cause the prisoners to erupt in celebration.

October 20: The hopes of liberation for those at Los Baños and other prison camps in the Philippines intensify when General MacArthur's forces conduct an amphibious assault of Leyte, an island four hundred miles southeast of Manila.

December 13: The Japanese jam more than 1,600 prisoners, including Fathers Duffy and Carberry, onto the transport *Oryoku Maru* for shipment to Japan.

December 14–15: American carrier aircraft, unaware that the *Oryoku Maru* contains American prisoners of war, attack and sink the transport in Subic Bay, fifty miles northwest of Manila. Fathers Duffy and Carberry survive a one-mile swim to shore, but the attacks kill more than two hundred prisoners.

December 16: Father Sampson and the 501st Parachute Infantry Regiment are ordered to rush to Bastogne, Belgium, to reinforce a faltering American line and help halt Hitler's desperate December counteroffensive.

December 20: While driving into dangerous territory in front of American lines to aid wounded and dying American troops, Father Sampson is captured by German forces. He begins a trek on foot covering more than 150 miles to trains inside Germany, which take him to his prison camp north of Berlin, Stalag II-A.

January 9: American forces land at Lingayen Gulf, placing friendly units closer to Philippine prison camps and bringing liberation nearer. Unfortunately for the captives, treatment at the hands of their Japanese captors worsens.

January 14: The *Brazil Maru*, a Japanese "Hell Ship," leaves the Philippines to take prisoners of war, including Fathers Duffy and Carberry, to prison camps in Japan.

January 26: With Father Duffy administering the Last Rites to him, Father Carberry succumbs to wounds, starvation, and disease.

January 30: The *Brazil Maru* arrives in Japan, where Father Duffy is taken to Omuta Camp #17 on Kyushu.

February 19: Three Notre Dame chaplains operate with their forces at Iwo Jima in the Pacific: Father Heintskill aboard the U.S.S. *Tulagi*, Father Francis J. Boland aboard the transport U.S.S. *Highlands* (APA-119), and Father Dupuis with the Fourth Marine Division.

February 21: After learning that the Japanese plan to massacre every person at Los Baños, General MacArthur orders U.S. Army Rangers to parachute into the camp to free the inmates.

February 23: In a daring raid, paratroopers liberate everyone at Los Baños, including the six Notre Dame missionaries.

March 17: Father Maurice E. Powers, C.S.C., approaches the German border with members of the U.S. Army's 101st Mechanized Cavalry.

March 29: Father Powers and the 101st Mechanized Cavalry cross the Rhine River and thrust into Germany.

April: In mid-April, Father Barry and the 157th Regiment approach Nuremburg, the center of Nazism; near the end of April, the Japanese move Father Duffy to a prison camp in Mukden, Manchuria. Father

Heintskill, aboard the U.S.S. *Tulagi,* arrives off Okinawa. Father Boland, aboard the U.S.S. *Highlands,* arrives off Okinawa, where his ship and nearby vessels come under repeated attack from Japanese kamikaze aircraft. After seeing action in the Aleutians and the Marshall Islands with the U.S. Army's Seventh Infantry Division, Father Joseph Corcoran, C.S.C., arrives at Okinawa.

April 18: Fathers Lawyer and McKee, along with Brothers Rex and Theodore, return to Notre Dame.

April 28: Soviet military forces enter Stalag II-A and liberate Father Sampson and the other captives.

April 29: Father Barry and the 157th Regiment liberate Dachau.

May 8: V-E Day, Victory in Europe, is celebrated around the world; Father Barry ends more than five hundred days in combat since his landing in Sicily almost two years earlier.

May 21: Sisters Olivette and Caecilius return to Saint Mary's.

August 6: An atom bomb destroys the Japanese city of Hiroshima.

August 9: An atom bomb destroys the Japanese city of Nagasaki.

August 12: A Japanese torpedo plane launches a torpedo at the U.S.S. *Pennsylvania,* aboard which Father Burke serves as chaplain. The torpedo explosion kills twenty men and wounds another ten.

August 15: Hostilities cease with Japan and terminate action in the Pacific Theater.

September 2: V-J Day marks the official end of the war in the Pacific, and with it, World War II; the Notre Dame chaplains gradually make their way back to the United States and to the university.

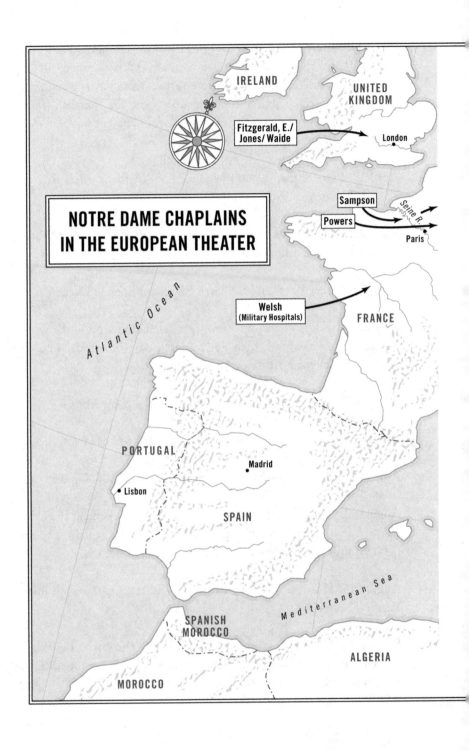

NOTRE DAME CHAPLAINS
IN THE EUROPEAN THEATER

IRELAND

UNITED
KINGDOM

Fitzgerald, E./
Jones/ Waide

London

Sampson

Powers

Seine R.

Paris

Welsh
(Military Hospitals)

FRANCE

Atlantic Ocean

PORTUGAL

Madrid

Lisbon

SPAIN

Mediterranean Sea

SPANISH
MOROCCO

ALGERIA

MOROCCO

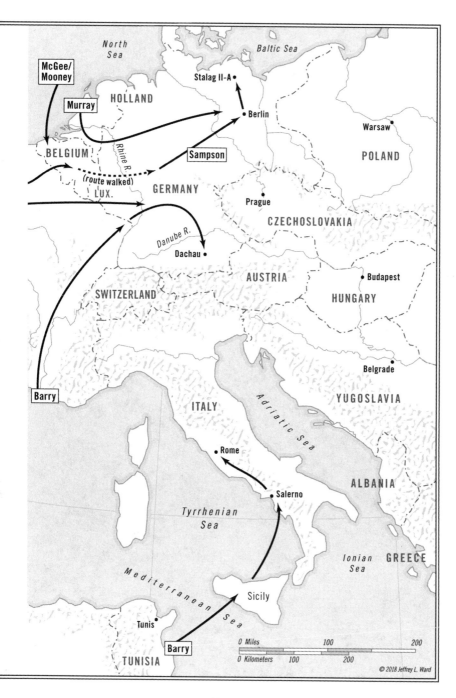

Notre Dame Chaplains in the European Theater

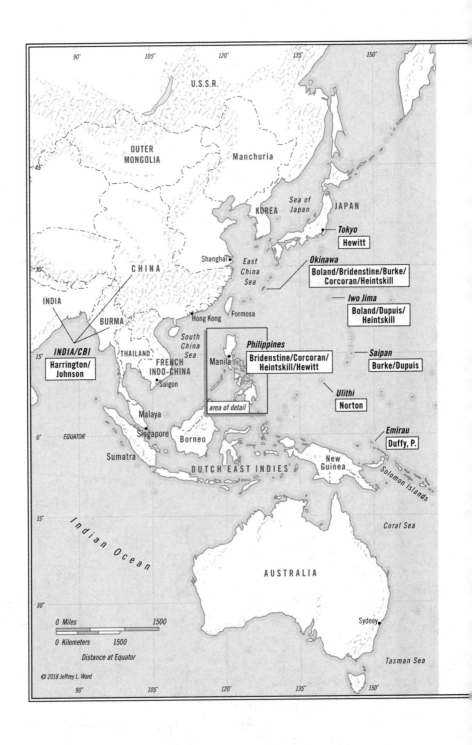

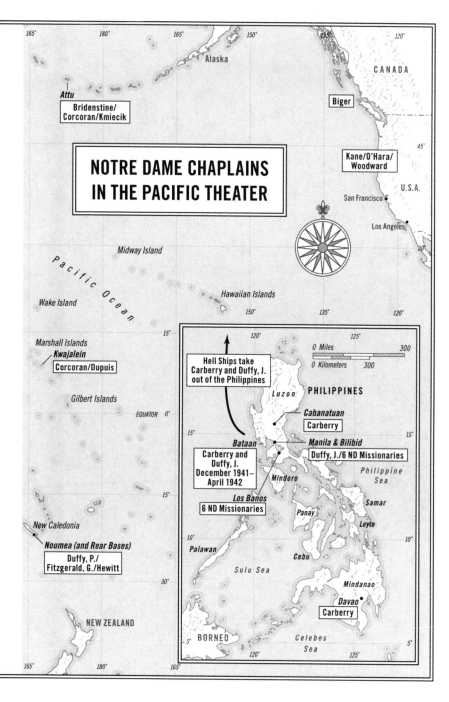

Notre Dame Chaplains in the Pacific Theater

THE CHAPLAINS
HEAD TO WAR

1920s to December 1943

PROLOGUE

Even for a war that exceeded the boundaries in military accomplishments, for the United States the nine-day period from June 6 to June 15, 1944, stood on its own plateau. On opposite sides of the globe unfolded the two largest amphibious operations in history: the massive Normandy invasion on June 6, 1944, against Hitler's Fortress Europe and the second nine days later against a linchpin of Japan's Pacific defense line, Saipan in the Marianas. That same week American forces entered Rome, from ancient times the symbol of power, after completing an excruciating campaign through Italy's mountains and valleys.

That the United States could simultaneously mount complex campaigns at three diverse locations around the world was testimony to the astounding outpouring of American industry. American infantry, sailors, and marines waged war armed with the weaponry produced by their civilian factory and shipyard workers back home.

AMONG THE participants of these events were four men united by common bonds. At a British airfield on June 5, 1944, Captain Francis L. Sampson inspected his equipment along with his buddies in the 501st Parachute Infantry Regiment of the 101st Airborne Division. He double-checked his main parachute and auxiliary, knowing that an oversight now could lead to a lethal ending in France's farmland from a faulty apparatus.

Before leaving for Normandy, Sampson stood in formation with his unit and listened as the hard-nosed commander of the 501st, Colonel Howard R. Johnson, replete in battle gear that included his trademark Bowie knife strapped to his waist, delivered a fiery talk on the eve of battle. The words gushed out of the veteran officer, each phrase stirring the young soldiers before him who were about to engage in combat with Adolf Hitler's vaunted military. Johnson ended by brandishing his Bowie knife and shouting, "I swear to you that before the dawn of another day this knife will be stuck in the foulest Nazi belly in France. Are you with me?" When the men, Sampson included, shouted, "We're with you!" Johnson added, "Then let's go get 'em! Good hunting!"

As his aircraft approached Normandy, Sampson leaped into the darkness, hoping to catch the Germans by surprise. One second later he dropped all illusions. "Our jump was a surprise all right—for us. The Germans were waiting for us, and they sent such a barrage of bullets at us that it will always remain a mystery to me how any of us lived."[1] Sampson, a novice to combat, wondered if he would perish in his harness before he even reached the ground.

As CAPTAIN Sampson jumped into Normandy, nine hundred miles to the southeast Captain Joseph D. Barry walked into Rome. The man who had already lived through three horrific amphibious landings—at Sicily, at Salerno, and at Anzio—and had survived hundreds of bombardments and strafings, had no time to enjoy the accolades or flowers from adoring Italians that rained down on him and the men of the U.S. Army's Forty-Fifth Infantry Division. They still faced difficult fighting against a skilled foe that had made Barry's division pay in blood and death for every foot of advance up Italy's hills and through its valleys, forever scorching the names Anzio and Monte Cassino in Barry's memory.

"I can say that every day and night on this battle-front is a constant reminder of Death," Barry wrote to a friend about his experiences in Sicily and Italy. He added of the bombardments from German artillery, "Each shell came a little closer, and each prayer became a little more fervent."[2]

SEVEN THOUSAND five hundred miles distant, on June 15, Navy Lieutenant, Junior Grade (jg) John J. Burke watched from the U.S.S. *Penn-*

sylvania (BB-38), one of the battleships damaged during the war's opening attack at Pearl Harbor, as the rebuilt vessel methodically blasted targets on Saipan. A part of the Mariana Islands in the Central Pacific, the island was a prime objective standing on the long route toward Tokyo and victory.

The sight of the American flotilla gathered to seize Saipan impressed Burke. Under the overall command of Admiral Raymond A. Spruance, victor of Midway, 535 ships transported 127,571 troops to the target islands in two groups. He watched marines who had, mere hours before, stepped into landing craft as they now inched toward shore, exposing themselves to heavier fire from Japanese mortars and guns with every yard they advanced. Even at the seemingly safe distance of ten thousand yards, enemy shells splashed uncomfortably close to the *Pennsylvania*. Admiral Spruance's flagship, the cruiser *Indianapolis*, reeled from a hit, and near misses endangered others. Still, Burke felt safer than those marines huddling in the amtracs (amphibious tractors) then churning shoreward.

Navy Lieutenant (jg) John M. Dupuis rode in one of those amtracs. Intent on depositing Dupuis's Fourth Marine Division on Saipan, the landing craft churned forward as shells screeched over Dupuis's head and direct hits flipped amtracs into the air. Military observers, recalling that one prominent general predicted the invasion would produce many dead marines, hoped that the senior commanders knew what they were doing.

So terrible was the fire that Dupuis questioned whether he would survive the landing attempt and make it to the beach, where he could begin executing the tasks for which he had so intensely trained. He later wrote that the marines of the Fourth Division with whom he worked left Pearl Harbor in fourteen ships, but when they had completed their tasks, only four shiploads remained.

Though involved in separate operations conducted thousands of miles apart, Sampson, Barry, Burke, and Dupuis were hardly strangers to each other. While soldiers and marines battled the Germans or Japanese with rifles and grenades, these four—chaplains all—dodged bullets and shells to aid the wounded and bring comfort to the dying. Even more, a second bond united the quartet, for each had either graduated from or taught at the University of Notre Dame in South Bend, Indiana.

They were four of the twenty-nine chaplains and six missionaries, most belonging to the Congregation of Holy Cross (C.S.C.), who served the country's fighting forces in every theater of the war. That these priests mirrored American families sending sons off to war can be seen in the letters to each other and especially to their religious superior at Notre Dame, Father Thomas A. Steiner. As the order's provincial, Father Steiner managed the day-to-day activities of Holy Cross religious in the United States and decided which posts the priests and brothers received. Just as did sailors in the Pacific or army privates in Europe in their letters to parents or wives, they asked Father Steiner how their fellow chaplains were doing and where they were stationed, and inquired about the latest events at home, which in their case was Notre Dame. A sense of family percolated among these chaplains.

They headed to war as neophytes to war's brutality, but like the infantrymen and marines they served, they adapted and performed their tasks under horrifying circumstances. They may have been assigned the specific mission of tending to the Catholic boys, but they gave comfort to all—Protestants, Jews, atheists—in religious and nonreligious ways.

The world was their parish. They ministered on oceans and battlefields, in hospitals and barracks. They tended battalions and regiments at jump-off points for battle, and repair and supply crews at minuscule island outposts. "Our chaplains are pretty well scattered over the face of the earth," wrote Father Steiner from Notre Dame in 1944. "They are on all fronts except the Russian front. When they all get back there will be no country and no island that some one of them have not been on, or at least, have had a close look at. It may be a good thing for the University to offer a class in geography."[3]

No matter their age—thirty-one years separated the oldest from the youngest—they brought comfort to frightened young men, often with bullets nipping at their feet and mortar shells exploding nearby. They may have been men of God, but they were in equal measure soldiers and priests. Father Barry's crawling under fire to reach the wounded and dying matches the bravery of men storming a machine-gun nest and earned chaplains praise from Pope Pius XII, who called them the best of the best.

More than chaplains, they were soldiers of another cloth, no different than the men they served except in the accoutrements of battle, and to them, the accoutrements meant a Bible and a crucifix, a Rosary and a religious medal. "I take my hat off to those fellows," one infantry officer said of chaplains. "They go into action unarmed. Good God, think of entering battle with a Book for a weapon."[4]

At the Holy Cross Cemetery at Notre Dame, American flags often adorn the gravesites of the chaplains buried there. This simple, yet powerful, gesture attests to the esteem with which these men are still held by their congregation and university, and to the World War II service that stamped their priestly careers as remarkable.

CHAPTER I

"OUR FIRST BAPTISM OF BLOOD"

War Opens in the Philippines

Whether the chaplains were Holy Cross or diocesan priests, they benefited from the rigorous training and austere lifestyle they willingly chose before joining the military. Demanding seminary classroom work and rigid schedules occupied them from morning until night. Periods of silence and frequent religious services, including daily Mass (twice on Sundays) and recitation of the Rosary, yielded moments for reflection and introspection, all intent on preparing the men for the taxing life offered by the priesthood.

Those who joined the Congregation of Holy Cross took vows of poverty, chastity, and obedience, while the diocesan priests promised at their ordination ceremonies to observe celibacy and obedience. Beginning in 1933, Holy Cross seminarians spent one year at the order's farm in Rolling Prairie, Indiana, a small community of six hundred people thirty miles west of the Notre Dame campus, where they learned that, beyond praying and preaching, a call to the religious life required physical and mental toughness as well. "In many ways, Rolling Prairie was our boot camp (not unlike the Marines' Parris island, perhaps)," wrote Father Theodore M. Hesburgh, C.S.C., who later became the university's president. He added that Rolling Prairie was "complete with rigorous physical training and a hard-nosed drill instructor."[1]

At the six-hundred-acre farm, Brother Seraphim, a former German soldier who immigrated to the United States after the Great War (1914–1918), was the taskmaster who, minus the litany of profane words, matched the scowls of the sternest U.S. Marine Corps drill sergeant. Long hours laboring at the farm tested the youths who emerged from high schools and forced them to examine whether they possessed the dedication and capacity for sacrifice to be a priest. By the end of Hesburgh's first year at Rolling Prairie, for instance, twenty of the twenty-nine men who entered with Hesburgh had dropped out of the arduous program.

Following that year the students switched to Notre Dame, where they lived at Moreau Seminary on the campus's northwest side and joined the other students attending classes. They wore street clothes rather than a conspicuous cassock, and while they could not date, correspond with high school girlfriends, or join campus social clubs, they could form their own athletic teams and scrimmage Notre Dame clubs. The diminutive Joseph D. Barry of Syracuse, New York, played shortstop for the seminary team and for years relished that his squad defeated an opponent that included some of Notre Dame's most acclaimed athletes. With a touch of hyperbole, his army division newspaper later stated of its chaplain, Barry "takes special pride in recounting that his team beat the famous Four Horsemen at baseball."[2]

Once the men completed their years in either a diocesan or Holy Cross seminary, they were ordained as priests and given their initial assignments. Many entered parish work. Those with oratorical skills joined the Congregation of Holy Cross's Mission Band, a group of Holy Cross priests who journeyed to parishes around the nation to conduct religious missions, while the priests who exhibited classroom skills and management talent remained on campus, where they taught classes, worked as prefects in student dormitories, or served in the university's administration.

"If Anything Ever Broke Here, We Would Definitely Be Up against It"

While the priests commenced their religious careers, volatile world events threatened to drag the nation into war. A clash between the

United States and Japan had appeared almost inevitable since the mid-1800s, when American politicians proclaimed that it was the nation's "manifest destiny" to expand beyond its continental borders into the Pacific. Bounteous natural resources in the Philippines and eastern Asia were there for the taking, and American manufacturers longed to offer their products to an untapped Asian market. Emotions intensified after a victorious United States acquired the Philippine Islands following the 1898 Spanish–American War. The United States stationed a garrison army in the islands, standing 1,400 miles southwest of Japan.

Japan simultaneously cast covetous eyes toward the same region. Minimal farm acreage in the small island nation forced Japan to import vast amounts of food and other items to satisfy its population. Almost 70 percent of the country's supply of zinc and tin came from outside, as did 90 percent of its lead, and all of its cotton, wool, aluminum, and rubber. In order to decrease its dependency upon other nations, Japan had to control the rich natural resources of the Philippines and of the Asian mainland. As long as moderates in the Japanese government balanced the militants who urged expansion, hostilities with the United States seemed unlikely, but should the militarists gain the upper hand, war loomed large.

FATHER JOHN E. Duffy and six Notre Dame missionaries found themselves in the midst of that turmoil. Born June 28, 1899, in Lafayette, Indiana, a community northwest of Indianapolis, Duffy attended Saint Mary's Parochial School and Notre Dame Preparatory before enrolling at the University of Notre Dame, where he gained renown as a skilled speaker. He later claimed that two men at Notre Dame most influenced him: the university's president, Father John W. Cavanaugh, C.S.C., for whom Duffy was secretary and from whom he learned how to diplomatically manage influential people, and famed football coach Knute Rockne, who helped nurture in Duffy a love of sports and a desire to excel at whatever he did.

After receiving his bachelor's degree in 1923, Duffy spent one year teaching and coaching at an Indianapolis high school before opting for the priesthood. Since he was familiar with the Congregation of Holy Cross from his time at Notre Dame, he considered joining that organization, but instead enrolled at a diocesan seminary, Mount Saint Mary's of the West in Norwood, Ohio, so that he could work in Ohio parishes.

After his ordination in June 1928, Duffy served parishes in three Ohio cities, including Toledo, before inquiring about duty as a chaplain. In October 1933 officials at the Diocese of Toledo approved his request and granted Father Duffy a ten-year leave to become an army chaplain.

After training and a brief stint as an assistant division chaplain in Texas, in May 1934 Duffy departed for three years' duty as assistant post chaplain at Fort Stotsenburg in the distant Philippine Islands. A three-year interval at a military post in the United States preceded Duffy's return to Fort Stotsenburg in April 1940.

He stepped into a hotbed of international developments. Seven months earlier, President Franklin D. Roosevelt had shifted the Pacific Fleet's home base from San Diego, California, to Pearl Harbor, Hawaii. He took this step as a caution to the Japanese government that he planned to oppose any overt military action by Japan against Asian states and the Philippines.

Roosevelt reacted again when Japanese troops moved into Indochina in July 1941. He severed trade with the aggressor nation and vowed to continue the embargo until Japan withdrew from both China and Indochina. Japanese leaders could either yield to Roosevelt's pressure and reestablish the flow of goods from the United States, or they could ignore it and risk war with a nation that possessed vast amounts of natural resources.

As the drumbeats of war intensified, Father Duffy keenly followed international developments. General MacArthur's presence as commander of U.S. Army and Philippine forces in the Far East brought welcome reassurance that steps were being taken to improve American military might in the islands, but Duffy thought that the still-inadequate defenses existing in the Philippines—an underequipped U.S. military backed by an undertrained Philippine military—invited an attack. He noticed arrogance and apathy among some of the American military, who failed to understand recent developments and dismissed the Japanese as a threat that they could readily dispatch. Servicemen's wives had been sent home, but each evening soldiers and sailors continued to enjoy sumptuous dinners at the Polo Club and entertainment at the Jai-Alai Club. Duffy was "convinced that if anything ever broke here, we would definitely be up against it. That was because of the apparent impossibility of getting any of the new officers to realize the seriousness and precariousness of the position of the handful of Americans that were on hand for even a token resistance against the military might of the Rising Sun."[3]

An alarming number of military still considered duty in the Philippines as a pleasant alternative to the more rigorous conditions found at most military outposts. "We had an easy life out there, with frequent parties and dances," said Staff Sergeant William Nolan, who worked at Fort Stotsenburg with a coastal artillery unit. "Talk about preparedness for war. Those men in the Philippines were no more an organized Army than the man on the moon."[4]

The outlook improved in October and November 1941, when American B-17 bombers flew into Clark Field and reinforced Mac-Arthur's arsenal. Their arrival "filled us with a great deal of pride," wrote Duffy. "It was considered the best battle plane in existence at that time and the longest range bomber." However, he and a handful of his officer friends "commented on the lack of discipline in the Air Corps and the ease with which the whole place could be wiped out and how a paratroop landing of a surprise nature could be made in the vicinity of Stotsenburg."[5]

"Japan Would Not Dare Attack Us"

The next month a group of nineteen missionaries from the United States, six of whom were Holy Cross from Notre Dame, arrived in the Philippines. Father Jerome Lawyer had been devoted to the Holy Cross Congregation since his teenage years, when he entered the Little Seminary at Notre Dame on September 1, 1926. He loved the communal feeling he shared with the other young men, an attitude he described as family. "I use the word family because that was the first word given to me to describe Holy Cross when I entered." He said, "It was love at first sight. That love brought me happiness."

That feeling was reinforced after supper on his first day when the group filed into the chapel to visit the Blessed Sacrament. Before entering, each man received a piece of paper bearing the name of a deceased Holy Cross member. They then walked to the cemetery a short distance away and recited a prayer at the gravesites. "This touched me emotionally," he said, referring to the tradition and to the rows of white crosses marking the graves of Holy Cross priests and brothers who had gone before him.

Lawyer was ordained June 24, 1939, at the campus's Church of the Sacred Heart (which would be designated in 1992 as the Basilica of the Sacred Heart). He studied Arabic, as he planned to devote his time as a missionary in areas such as Bengal (now Bangladesh), heavily populated with Muslims. "From age 13 on I was obsessed with the idea of going there as a missionary."[6]

Lawyer's classmate, Father Robert McKee, and four Holy Cross companions accompanied Lawyer to the Philippines, a temporary stop along the route to their mission destinations. Brother Theodore Kapes and Brother Rex Hennel, who had been a star guard on the 1935 Indiana high school state championship football team, and Sisters Mary Olivette Whelan and Mary Caecilius Roth (hereafter referred to as Brother Theodore, Brother Rex, Sister Olivette, and Sister Caecilius), planned to labor as missionaries alongside Lawyer and McKee in Dhaka, Bengal.

In late October 1941 the group left South Bend aboard a train bound for San Francisco, where they would settle in on a passenger ship for the lengthy voyage across the Pacific. The group toured San Francisco for a few days, and that Saturday they listened via radio broadcast as Notre Dame's undefeated football squad took on unvanquished Army in a game held in New York. In the bitterly contested clash, the rivals played to a scoreless tie, the only blemish that year for coach Frank Leahy's boys on their way to a third-place finish—behind Minnesota and Duke—in the Associated Press poll of top college football teams.

With Hitler already embroiling Europe in war and the Japanese creating rumbles in the Pacific, on November 9 the group boarded the liner *President Grant* for the six-week ocean voyage to the other side of the world. Concerns that they might be wandering into an area about to erupt in flames intensified with the air of intrigue surrounding their departure. "After much secrecy about the time, pier and date of sailing," Sister Olivette, a broad-smiling, wiry dynamo, wrote to Mother M. Vincentia, her superior general at Saint Mary's, "we finally got away at 6:00 P.M. Sunday 'unheralded and unsung.'" She called the transport "a missionary ship," as the complement included nineteen Catholic and twenty Protestant missionaries, but because their Protestant companions brought aboard wives and children, "We're outnumbered though three to one." A look at the lengthy passenger list however, dispelled their concerns that war might flare while they were on the high seas. Those businessmen and consular officials, thought the Notre Dame contingent, would never endanger their families by inserting them into a maelstrom. Sister Olivette felt confident enough that she discussed Christmas and wrote home that she would "send our Merry Christmas to you from Manila," and Father McKee commented that, "If there was danger, why had the State Department issued us passports for travel in this area?"[7]

The presence of their escorting ship, the light cruiser U.S.S. *Boise* (CL-47), also reassured the group. "Our cruiser was like a mother hen to our five merchant vessels," wrote Sister Olivette, "skirting around us, sometimes in front, sometimes in the rear but always on the alert sending out scouting planes which it was our delight to watch being catapulted from the cruiser and later picked up with a crane. The pilots knew we were an appreciative audience and usually flew low and close to give the *Grant* passengers a cheery wave."[8]

An uneventful six-day trip delivered the six to Honolulu, Hawaii, on November 15, 1941. When an army officer took them on a tour of the military installations on Oahu, including Pearl Harbor, the weaponry posed an impressive spectacle. The sisters marveled at the array of battleships, cruisers, submarines, and torpedo boats that filled the harbor, which Sisters Olivette and Caecilius described as "the pride of the Pacific Fleet." They scanned the thousands of mines neatly lined up and the aircraft that constantly arose from or landed on a massive aircraft carrier that dwarfed nearby vessels, and "were comfortably confident that no nation in the world would ever dare attack America, or Americans, no matter how far we might go."[9] The six sensed a heightened awareness among the soldiers that hostilities with Japan might soon occur but believed that if war erupted, it would never happen at the American naval bastion at Pearl Harbor.

Three days later the group gathered their belongings for the next leg on their journey, the Philippine Islands, which would be their final stop before reaching India. A convoy of four ships, again escorted by the cruiser U.S.S. *Boise*, lifted anchor on November 18, but military restrictions introduced a mood more somber than that of the pleasant trip to Hawaii. Passengers were required to adhere to a rigid blackout each night and refrain from smoking on deck after dusk. Rather than approach Manila from the usual northern route, which placed the ships between Japan and the Philippines, the convoy entered through the San Bernardino Strait hundreds of miles to the south.

On December 4 the convoy passed the military stronghold of Corregidor, an island that safeguarded the entrance to Manila Bay, and docked at Pier Seven in Manila. Each day the missionaries left the ship to visit Manila's attractions, but returned with the other passengers every evening to spend the night aboard ship.

On one of their jaunts into the city, Brother Rex and a few others shared a leisurely evening stroll through the city's avenues with a Filipino engineer named Mr. Lim, a daily communicant who worked for the Philippine government. When their conversation turned to the possibility that Japan and the United States would soon be at war, Mr. Lim expressed his fear that hostilities between the two governments were likely to erupt. "Of course," explained Brother Rex, "we told him that Japan would not dare attack us. And if they were so silly, the American fleet would sail boldly up and let loose with guns, and that would be the end of that."[10] A practice air raid on December 6 hinted that rather than being a distant specter, war loomed near, but the six missionaries remained confident that they would reach their postings in India.

AFTER FAILING to convince President Roosevelt to lift the embargo on oil and other products, the Japanese prepared for war. Tension mounted in Washington and Tokyo, and Father Duffy, now promoted to major and named force chaplain, Northern Luzon Force, by MacArthur, saw little prospect for continued peace. The military canceled all leaves and placed its forces on alert.

When American codebreakers intercepted a Japanese message to diplomats in Washington ordering them to destroy sensitive documents and to present a note to the United States at 1:00 p.m. on December 7, Roosevelt knew that war was imminent. Warnings raced to every American military post in the Pacific, cautioning that hostile action by Japan could be expected within days. Most observers believed war would start either in the Far East or in the Philippines and discounted Pearl Harbor as a likely target. In the event of war, the United States would have time to organize its navy in Hawaiian waters before sending it across the Pacific to engage the enemy.

"It Was the Bloodiest and Goriest Mess I Have Ever Seen"

In the Philippines, Father Duffy tried his best to maintain a normal schedule. With war clouds gathering, Father Duffy figured that a typical sermon for his Mass on December 7—December 6 at Pearl Harbor, which rested on the other side of the International Date Line—focusing on charity or on treating one another with decency would miss the mark. His congregation, all of whom might be dodging bullets and bombs before Christmas, required more.

Father Duffy reminded his audience that both he and they must be prepared to meet God, "for we know not when God would call us." He emphasized that "some of us might not be here tomorrow for we know not the day nor the hour when we would be called to give an account of our stewardship,"[11] and reminded them that he would be available at any time to hear confessions.

Father Duffy had just finished his morning Mass on December 8 when he heard over the radio that the Japanese had attacked the Hawaiian naval base. The men around him reacted calmly, as they had long assumed war with Japan was inevitable, but the location for the opening assault surprised most. Duffy met with two officers, and the trio agreed that the Philippines would soon be attacked.

They were correct. Fifty-four Japanese bombers and thirty-six fighters from Taiwan struck Clark Field shortly after noon. Men leaving the mess hall after lunch gazed skyward at the noise and, for a moment, marveled at the stunning V formation of the incoming aircraft. Their reverie ended when the fighters dropped bombs and strafed the neatly parked American aircraft. The announcement, "Tallyho! Bandits over Clark!" shot through the base. Don Bell, a popular radio news commentator, somberly told his audience, "There is an unconfirmed report that they're bombing Clark Field."[12]

Duffy grabbed his helmet, jumped into his car, and raced toward headquarters, eluding the bullets and bombs that at one point forced him to abandon the vehicle and take refuge in a trench. Smoke and fire enveloped nearby hangars and buildings, and smoldering heaps of mangled steel were all that remained of those shiny fighters that once gleamed on the runway.

Duffy ran to the field, littered with dead and wounded, to hear confessions and administer Last Rites. He then rushed to the Fort

Stotsenburg Hospital, where he again administered Last Rites to any dying serviceman he came across, opting to avoid wasting precious moments by checking about the soldier's faith. "I knew it would be effective for the members of my faith & that it would do the others no harm," he explained later. "There wasn't sufficient time for inquiry about religious tenets of the wounded."[13]

The attack ended in minutes, leaving Clark Field in shambles. Every American fighter and all but three of the large Flying Fortress bombers lay in ruins, a total of ninety-six American aircraft now resembling crushed metallic spiders more than weapons of war. Combined with the successful raid against Pearl Harbor, the Japanese had neutered the two main American military bastions in the Pacific.

Tension dominated the ensuing hours. Soldiers slept next to their weapons so they could be ready to repel the Japanese invasion force expected to follow. Father Duffy comforted the wounded at the hospital before hurrying to the morgue, where he anointed the Catholics and participated in a multidenominational funeral service for almost one hundred dead. Father Duffy had witnessed much in his time as a priest, but nothing compared with the bodies of men so disfigured that they had to be buried without identification. "It was the bloodiest and goriest mess I had ever seen up to that time," he later wrote.[14]

After an exhausting day, Father Duffy returned to his quarters, where he shared a quick drink with two officers and tried to comprehend the day's stunning events. A phone call from headquarters informed Duffy that because the navy had sustained such devastating damage at Pearl Harbor, the likelihood of reinforcements or supplies filtering through to MacArthur's forces in the next six weeks was negligible. He would not have much time to think about food or additional troops anyway, as over the next four days he buried 112 soldiers and Filipino civilians.

THE LACK OF reinforcements was dire news for another Notre Dame graduate, Captain Richard E. Carberry, who served with the Forty-Fifth Combat Team, Philippine Scouts, not far from Duffy. After completing graduate studies at Notre Dame in 1931, the native of Panora, Iowa, turned to the priesthood and became an army chaplain in 1940. Born October 15, 1905, he came from a long line of Domers: his brother, John, played offensive end on Knute Rockne's 1929 undefeated national championship team, and his two other brothers graduated from Notre Dame. Carberry was well respected in his unit by officers and enlisted, Catholic and Protestant. He enjoyed working with the elite scout unit but, like Duffy, feared that the forces then in the Philippines would be inadequate to counter any Japanese assault. No matter what, Carberry intended to be with his combat team, tending to their spiritual needs on the front lines while the soldiers handled military matters.

"Her Days of Suffering Were at Hand"

Aboard the *Grant*, the Holy Cross missionaries also experienced a torturous first day of war. Fathers McKee and Lawyer turned on a radio after enjoying supper in a Manila rectory. A Dutch news broadcast out of Indonesia described the fragile Pacific situation, and when the commentator explained that communications in that area with Japan had been severed, one of their hosts muttered, "That means war in this part of the world."[15] Father Lawyer relayed the news to Brothers Rex and Theodore, who reacted with stunned silence.

After witnessing the assemblage of naval power at Pearl Harbor only a few weeks earlier, Sister Olivette had trouble digesting the information. "I think maybe we were even more shocked because having just been there and seen the mighty array of ships and planes and the defense preparation it never occurred to us that such a thing could happen," she wrote in a letter to her friends at Saint Mary's. "It seemed like we were so well prepared." Sister Olivette and her companions hurried to the radio, hoping to learn more about the calamity. "But sudden fear was soon overruled by confident indignation. America, we knew, would settle the attack vigorously, promptly, effectively."[16]

That afternoon the captain of the ship assembled the passengers and told them that for their safety, they had to leave the vessel and find quarters in the city, as the ship would likely be a prime target for Japanese bombers. He added that once they had found quarters, they should leave the address with him so he could contact them when the ship was ready to depart. McKee, Lawyer, and the two brothers found housing at a Jesuit college, the Ateneo de Manila, while the nuns took refuge with a group of Maryknoll Sisters at St. Paul's Hospital. The six missionaries assumed they would only temporarily be at their new quarters, as, according to Sister Olivette, "we all thought it would be only a few weeks and our army and navy would settle this upstart of an enemy!"[17] They decided to send one person from the group back to the ship each day for updates.

Their journey from the vessel to their new quarters in Manila, now blacked out, provided an eerie introduction to war. Gunshots interrupted the calm, guards manned posts, and buses collected Japanese residents to take them to holding centers. When Sisters Olivette and Caecilius arrived at the hospital, they had to use flashlights to find their way in the blacked-out building. Illumination emitted only from the surgical and delivery rooms, but workers had painted the windows black to prevent light from shining outside.

Tension heightened during the night, when two Japanese air attacks lambasted military installations. "At midnight the siren sounded its first mournful wail," wrote Sister Olivette, "warning Manila that her days of suffering were at hand."[18] The nuns gathered the Filipino nurses in the chapel adjoining the first-floor patient wards, where the group recited the Rosary to keep their minds off the bombings.

At the Ateneo, the bombing of Nichols Field two miles to the south knocked Brother Rex and his companions from their beds on the third floor. When Japanese aircraft arrived for a second air attack an hour later, Rex and a large group rushed to a bomb shelter, where they remained for the rest of the night. The next day sixty Japanese aircraft flew over Manila and bombed the massive navy yards at Cavite ten miles distant, while other planes dropped leaflets informing Filipino residents, "We are here to finish the war and liberate the Filipinos from American rule."[19]

The four male Notre Dame missionaries offered their assistance to the wounded and dying, now tending to bodies disfigured by bombs and sliced by shrapnel instead of ministering to civilian parishioners in India as planned. "We had our first baptism of blood as we walked among the many Cavite victims brought from that raid to nearby Philippine General Hospital,"[20] wrote McKee.

Their spirits rose when they listened to the radio broadcast of President Franklin D. Roosevelt's powerful speech asking Congress to declare war. "Our patriotism and sense of injustice done were stirred by a rebroadcast of President Roosevelt's speech,"[21] wrote Sister Olivette of Roosevelt's "Day of Infamy" address.

Sisters Olivette and Caecilius treated numerous patients pouring in from the Cavite naval base as well as civilian families injured in the bombings. One Chinese family, consisting of an aunt, a grandmother, two young boys, and an infant, hobbled in to be treated for lacerations. Despite witnessing the recent death of the mother of the three children, the group impressed Sister Olivette with their stoic demeanor as the sisters mended their wounds. "They were so wonderfully patient I marveled at them," wrote Sister Olivette, "even the little children didn't utter a sound and they all had shrapnel wounds."

The grandmother, in particular, stood out. "The old lady was a marvelous study of patient, resigned suffering and seeing her one realized that the Chinese would never be conquered by bullets, that anyone who could take pain and suffering like that would conquer in the end." The elderly woman served as an example for Sister Olivette as to how she might deal with issues she had never imagined she might one day face.

While Fathers Lawyer and McKee visited as many hospitals as possible to comfort the wounded and dying, at the U.S. Army's invitation the sisters and staff of St. Paul's Hospital commenced a move to a building of the Philippine Women's University being used as a military hospital. Throughout December 13 the staff moved every item from St. Paul's to their new location, a three-story structure offering patient wards, operating and X-ray rooms, administrative offices, and a chapel on the first floor, a second floor for patients able to climb the stairs, and dormitories on the third floor. In scouring the walls, windows, and floors, the sisters encountered roaches so large that one soldier told Sister Olivette, "If we had those in Texas we'd saddle 'em and ride 'em."[22]

"Nobody Seemed to Know If They Were Coming or Going"

Despite the gloomy outlook, MacArthur and his top aide, Major General Jonathan M. Wainwright, had to mount an effective defense and hope that they could hold off the Japanese until reinforcements arrived. The island of Corregidor, thirty miles from Manila and two and a half miles south of Bataan Peninsula, stood guard at the approaches to Manila Bay. The "Rock," as the island was called, housed artillery and machine-gun emplacements along with Malinta Tunnel, a vast, labyrinthine complex able to hold supplies, hospital wards, and ten thousand soldiers. MacArthur counted that his forces on Corregidor could prevent enemy shipping from entering Manila Bay and give his land units time to hold off any Japanese assault until help appeared.

Father Duffy doubted MacArthur could succeed. Troops meandered about Clark Field with little apparent guidance, and "nobody seemed to know if they were coming or going."[23] Shorn of his air force by the Japanese on the first day, MacArthur possessed little with which to prevent further bombing raids.

By the middle of December Father Duffy had joined Wainwright's Northern Luzon Force, situated near Rosales, north of Manila. MacArthur had posted forces to that area to counter the expected Japanese landings in Lingayen Gulf to the north and ordered Wainwright to hold at the beaches as long as possible before falling back to the second line of defense along the Agno River, one hundred miles north of Manila.

Three days before Christmas, 43,000 Japanese troops of Lieutenant General Masaharu Homma's Fourteenth Army stormed ashore in Lingayen Gulf. Homma outfoxed Wainwright, who expected them to arrive near the mouth of the Agno where he and his men waited, by landing forty miles up the coast where few defenses existed. Within twenty-four hours Wainwright informed MacArthur that he could not hold the Lingayen beach area against Homma's fast-moving forces and asked permission to withdraw behind the Agno River. MacArthur approved and implemented the war plan that called for an orderly retreat of American and Filipino forces into Bataan Peninsula, where they would hold out until reinforcements arrived.

Wainwright named Duffy chief of army chaplains for the First Philippine Corps and assigned him to a tent with Colonel Frank Nelson, a member of Wainwright's staff. Much as he found elsewhere, however, the enemy controlled the skies, and most of the inexperienced Filipino troops had been rushed to the front with little training.

Conditions deteriorated December 24 when a second Japanese force landed in Lamon Bay, southeast of Manila, and hammered MacArthur's line on another front. Combined with Homma's men near Lingayen Gulf, a Japanese pincer closed from the north and southeast on the already weary American and Filipino units. Realizing he could do little to halt the enemy, MacArthur hastened the withdrawal into

Bataan, established his headquarters on Corregidor, and hoped that he could collect enough supplies in Bataan and extricate all his units before the Japanese cut across the peninsula's top and sealed the door.

Stationed with Wainwright's forces in the north, Father Duffy faced a 150-mile retreat through dense jungles laced with streams. Their task was to hold the enemy along the Agno as long as possible before falling back to three more defensive lines standing between Homma and Bataan, mounting a defense at each barrier to impede the Japanese before withdrawing to the next line. Realizing he might not have a second chance to contact family in the United States, Duffy sent a hurried cable: "Well. Merry Christmas."[24]

Father Duffy worked around the clock tending to his men and looking after some of the thousands of Filipino civilians hoping to evade Homma's soldiers and reach Bataan. Parents grasping children struggled to keep pace with the stream of soldiers, trucks, and oxcarts as the forlorn columns meandered along dirt highways and jungle paths toward Bataan. Clouds of dust and silent prayers from despairing parents spiraled heavenward amid the chaos.

MacArthur ordered Wainwright to delay Homma until January 8, at which time the final units would have reached Bataan and the main bridges could be blown. When the Japanese crossed the Agno River the day after Christmas, however, Homma enjoyed a clear path to Manila. In hopes of preventing further damage, MacArthur declared Manila an open city, meaning he did not intend to make a stand in the urban center. He revised his plan and ordered the key bridge at Calumpit and other locations destroyed on January 1.

MacArthur's army, including Father Duffy and Father Carberry, was now sealed in a peninsula, with the sea on three sides and Japanese on the fourth.

"We Were Well Aware That We Were Prisoners"

In the meantime, the six Notre Dame missionaries made certain that each day one of their number journeyed to the harbor to check on the passenger ship due to transport them to India. They recoiled in dismay when, one day, the individual discovered that, without notice to anyone, the ship had departed and stranded the missionaries in Manila. They could now do nothing but help the burgeoning number of wounded, hope that American relief forces rushed to their rescue, and attempt to get word home that they were unharmed. "Greetings," Sister Olivette and Sister Caecilius wrote in a December 22 telegram. "Safe. Army nursing with Maryknolls."[25]

To pass the time and to improve morale, Brother Rex and Father McKee joined a choir organized by the Jesuits that moved from hospital to hospital singing Christmas carols to the patients. Brother Rex had attended many Christmas Midnight Masses and other celebrations set amid the beautiful surroundings of Notre Dame's Church of the Sacred Heart, but he could not think of one that topped his Christmas in Manila that year. He was overjoyed that "they were able to help the wounded boys thrill once more to the songs that they had grown up on." As the choir sang, Rex scanned the crowd of wounded and noticed tears coursing down their cheeks while they listened to "the strains of 'Silent Night,' and the other songs they knew so well." The image moved him, and "it made us feel good to know that we had brought a little bit of Christmas to the poor boys." As a youth he had reveled in the family Christmas tree, bedecked with shiny ornaments and bulging with gifts underneath, but "Christmas of 1941 will live in my memory as one of the happiest I have ever spent. With all the tinsel taken from it, one had to go back to the real spiritual meaning of the feast."

Dismal news soon dispelled the joy. On Christmas morning army officials informed the group that Japanese forces would enter Manila some time that evening. Tanks and trucks, accompanied by lines of retreating American and Filipino soldiers, coursed through Manila on their way to Bataan Peninsula, thirty miles west of the city across Manila Bay. "It was a discouraged and saddened group of priests and brothers who waited through the long Christmas afternoon," wrote Brother Rex. "Not much was said, but the general atmosphere was one of discouragement and fright. We had heard of the rape of Shanghai, and other acts of the Japanese, and all of us made sure that we were ready to face the worst when the Japanese arrived."[26]

The stories of Shanghai, Nanking, and other conquered regions, where raucous troops plundered the towns, slaughtered thousands of civilians, and raped the women, had widely circulated. The missionaries hoped for fair treatment but feared the worst, especially for Sisters Olivette and Caecilius. Even before the Japanese arrived, looters had turned once-proud Manila into an orgy of crime and mayhem. "Wholesale looting continues," Sister Olivette recorded in her diary. "Army gone. Constabulary disarmed."[27]

The Japanese failed to enter the city that day as warned, but the missionaries, remaining by the side of their civilian patients, concluded that incarceration by the Japanese was imminent. Ignoring the risks, the priests and brothers left the comparative safety of the hospital to search for wounded and dying among the rubble of destroyed buildings, a mission of mercy that revealed some of war's most hideous images. They found one man pinned beneath a huge wooden girder with one leg almost totally severed, and another man so badly burned that when they tried to move him his skin slipped off "like the peeling coming from a boiled potato." Brother Rex wrote, "It was the first time that any of us had come so close to death, and the experience was upsetting." He added that "it was pitiful to see the poor people carrying their few belongings from their homes. Bundles of clothing; sewing machines; a pan or two. They never had much. Now they had nothing. I was beginning to understand the meaning of war."

He described MacArthur's designation of Manila as an open city "a shattering blow" but held onto the slim hope that help might yet arrive. When on December 29 American military forces systematically destroyed anything the Japanese might be able to use, setting afire reservoirs of oil and destroying facilities at the naval base at Cavite, "Spirits were down, tempers were short, and depression was great."

The Japanese arrived in the early morning darkness four days later. With daylight, Brother Rex saw that Japanese soldiers manned machine guns and stood behind sandbag barricades in front of their building. "We were interned,"[28] he gloomily concluded.

"The city was ringed by fire, ships in the nearby bay burning, buildings all over the city on fire," wrote Father McKee. "We waited for the Japanese, hoping for some sort of peace and order. Finally on January 2, 1942, in the dark of the night, we heard trucks and tanks as the Japanese Army entered the city."[29]

Sister Caecilius first noticed the Rising Sun emblem when a troop carrier came into view a block away. "We waited in anxious suspense for the first contact with the enemy," she recalled. At 2:00 a.m. Japanese soldiers stood outside their front gate, demanding to be let in. Upon opening it, a squad rushed into the courtyard but neither entered the building nor molested anyone. However, when the soldiers searched the missionaries and everyone else, "We were well aware that we were prisoners."[30]

Eager to gain the cooperation of the Filipinos, who as fervent Catholics were devoted to the priests and nuns, the Japanese at first refrained from mistreating the missionaries. Japanese officers met with the priests living at the Ateneo and decided that, instead of being confined with the American civilians interned at the University of Santo Tomas campus, the priests would remain at the college, where they could continue to assist nearby parishes. The Japanese gathered the Holy Cross and Maryknoll nuns at the Convent of the Assumption, then operated by a French order of sisters. The missionaries, who had earlier expected a quick resolution to the conflict, had now begun what would turn out to be a lengthy incarceration.

"What lay ahead of us?"[31] wondered Father McKee.

"I Held Mass in a Different Place Each Day"

From January until early April, American and Filipino forces on Bataan battled the numerically superior and better-supplied Japanese. Although President Roosevelt had promised to send reinforcements, MacArthur could count only on the 15,000 American and 65,000 Filipino troops, most exhausted and hungry, already mounting defenses in Bataan, and on the supplies they brought into the fifteen-mile-wide and thirty-mile-long peninsula. The general hoped that Bataan's mountainous terrain and thick jungles would impede the enemy long enough for him to strengthen his line of defense. Wainwright's units, including the men served by Father Duffy and Father Carberry, occupied the western half of the peninsula.

Like the soldiers around him, Duffy went on half rations— approximately two thousand calories a day—to stretch the meager food supplies. Dry cereal, canned fruit, and onions provided the main sustenance, prodding soldiers to scour the jungles for other edible items.

Despite heroic efforts to halt the enemy from January 18 to 19, Wainwright had to pull his weaker forces back toward the peninsula's southern half. Father Duffy accompanied the soldiers as they trod over rocky terrain and through jungles. He heard confessions and said Mass for Filipino troops, and one night, when alerted that the Japanese were flanking the line, he volunteered to hurry back to an ammunition dump and arrange for bullets and artillery shells to be brought forward. The officer in charge of the artillery, Major A. L. Fitch, later told Duffy that his artillery shells helped detain the Japanese until the men could fall back to other positions. When Father Duffy asked how, the major replied, "Padre, it was an artilleryman's dream. There were targets in front of me, targets behind me and targets on both sides of me and we really had a field day until all the ammunition was expended. Thanks to you we had all there was in the area. We expended a lot of Japs."

By January 26 the weary soldiers had dug in along another defense line farther down the peninsula, hoping to slow the military juggernaut heading their way. Japanese snipers infiltrated the area, and the nonstop fighting littered the region with bodies. "Six weeks after," Duffy recalled, "the entire area stunk to high heaven tho we had buried everything we could recognize as a human."[32]

As January waned, soldiers began to realize the futility in pinning their hopes on a reinforcement convoy. They scoffed at MacArthur's mid-January message that thousands of troops and hundreds of aircraft rushed their way from the United States and laughed when the general claimed that if they could hold on awhile longer, assistance was certain to arrive. Father Duffy later said that they were so short of everything, the men used to joke that "we ought to send Roosevelt a message and tell him our P-40 [fighter] was about worn out, and wouldn't they please send us over a new one." Conditions grew so desperate that in the middle of the month, in Washington, D.C., Secretary of War Henry L. Stimson could see no way that the nation could transport enough men and material to save the trapped men in the Philippines. Stimson concluded of the fighting, "There are times when men have to die."[33]

WHILE SOLDIERS battled the Japanese and the hunger and malaria that daily ground them down, Fathers Duffy and Carberry faced one overriding duty: to bring God's comfort to those men. More accustomed to the peace and calm of a sacristy and pulpit, they made the jungles of Bataan their church and the infantry fighting and dying on the front lines their congregation. As head chaplain, Duffy told those he supervised, including Father Carberry, to be with the men at the front rather than spending time behind the lines. Duffy could have remained at headquarters or at one of the two hospitals set up in Bataan, but he also chose to labor in the combat zones, knowing that location was where he was most needed.

"I held Mass in a different place each day,"[34] Duffy wrote of his attempts to make himself available to as many soldiers as possible. His churches ranged from small huts to open fields, where he celebrated Mass on altars made from used crates and broken wooden tables. He buried the dead, marked and registered grave sites, heard confessions from young men soon to face death, delivered orders under fire from commanders to troops, walked miles through the heavy jungle to join men at the front, and used a shortwave radio to relay hurried messages from soldiers to family back home. He was parent, friend, and confidant to young men in their time of greatest peril, and he remained with the men even after suffering minor wounds on January 1, for which he received the Purple Heart. He performed so capably that he earned praise as the World War II counterpart to World War I's acclaimed Father Francis Duffy, whose exploits with the Rainbow Division in Europe were legendary.

A United Press feature on the chaplains of Bataan stated, "Before a crude altar of stacked-up ammunition boxes over which a shelter tent had been placed as a cover, a middle-aged slightly-built American priest celebrated the Roman Catholic Mass." The article added that Father John E. Duffy of Toledo was now laboring somewhere in Bataan, "close enough to the front so that the rumble of guns provided an accompaniment for the priest's words." The article continued, "The chaplains on Bataan have many duties," a statement that was true for Father Carberry and the other chaplains for whom shell bursts and bullets became commonplace. "They aid in burials, operate aid stations and even deliver messages under shellfire as well as aid in bringing up supplies."[35]

Father Duffy's work became so celebrated that the *New York Times* profiled him in an article and *Time* Magazine lauded his work in its February 23, 1942, issue. "Father Duffy, World War I chaplain of the famed Fighting 69th, has a namesake in Bataan, Father John E. Duffy of Toledo, who received the decoration of the Purple Heart for 'singularly meritorious action' when slightly wounded in action on New

Year's Day. He celebrates Mass at the front on an altar of ammunition boxes."[36]

The noted magazine correspondent John Hersey mentioned the work of Father Duffy and other chaplains in his 1942 book *Men on Bataan*, published not long after the fighting in the peninsula had ended. Hersey explained to his audience in the United States that these religious individuals "did not just visit the fronts, but stayed there, bound by a duty which they considered just as imperative as military orders." Hersey added that "The things they did were many. They held divine services and said mass. They gave men decent burial. They comforted the wounded and cheered up the whole. They helped doctors at aid stations. When necessary they delivered messages under fire and pitched in on chores of supply. And they shared every peril."

Hersey singled out Father Duffy for praise. "There was a famous Father Duffy with MacArthur in the Rainbow Division in France; there was another with him on Bataan, Major John E. Duffy of Toledo, Ohio. This Father Duffy, of middle age, slightly built, and with a little gray among his blond hair, was a graduate of Notre Dame and of the Seminary of Mount Saint Mary's at Norwood, Ohio. He had been in the Army nine years when war came." Hersey continued, "You could see this Father Duffy, on a Sunday morning, saying mass in the jungle with some ammunition boxes for an altar and a shelter tent for a cathedral. Or you might find him taking the fingerprints of dead men, putting one set in a sealed container to go into the grave and keeping another for the records. Or you might find him with just one boy, away from the crowd, hearing the lad confess that he had cursed, that he had been afraid, that he had killed men."[37]

The men who escaped the day's fighting, however briefly, to kneel at Mass and receive Holy Communion gained a sense of peace and comfort. "Went to church this morning to 8:30 mass said by Fr. Duffy in a leafy covering of jungle," Captain Tom Gerrity wrote in a February 15 diary entry that appeared in home-front newspapers. "During mass I pondered over the many masses I've heard under other circumstances, and yet how peaceful was this one even with gunfire and the drone of enemy planes."[38] Gerrity was able to elude the war, including the ear-splitting artillery exchange that flared during the Mass, while Father Duffy intoned the familiar Latin words and lifted the host and wine during Consecration. Those moments forged a connection with home, with all that was familiar, with religion and decency.

By February 10, subsisting now on one-third rations, battling the sapping effects of malaria, and placing their dwindling hopes in a reinforcement convoy that seemed more mirage than real, morale slumped. "We were down to some rice and salmon, plus anything you could shoot and skin," recalled Staff Sergeant William Nolan. "It was right about this time I began thinking our situation was hopeless, although a lot of the guys wouldn't admit it and kept hoping for the convoy. We were thousands of miles from the States, on a peninsula being attacked on land by Japanese units and surrounded at sea by the Japanese Navy. Morale started to get lower and lower as soldiers got weaker and weaker. We had no cover from mosquitoes at night because we slept at our positions, and guys were so sick they couldn't do a hell of a lot."[39]

NOT FAR from Duffy, Father Carberry fended off exhaustion to aid his weary, famished men. "I am on my way to Corregidor to see if I might get a few cigarettes for the officers and men," he wrote on February 16 to his family. "I think no one will argue about the brand anymore so will not have to get a few of each kind." Carberry admitted that the last few months, during which he had helped almost 900 dependents of soldiers evacuate the islands and had anointed 230 dying troops at aid stations near the front lines, had taken a heavy toll. "There have been times when I have longed for the hills of Guthrie County [Iowa], but have always thanked God daily for the jungle of Bataan as that has been our friend daily since the start of the war." The priest lost all his belongings when Manila fell into Japanese hands and, he noted, "I killed a cobra snake one night with my bolo when I was about to pitch my blanket," but he termed the fighting by United States and Filipino troops "our glorious stand." While he wished that he had news from home—he had heard nothing about his ailing father since November—he told family, "Do not worry about me. I am saying Mass here for the troops and really liking the war."[40]

Father Carberry followed the men of the Forty-Fifth Combat Team wherever they moved, whether to a static defensive line or into combat. When danger was at its greatest, Carberry inspired the men not with a stirring Knute Rockne speech, but with his actions. When the column of vehicles in which Carberry rode came under intense mortar, machine-gun, and small-arms fire, Carberry repeatedly ran up and down the length of the convoy, ignoring shell bursts and bullet ricochets to help the wounded and calm the others. He lent hope "at the height of danger," according to the citation for the Silver Star he received for this valor, with his "utter disregard of his own safety"[41] in ministering to the men.

"At Last, the Blow Fell"

In their Manila convent, Sisters Olivette and Caecilius kept track of developments by surreptitiously listening to broadcasts over a radio left behind by an army nurse. Each evening, alone in the dark and with the radio tuned to a low volume, the nuns heard daily reports from Corregidor and prayed that Japanese guards did not burst in and remove their sole contact with the outside world.

Their morale at first remained high, as they believed that a relief force rushed to their rescue. "We were sure that reinforcements from home would arrive," wrote Sister Olivette, "that MacArthur was winning all the battles, that it was only a question of time, and not too long a time, before the tide turned." The sisters, along with thousands of other civilians trapped in the Philippines, failed to grasp that MacArthur's military units fought a hopeless cause. "That a desperate beleaguered garrison was 'whistling in the dark' to keep up its courage and that of its listeners did not occur to us,"[42] Sister Olivette later wrote.

Little by little, however, their hopes dissipated as first one American-Filipino unit, and then another, yielded. With defeat almost a certainty, on February 22 President Roosevelt ordered MacArthur to leave the Philippines, reestablish his command in Australia, and organize American forces for future offensives against the Japanese. On March 11, one day after he handed command of all troops on Luzon to Wainwright, the general and his family departed. Upon arriving in Australia, MacArthur uttered his famous words, "I came through and I shall return!"[43]

Six days later Father Duffy alerted his superior in Toledo, Bishop Karl J. Alter, that he was holding up under the trying conditions. "Just a line to let you know I'm still among the living and continuing daily to do the work assigned me among our Catholic men." He informed Alter that he had been wounded in January, "but only slightly. It was taken care of by a medical officer but I did not have to go to a hospital." Despite inadequate food, enemy assaults, exhaustion, and diarrhea, he kept busy administering the Sacraments and saying Mass, and added that "Everything is going along as well as we could hope for under the circumstances."[44]

Conditions deteriorated in the face of swift advances by the numerically superior Japanese. At one location Duffy came upon Japanese bodies piled forty high. "Constant feints at our front lines in both corps," he wrote of this desperate time. "Continuous daily air raids with little effect. Starvation diet of 6 ounces of food per day per man doing most damage. Hospital filled. Men down with malaria, dengue, dysentery, in the lines so weak hardly had strength to pull triggers on guns but constant artillery fire kept enemy off balance."[45] In early March the chaplain sustained a second wound, which required hospitalization for ten days, after which Duffy returned to the front lines.

Later that month Wainwright informed Washington that he had only enough food to last until mid-April. In the few moments when Father Duffy was able to visit his friend behind the lines, he and General Wainwright discussed the swirl of events, "and legion are the times that I have seen his eyes fill and the tears roll down his strong manly face for the men lost in that day's battle." One night Wainwright told Duffy about the two officers he dispatched with orders to stem a Japanese assault threatening to break the lines. Both died carrying out the order, "and that night as we sat around our headquarters, the tears streamed down the General's cheeks because those men had been lost. In fact there was not a day during the dark days in northern Luzon and the darker days in Bataan that the General did not worry about his wounded and his dead." While General MacArthur received the lion's share of praise, Duffy contended that Wainwright's calm presence and simple decency "did more to encourage the men and give them a will to fight, and was more responsible than any other single factor for the courageous stand that a handful of Americans and some untrained Filipinos made against the invading hordes of Bushidoists."[46]

As Wainwright prepared to leave Bataan to succeed MacArthur on Corregidor, Duffy told Wainwright that, like MacArthur, he would likely be ordered out of the Philippines as well. "No, Duffy, I will never leave my men," replied Wainwright, who vowed to continue to fight from the island fortress until either help, death, or surrender came.

While his friend relocated to Corregidor, Father Duffy remained in Bataan with two of Wainwright's aides, knowing there was nothing anyone could do but wait for the inevitable: surrender and likely an indeterminate stint in captivity. The priest, however, remained defiant. "Lack of food, disease and death finally defeated us, not the Japs."[47]

DURING THE first week of April, General Homma sent a message asking Wainwright to surrender all forces on Bataan and Corregidor. After receiving the American general's refusal, on April 3, Good Friday, Homma unleashed an assault that six days later forced Major General Edward P. King Jr., commander of the Luzon forces following Wainwright's move to Corregidor, to capitulate and relinquish the men under his command, including Fathers Duffy and Carberry.

"At last, the blow fell. Huddled in the darkness about our radio we heard the ominous words: 'Bataan has fallen!'" wrote Sister Olivette. Soldiers on Bataan reacted with a mixture of incredulity and resignation. Though it was a bitter pill to swallow, most had already accepted that their predicament would end either in death or captivity. "Actually, the surrender came as kind of a relief," remembered Staff Sergeant Nolan. "We'd no longer have to fight, and we thought we'd be treated halfway decent, maybe even be swapped for Japanese diplomats. There was a feeling of, 'Oh boy, this is over!' Little did we know how much worse it was to get."[48]

While the Japanese celebrated with parades through Manila's streets and salutes to their emperor, Father McKee refused to yield the slim hope for an American relief expedition, dimmed though it had been with the fall of Bataan. "Our question now was: could the small force now left on the tiny island of Corregidor, two miles south of the tip of Bataan, hold out until help would come from America?"[49]

"Lord, Have Mercy on Your Servant"

With word of the surrender quickly spreading, on the dusty, winding roads that inched along Manila Bay on Bataan's eastern coast there occurred a ten-day atrocity that would soon be labeled by a shocked world as the Bataan Death March. Hastily drawn Japanese plans for prisoner evacuation produced chaos and brutality for the priests and soldiers.

According to those plans, the prisoners would be gathered at San Fernando after a march of up to fifty-five miles and then transported thirty-three additional miles by truck and train to Camp O'Donnell, seventy miles northwest of Manila. Four food stops existed along the route, supplemented by rest stations with water and sanitary facilities every mile, and the Japanese established two hospitals for those too weak or injured to move.

Unfortunately, plans never became reality. The Japanese, already logistically stretched by their advances in British Malaya and the Netherlands East Indies, lacked enough food to share with the American and Filipino captives. They underestimated the physical condition of the prisoners, many of whom were in no shape to walk the miles asked of them, and the Japanese assumed they would have to care for only 25,000 to 35,000 prisoners, one-third of the actual number.

What was to be an organized movement of prisoners quickly disintegrated. As men shuffled north along the peninsula from Mariveles on Bataan's southern edge on April 10, Japanese troops advancing in the opposite direction looted and beat the prisoners. Father Carberry learned to be especially wary of trucks filled with Japanese soldiers, who made a gruesome game out of smacking prisoners with their rifles. The captives trudged along hour after hour on the dusty road, stumbling without water to quench a thirst aggravated by the ninety-five-degree heat. More than once, a parched prisoner dashed from the line toward muddy water along the road, only to be shot dead before he reached the puddle.

"Extreme Unction, Baptism, Confessions administered daily on march," wrote Father Duffy. "Death, pestilence, hunger, exhaustion, depleted all. Beatings, decapitations, executions beleaguered an exhausted, defeated army that had fought three months on seven ounces of food per day until there was no more food, medicine, or ammunition. In disgrace, exhausted, we were driven like cattle along that march, and the weak, exhausted and sick were slain or left to perish."[50]

"It was terrible to keep walking when you were barely able to lift your feet above a shuffle," said Staff Sergeant Nolan. "Those who fell on the side of the road were either bayoneted, shot, or trucks ran over them. I kept going by focusing on what I was doing and not thinking about the atrocities. More men died each day, but they gradually became simply more men dead—I was alive and concentrated on that."[51]

At one point Reverend Robert P. Taylor, a Baptist chaplain and one of Father Duffy's closest friends, rushed over to assist men to their feet before guards could beat them. He heard a familiar voice say, "Down but not out, eh, Preston?" When the cleric realized it was his fellow chaplain, also helping men rise, he replied, "Never out, Duff. Never out."

Taylor glanced at the priest, normally bedecked in a crisp uniform and priestly accoutrements, and realized how much of a toll the recent weeks had been on Duffy. The tattered pants of the now-barefoot priest hardly covered his legs, and the usually clean-shaven man sported a thick, matted black beard. "If your bishop catches you without your robes, he'll excommunicate you," joked Taylor, trying to lighten the misery a bit. "If he saw me now, he'd vomit, I stink so bad,"[52] answered Duffy.

The lengthy line of men sometimes walked through dust so thick that that they could barely see ten yards ahead. They discarded packs, helmets, and other items to lighten their load, but nothing could block out the bloated, decaying bodies, bayoneted earlier by Japanese guards, that lay by the roadside and emitted a sickening stench.

Guards stationed every twenty to thirty feet prodded the captives with their bayonets to maintain a steady pace. One guard, nicknamed the Shadow by other prisoners, glared so often at Father Duffy that Taylor warned him to immediately obey any order, but the Shadow seemed to have selected Duffy as his personal target. On one occasion, the guard stared at the crucifix dangling from a chain around Duffy's neck, thrust the tip of his bayonet toward Duffy, severed the chain, and flung the crucifix into the dust. Any time Duffy slowed his walk, the Shadow battered the priest's face with the butt of his rifle, so Taylor purposely started to walk behind Duffy so he could help support his friend should he begin to falter.

The Japanese often made the prisoners stand in the tropical sun for ten to twelve hours and then resume marching to see which of the exhausted men collapsed. Failure to keep pace with the line usually resulted in a bayonet thrust to the back. Duffy said later that at that time, "it was all that I could do to carry my own freight."[53]

Duffy's group reached the first stop midway up the peninsula within two to three days. For the first time since surrendering, the men enjoyed a little rest, water, and a small portion of rice and salt. Duffy used the time to administer Last Rites to a group of twenty-five Americans teetering on the brink of death. Though three other stops stood along the route, they offered little comfort. A rice paddy enclosed by barbed wire housed the prisoners at Orani, but by the time Duffy reached the town, the stench from human waste and dead bodies from earlier arrivals was more than anyone could bear.

Five days after he started the excruciating march, just above Orani, Father Duffy witnessed charity and compassion from the least-expected place. When Duffy again stumbled and fell, a group of guards beat and kicked the exhausted priest. After they left, another guard lagged behind and asked the prone Duffy what he might do to help. When Duffy pleaded for a drink, the guard left, but soon returned with a cup of tea. The Japanese soldier helped Duffy take a few sips, handed him biscuits, and cautioned him to catch up with the group ahead before other guards bayoneted him. Duffy, refreshed by the tea and biscuits and uplifted by the guard's humanity, struggled to his feet and, with agonizing effort, rejoined Reverend Taylor and the other fatigued men. He avoided certain death due to what Duffy later described as "one Jap's act of kindness."[54]

The unforgiving sun intensified as the morning hours stretched into the afternoon and transformed the roads into suffocating, dust-covered paths. Dirt matted their hair and clogged their nostrils, and the perspiring men trod paths littered with the human waste left by dysentery-stricken captives. Duffy kept pace by placing one foot in front of the other, focusing on one step at a time while blocking out the brutality so shockingly evident along the road.

"We plowed along like cattle, and played mental tricks with ourselves by thinking that something better waited for us just up the road," said Staff Sergeant Nolan. "Every once in awhile, if the guards weren't looking and there was some water by the road, we'd try to quickly scoop some up, even though we could see dead Americans lying in it."[55]

The ragged line of prisoners meandered past ditches clogged with American and Filipino bodies—many beheaded. One American officer counted twenty-seven headless bodies before forcing himself to keep his eyes fixed on the man in front of him to banish the gruesome sights.

Reverend Taylor slowed his pace to rejoin Father Duffy and encouraged the obviously weakened priest to keep moving. "It'll soon be night, Duff. Then they'll let us rest." The priest complied but asked the

Baptist minister to recite the words of the Catholic Last Rites over him, should he be unable to continue. "Don't think about it, Duff," the chaplain replied. "Think of night and rest."[56]

On April 22, eleven days after the march began, between the towns of Guagua and Bacolor, an elderly Filipino woman risked the guards' anger by offering water to Father Duffy. He had started lifting the cup to his mouth when his nemesis, the Shadow, smashed Duffy's face with his rifle butt, thrusting the cup inward with such force that the priest spat blood and teeth. Duffy dropped to his knees and was uttering a prayer when the Shadow ran his bayonet through Duffy's side, put his foot on the slumping priest, and yanked the blade out.

Neither knowing nor caring how the guard would react, Reverend Taylor knelt beside his friend and held Duffy's head in his hands. "Lord, have mercy on your servant," said Taylor of the priest he assumed was dying. "He's a good man who served you well. Receive his soul."[57] A Paulist priest, Father Thomas Scecina, came upon the scene and, also thinking the priest was dying, anointed Father Duffy.

Taylor left his companion when the Shadow threatened to do the same to Taylor if he did not rejoin the line. Before he had gone far, though, Taylor glanced back to see some Filipinos dragging Duffy, still alive, into the jungle. Taylor hoped that Duffy might somehow survive but doubted he would ever see the priest again.

While kind Filipinos carried Father Duffy away, at another point in the line Father Carberry reached the final resting place at San Fernando, an important rail center nine miles from Lubao. A twenty-five-mile train ride from San Fernando to Capas preceded an eight-mile march into temporary quarters at Camp O'Donnell. Guards crammed Carberry and one hundred captives into boxcars designed to carry forty and heated by a blistering midday sun. "We had to stand up because there was no space to sit down," said Staff Sergeant Nolan. Soon, as vomit and fecal material from dysentery sloshed about the floor, some yielded hope. "Guys were so sick and weak," explained Nolan, "that they didn't care anymore"[58] and perished in the oppressive heat of the boxcars.

The Death March ended in late April 1942, by which time an estimated 600 to 650 Americans had succumbed. Any slim hopes of rescue disappeared on May 6 when General Wainwright, realizing the futility of the situation and hoping to save American lives, announced the surrender of all forces in the Philippines to the Japanese. The general sent a message to President Roosevelt which included the moving words, "With broken heart and head bowed in sadness but not in shame, I report to your excellency that today I must arrange terms for the surrender." He added, "There is a limit of human endurance and that limit has long since been passed."[59]

For Fathers Duffy and Carberry, as well as for the missionaries in Manila, the war would now be fought in a series of prison camps while the United States geared up for a lengthy and bloody march across the Pacific. The soldiers on Corregidor had comprised their last shred of hope, but its surrender doomed them to isolation in a Japanese-controlled country. "Finally, on May 6th," wrote Sister Olivette, "we listened in helpless silence as the voice of General Wainwright read the order to his forces on the Philippine Islands to join him in surrender. We were prisoners of war!"[60]

AT THE same time that Duffy, Carberry, and the six missionaries disappeared into prison camps, America's military opened the doors to millions of young men and women who rushed to serve their nation in its battle against Germany and Japan. Among those millions were twenty-seven other Notre Dame priests, each wanting to minister in the arena where soldiers most needed their services: the battlefield.

American military units were commencing the long road to victory in Europe and the Pacific. Rescue at some distant point was on the way, but would it arrive too late for Notre Dame's eight religious held captive by the Japanese?

CHAPTER 2

"THE CHAPLAIN IS THE SERVANT OF GOD FOR ALL"

Chaplains in War Training

With war operations dominating the news that spring of 1942, other Notre Dame priests sought permission to become chaplains and serve at the front lines with the soldiers and sailors who battled Japan and Germany. The men had taken various routes to the religious life, but the path of each wound through Notre Dame, where they studied at either the university or the Holy Cross Seminary on campus. They came from every section of the nation but fashioned a common bond with one another at Notre Dame, where the university's academics, sports, and spirituality strengthened positive traits and molded newer ones. Throughout their lives, all retained their ties to Notre Dame and, if a member of the Congregation of Holy Cross, to one another. Like every religious association of priests, brothers, and nuns, the Congregation of Holy Cross was during World War II, and still is, a family. The members share everything, including their earnings, and think of one another not as coworkers but as brothers and sisters.

Whether the priests were Holy Cross or diocesan, their top priority was to bring the benefits of religion to others. What better way, some thought, than to volunteer to be a chaplain?

The word *chaplain* originated in the fourth century when, one cold, wintery night, a soldier named Martin gave half of his cloak to a beggar. After experiencing a vision showing Christ wearing that cloak, Martin left the military to devote his life to the Catholic Church, donning the remaining half of the cloak he had shared. His reputation for holiness and for performing miracles earned him a loyal following during his life as well as after his death, when the Catholic Church bestowed sainthood on him as Saint Martin of Tours. To rally their troops subsequent French kings carried into battle Martin's cloak, or *cappella* in French. The king's religious adviser tasked with keeping the cloak safe was called *cappellanus*, a word that in Old French became *chapellain*, and eventually *chaplain*.

In the New World, George Washington often advocated for chaplains' use in the military. On September 23, 1756, during the French and Indian War, he wrote to Robert Dinwiddie, lieutenant governor of Virginia, of his contention that the presence of a chaplain could boost morale and reduce drunkenness among his troops. Washington persisted in this belief during the American Revolution twenty years later, when he added, "While we are duly performing the duty of good soldiers, we certainly ought not to be inattentive to the highest duties of religion."[1] At his and other leaders' urging, on July 29, 1775, the Continental Congress adopted a pay scale for army chaplains granting them twenty dollars per month, the same pay as captains. This date is recognized as the official beginnings of the U.S. Army chaplaincy.

During the Civil War, priests from the Congregation of Holy Cross, including Father William Corby, C.S.C., who gained fame at Gettysburg, offered their services. They and other chaplains became so valued that an officer with the Tenth Connecticut Regiment concluded, "We count our chaplain as good as a hundred men in a fight, because the men fight so much better when he's with them."[2]

The establishment of an official army chaplain school during World War I (a navy chaplain school followed during World War II) and the designation of chiefs of chaplains for the army and navy gave further official recognition of their value to the military. "We who are in authority recognize it as a trust to return to wives and mothers at home husbands and sons who are not only all that they were before they came to France, but something bigger and finer," wrote General John J. Pershing during World War I. That concern lasted through the conflict two decades later, when General George C. Marshall explained, "There should be no fear that any young man will suffer spiritual loss during the period of his military service. On the contrary, we hope that the young soldier will return to his home with a keener understanding of the sacred ideals for which our Churches stand."[3]

THE ROMAN Catholic Church recognized the importance of chaplains as well. On November 29, 1939, Pope Pius XII appointed Bishop Francis J. Spellman to be military vicar for the United States. The next month Bishop John F. O'Hara, C.S.C., Notre Dame's president, was appointed military delegate to assist Spellman at what became known as the Military Ordinariate. His task was to oversee the rapid inclusion of Catholic priests into the military. Under O'Hara's guidance, the number of Catholic chaplains in the army and navy rose from 55 in 1939 to more than 3,000 (plus 1,700 auxiliary chaplains) by 1945.

The expansion did not come easily, however. In a letter sent to the superiors of religious orders throughout the United States a year and a half before Pearl Harbor, O'Hara cited the need for fifty-three chaplains as the military expanded in response to alarming developments in Europe, where the German dictator Adolf Hitler had already engulfed the continent in war, and in the Pacific, where the Japanese threatened to disrupt the peace. O'Hara emphasized that the men selected from those orders, including his own Holy Cross, should be deeply spiritual and able to "lead the lonely sort of spiritual existence that is usually the lot of the Chaplain." He advised that the men be sound physically "and fitted by nature and grace to meet men on a man's level." O'Hara cautioned that if he was unable to fill chaplain vacancies with Catholic priests, he might be forced to turn to Protestant clergymen to fill the chaplaincies—"And be it said to the credit of the Protestant ministers, that they are applying for chaplaincies at the rate of thirty or forty a day."[4]

With war yet seventeen months away, and with the clutches of the Great Depression losing traction, in mid-1940 the nation's mind was on anything but military concerns. A handful of Catholic volunteers trickled in, including some C.S.C., but the situation grew so desperate that on November 28, 1941, only nine days before Pearl Harbor, O'Hara dashed off a personal appeal to the Holy Cross superior at Notre Dame, Father Thomas A. Steiner. He told Father Steiner that the War Department had informed him that because of "the prolonged lack of Catholic chaplains" it would soon be necessary to either fill the vacancies with Protestant or Jewish chaplains or to keep them vacant. Adding that "the situation is acute,"[5] O'Hara asked his fellow Holy Cross priest to consider sending men under the age of forty who might qualify.

O'Hara's congregation responded. Less than three weeks after Pearl Harbor, Father Steiner wrote to Father Edward Fitzgerald, C.S.C., of the need to free the order's priests from their peacetime duties so they could become chaplains. "These are critical days," he wrote, "and much sacrifice must be made, so we may just as well begin immediately."[6]

Unlike the hundreds of thousands of young men soon to be whisked away by the draft, the twenty-nine priests (counting Fathers Duffy and Carberry) volunteered, not from a sense of adventure or a willingness to bear arms, but rather from the desire to aid those young men about to endure life's most crucial test: that of facing on the battlefield another human being intent on killing them.

On December 7, 1941, these men averaged 36.4 years of age, ranging from twenty-seven-year-old Father John McGee to forty-nine-year-old Father Vincent Mooney. (Fifty-three-year-old Bishop John O'Hara, remained at the Ordinariate.) They felt the same emotions, the same patriotism, and the same fears as the hordes of young men who left job or school to enter the military, and like their fellow countrymen, they wanted to do their part in helping defeat the nation's enemies. Unlike those countrymen, however, soon to be armed with powerful new weapons, they would bring to the war the same tools they used in peacetime: chalices instead of rifles, prayer books instead of hand grenades, sympathetic ears and calming words instead of bombs.

By the end of 1942, nineteen of the twenty-nine chaplains (not counting the six missionaries, two of whom were priests) were in service, with eight more joining in 1943 and another pair in 1944. Older than the soldiers and sailors they ministered—partly because they had already completed not just college but also additional years in seminary training, and partly due to the government's desire to take only experienced priests—65 percent were in their thirties, and all enjoyed good health.

Three were already chaplains when war broke out. Besides Fathers Duffy and Carberry (the latter of whom became a chaplain in 1940) in the Philippines, Father Barry, a pint-sized man with the heart of a lion, had been posted since April 1941 with the army's Forty-Fifth Infantry Division, a Colorado National Guard unit that would serve with renown in the European theater.

Priests entered the chaplaincy for different reasons. Some wanted to join the legions of young men willing to sacrifice life and limb for their country, a duty they felt they had no right to shirk simply because they were priests. Others wanted to do their part in making the world a safer place, or to answer the call of repressed nations suffering under the Nazi boot in Europe or the Japanese sword in the Pacific. All saw it as an opportunity to bring Christ's words to soldiers and sailors facing the direst of tests.

They left posts at Notre Dame, as did Father Francis J. Boland, dean of the university's College of Arts and Letters; and Father Robert W. Woodward, who in addition to teaching philosophy at Notre Dame also served as rector of Morrissey Hall, one of the campus dormitories. Others transferred from parish duties and headed to the army.

"Every priest who can possibly be spared is badly needed at the present moment," wrote Father Gerald Fitzgerald (no relation to Edward) to Father Steiner of his own eagerness to become a chaplain. From his post in Austin, Texas, where he taught high school, Father John Biger heard that some military units lacked Catholic chaplains. He volunteered and explained to Father Steiner, "My chief concern is the welfare of the boys. Certainly, we cannot deny that they need moral and spiritual support." In explaining his desire to be a chaplain, Father Henry Heintskill wrote, "I have thought over this matter and believe that in this request I am motivated by considerations of patriotism and the desire to be of spiritual help to those who will most need that help."[7]

Personal issues sometimes provided the reasons for volunteering. Father Thomas A. Gleason, whose duties in Massachusetts included serving the local police department as chaplain, sent a stream of unsuccessful requests Father Steiner's way in hopes of joining his brethren priests in the military. "I have been watching the mail daily for a favorable reply. Some of my former comrades in the Police Department are terribly disappointed that I am not in the Army. In fact, some of them think that I have not the 'guts' to enter the Army as a chaplain. I am hoping for an early approval of my application."[8]

They turned to Father Steiner because the first step in becoming a chaplain was to obtain the permission of either their diocese or, as was the case for a religious order such as the C.S.C., their superior. If Father Steiner approved, he forwarded the name to the Military Ordinariate in New York City, which then sent the names of those it endorsed to the U.S. Armed Forces.

Although the requirements changed during the war according to the branch of service and as the need for additional chaplains soared, in December 1941 army regulations stipulated that chaplains be male citizens between the ages of twenty-three and forty-three, ordained and accredited with a recognized religious denomination, graduates of both four-year college and three-year theological seminary courses, and priests with three years of experience. Their appointments would last until six months after the war. After receiving approval, the chaplain-to-be filled out an array of questionnaires, attached a photograph, and headed to the local police station to be fingerprinted. He finally submitted his papers and waited for a telegram telling him where to report for training and chaplain school.

"Life in the Army Is Quite Different from Civilian Life"

As was true for those young men entering the U.S. Army, Navy, or Marines, a training period began each chaplain's transition from the civilian to the military life. Inside the classrooms, the novice chaplains studied military customs, laws, disciplinary codes, and histories, while outside, the exacting physical training handed them no breaks.

The army opened a chaplain school in February 1942 at Fort Benjamin Harrison, Indiana, but only four classes finished the monthlong course—eventually lengthened to six weeks—because the facilities could not handle the increasing numbers flowing into the military. As a replacement location, the government turned to prestigious Harvard University in Boston to house its prime chaplain school, which accepted its first candidates in August of the same year. Harvard served as host school for two years, after which the army shifted its operations to the massive military complex at Fort Devens, Massachusetts, and then to Fort Oglethorpe, Georgia.

The navy's chaplain school started at Virginia's Norfolk Naval Station but in spring 1943 the location switched to the College of William and Mary in Williamsburg, Virginia, to handle the larger numbers. The course consisted of six weeks of training—the navy added extra academic classes on naval customs and regulations—and two weeks at a navy post.

Father Joseph D. Barry, C.S.C., found out how harsh, and invigorating, was the alteration from civilian to military. Small in size at 5'3", Joseph Barry made up for it with intensity and grit. Born to Irish immigrant parents from Galway and Cork on December 7, 1902, in Syracuse, New York, Barry excelled in the athletic arena. A key member of his Catholic high school's baseball nine, Barry also quarterbacked the school's football squad to the Syracuse city championship.

The serious-minded Barry, however, paid attention in the classroom, where he raptly listened to nuns spin their stories about the summer classes they had taken at Notre Dame and the joys of the religious life. Intent on becoming a priest, Barry enrolled at Notre Dame in 1925, graduated four years later, and spent four additional years at the Holy Cross Seminary on the university's grounds before being ordained in June 1933. It was during his time preparing for the priesthood that Barry, playing shortstop for the seminary baseball team, helped defeat a Notre Dame squad supposedly featuring the Four Horsemen.

As tough as the gridiron quartet might have been, Barry now faced a rigorous test that made Rolling Prairie appear tame by comparison. "Let me say this is no snap," reported Father Barry to his superior, Father Steiner, of his time in chaplain school at Harvard. "Still suffering from the pains and aches of the first three days of shots in the arm, vaccination, X-ray, blood test, physical exercise, swimming and marching,"[9] lamented Barry's fellow South Bend chaplain, Father John J. Burke, C.S.C.

Barry, like the other Notre Dame chaplains at the school, awoke between 5:30 and 6:00 a.m. each day to face a demanding sixteen-hour schedule that alternately packed military jargon and information in their brains and strained every heretofore-unchallenged muscle. At the navy's chaplain school, twenty-nine-year-old Father Heintskill hustled out of bed to the parade ground, where he and the other candidates marched to breakfast. Thirty minutes later he again stood in formation before racing to a morning packed with classes instructing the initiates in military law, map reading, medical sanitation, military insurance, first aid, military etiquette, and a hundred other items. A one-hour break for lunch preceded two additional hours of classroom instruction.

After the final lecture, when students at civilian universities retired to leisurely pastimes, Barry and the chaplains faced hours of physical training, leading thirty-five-year-old Father Joseph Corcoran, C.S.C., to moan, "and it seems like we already went through a full day already."[10] They swam, ran across nearby farmland and fields, and marched along dusty roads—tasks designed to toughen the chaplains, who would be expected to face the same rigors as the men they served. Three nights a week the men sat through two-hour lectures about hygiene, military history, or other relevant topics, and they often spent weekends reading classroom assignments and completing what seemed hundreds of reports and questionnaires.

Introduction to the military life took a toll on the chaplains, all of whom were older than the recent high school graduates quickly filling the ranks of the expanding armed services. "For ten days we had the pants drilled off of us," reported Father Heintskill. He claimed that the camp was "alternately the dustiest and muddiest hole this side of Russia" and that his fellow Holy Cross priest, forty-seven-year-old Father Boland, one of the oldest chaplains present, "is taking something of a beating . . . but he looks very healthy." In his reply, Father Steiner expressed his concern that Boland was not up to the task, as he "is not as young as he used to be. However, he will probably toughen up, and become a regular."[11]

The long-distance runs and demanding classroom hours introduced the priests to military life, gave them a glimpse of what they would face in combat, and established the foundation for them to be more effective chaplains. Barry calmed trainees as the young men crawled through obstacle courses while real bullets zipped inches above their heads, and he returned from exercises to the cheers and backslaps of men who appreciated his refusal to back down from arduous activities. Having endured the same adversities as the men with whom they were about to work, they were more readily accepted by the soldiers and sailors.

"As you know, life in the army is quite different from civilian life," wrote Father Barry. "Here in the service, the troops or officers don't care where you come from or who you were before; but they are keen to see what you can do and above all, how much you can take." Barry found the daily three-hour drills and the twenty-five-mile night marches stimulating but was not as certain about his older comrades. "Many of the older men find this 'subject' very hard on their feet, but it's a taste of what's coming."[12]

After completing chaplain school, Barry and the other army chaplains were commissioned as second lieutenants, while Heintskill and his navy comrades became lieutenants (jg). They enjoyed a brief leave before reporting to the next post, where they joined army infantry or navy seamen for additional training in specialized areas.

Father Barry was attached to the 157th Regiment, a Colorado National Guard unit of 2,600 men that was one of three regiments forming the Forty-Fifth Infantry Division. Going into combat with the motto "Eager for Duty," the 157th Regiment enjoyed a famed past. The unit fought nobly during the Indian Wars and raised the American flag above Manila in the Philippines during the 1898 Spanish–American War. In 1916 the regiment chased the Mexican outlaw and revolutionary Pancho Villa along the Arizona–Mexico border before deploying to France for service in World War I.

Many of the men to whom Barry ministered had scratched out meager existences during the Great Depression, living in economically depressed areas also hard hit by the massive storms that created the Dust Bowl. They originally joined the regiment to collect the twelve-dollar quarterly check offered by the National Guard. As the Forty-Fifth Infantry Division drew from Colorado and Oklahoma, areas containing a large population of Native Americans, Father Barry became accustomed to working with members of the Cherokee, Choctaw, Sioux, and other tribes. He found that most of the white soldiers accepted their Native American brethren, mainly because they repeatedly exhibited courage in training exercises and would be welcome companions when the unit met the enemy. In 1939 the regiment adopted the nickname the Thunderbirds, after the mythical bird with extraordinary powers of Native American lore.

In February the Forty-Fifth Division moved to Camp Barkeley, near Abilene, Texas, a facility soaked with so much standing water that the men joked they had arrived at a naval base. They griped about the mud that stuck to their boots and impeded their movements, but later appreciated the experience when they faced worse conditions in the downpours of the Italian campaign.

"Camp Barkeley, Texas—BAH!" wrote Barry of his disdain for their new location. Blistered feet joined the rain and mud as the worst tormenters during long marches and military exercises. "Never did I spend such an unholy Holy Week, & never did I do so much penance (God knows I needed it) in so short a time," Barry wrote to Father Steiner. "We were on the march all day Holy Thursday, all night, until 4 a.m. I stumbled in a rut made by a weapons carrier truck and I stayed just as I fell. I used my steel helmet for a pillow, a rain coat for a blanket, and the black sky for a roof. We had marched 31 miles—and I marched. I saw kids with blisters as big as dollars."[13]

The week Barry referred to was the regiment's April 1941 field exercise against the Second Infantry Division, the first time the National Guard unit competed against a Regular Army outfit. Both vied to be the first to reach a pass on a plateau near Abilene, and even though Barry and his regiment had to cross more miles over more adverse terrain, they handily reached the pass before their rivals.

During that Holy Week exercise, on Good Friday a soldier from the South walked up to Barry as another soldier showed Barry how to operate a machine gun.

"You all a chaplain?" asked the young soldier.

"Yes, soldier. Why?" replied Barry.

"Well, this is the God-damnedest Good Friday I ever spent," he answered. "How about you? We should be praying and not learning to shoot other folks."[14] Barry agreed with the sentiment, but in those years the war took preference, even if it meant interrupting the most solemn religious period of the year for Catholics.

Later, after celebrating one Mass in a recreation tent and a second in a larger "Big top" tent (Barry's description), Barry, disappointed in the sparse attendance at service, improvised a scheme to attract more men to Mass. After a soldier walked up and handed Barry $1.20, which Barry explained was "a lot of $ for a soldier boy to have," he asked what the money was for.

"I won it in a poker game and I promised St. Joseph I'd give half of my winnings to the Church," answered the soldier.

"What a time I had keeping a straight face," Barry wrote to Father Steiner. "I took it, looked at it and said, 'Now, you've paid your promise. Now I'll give you $1.20 if you bring in a boy who had not made his Easter Duty'—and he did the next Sunday."[15]

While Barry enjoyed interacting with the troops, he did not appreciate the weekly Monday morning chaplains' meeting, which in his opinion consisted mostly of chaplains complaining about a lack of typewriters and Bibles. "What a gang of cry babies,"[16] he wrote. Barry preferred to be out in the field with his men instead of wasting time in an office.

Weekends, when the soldiers flocked to San Antonio for a few hours of fun, provided interesting challenges. Although the city offered many historic places, including the famous Alamo where Davy Crockett and others had perished, Barry understood that the soldiers preferred bars and places of ill repute over tourist spots. "I don't know how much history the boys learned,"[17] Barry wrote; he told Father Steiner he often had to accompany an officer into San Antonio to bring back the men who had landed in the slammer.

Barry's unit made history by participating in the September 1941 Louisiana maneuvers, the largest peacetime military exercise to date, which pitted the Second Army against the Third Army. Almost half a million men operated across 3,400 square miles of Louisiana's hills, ravines, and wetlands while generals evaluated prewar military doctrine and isolated areas of training that needed improvement.

"This business of marching 20 and 30 miles a day, wading through swamps, certainly gives a fellow a tiger appetite and the will to fall asleep while walking," wrote Barry to Father Steiner. "Heard of drivers falling asleep, but I've seen soldiers walk off the road and land in a ditch." At night he pitched a pup tent, which "is supposed to care for one pup or two men." Despite the cramped quarters, the exhausted priest noted, "Had a good sleep. It's getting so now I can sleep wherever I fall. No fooling."[18]

Father Barry had to catch his rest whenever possible, for he served under a man who would become one of the army's most heralded and controversial commanders, Major General George S. Patton. The officer, said Father Barry later, loved to drill and thought nothing of yanking him and the men out of their tents for marches lasting until dawn.

Like everyone else, Father Barry battled temptation. Early one rainy morning, Barry thought of staying under the warm blanket and catching a few extra hours of sleep, but duty beckoned. He concluded that "the kids will be looking for you, rain or shine," and made a silent bargain with himself: "Get up, Joe, and I'll take you to the officers' club for a night cap."[19]

During the exercise, soldiers faced their tasks seriously, but Barry noticed that at times they could suddenly lighten the mood by "liberating" homes occupied by pretty girls or "seizing" cold drink stands. At one point in the maneuvers his unit captured thirty men from the opposing army. When the prisoners, all from Indiana, learned where Father Barry had studied, they pestered him with questions, none of which pertained to the military. "When they heard I was from Notre Dame," wrote Barry, "their interest was, 'what kind of team you gonna have?'"[20]

Although Roman Catholics comprised one-quarter of the regiment's roster, Father Barry ministered to every faith, including Protestant and Jewish soldiers, as well as men who lacked religion or who had never been baptized. Rather than remain in his office and wait for men to come to him, Barry dropped by the post exchange—a popular place for men to gather—orderly rooms, and barracks. He shared jokes and laughter as he handed out Bibles and prayer books, religious medals and Rosaries. For those with serious matters on their minds, at the end of a long day Father Barry camped out at the chapel, where he listened to soldiers unravel their woes and offered advice. In the field he said Mass wherever he could, setting up makeshift altars on the turned-down tailgates of trucks. From March to June 1943, he conducted an average of six personal interviews each day and heard seven hundred confessions each month, and also organized company singalongs, delivered sex morality lectures, and arranged hospital visits. While he had little difficulty in locating soldiers to be altar boys, Barry was sometimes disappointed with the small turnout at some of his Masses. He even resorted to suggesting to sergeants that they tell their men they would receive a pass into town if they attended Mass. "It works,"[21] he told Father Steiner.

On another occasion, hoping to entice men to seek out the priest for counsel, Father Barry enlisted the aid of the roughest-looking sergeant he could find, handed him one thousand religious medals, and posted him where the soldiers washed their mess gear. As the sergeant passed out the medals, he told them that the medals were no good unless the chaplain blessed them. "It ain't blessed, you see. It ain't no good that way. Go over and have the padre bless it."[22] A steady line of soldiers filtered over to Barry's quarters, giving the priest the opportunity to inquire about their needs, gripes, and religious state.

Father Barry quickly learned that rules, the linchpin of his religious life and the code of behavior he strove to follow, often meant little on the battlefield. When the tanks of Barry's unit were in danger of running out of gas, Patton had them filled up at gas stations outside the maneuver area. Opposing commanders later complained that he had ignored the rules, but Patton brusquely replied that there were no rules in war. Victory was all that mattered, and he planned to do anything necessary to achieve that end. Barry, who had lived according to rules his entire life, understood that he now operated in a realm where rules might be handily discarded.

Less than three months later, training intensified for Barry and the soldiers of the 157th Regiment when the Japanese attacked Pearl Harbor. Longer marches and field operations occupied most of their time. "It was simply a matter of learning how to kill as an alternative to being killed," wrote Second Lieutenant Felix L. Sparks, an officer in Barry's 157th Regiment. "Boys suddenly became men."[23]

While they may have transformed into men as far as war was concerned, in Barry's eyes they remained boys in need of spiritual guidance, a boost to their morale, or a shoulder to lean on.

"Keep Your Fingers on the Pulse of the Regiment"

In another training facility, Father Francis L. Sampson questioned his sanity as he, along with the other novice paratroopers, prepared to take their initial leap from an aircraft soaring disconcertingly high above the Georgia pastures. He was too proud to back away and earn the disdain of his comrades, and besides, he had found alluring the prospect of serving with an elite unit like the paratroopers. If he hoped to minister to those men, he had to ignore his anxieties and leap from the airplane toward trees that now appeared to be the size of toothpicks.

Born February 29, 1912, in Cherokee, Iowa, Sampson graduated from Notre Dame in 1937 before enrolling at Holy Cross Seminary. He handled the rigors of Rolling Prairie but soon decided that he preferred the duties of a diocesan priest to that of a religious order. After transferring to the Saint Paul Seminary in Minnesota, Sampson was ordained in June 1941 and following Pearl Harbor received permission to become an army chaplain from his bishop, the Most Reverend Gerald T. Bergan of Des Moines.

While in chaplain school at Harvard, Sampson volunteered for the paratroops, unaware that his training entailed far more than he expected. "Frankly I did not know when I signed up for the airborne that chaplains would be expected to jump from an airplane in flight,"[24] Sampson later wrote.

His arrival at Fort Benning, Georgia, in May 1942 to begin work with the paratroopers did not help. An adjutant informed Sampson that the two chaplains who preceded him now lay in hospitals, one with a broken leg and the other with an injured back. As the color drained from Sampson's face, the adjutant burst into laughter and confided that three or four other chaplains had safely made it through paratrooper school.

The school offered four weeks of training—Stages A, B, C, and D—each conducted by a sergeant. Like despots of old, the sergeants ruled over every student, officer and enlisted. Lest the trainees doubt their authority, they had the example of the unfortunate lieutenant colonel who made the mistake of disagreeing with and berating his training sergeant. The school's senior commander forced the lieutenant colonel to apologize in front of the unit before drumming him out of the school. The sergeants "meant business here," wrote Sampson, "they played no favorites, and any man who failed to fulfill the rugged requirements was washed out."[25]

As he explained in his book, *Look Out Below!*, Sampson and seventy-seven other officers reported for Stage A, which concentrated on calisthenics and running. The first morning workout exhausted Sampson, who nursed pains from muscles he wished he no longer had. One-quarter of his group collapsed in the withering Georgia heat, and the men who survived fell onto their cots, sweaty fatigues and all, until they had to report for afternoon exercises. Sampson pushed himself to complete the obstacle course, squats, judo, and fifty pushups while hoping to retain enough energy for after-dinner consultations with soldiers and a visit to the chapel to recite his daily Breviary.

He and his fellow trainees had to run to and from each activity, and no one could lean against anything throughout the arduous days. Sampson once yawned while the sergeant demonstrated an activity and quickly found himself on the ground, sweating as he completed the fifty-pushup punishment. By the end of the week forty of the seventy-eight candidates had dropped out of the rigorous program.

In Stage B, the second week of training, instructors taught the correct way to parachute. Practicing first from the fuselage of a plane without wings, instructors illustrated how to stand properly in the plane, how to hook up the strap that rips the top off the parachute pack, and how to check fellow soldiers' equipment. They then marched the group to the landing trainer, where Sampson and his fellow trainees were fastened in a jumper's harness attached to a roller that slid down a long incline. As Sampson plunged downward, the sergeant pulled a lever and Sampson suddenly dropped to the ground, at which time he was to hang on to the risers (straps connecting to the canopy lines), duck his head between his knees, and roll along the ground like a ball.

Any man who failed to properly execute the landing incurred the sergeant's wrath, who made the offender double-time around the area several times, holding his parachute risers above his head and shouting out his misdeed. Sampson, like most everyone else, bungled the first few attempts and had to run around the field eight times, shouting, "I'm a bad chaplain, I dropped my risers!"

After next sliding down a long cable extending on an incline from a thirty-eight-foot-high platform toward a pile of sawdust, for the rest of this stage and all of Stage C, each man in the group trained by being hoisted to the tops of 250-foot towers and then suddenly released. Sampson listened attentively as the sergeant showed them how to pack their own parachutes, stimulated by knowing that he would make his first five jumps with the parachutes he assembled.

The final step in becoming a paratrooper came with the actual jump in Stage D. Immediately before that moment, which many of the men dreaded, a long line of paratroopers waiting for Confession swamped Sampson. He understood their motivation, as he shared the same concerns. About to make their initial jump from an aircraft, all that kept Sampson and the other trainees from a sudden death was pieces of cloth packed by the men themselves.

Once aloft in the plane, Sampson was surprised at how small everything looked from the air. The orders "Stand up!" and "Hook up!" preceded the command to "Check your equipment!" at which time each soldier inspected the parachute of the man ahead. The final paratrooper in line then began the rhythmic "Ten O.K.!" and slapped the leg of the man ahead. When the countdown reached Sampson, he shouted, "One O.K.!, Sergeant."

A flaring red light above the door signaled the jumpmaster to slap Sampson's leg, at which the priest leaped out the door. The prop blast spun him around as he plunged downward, helpless in the void. He remembered to keep his chin pressed to his chest, but the chute opened with such a jerk that it almost knocked him unconscious. The chute slowed his descent and all was "peace and quiet," which he later called "a pleasant sensation. The thrill was nothing at all like what I had expected. The excitement, nervousness, and tension were gone, replaced by a feeling of great satisfaction and genuine enjoyment."

Sampson landed hard and felt a sharp pain in his leg. He briefly entertained the thought that if it were broken, he had the chance to exit gracefully from the program, as "jumping is a boy's racket, not something for a thirty-year-old man," but other than a few frayed nerves, the chaplain was fine. He carried his parachute to waiting trucks, where he joined an exuberant group of trainees, proud of their success and boasting that paratroopers had no equal in the military. "It was impossible not to share their good spirits. We sensed, too, that our mutual experience really made us brothers in the airborne family." On the ride back they started singing a refrain common to paratroopers— sharing the tune to the Civil War melody, "The Battle Hymn of the Republic"—"Gory, Gory, What a Helluva Way to Die."

Sampson's group completed five jumps by end of the week, at which time each received a certificate and the school commandant pinned wings above their left breast pocket. They proudly donned the shiny jump boots and sewed the paratrooper patch on their caps, both of which were "badges of such distinction that the jumper considered himself outside the law, above observing the customary courtesies toward civilians, and in a position to scorn all other branches of the service."[26]

Sampson had successfully completed his training and entered the paratrooper corps. He eventually received orders to join the 501st Parachute Infantry Regiment, then training at Camp Mackall, North Carolina, where he easily ingratiated himself with his superior officer and the men. When Sampson met Colonel Howard R. Johnson, the no-nonsense, gritty commanding officer who had taken his unit through training at Camp Toccoa, Georgia, Johnson dispensed with pleasantries and told the priest that he expected Sampson to be his conduit of information concerning the regiment. He ordered his new chaplain to keep track of the men's morale and to participate in every military exercise. "I want you to keep your fingers on the pulse of the regiment. You will know before anyone knows, before I know, if anything goes wrong with the morale, and I want you to come in as soon as you see something wrong and tell me. I want you to be with the men all the time, on their marches, on their night problems, in the field. Jump with them when they have to jump. This is what I expect of a chaplain. This is what I expect of you, if you are going to play on my team, fella."

Sampson, hoping to gain Johnson's approval, scrupulously followed the officer's directions but gained both Johnson's and the unit's respect from a comical mishap. When Sampson unknowingly ruffled a junior officer's feathers, the officer barged into Sampson's office and berated the chaplain for interfering with his authority. As the irate officer wheeled about to leave, he tripped over a loose floorboard, crashed through the screen door, and tumbled down the stairs, leaving the bewildered chaplain alternately stifling laughter and wondering what had so enraged the man.

Rumors shot through camp that Sampson, the unit's new chaplain, refused to be intimidated by the officer and, offended by the man's complaints, had knocked the officer through the door. Colonel Johnson summoned Sampson for an explanation, but the skeptical officer let the matter slide when Sampson claimed the affair was an accident. However, still believing that his priest had cold-cocked his junior officer, as Sampson left the office Johnson winked and said, "I like to have a chaplain be able to handle his dukes."[27] Sampson, who had never before been involved in a fight, left with the respect of his combative commander and of the paratroopers, who admired that they had in their midst a "fighting" chaplain.

"I Felt That I Ought to Be Five Priests"

Other duties with which the army infantry or navy seamen did not have to contend made the roles of Barry, Sampson, and the other chaplains more challenging. They were priests first and soldiers second, and in that primary role, they counseled and ministered while the rest of camp enjoyed leisure hours.

The military encouraged the inductees to see their chaplain if they faced any personal issues. The calm voice of a chaplain could not only settle their nerves during the challenges of training but also help them adjust to the jarring transition from the civilian to the military world. Soldiers barely out of high school faced the prospect of killing fellow human beings, an action that shattered every standard of civilized society and violated every dictate of their religious upbringings. In addition, war wrenched the young men from families, friends, and everything to which they had become accustomed. In these tumultuous times, chaplains represented normalcy in the midst of change and a touch of home in a foreign world.

To keep morale high, chaplains delivered lectures on morality, visited hospitals, and arranged sporting events and singing contests. They helped men fill out life insurance forms or obtain emergency leave when a parent passed away. They answered letters from wives complaining that their soldier-husbands had not written in months and from parents asking the chaplain to look out for sons who suffered from maladies ranging from timidity to gambling issues.

To be effective chaplains, Father Barry and the others had to be attentive listeners, for men filed into their quarters plagued by a variety of issues. Barry had to find the right words to soothe a soldier with an ill child at home, a brother who drank too much, or a wife who found comfort with another man. Soldiers sought counsel on whether to immediately marry the girl of their dreams or wait until after the war and risk that their separation might irreparably alter their situation. Thirty-four-year-old Father John M. Dupuis, C.S.C., with the Twentieth Marine Regiment Reinforced at Camp Lejeune on the New River near Jacksonville, North Carolina, made files for each Catholic marine in the regiment. He intended to talk to each man before they headed overseas to make certain they all approached combat with clear consciences.

"There are all sorts of problems the men have," Father Heintskill wrote to Father Steiner, "they're worried about conditions at home, etc. We have to do what we can." He explained that after one Friday evening service, at least two hundred men gathered for Confession, requiring him to remain an hour after lights-out at 9:30 p.m. "If ever I felt that I ought to be five priests it was that week."[28]

Father Heintskill became accustomed to constant interruptions from his sailors. "Maybe I should know better than to try to write a letter in my office," he mentioned to Father Steiner. "Every time I try to do it, it seems that I'm inviting interruption." As an example, he pointed out that the day before, he had started one letter, only to stop when a sailor asked to see him. Later in the day, when he returned to the letter, "I found it scratched up with notations I had made concerning some boy who wanted a discharge from the Navy." For much of the day Heintskill listened to sailors insisting they had to get home—"and the worst part of it all is that there is nothing we can do about it"—or read the plaintive letters sent by women trying to locate missing sons or "wives trying to get more of their husband's money."[29]

At the same time, like the soldiers they counseled, the chaplains were hardly immune to personal problems. A priest did not shed the joys and tribulations of family and friends because he entered the religious world. Personal issues followed them into the service, and they had to find ways to handle those issues while dealing with everything else the military tossed at them.

Since Father Barry's father had been deceased for a decade, he and his siblings financially supported their seventy-four-year-old mother. With all but one of his brothers and sisters married and unable to contribute, Father Barry tried to complement the fifteen dollars each week his single sister could afford.

As a member of the Holy Cross Congregation, though, Father Barry had taken a vow of poverty. The community, not the individual, owned everything, and he had to ask Father Steiner for permission to retain part of his wages. "May I give some financial assistance to my mother?" he wrote Father Steiner. He explained that his mother owed "all kinds of bills," that she had borrowed five hundred dollars "to save the home," and that coal and repair bills "are mounting and she is not getting any younger."[30] Father Steiner readily granted his permission, enabling Father Barry to help his aging mother.

LONG BEFORE they reached the battlefield, the priests dealt with seismic changes once they became chaplains. They emerged from religious worlds populated by Catholic priests like themselves, but once in the military, they stepped into an interdenominational domain comprised of Catholics, Protestants, and Jews. Before the war, different faiths rarely interacted. Catholic priests knew comparatively little about their Protestant or Jewish brethren who, in turn, professed ignorance of the Catholic faith. That changed once the candidates arrived at their chaplain schools.

At Harvard, whenever possible the army grouped together student-chaplains of different faiths so they could better understand each other's beliefs and practices. Father Barry shared a room with four other clerics: a Baptist, a Methodist, and a Congregationalist minister, and an Anglican priest. Practicality, not ecumenism, was the military's prime goal, for under fire, when the bullets flew and men died, the chaplains would have to minister to soldiers of every faith and denomination. "The chaplain is the servant of God for all," the *Army Chaplain Technical Manual* reminded every candidate, "and no narrow sectarian spirit should color his utterances, nor should his personal work assist only a special group."[31]

Chaplain school was thus the first time that most Notre Dame chaplains lived and worked with ministers of different denominations. They studied the basic prayers and services of every faith and engaged in late-night chats with Protestant and Jewish chaplains. Father Barry learned how to conduct Seder services for men of the Jewish faith, while Father Sampson instructed his Protestant candidates on how to properly say the Rosary. Protestant and Jewish chaplains were barred from hearing confessions or presiding at Mass, and only rabbis could conduct certain Jewish services, but the chaplains gained insight into other denominations that their Holy Cross brethren at Notre Dame missed. During training, they began to view Protestant and Jewish chaplains as human beings rather than as caricatures, and they followed the precept of "cooperation without compromise"—in other words, they would open their religions to other faiths, even conduct services for other denominations, without yielding on key issues such as distribution of Holy Communion. Multipurpose chapels hosted Catholic

Masses and Confession, followed by Jewish and Protestant services. Protestant chaplains often obtained blessed religious medals from Barry and other Catholic chaplains to distribute to the Catholic men in their units. Long before the 1960s reforms of Vatican II, the Notre Dame chaplains engaged in ecumenism.

Even holy men are not immune to prejudices, however. The Reverend William R. Arnold, a Catholic monsignor and the army chief of chaplains, complained that he spent an inordinate amount of time dealing with fractious clerics. Some Protestant ministers believed that their Catholic counterparts dismissed them as religious heretics, and some Catholic chaplains countered that Protestants scoffed at their practices.

During one nighttime air-raid drill, Father Corcoran and his fellow chaplains at Harvard rushed to the basement, where they sat in the dark for nearly an hour. "It was not so bad at first," he explained to Father Steiner. "But soon the Southern Baptists started their hymn singing. The only escape from there was the other end of the basement. And when we got down there, the Methodists were shouting their lungs out. The next time a black-out practice comes, the Padres are going to bunch together and out-shout both factions."[32]

Thirty-one-year-old Father Thomas Hewitt, C.S.C., who attended chaplain school with Father Barry, called his time at the school "one of the most peculiar experiences that I have met in my priesthood." He roomed with a Lutheran, a Christian Scientist, a Baptist, and a Reformed Evangelical, but he was not certain if their respect for Catholic priests was real or feigned. Along with other priests, Hewitt snickered at how the ministers called each other "Brother" and concluded that "they may detest the Catholic Church, but one thing is sure: they detest the sect of each other."[33]

Disapproval of other faiths crept into the letters mailed to and from Father Steiner. Father Heintskill, then studying at the navy's chaplain school in Williamsburg, Virginia, claimed that the Catholic chaplains mingled well with the chaplains of other faiths but then undermined his statement by adding, "For one thing we've found out they are a pretty dumb lot. In classes they ask the most asinine questions. But there are a couple of good Protestants—some are definitely interested in the Church."[34]

Two months later, Heintskill had not moderated his stance. "As we go along in the school it appears that one of the primary objectives is to teach chaplains—Catholics, Jews, and Protestants to cooperate," he wrote to Father Steiner. "I don't know that I've been too apt a pupil. There are several Protestants for whom I've come to have a genuine respect; but on the whole they still strike me as an insincere, selfish and hypocritical lot. I can't help but feel sorry for the sailors who will have to rely upon these chaplains for help. They are a pretty ignorant bunch when it comes to spiritual information." Father Steiner trumped his fellow Holy Cross priest by replying, "There is little sincerity in any of them. They are a selfish, hypocritical, four-flushing lot."[35]

Despite the divisions, Father Barry, Father Sampson, and most of the other Notre Dame chaplains realized that while significant differences existed with their Protestant and Jewish brethren, in the heat of combat those variances would dissipate. Under fire no one would be a priest or rabbi, but rather simply a human being bringing solace to another in distress. When a dying young boy cried for his mother, the faith of the chaplain ministering to him meant little.

While in the Pacific Robert Sherrod, the gifted military correspondent for *Time* Magazine, observed in 1943 the cooperation between the Catholic and Protestant chaplains aboard the troop transport as the vessel steamed near its destination, Tarawa, where a bloody three-day island battle was about to unfold. Sherrod, who had covered epic events for the magazine throughout his career, wrote of the impressive collaboration, "Denominational distinctions did not mean much to men about to offer up their lives."[36]

In civilian life the Catholic, Protestant, and Jewish ministers had rarely mingled. Once in training camp, however, they began to shed their differences and started treating each other as individuals sharing the same goals and facing the same dangers instead of members of a particular group. As another Catholic chaplain said, "Prejudice had no part for those who might die together."[37]

No matter how widespread their posts or how tumultuous their lives, the chaplains found an anchor of stability in Notre Dame. In their letters to Father Steiner, they constantly referred to the university. While in training, thirty-eight-year-old Father Edward Fitzgerald attempted to accompany an army convoy traveling to Fort Wayne, Indiana, ninety miles from Notre Dame. When his superior officer denied permission, Fitzgerald joked to Steiner, "Perhaps they suspected I'd take a little jaunt to Notre Dame!"[38]

Father Barry inevitably asked about the football squad, writing Father Steiner from the army chaplain school at Harvard, "We of 'Harvard' were glad to see Notre Dame come thru. The school has thousands of friends here in Boston." Father Steiner replied in kind, once concluding, "The team looks and acts like it is well coached and speedy."[39]

Father Steiner also commented on the remarkable transformation then occurring at the university. The navy, in need of facilities to train the thousands of fresh officers required by the war, had concluded an agreement with the university for Notre Dame to house successive groups of 2,500 midshipmen for three months' training each. The arrangement not only aided the navy but also helped keep Notre Dame financially afloat at a time when most prospective students delayed college until after the war to enter the military.

As TRAINING wound down, Monsignor Arnold, chief of chaplains, discussed the perils that Barry, Sampson, and every other chaplain would soon face. In a letter sent to each man he wrote, "We know something of the real sacrifices you have made in leaving organized, well-equipped parishes and comfortable homes to preach the knowledge and love of God and to bring the safeguards and consolations of religion to the officers and soldiers of our defensive forces." So that there would be no misunderstanding of what they were about to experience, he bluntly emphasized that "your responsibility is tremendous" and stated that "inconveniences, difficulties and hardships will be your portion. Your only sure reward will be God's blessing and the fruits of your ministrations in the lives of your men. Military life is a life of discipline, and the essential military virtues of courage, loyalty, obedience, devotion, and self-sacrifice are also religious virtues."[40]

By the time training ended, both military personnel and the chaplains were prepared to step onto the battlefield. "The men are ready for action," wrote Father Hewitt, "straining at the leash, being trained to a fine edge over a period of two years." He added that he, too, was ready. "Now is my great opportunity, with God's help, of instilling a greater devotion to God that will bring them divine courage at the moment of battle."[41]

"Believe Me, These Kids Are Soldiers"

Father Barry was ready, too, but his unit faced additional training before the soldiers could head overseas. In April 1942, the 157th Regiment marched through cheering crowds of Abilene citizens to board a train out of Texas. Father Barry and the regiment settled in for the journey through nine states to Fort Devens, Massachusetts.

The training intensified once the regiment reached Fort Devens. As always, Barry shared every exercise with his unit, including twenty-five-mile speed marches in which he was burdened with so much equipment that soldiers near him marveled that the 5'3" chaplain did not collapse.

"Barry was a short man," said Lieutenant Kenneth P. Stemmons. "He had all this gear on, and he was almost like a little kid. We wondered how he ever carried it all around, because it was made for six-feet guys. It was kind of comical. He was so small in stature compared to all those soldiers, and they were impressed that this little guy could do all that he could do. He was very popular with everyone. They all joked with him, but he'd laugh like the rest."[42]

During the summer, when the division added amphibious assault training on Cape Cod to the schedule, Barry donned his equipment, climbed the large tower that substituted for a ship, and then slid over the side onto netting to master the intricate drop from transports to landing craft. Ship-to-shore movements from actual vessels followed, forcing seasick soldiers to navigate the swaying netting toward choppy waters and bobbing landing craft.

Near the end of 1942 the division moved to Pine Camp near Watertown, New York, a location so bitterly cold and wintry that the soldiers labeled it the place "where blizzards rage."[43] Training slowed and morale slackened in the grueling conditions, producing a rash of fights in Watertown bars and one shooting.

Watertown residents welcomed the division's departure in January 1943, when the unit shifted to Camp Pickett, Virginia. Training again intensified, with the division operating in the Blue Ridge Mountains and conducting amphibious exercises on the Chesapeake Bay. Although Barry heard numerous gripes about the demanding activities, the men would appreciate these weeks of preparation when they hit the shores and mountains of Italy.

In a letter to the priest, Father Steiner remarked that Barry shifted around so quickly that "it would not surprise us either if this letter reached you at some other place miles from Fort Devens. Things move rapidly these days." He then added words of encouragement for Barry, who was one of the first priests from Notre Dame to serve as a chaplain in the conflict: "The war is becoming more serious every day, so you may expect to move at any time on short notice. We hope and pray that all will go well with you. Keep up your courage, and frequently renew your confidence in Divine Providence. You are doing God's work."[44]

From April into June, the Forty-Fifth Division embarked upon its final preparations for overseas duty. Barry informed Steiner that they were part of a task force, "the commander of which is rough, tough, outspoken General Patton. Recently he addressed us and left no doubt in the mind of any officer. There's a task to be done and we must expend all the force at our command."[45] Barry said that no one except their senior commanders knew the division's destination, but most guessed Egypt.

His days were filled with Mass and visits with troops, men for whom Barry developed a deep attachment. He posted a sign near mess hall stating "Heavenly Bread before daily bread" to entice the soldiers to think of their spiritual as well as their physical needs, and he became so exhausted hearing confessions that he nearly collapsed. He nudged his ailments aside when he looked at the young men who needed his assistance. "It got very tiresome, but love, I'm told, does not count the cost."[46]

Through outstanding performances in training and maneuvers, the division built a reputation as a crack outfit. Even the citizens of Watertown later gave grudging admiration to a division that had kept the town's constables occupied. An editorial in the Watertown newspaper called the Forty-Fifth "a rugged, rollicking group" that made other units that trained there "appear as docile as Dagwood Bumstead." The editorial added that while the soldiers "gave local police and MPs a real workout, . . . They were fighting men," and suggested that if a commander wanted an enemy location seized, "let him shove the 45th into battle. They will deliver the town, mussed up perhaps, but thoroughly conquered."[47]

On June 3 Father Barry and the 157th Regiment boarded five transports earmarked to take them across the Atlantic and into battle. Before embarking, men who had yet to make out their wills or purchase government life insurance scurried to complete the forms, many with the assistance of Father Barry, and scribbled notes to loved ones. Once aboard ship, the men played cards, listened to the radio, and mused over what the coming weeks might bring.

At 8:00 a.m. whistles sounded, and the convoy slowly steamed out of Hampton Roads, Virginia, bound for North Africa. As the U.S. coastline receded, men stared shoreward, thinking of loved ones and of the homes they were now leaving to defend. Father Barry thought of the Grotto at Notre Dame, where meditation and prayer in a tranquil setting had brought him hours of serenity, of the lakes, and of the stadium and its football games.

He hoped the strength that he absorbed at the Grotto could sustain him in battle. He believed that he and the regiment were ready for combat and claimed in a letter to Father Steiner that "the men are quite eager to shoot. Believe me, these kids are soldiers; coming from the Rockies and reared in the wide-open spaces they take to this Army life like the proverbial duck to water." The large numbers of Native Americans, he said, "are tops" for scouting an enemy, and "they can run for miles and come back for more."

Barry freely admitted his love for the division and confided with Steiner that he was ready to accept whatever lay ahead. "Seventeen months of training has prepared me well. I can eat anything," and "after eight or ten hours of marching I can sleep standing up. I've seen kids in night and forced marches go to sleep on their feet." The priest admitted that the rigorous training created deep bonds between them. "Strange do we act when we sit down to a table with cloth. Hardship seems to make for fellowship and fellowship develops some worthwhile friendships."[48]

Those friendships would be sorely tested in the coming weeks, a time that would toss the undersized Father Barry into battle and challenge him physically and mentally.

FOR BOTH the military and the chaplains, the conclusion of training marked the end of one phase of their military lives and the beginning of another. While no doubt arduous, the training at least occurred in familiar territory. The men had left home—which for the chaplains meant Notre Dame—but they still operated in stateside camps, thousands of miles distant from the war and its horrors. The eastern and western coastlines hoisted mental barriers that, for a time, kept the bullets and bombs at a safe distance.

With training completed, the war now moved front and center in their thoughts. The transports would whisk them away from all that was safe and familiar, toward the perils of the combat zones. War and its accompanying hazards drew nearer with each mile that the familiar coastline receded.

CHAPTER 3

"SURELY WAR IS A DIRTY GAME"

The Chaplains Go to War

With U.S. training camps sending hundreds of thousands of soldiers and sailors to war, the demand for chaplains rocketed. Within one week after Pearl Harbor, O'Hara's Military Ordinariate in New York City issued a letter to the country's Catholic organizations announcing that the military immediately needed two hundred priests and would require more as the war continued.

In a subsequent letter, O'Hara challenged fellow priests by stating, "The greatest missionary responsibility ever faced by the Catholic Church in the United States is presented by the Catholics in the Armed Forces today." He called the more than one million Catholics in service, "heads of a million future Catholic families [underline his]"[1] who deserved to receive the same comforts from their religion as the people back home. O'Hara needed to fill one hundred chaplain openings each month, and he argued that even though stateside parishes required priests, the congregations should be willing to endure inconveniences so that those young men placing their lives on the line for their nation could receive the benefits of a Catholic chaplain.

Bishop O'Hara even appealed to priests' emotions. He quoted from one soldier's letter to his pastor back home about the shortage of chaplains: "Boy, a Catholic chaplain is really a treat for sore eyes in the Army. But the only time we see one is on Sunday, that is if we can get to Mass. Our Mass is at 7:00, and that's the same time we eat, so the boys who go to Catholic church don't eat. I don't care if I ever eat breakfast, as long as I can get to church."[2]

Father Steiner accepted the challenge. In July 1942 he forwarded the names of five additional Holy Cross candidates from the fifteen who had asked permission to become chaplains. "No doubt as the war continues more chaplains will have to be offered," he wrote to a friend, Father Bernard E. Ransing, C.S.C. Steiner had to walk a fine line between the needs of his religious order and the military's demands—already twenty-one of the approximately three hundred Holy Cross priests had become chaplains—but he admitted to the dilemma of halting domestic religious programs and teaching positions to provide more chaplains, writing, "I am afraid that soon we will be obliged to make real sacrifices."[3]

The War Department gradually raised the age limit to enable more priests to apply for the chaplaincy, nudging the upper age to fifty-five from fifty in the army. However, a shortage of chaplains persisted for the duration of the war, forcing Bishop O'Hara to send repeated missives to all dioceses and religious orders requesting more candidates, not merely to replace those lost to death or injury, but also to minister to the expanding numbers pouring into the armed forces.

"I'm Paid to Die for My Country"

While Father Barry and the 157th Infantry Regiment prepared to storm Sicily's beaches to engage German and Italian foes, the Notre Dame religious in the Philippines struggled to remain alive as captives of the Japanese. Father Duffy could credit Lady Luck and Filipino compassion with saving him from the Death March. After the column of prisoners and Japanese guards passed by the bayoneted priest, two Filipinos had carried the unconscious chaplain into the brush, thinking him dead. When Duffy regained consciousness, he found himself in a bamboo shanty on the dykes of the fish ponds near Guagua, Pampanga, along with eight other Americans whom local inhabitants had whisked away from that deadly trail. Unfortunately, as Father Duffy recalled, in the next week five of the eight succumbed "from the ravages of the ordeal they had just passed through." Filipinos dug holes in the dykes into which they gently lowered the bodies and then covered the site with banana leaves topped by a layer of dirt.

Because Father Duffy could not walk, the Filipinos brought him food twice a day, and doctors daily treated his bayonet wounds. Duffy hovered between life and death as he gradually rebuilt his strength. "Filipinos' loyalty superb," Duffy later wrote. "They fed and clothed us and braved enemy activities at all times to protect Americans both in and outside of prison camps."[4]

One night in early May 1942, guerrillas carried Father Duffy, still too weak to walk under his own power, to Santa Rita, Pampanga. There, at the Santa Familias Hospital, operated in part by the Missionary Sisters of St. Dominic, the nuns nursed Filipino soldiers wounded in the recent fighting and the Death March. The Japanese dismissed their work as Filipinos tending to other Filipinos and thus only occasionally checked on them. Duffy's presence, however, endangered the hospital staff, who would suffer harsh retribution should the Japanese discover they sheltered an American. The nuns dismissed the risks and treated Duffy for three months while his wounds healed.

As his strength returned, Father Duffy became more active. When he learned that thousands of American prisoners in nearby Camp O'Donnell lived in such squalor that men "were dying like flies, hundreds a day,"[5] he organized a daily messenger service to and from the camp to smuggle in food, medicine, and information on the war.

By the latter part of June, Duffy had regained enough strength to visit Lieutenant Colonel Claude A. Thorp, left behind by MacArthur to direct guerrilla activities, at his headquarters in the Zambales Mountains northwest of Manila. Duffy offered his assistance, mainly in conducting religious services and hearing confessions, but hinted that he would not shrink from picking up arms if the situation called for it. Over the next four months, while still in the hospital, Father Duffy, under Thorp's supervision, helped organize guerrilla activities in five Philippine provinces in the Bataan region. When the Archbishop of Manila learned of the priest's activities, he warned Duffy to be careful to avoid the Japanese, but the priest refused to slow down.

As a chaplain, Father Duffy was forbidden to take up arms, but he had reason to ignore the dictate. In the latter part of June 1942, the guerrillas received a report that the Japanese operated a bayonet course near Malolos, the capital of the province of Bulacan. Duffy accompanied a band of guerrillas sent to investigate. When they approached Malolos, Duffy spotted a squadron of Japanese using Filipinos "as live targets on a bayonet course. I was screened by bamboo trees and saw about ten or twelve Filipinos being so used."[6] Duffy's small group could do nothing to intercede, but the incident made him more determined to help the courageous Filipinos.

He barely avoided capture a few times. "Nips searched the hospital twice for an alleged American," wrote Father Duffy, who eluded detention by donning nun's garb. "Succeeded in hiding from them but after second search left on August 20th so as not to endanger others who were caring for Filipino soldiers."[7]

Until the end of 1942 Duffy ministered to isolated groups of American soldiers and their Filipino guerrilla allies. He traveled from unit to unit, saying Mass and giving Communion. Blood poisoning in his bayoneted foot slowed him for a month, but care from a Filipino doctor and nurse brought him back to health.

Duffy and his band operated through back roads and across fields and rice paddies, encouraging people in numerous towns, visiting U.S. officers, and commanding different guerrilla units. Filipinos warmly greeted them and readily opened their homes and shared their food with the guerrillas. Duffy rejoiced when he learned of the smashing June 1942 naval victory at Midway, where American carrier aircraft sank four Japanese carriers, and called the August landings at Guadalcanal "a great boon"[8] to morale.

At the small village of Tibuc-Tibuc, Duffy encountered Staff Sergeant Ray C. Hunt, an American who, like Duffy, had escaped from the Death March, taken refuge with the local population, and helped organize guerrilla activities. Hunt immediately warmed to Duffy, whose choice words made him seem more like an old military salt than a veteran priest. "I remember him chiefly because he had what seemed to me a remarkable vocabulary of profanity for a clergyman," Hunt wrote in his memoirs after the war. "I used to wonder if he could swear as impressively in Latin as in English."[9]

The Japanese nearly trapped the elusive priest in a September raid in which they killed three Filipinos and captured five American soldiers, but they overlooked Duffy, who had taken shelter 150 yards away. Guerrilla forces continued to harass Japanese locations, but the most successful raid occurred between Guagua and Macabebe in early December, when the guerrillas, accompanied by Father Duffy, captured a battery of Japanese field artillery. They immediately turned it on the Japanese and fired until they exhausted the supply of shells. During the action, Father Duffy found an American flag and tucked it beneath his shirt; he retained the flag for the next two years, often wrapping it around his body to prevent its discovery. Duffy and the flag, which stood as a reminder of freedom and a symbol for why he resisted the Japanese, became inseparable.

Near the end of 1942, a Japanese general's son was killed at San Luis and the Japanese exacted swift punishment. Aircraft bombed suspected guerrilla locations, killing many men, women, children, and tank-supported troops scoured fields and wooded areas. The attacks forced Duffy and the guerrillas to halt their activities until the flurry of reprisals terminated.

Ironically, a Catholic cleric proved Duffy's undoing. When Bishop Paul Y. Taguchi of Osaka, Japan, who traveled with the Japanese troops, visited the hospital in early January 1943, one of the sisters, thinking the bishop would honor her confidence, mentioned Duffy's presence. Instead of keeping the secret, Yaguchi speedily alerted Japanese authorities, who seized and imprisoned the priest.

The Japanese interrogated Duffy to gain information about the guerrilla forces. They smacked the priest with a baseball bat and subjected him to the water cure and other tortures, but he refused to talk. "Even if I knew anything I wouldn't tell you," Duffy warned his captors. "I'm paid to die for my country, so cut out this foolishness and either chop my head off, like you've done with others, or shoot me."[10]

The Japanese put Father Duffy on trial, a formality leading to execution. Two spies testified that the priest had actively fought with the guerrillas, but Duffy countered that although he provided aid to the Americans in Camp O'Donnell, he never took up arms or fired a weapon.

Surprisingly, his arguments carried the day. After a Japanese court martial declared that Father Duffy was not a guerrilla, but had only accompanied them after being rescued, the Japanese incarcerated Duffy in a penitentiary in San Fernando for two weeks before transferring him to Bilibid Prison in Manila. "Expected to be executed by the Nippers but managed to beat the courtmartial,"[11] he later wrote.

Duffy had evaded the clutches of the Japanese military court, but could he expect the same good fortune in the future?

"We Have Been Much Worried about Our Missionaries"

Father Carberry also survived the Death March, but unlike Father Duffy, he was first confined at Camp O'Donnell along with the other men taken at Bataan and then, in June, moved to Camp Cabanatuan. A complex of three training camps formerly used by the Filipino army to sharpen its forces, some ninety miles north of Manila on the Pampanga River, Cabanatuan became a prison camp after the Japanese defeated the combined American and Filipino forces. Family in the United States learned of Father Carberry's incarceration in a February 23 telegram from the adjutant general that informed them, "Your son Captain Richard E. Carberry, Chaplains Corps has been reported a prisoner of war of the Japanese Government in the Philippine Islands."[12] The telegram proved to be a mixed blessing, for while family at least knew that their son was alive, they now faced the specter of the unknown, but most certainly hostile, conditions of the prison camp in which he languished.

A second letter from U.S. military officials arrived in March. It directed the Carberry family to address any correspondence to Father Carberry in care of the Japanese Red Cross, which would forward it to their relative. Letters were to be as brief as possible and subject matter confined to personal issues while avoiding international developments. The family was to inscribe "Prisoner of War Mail" in large letters in the upper left-hand corner of the envelope, which could be sent free of postage.

Two months later, Father Carberry's parents received a welcome letter from their son. He told his family that he had endured "all that the enemy has to offer so far," and added that "There are many things to say to all of you, but as our Lord said, 'You can not bear to hear them now.'"[13] His parents must have winced upon reading these disturbing words, but they at least knew their son was alive.

In the midst of squalor, Father Carberry found a calling in tending to the Americans who wound up in Cabanatuan's overcrowded, ill-equipped hospital. Meant to hold no more than forty patients, each of the thirty wards bulged with up to one hundred soldiers, some weakened from dysentery or malaria, while others battled infections and severe injuries. A separate quarantined section, labeled Zero Ward by the prisoners, housed patients likely to die.

Cabanatuan became Carberry's parish. Though himself weakened and weary, he sat beside dying patients, heard confessions from frightened soldiers, and offered soothing words to those on the brink of despair. Cut off from civilization, Father Carberry became their avenue to God.

On July 16, 1942, he sat at the side of Staff Sergeant Ralph J. Kearney, administering Last Rites moments before the soldier succumbed. Kearney was too far gone to be helped, but Carberry could at least provide words of comfort and prepare him for what lay ahead. When Kearney's family learned of his death, they were consoled that a priest had been at hand. "Father, you have no idea of the happiness we received when we heard my brother had a priest with him to help him on the way to God,"[14] Kearney's sister wrote in a letter sent to, but never received by, Father Carberry. She explained that her parents were daily communicants who had prayed every day for their son's safe return, and while they were inconsolable with news of his death, they were comforted that Father Carberry had taken care of their son's religious needs at a time when he most required it.

THE CARBERRYS were not the only family worried about captive relatives. In South Bend, Father Steiner and the other Holy Cross priests and brothers said Rosaries and recited prayers for the well-being of Father McKee and the other Holy Cross missionaries trapped in the Philippines, while the nuns at Saint Mary's offered daily Mass and prayers for Sisters Olivette and Caecilius. They may not have been related by blood, but they were tightly bound by their devotion to God, their desire to aid their fellow man, and their love for their congregation.

"We have been much worried about our missionaries who had to disembark at Manila," Father Steiner wrote to Father Edward Fitzgerald in January. "We trust that so far they have escaped injury or worse, and that we may soon hear from them. No telling, though, what to expect from the Japs."

Father Steiner told Father Fitzgerald, himself soon to head to war as a chaplain, that he hoped Fitzgerald had "physically and mentally become inured to the life of a soldier." Steiner added that the uncertainties surrounding their comrades in the South Pacific were cautionary signs as to Fitzgerald's future endeavors. "Strenuous times are ahead of you, but with implicit confidence in God you will surely weather all the storms that may await you."[15]

Four months later Bishop O'Hara visited with Father Pacifico Ortiz, S.J., a Filipino army chaplain then in the United States. Before fleeing to Corregidor on Christmas Eve with Philippine President Manuel L. Quezon, Ortiz had seen the Holy Cross group in the Philippines. He told O'Hara that the missionaries had been interned with other Americans, that "They were not molested in any way," and that some members of the group had at times been permitted to go into Manila. This decent treatment, he explained, came from two sources: Japan's apparent desire to maintain "the good will of the Vatican," and the presence among the occupying troops of two Japanese Catholic chaplains. "In view of these facts, I believe that we can all rest assured that our Holy Cross representatives in Manila are suffering less hardship than they would have undergone had they reached their mission field in India. Perhaps God wants them in the Philippines for some particular purpose."[16]

Over the next three years Father McKee, Brother Rex, and the others would arrive at that same conclusion. While they operated from behind barbed wire and stone walls instead of in Asian missionary settlements, they gradually realized that the new work so suddenly thrust upon them possessed a depth and grandeur that they might never have experienced in their original assignments.

The Japanese permitted Sisters Olivette and Caecilius to teach religion for the next two years at Manila's Convent of the Assumption, a short distance from the Ateneo, and granted them access to a short-wave radio. When the nuns tuned in to a San Francisco radio station and heard American songs and news broadcasts, they remembered, "our spirits picked up." In July the Japanese allowed the nuns to travel into Manila where, wearing red armbands that granted them safe passage, they could shop for necessary items or see a physician. "These outings," the nuns recalled, "were a blessed relief from our confinement."

The nuns found rewarding their efforts in nursing prisoners of war confined in the American medical unit in Santo Tomas. Sister Caecilius worked in the children's ward, tending to the dependents of U.S.

military and diplomatic personnel trapped in the Philippines by the outbreak of war, while Sister Olivette treated patients suffering from dengue fever. The Japanese also allowed Father McKee and Father Lawyer, confined at the Ateneo one block away, to visit the convent to obtain wine and hosts for the Masses they celebrated.

Local Filipinos came to their aid by smuggling items brought to the islands by U.S. submarines. Interspersed in bags of apples were candy bars wrapped in red, white, and blue paper, bearing the victory *V* and MacArthur's pledge to return. "All were messages from home, prized out of all comparison with their actual value,"[17] wrote Sister Olivette.

Down the street from the nuns, the two priests and two brothers enjoyed similar conditions, but Brother Rex became convinced that the Japanese suspected them of being military personnel rather than religious. During their stay at the Ateneo, Japanese spies resided across the street, and whenever the four men left to visit a parish in Manila or elsewhere, the spies followed close behind.

They lived a relatively normal daily schedule that was denied to American and Filipino personnel confined in Cabanatuan or Bilibid. Brother Rex's typical day began with 6:00 a.m. Mass. After joining Brother Theodore and the others at the Ateneo for breakfast, he and Theodore labored in a garden until lunch. Thirty minutes of leisure preceded the afternoon siesta, a break lasting until 3:00 p.m., after which Rex coached a group of Filipino boys in basketball and trained them how to serve at Mass. Dinner at 6:30 p.m. preceded an hour in the recreation room, after which Rex read a bit before lying down for the night.

Like the Holy Cross sisters a few blocks away, Rex and Theodore considered their concealed radio a vital link to home, although they had to be more circumspect as the Japanese denied them permission for the device. Home-front music and news broadcasts connected them to their families and countrymen. Although the men resided thousands of miles from the United States, the voices of American radio commentators, and especially the melodies of popular songs coming in from San Francisco radio stations, made them feel as if they were still a part of events occurring in the United States, and bolstered hopes that they had not been abandoned. They heard the same news their families heard; with their fingers they tapped beats to the same tunes. "One of the most important things to people in an occupied country is news," wrote Brother Rex. "Without it you become discouraged. With it, even when it is not too encouraging, you continue to have hopes."[18]

In March 1943 the Japanese confiscated the nuns' radio. When guards returned the item shortly afterward, the radio had been altered to pick up only those stations broadcasting Japanese programs. Thus cut off from an outside source of news, the nuns had to rely on rumor and tidbits relayed by Filipinos to supplement the information brought in by the male religious.

MORE FRUSTRATING than a lack of communications from the United States, however, was the uncertainty about what news family in the United States had learned of their plight. Did their mothers and fathers believe they were still alive, or were they in the dark about their fates? Severed from any meaningful communications, they could only hope that word of their survival had reached their parents and siblings to ease their burdens.

In fact, a few letters written by the religious in the first year of the war reached the United States aboard the Swedish exchange transport M.S. *Gripsholm*, hired by the U.S. State Department to ferry Japanese diplomats and nationals out of the United States in exchange for groups of United States diplomats and nationals caught in Japan or the Philippines. A September 1943 letter from Brother Rex to his parents informed them that the Notre Dame religious were "fine. We are getting plenty of everything, and all of us are in excellent health." He tried to reassure his mother by adding that "I have put on about ten pounds since I got here, so you see there is nothing to worry about in that regard." He explained that they were living with the Jesuits at the Ateneo, and that "I like the Philippines immensely, and it is going to be very hard to leave when it comes time to go to our mission."[19]

Father Steiner sent separate letters on December 13 to the fathers of Brother Theodore and Brother Rex, explaining that he had also received word from Father Lawyer that their sons were doing well. This initial word from the Philippines brightened their Christmas and prodded John Kapes to reply, "I can't begin to express our feelings in hearing about our beloved brother and son."[20]

Unfortunately, the Notre Dame religious in the Philippines remained unaware that the updates had been received by their families.

The thought that their families might believe they were dead added to the burdens of incarceration in a distant land.

"How Welcome Your Letters Always Are!"

While by mid-1943 Fathers Duffy and Carberry and the Notre Dame missionaries had been captives for a year, and Fathers Barry, Dupuis, and Sampson had either finished or almost completed their training for the European and Pacific battlefronts, other Notre Dame chaplains, willingly or not, operated on the war's fringes. "I said Mass in a different place every day and three other places on Sunday,"[21] Father John J. Harrington, C.S.C., wrote to Father Steiner from his station in India. Born in Eureka, Utah, in 1905, Harrington arrived in Bombay in late November 1942, on his way to duty with the Fifty-First Fighter Group in New Delhi and Assam. Harrington never saw the front lines, which lay hundreds of miles to the northeast, but he counseled men of the Army Air Force who faced some of the war's most hazardous missions: flying supplies five hundred miles over the Himalayas to Chinese forces fighting the Japanese.

The route across the Himalayas, called the Hump, challenged the most expert flier. Strong winds buffeted aircraft, and thick cloud cover masked mountain heights. Pilots joked that if they could see the runway through the fog and rain, they were approved for takeoff. Harrington was never allowed to accompany the crews during their missions, but he made certain he was available before and after each flight, hearing confessions, giving Holy Communion, and lending an ear or a consoling word. Harrington, the only Catholic chaplain posted to an area that contained seventeen different Allied installations, might not have been at the side of a bloodied soldier as he succumbed on the battlefield, as Fathers Barry, Sampson, and others were soon to do, but the priest provided reassurance to men who faced death each time they lifted off the runways.

In May 1943, five thousand miles northeast of the Hump, for the only time in the war, American forces attacked enemy units entrenched on American soil. The previous June, Japanese garrisons had occupied Kiska and Attu, two sparsely inhabited islands in the Aleutians, off

Alaska's mainland. The islands held little military value, but Japan's seizure of what had been U.S. territory since 1867 enraged people on the home front. Embarrassed and angered by Japan's bold affront to the nation's honor, people demanded a speedy reply.

That answer came when the Seventh U.S. Infantry Division landed at Attu to eliminate Japanese units defending the island. Before month's end the outnumbered Japanese, realizing the hopelessness of their situation, conducted one of the war's largest suicide charges. Shouting wildly, Japanese soldiers crashed through American lines and threatened command posts before American gunfire cut them down. When the fighting ended, more than two thousand Japanese dead littered the ground.

Among the forces placed on the island was Father Joseph M. Kmiecik, C.S.C. He arrived after the May fighting, but along the way he survived a scary moment at sea when a Japanese torpedo barely missed his transport, a ship loaded with aviation fuel and ammunition. A hit would most likely have ignited a ferocious explosion and killed everyone aboard.

Kmiecik shared a tent at Attu with two doctors and a supply officer. After his first meal, a tasteless concoction from a C-ration, Kmiecik placed a sign over the door reading, "Worries—My Work. Beefs—My Meat."[22] He dispensed with the usual assortment of chaplain duties, but found that in the bitter cold of those islands, most casualties came from frozen feet rather than from Japanese bullets. Kmiecik hoped to be transferred farther west to where the island battles would unfold, but until then, he ministered to the men in the frigid Aleutians and waited for a combat assignment.

FATHER JOHN McGee, C.S.C., likewise bided his time in a cold region. One of two Holy Cross priests from Canada who asked to return to their homeland to serve as chaplains in the Canadian Armed Forces, McGee named his log chapel Notre Dame de Labrador. Duty in the Canadian province of Labrador consisted mainly of routine matters, but he prayed that his posting would change once the Allied nations converged on Hitler. He longed to serve with combat troops and attempted to alter the situation, but admitted that his prior Holy Cross postings had been tame by comparison, writing, "This work in the army is an education itself."[23]

IF HE COULD have read McGee's words, Father Edward Fitzgerald would have nodded his assent. Born in July 1903, the priest from Roslindale, Massachusetts, was ordained at Notre Dame's Church of the Sacred Heart in 1932. Nine years later he entered the military and was assigned to the 208th General Hospital, then operating in Iceland—"Away up here on the top of the world," he informed Father Steiner. Because the men were so busy at the hospital, he adjusted the times of Sunday Mass to accommodate their hectic schedules, celebrating it in the afternoon as well as the morning. "Conditions here are quite different than back home, and an hour any time on a Sunday would be ideal. We would have to accommodate ourselves to the time when the boys are free. A seven day work week really means that up here."

He assured Father Steiner that should he volunteer more Holy Cross priests to be chaplains, they would lack for neither work nor appreciation. "The men you are sending to the service will find plenty of work to do and a welcome by the Catholic men, officers and others that will give them a real thrill." He added, "And we could use plenty of them."[24]

Like other Notre Dame chaplains, Fitzgerald found time to inquire about the university. He asked about the program instituted at Notre Dame in which the navy employed the university's facilities to train its young officers. "Need I tell you how welcome your letters always are!" he wrote to Father Steiner. "Golly, I sure look forward to them and the news about Notre Dame, and the good work the Holy Crossers are doing to whip the Navy into shape to fill the demand for officers."

Fitzgerald heard abundant praise for Notre Dame from the navy officers with whom he worked. "Notre Dame seems to facinate [sic] everybody and as a result one can't help but feel the old Adam's apple pulsate and the swallowing made difficult when all these deserving praises are heaped upon Our Lady's school." Fitzgerald was delighted to report that he met a number of Notre Dame students and graduates, and "you can well imagine what we talked about. It sure is a small world after all."

The priest enjoyed his work in the military, but he missed walking around campus, strolling down by the lakes, and visiting the Grotto. "I can well imagine what N.D. looks like during these Spring days," he wrote in June 1942. "Altho the picture is somewhat different now with the boys in blue marching around, I suppose."[25]

Fitzgerald's devotion to the university's football squad peppered his letters to Father Steiner. "One really feels bad during this time of year especially when one is away from the States and Notre Dame is throwing that pigskin around," Fitzgerald wrote in October 1942. Via shortwave radio he listened to the Wisconsin game that ended in a disappointing 7–7 tie against a team that featured the running exploits of Elroy "Crazylegs" Hirsch, and he tried to forget the 13–6 loss to Georgia Tech. "The Georgia game we will skip like all true sons of N.D. and offer the excuse that we can't win them all."

Fitzgerald worried about the game against the undefeated Iowa Pre-Flight Seahawks, a team at the University of Iowa comprising naval officers in training and featuring mostly former All-Americans and professionals. Navy personnel stationed in Iceland boasted that Fitzgerald's Irish had no chance, "and believe you me I took much ribbing from the boys here about just how badly we were going to take a shellacing [*sic*]." He had the last laugh, however, as Notre Dame laid four touchdowns on the Seahawks to prevail, 28–0. Fitzgerald had held his tongue when teased before the game, "but when I heard the score I went around as tho I had coached the team myself."[26]

After a furlough in September 1943 to visit the British Isles, which had already witnessed the ravages of war and were a likely gathering spot for armies designated to invade the occupied European mainland, Fitzgerald asked to be assigned to the active front. He hoped to share the hazards faced by the young men in combat but feared that he might remain in Iceland for the duration. Other priests from Notre Dame had completed their training and begun to join Father Barry in the combat zones. Naval chaplain Father Patrick Duffy, C.S.C., was working in the South Pacific on the U.S. Naval Construction Battalion (Seabee) bases, and army chaplain Father Joseph Corcoran, C.S.C., had joined the Thirty-Second Infantry Regiment of the Seventh Infantry Division in the Central and Southwest Pacific. Father Fitzgerald hoped that he might soon complete a trio.

"Father Barry Was Never Too Busy to Talk to You"

Father Barry could have cautioned Fitzgerald about a desire to serve at the front, for he had already experienced his first combat. After completing his training with the 157th Regiment of the Forty-Fifth Infantry Division, nicknamed the Thunderbirds, in June 1943 Barry stepped onto a troop transport for the two-week journey across Atlantic waters to the war zone. He had witnessed imposing spectacles at Notre Dame, both religious and secular, but few matched the grand assemblage of twenty-five vessels, mostly transports, escorted by a dozen destroyers as the convoy fanned out over a vast stretch of ocean and steamed eastward. Lumbering transports strained against the waves, while sleek destroyers sliced through the waters, vigilantly shepherding the formation across enemy-infested waters as they searched for German submarines.

Barry now replaced everything that was familiar and comfortable with an unknown future fraught with peril. The war had remained distant during training—headlines in newspapers more than a reality to be faced—but took on a more sinister context once the coastline of Virginia receded. They were now steaming toward the fighting, not practicing for it, and within weeks they would engage in battle the vaunted German Army.

As soon as the formation departed, each man received a pamphlet titled *Pocket Guide to North Africa*. The pages described their initial destination, but as fighting in Africa had recently ended with the German forces in retreat, everyone concluded that this would be an interim stop. After additional training and preparation, they would be thrown against the enemy, and soldiers placed wagers on France, Italy, Sicily, or Sardinia as the most likely locations.

They also bet on whether enemy U-boats would attack the formation before it reached Africa. A red line inching eastward across a large chart in the mess hall informed them of the convoy's progress, and while German submarines failed to materialize, the handful of occasions when destroyers dropped depth charges, on what turned out to be schools of fish, whales, or underwater land formations, put most on edge.

The taunts of Axis Sally, the name given to female radio personalities in Berlin and Rome who broadcast English-language German propaganda to Allied troops in Europe and Africa, also left them uneasy. Barry and the soldiers enjoyed the current songs Axis Sally played, but they fell silent when the propagandist announced, "You boys in the Forty-Fifth Division know you are on the high seas and I'm going to play a song for you. It's 'The Last Roundup' and it's going to be the last roundup for many of you."[27] Reading news stories at home was one matter, but listening to a threat directed specifically at you was another.

Lectures on everything from how to react to a mortar attack to prisoner of war treatment kept the troops occupied, as did the Hollywood films shown several times each day, but Father Barry still lacked enough hours to handle the crush of men who wanted to see him. He was relieved that, unlike many others, he had not become seasick, and he enjoyed the comments about Notre Dame made by naval officers who had attended midshipman school on campus, "all good boys and forever saying nice things about their short stay at school." Other than time taken to send a handful of letters to Father Steiner and to family, however, Barry's day was packed with visits to the soldiers. In addition to hearing confessions and giving a daily talk over the loudspeaker, Barry celebrated Mass either on the fantail (a ship's rear section) or, in poor weather, the mess hall. Now that they were on their way to war, he informed Father Steiner, "my 'congregation' was overflowing."[28] He found that, in deep contrast to home-front celebrations of Mass, where those in attendance often gave mere lip service to prayers they recited by rote, religious observance aboard a ship heading to war possessed a devotion and sincerity not always witnessed at home.

On June 21 the convoy exited the Atlantic Ocean and steamed by the Rock of Gibraltar into the clear blue waters of the Mediterranean Sea. The next day the ships docked at Oran in French Algeria. "No doubt you received a card by this time telling you of my safe arrival," Father Barry wrote to Steiner. "Maybe Uncle Sam told you where—I can't."[29]

Barry and the 157th Regiment were immediately thrown into more training. In the following days officers informed their men that they were about to attack well-emplaced German and Italian units across rugged terrain sowed with land mines. Barry, bedecked in full battle gear, joined the troops as they practiced scaling down rope ladders into landing craft. A sergeant bellowed that once they started to descend the ladder, they must keep moving or risk having their knuckles stepped on by the man above. Barry explained to Steiner that if the man below stopped, the sergeant told them to "use the butt of your rifle to let him know you are alive and you want to go down." No one, Barry wrote, whether soldier, officer, or chaplain, was exempt. You "just knock the knuckles of the guy below you. And he will get going."[30]

Before they embarked on transports for the actual assault, Barry visited as many ships as possible to look after the units aboard. Carrying his priestly implements, including a prayer book and Mass kit, "off we went to visit battleships, cruisers, destroyers and what have you," he wrote to Bishop John O'Hara at the Military Ordinariate. "Mass was said wherever we found room: quarterdeck, fantail, officers' country, bridge, and wardroom."

Barry, never shying from relating a humorous incident, told O'Hara of the skipper who went out of his way to make sure Barry had everything he needed when the priest visited his ship. When Barry asked the officer why he took such pains to ensure Barry's comfort, the officer answered that he had seven reasons for welcoming a chaplain. The first six were "to make his crew happy and No. 7 was to make his [Catholic] wife happy."[31]

While on campus at Notre Dame, Barry had occasionally celebrated Mass in the beautiful Church of the Sacred Heart, splendid with its paintings, sculptures, and adorned altar, but preferred to do so with small groups of students in the more intimate surroundings of one of the tiny chapels that are a fixture of every student dormitory. In Africa, thousands of miles from campus, he now conducted services in cramped wardrooms and on swaying decks to boys who, minus the uniforms and military accoutrements, reminded him of those young Notre Dame students, with one major difference: squeezed into those confining quarters, Father Barry brought Christ directly to men who might soon be dead. As one soldier wrote to his parents of his chaplain, "His cathedral is in a corner of the mess, and its stained-glass windows are portholes, small and round, stained only with salt water. We ourselves built for him the table he uses for an altar."[32] Father Barry felt at home laboring in such quarters.

As was true of every chaplain, Father Barry found that the closer the soldiers of the 157th Regiment moved to battle, the more avid became their prayers. They attended Mass more frequently, not solely because they were scared, but mostly because they hoped to perform well in combat and to come through when their buddies needed them. Barry recognized that each Mass could be a soldier's final Mass and each confession his last plea for forgiveness, a gravity he refused to overlook. Whether in the form of Mass, a gathering to recite the Rosary, or a hushed Our Father or Hail Mary whispered with a frightened soldier in a lonely corner of a transport, Barry gave reassurance and comfort to boys who were about to face life's sternest test.

Barry ignored exhaustion and skipped meals because, at a time like this, a chaplain's hours were not his to hoard. Rest and leisurely suppers would come later, but until then Barry intended to be available whenever one of his lads, Catholic, Protestant, or Jew, needed him. On the eve of combat he became the soothing mother and the sage father to sons. "Father Barry was never too busy to talk to you," said Lieutenant Stemmons. "He never asked if you were Catholic and treated us all the same. Barry was always there for everybody. If anyone had a problem, he'd talk to them."[33]

The soldiers' fondness for Barry was universal, as shown in articles written during the war and in interviews conducted more than seventy years later. "He was a very gentle guy. Everyone admired him," said Sergeant Vinnie Stigliani of E Company, 157th Regiment. "I have a lot of respect for him. He cared for the soldiers he served. He was very important, especially before going into combat. Probably more than seventy-five percent of the men attended services then."[34]

Father Barry was a prime example of what General George C. Marshall, army chief of staff during the war, said of the important role played by chaplains. "I look upon the spiritual life of the soldier as even more important than his physical equipment," Marshall explained. "The soldier's heart, the soldier's spirit, the soldier's soul are everything. Unless the soldier's soul sustains him, he cannot be relied upon and will fail himself and his commander and his country in the end." Marshall added, "It's morale—and I mean spiritual morale—which wins the victory in the ultimate, and that type of morale can only come out of the religious nature of a soldier who knows God and who had the spirit of religious fervor in his soul. I count heavily on that type of man and that kind of Army."[35]

"One Has a Funny Feeling When Death Looks One in the Face"

With battle against the Germans less than two weeks away, hard-nosed Lieutenant General George S. Patton used every trick in his bag to prod his men to victory. His utterances, heavily laced with profanity, won him both a vast following among the soldiers and with people at the home front, as well as a legion of critics. On June 27, the colorful commander of the Seventh Army, of which Father Barry's 157th was a part, gathered the division's officers to discuss their impending operation, an assault against German and Italian forces on Sicily.

"Gentlemen, in a few days we're going to hit the mainland of Europe for the first time," he said in typically gruff fashion. "Most of you have never been in combat before and you may be afraid. But don't be afraid! You can stick a red feather up your ass and run around in front of them and they can't hit you." Patton cautioned that the Italians and Germans might try to fool them into thinking they were about to surrender, when in actuality they planned to open fire on American troops when they drew closer. The general added that he had no problem if the enemy wanted to surrender, but asserted that it was equally acceptable to "kill the bastards"[36] if they declined or displayed any deviousness.

FATHER BARRY had less bellicose thoughts in early July as he visited soldiers aboard the troop transport that would take them into their first battle against the German Army. As he filed past the sweating bodies Barry, unlike Patton, distinguished between the soldier, rifleman, or mortarman who was forced to kill and the innocent young man he was there to serve. He dealt with the latter profile of each person, and throughout the war, in every correspondence with Father Steiner, every letter to family or friends, every conversation with other chaplains, Barry referred to them not as soldiers but as his "boys" or his "lads." They had been boys before the war; to Barry they were still boys. To see them as anything else would denigrate that docile side and would negate everything they had been and now fought to rejoin. Father Barry personalized a war that, by pitting thousands of armed men against each other, was innately impersonal. This tendency to see soldiers as individuals was the quality that made Barry an outstanding chaplain. This trait also caused the priest devastating grief and anguish, but it allowed Father Barry to fulfill one of his principal tasks, that of being a substitute during the war for the mothers and fathers his boys had left behind.

With the regiment leaving Oran on July 5 aboard five transports, Barry shuffled from boy to boy, checking with one to see if he had any requests, patting another on the back to bolster confidence, and bending over a frightened private to hear a hurried confession.

As the armada moved eastward along the coast of North Africa, other transports joined, bringing General Bernard Law Montgomery's British Eighth Army and the remainder of Patton's Seventh Army from Algiers and Bizerte. From the initial collection of transports, the force expanded to nearly two thousand ships, at that time the largest invasion fleet in the history of the world. At least they now knew their destination. The small, government-issued book *The Soldier's Guide Book to Sicily* left no doubt.

As the soldiers joked with one another or prepared for the coming action, Father Barry found a quiet corner on the transport to begin a letter to Father Steiner. He had sent such missives in the past, but this letter was remarkable, not for specific details of the assault, which censors would never allow, but for the self-examination in which Barry engaged. He had already written a friend, Father J. P. Wagener, that he hoped to make up for any shortcomings "to Christ and Notre Dame by spending myself on the battlefields ahead,"[37] but he now went further.

Utilizing Father Steiner as a long-distance counselor, Father Barry divulged his concern not so much for personal injury or death as for whether he would be worthy of his boys. He had endured everything with them, including the rigors of training and the transatlantic voyage, but now that they approached death's door, he wondered if he would be up to the task of providing solace and religious comfort to boys under fire. Barry realized that in war, when a chaplain's main duty was to tend to soldiers on a battlefield, severe wounds and death were the norm. He hoped that when the time came, he could ignore his fears and perform as well on Sicily's mud, amid flying bullets and exploding bombs, as he had in training or at Notre Dame.

"By the time you receive this note the news of this coming engagement will be old," he wrote to Father Steiner on July 8, as the Mediterranean's waters slapped against the ship. "At this date we can only guess what is to happen. I hope and trust the greater part of that news is good. However battles are not won without someone getting hurt. Is it I Lord, for only Christ knows now. In a few days the whole country will know." As would Father Barry. "It is hard to realize what lies ahead," he confided in Father Steiner. "This morning after breakfast I went topside; as I strolled about the deck I looked up at the sky, a marshmellow [*sic*] mountain of clouds hung overhead, the sea was calm and beautifully blue, everything was so peaceful. What a contrast to the smoke and noise and blood and broken bodies that must come in the next few days. Surely war is a dirty game. What a price we have to pay for a few years of liberty."

Father Barry hoped he would be spared "to minister to my boys. I have a good number to care for," but accepted that he had little to say in the matter. A bullet cared little for rank or background, and Barry figured that if he perished on the battlefield he was at least giving his life performing priestly deeds. "If however it is God's will that I pay the price, I shall ask Our Lord to accept my sacrifice in reparation for my sins. I also ask your forgiveness," he added to Father Steiner, "for any negligence in this post, especially for my callousness in writing." Father Barry concluded, "I hope this does not sound too pessimistic, yet one has a funny feeling when death looks one in the face."[38]

Father Barry would agree with, and most certainly appreciate, the words offered by two of the war's top commanders. Marine General A. A. Vandegrift, who had the previous year guided American land forces to victory in the bitter fighting with the Japanese at Guadalcanal, spoke to a group of chaplains about their effect on the soldiers. "America's young men travelled far from home, but they did not go one step away from their churches," said Vandegrift. "Their faith could not, and did not, fade. Stated calls to worship, and the salutary influence of example, went with them even into the thick of battle." Vandegrift added that he was always impressed with those chaplains who wanted to be at the front lines, "and I assume that that was because, as one put it, at the time: 'That is where the fighting man needs God most—and that's where some of them know him for the first time.'" Or, as General Marshall said, "A good chaplain does not require a church; a poor one will empty a cathedral."[39]

Death and debilitating injuries loomed closer as the transports approached Sicily, for they were part of a massive attempt to first dislodge the German Army from Sicily and then move onto the Italian peninsula and the European mainland. Operation Husky, as the military designated the invasion of Sicily, called for ships to land 66,000 American soldiers, including Father Barry's 157th Regiment, and 115,000 British infantry along one hundred miles of the Sicilian coast. In expectation of an attack the German commander, Albert Kesselring, reinforced his ten Italian divisions with two of Germany's best, the Fifteenth Panzergrenadier and the Hermann Goering Panzer Division. Kesselring planned to throw everything he had at the invaders as soon as they attempted to break out from the beaches and move inland.

Two regiments of the Forty-Fifth Infantry Division would land north of the small fishing village of Scoglitti, while Barry and the 157th would storm ashore eight miles south to seize Santa Croce Camerina three miles inland and high ground to the northeast. The regiment would then join the 179th Regiment in taking the Comiso airfield before linking up with Montgomery's units to their right. Once ashore, Patton's troops would support Montgomery's drive up Sicily's east side by guarding the British commander's west flank. That required Patton's units, including the 157th Regiment, to operate over arduous mountain terrain.

With time before the battle dwindling, Father Barry was far from alone in grappling with his thoughts. Unless they were veterans of combat—and only a handful of the officers could lay such a claim—each soldier asked himself if he would ably perform when the battle commenced. "It was a regiment made up of United States citizens who were facing their first combat," wrote the 157th Infantry Regiment's historian immediately after the war, "pretty damned scared of what was coming, but determined to do the best they could. What they wanted most of all just then was to get off those damnable, bouncing, weaving boats."[40]

Father Barry never succumbed to seasickness, but most around him turned blue as strong winds on the journey's fifth day created heavy swells that rocked the ship as if it were a cork. In the hold of some transports, men carefully navigated their way to the head (restroom) through vomit an inch thick. Soldiers checked their ammunition and gear, wrote hurried final letters to loved ones, or fell into a stoic silence. In the predawn darkness, cooks on each ship served the soldiers a hearty breakfast, which some gloomily compared to a murderer on death row being given his last meal. "For us, the war had finally started,"[41] wrote Sergeant Don Robinson, creator of the *45th Division News*, which operated during the war.

The landings on July 10, 1943, amid blustery winds and rough seas, proved as difficult as many feared. With waves buffeting the craft and threatening to smash them into the transports' hulls, the climb down chain ladders from the troop transport into a landing craft was perilous. Men of Barry's 157th Regiment went over the side at 3:45 a.m., taking care to place their hands on the sides of the ladder rather than on the rungs, where they were easy targets for the boots of the soldier above. Several soldiers fell, and one drowned, in the attempt.

Naval gunfire startled Barry when the big guns commenced their shore bombardment. As booms rumbled toward the beaches, the assault craft nudged away from the transports, formed a huge *V* pointing landward, and started toward shore, their engines groaning to make progress against nine-foot swells that lifted and bounced the craft as if they were toys. Men again fell ill, filling the bottoms of the landing craft with their breakfasts. Before they reached the landing spot at Bailey's Beach, five miles south of Scoglitti, more than half the vessels were damaged or sunk in the swirling surf, with twenty-seven men in F Company alone drowning when their boats collided or flipped over in the surf.

By the time that Father Barry climbed off his transport, German mortar and artillery shells splashed among the landing craft. According to Barry, the Germans seemed to know the 157th Regiment was coming, "and we were shot up quite a bit."[42] When his boat neared shore, one shell crashed so close that Barry had to jump out and swim toward the beach. Weighed down by equipment that dragged him under the waves, he nearly drowned in the turbulent water. Holding his breath, Barry slipped off items until he reached the surface, but instead of seeking refuge on the beach from German machine-gun bullets and mortar shells, he dove under to locate what he had dropped, especially his Mass kit. As bullets sliced through the water only feet away, Barry found his Mass kit and began a hasty trek to shore.

"I always wanted to swim in the Mediterranean but did not relish being dumped in bag & baggage," he wrote to Father Steiner the next month of his first amphibious landing. To Bishop O'Hara, five months later, he joked, "I did not land on the coast of Sicily. I swam to it."[43]

Before day's end the 157th seized the high ground above Santa Croce Camerina. Sicilians draped white flags from windows to alert the Americans that they would meet no resistance, and five hundred Italian soldiers quickly surrendered. In early evening soldiers dug temporary graves three miles inland for their fallen comrades, a sight that would soon become all too familiar to Father Barry.

The day's landing placed 181,000 Allied soldiers on Sicily. In the coming weeks the forces mounted two drives, with Montgomery's

British forces heading up the east coast toward Messina, only two miles from the Italian mainland, and the 157th and other American troops moving along his left flank.

Father Barry prayed that no subsequent action would match the terror of this first landing at Sicily where, he said, the regiment lost so many men because "we were concentrated, they knew we were there." He added, "I spent the first two days and two nights fishing boys out of the Mediterranean. Boys who were shelled and got out of their boats loaded with their gear and all the things, and just sunk and drowned. There were hundreds of them."[44]

"I'm Generally Up Front with My Boys"

The rapid advances by Father Barry's regiment in the next three weeks would dramatically slow farther inland, where the unit, according to the regiment's historian, "for the first time ran into the bitter German resistance that was to oppose the regiment until V-E Day [May 1945]."[45]

The 157th liberated three Sicilian towns on July 13 but ground to a halt when the Germans launched at Licodia Eubea a tremendous counterattack, backed with artillery, flamethrowers, and tanks. Both sides searched for openings in their opponent's lines, and officers employed every tactic in the book to stem the enemy drive. "First we'd hit center, then smash the tackle, and now and then we'd make an end run,"[46] Father Barry, the avid Notre Dame football fan, described the action in a letter home.

Father Barry spent part of his time at aid stations situated a short distance from the fighting, where he could assist the wounded or dying, but he preferred to be with the boys at the front lines, where he could lend an encouraging word to scared soldiers or rush to the side of a dying boy moments after he had been hit. The soldiers of the 157th grew accustomed to seeing Barry, a white cross adorning his helmet, scurrying about the battlefield, ignoring the bullets and mayhem to bring religious comfort to the unit. Barry was not primarily concerned about a boy's religion. All that mattered was that these young boys, Catholic, Protestant, or Jew, needed him, and at Licodia, where the regiment suffered sixty casualties, they needed him.

"He was a dandy!" said Private First Class Isaac F. Caudle of C Company. "He was one great, great chaplain. It didn't make any difference what religion you were. You look around, and there he was. He was there for you, no matter who you were. It didn't make any difference how hot the shells were coming in. He was still doing his work."[47]

German opposition stiffened as the regiment moved into Sicily's mountainous center, where for a week they battled nonstop along the island's main north-south road. Attacking day and night, giving neither the soldiers nor Father Barry time to rest, the regiment reached Sicily's north coast and fanned out to the east and west along the coastal road.

German land mines planted along that route destroyed vehicles and eviscerated soldiers, while German artillery emplaced in mountain heights rained shells on the regiment. Despite the hazards, the regiment battled its way toward the next objective, the village of Santo Stefano di Camastra (known to the men as San Stefano), a gateway to Messina on Sicily's northeast coast and the door through which the Germans would evacuate to the Italian mainland a few miles away. To reach Messina, the 157th had to cross San Rosso, a mountain shielding San Stefano.

The 157th Regiment came to know the landform by a different name—Bloody Ridge.

"OUR MARCH was largely a matter of mopping up until we hit San Stefano and Bloody Ridge," stated the *45th Division News*. The article called it the "toughest fight in the Sicily campaign."[48] In the process Father Barry proved to every man in the regiment that he could handle the challenges brought by combat.

Bloody Ridge was a series of five peaks atop slopes so steep that vehicles could not navigate the ascensions. German artillery and mortars infested each ridge, bringing Barry and the infantry under fire each time they attempted to attack.

During the night of July 26 to 27 the 157th advanced toward the village of Motta D'Affermo. German soldiers, intent on holding off the Americans long enough to allow other units to escape across the Strait of Messina to the Italian mainland, waited with machine guns, mortars, and artillery on Bloody Ridge. While one battalion assaulted the ridge from the south, two others attacked from the northwest.

German artillery and mortar shells erupted on all sides, whipping razor-sharp pieces of rock and shards of steel among the men. German snipers decimated the ranks, and trip wires and mines, including the feared Bouncing Betty that sprang three or four feet into the air before exploding, ripped apart others. The unit ground through the butchery and swarmed into the German line, hurling grenades and engaging in hand-to-hand and bayonet fighting.

Barry crawled through a dry creek bed to reach wounded soldiers. He ignored bullets that ripped into the dirt close to his feet and explosions that shattered nearby foliage to pause over each fallen man, check the dog tags for their religion, and either hurriedly hear confession and give absolution to the Catholics or say a quick prayer for the non-Catholics before moving on. He dropped low to the ground to press his ear next to the mouths of the injured and dying men, straining to hear the whispered words amid the din of shell bursts, machine guns, and shouts. He hesitated longer over the dead, making himself for a few moments a prime target for German bullets and shrapnel, before tending to other fallen soldiers.

The 157th Regiment suffered 108 casualties that first day of fighting, but their task was far from complete. That evening officers stationed men three yards apart in a circular defense line, and during the relative calm Barry moved along the line to check on boys whose biggest concerns not that long ago had been what girl to ask to a prom or what shirt to wear to a party.

Dawn brought more of the same as the 157th again struggled to scale the ridge and dislodge the enemy. In the daylong fighting Barry, his uniform splattered in places with the blood of the wounded and dying whom he consoled, impressed the men with his calm demeanor under fire. The soldiers could rely on their rifles and hand grenades to answer the enemy, but Father Barry carried only his khaki uniform, his stole, and his prayer book. At times the priest operated mere yards from Germans trying to kill him. He lost count of the men to whom he gave comfort or administered Last Rites, and one time, after receiving orders to fall back from a German unit threatening to break through, he refused to leave a group of wounded boys until every casualty had been evacuated. He later organized a search party and, ignoring the obvious perils, led it into German minefields to retrieve the bodies of killed Americans.

In five days of bitter fighting at Bloody Ridge, the 157th Regiment lost 163 men killed or wounded. Barry's superior officer was so impressed with the priest that he added Father Barry's name to the list of his soldiers whose bravery deserved a medal. The next year, in recognition of his valor, the army awarded Barry one of its highest honors, the Silver Star. The citation stated that Barry's "cool efficiency under fire and cheerful acceptance of danger and hardship were an inspiration to all who served with him and aroused the troops to greater efficiency."[49]

In their first three weeks on Sicily, the Forty-Fifth Division suffered almost a thousand casualties in driving back the enemy and seizing more than eleven thousand prisoners of war. After twenty-two days of continuous combat, Barry and the Thunderbirds hopped into trucks for the short trip to a rest area near the port of Termini Imerese on Sicily's northern coast. "We weren't green anymore,"[50] concluded the division's newspaper.

Barry was momentarily out of danger, but he found little time to rest. He conducted outdoor services in pleasant olive groves, heartened by the larger numbers that attended Mass, but knew that bombs and bullets had more to do with that spike than anything he did or said. He counseled men who wanted to see a priest for a variety of reasons. The soldiers had left the United States, but their personal crises crossed the Atlantic with them; if Barry did not address those issues, the problems could affect a soldier's performance in battle and endanger him and others. Men sought consolation for the deaths of loved ones back home, worried over a lack of mail from sweethearts, or asked for advice on whether to divorce an unfaithful wife.

Barry often wished that people in the United States used better discretion in what they included in their letters. With the enemy close at hand, the last thing his boys needed was to read about family difficulties. One chaplain, Adolph Petersen, was so irate with the home-front problems brought up in mail to soldiers that he wanted to scream to every household, "Write often to your boys in the service but don't load your letters with griefs and difficulties at home that they can do nothing about. You owe it to them to keep things going smoothly at home, to keep harmony on the home front while they are training and giving their all on the fighting front."[51]

By so capably and bravely serving the troops, Barry set an example for the 157th Regiment. More persuasive than his sermons or prayer services, the priest's daily conduct illustrated that one could maintain and follow religious and moral precepts even in a world of death and destruction. On the Sicilian battlefield, Father Barry accomplished more in a few weeks than he might have in a year back at Notre Dame.

True to his nature, the Silver Star recipient deflected all praise to his boys. In a note to Father Steiner written during their rest period, he apologized for not being able to divulge specific details about his location or the regiment's activities, but expressed his admiration for those young soldiers who overcame their fears, engaged the more experienced Germans, and emerged triumphant. "America can be proud of her boys," he wrote to Steiner on August 3, "how they can fight and how the enemy knows it." Downplaying his role in a casual, almost humorous manner that belied the hazards he had just faced, Barry explained, "I'm generally up front with my boys doing everything possible, saying Mass while shot and shell whistle overhead—no need for bells—shells keep my congregation alert." Barry figured that their next operation would take them into Italy and northward to the Alps, but, he noted, after traversing the arduous Sicilian terrain, "I can't imagine the Alps being more difficult to fight over."[52]

In the face of the combined American–British offensive, the German Army retreated to Messina to avoid being trapped on Sicily. With Patton rapidly advancing from the west and Montgomery closing from the south, German units navigated three miles across the straits, dug in on the Italian mainland, and prepared for the inevitable American assault against the peninsula. Always fond of a show, Patton hoped to beat his rival, Montgomery, into Messina, and thus ordered parts of the 157th Regiment to mount an amphibious move behind German lines twenty-five miles west of Messina. Patton edged out Montgomery when elements of the 157th Regiment entered Messina on August 18.

With Messina secured, and after five weeks about which Barry joked, "I walked practically across the ancient island,"[53] the 157th Regiment enjoyed a longer break near Cefalú, midway across the island's northern coast. A Bob Hope United Service Organizations (USO) show boosted spirits, especially when the beautiful Frances Langford, midriff bared, sang and danced. Hope and Langford signed autographs afterward, with the comedian claiming he should be asking the soldiers for theirs.

Hope was not alone in that assessment. Ernie Pyle, the revered newspaper correspondent known for his affinity for the common foot soldier, praised the Forty-Fifth Infantry Division for coming straight from American training camps and proving that an American division could compete with the enemy. He wrote that "these quiet men of the Forty-fifth, the newest division over here, have already fought so well they have drawn the high praise of the commanding general of the corps of which the division is a part."[54]

Patton had, indeed, taken time to praise the Forty-Fifth Division. He remarked that before the invasion of Sicily he had doubts about the National Guard unit, but after the unit's outstanding performance, he was honored to command the men. The loquacious commander even took time to meet with the taciturn Father Barry. Patton heartily shook Barry's hand and blustered, "Good to have you, Padre. I want you to know, Padre, that I also read that God-damned good book that you read." Barry left the encounter believing that Patton would use profanity even if he were talking to the Pope, as "he could not talk without it. Especially the G.D."[55]

Barry spent most of the rest period in aid stations with the wounded. He moved from bed to bed in the cramped Red Cross hospitals and told an interviewer that he hesitated to ask about the soldiers' religion as he was there to help any boy, Catholic or not. Barry inquired as to what the boy needed and invariably discovered that more than anything, they simply wanted someone to talk to. "They had a lot to say, especially when they were stretched on the bed," Barry said.

One soldier asked Barry to hear his confession but worried that his fellow patients might eavesdrop. Barry settled the matter by lighting a cigarette, leaning over, and talking to him as if the two were engaged in a friendly conversation. Barry explained that "no one would think you were hearing a confession. The cigarette was lit but you did not take many puffs. But anyone coming along could see the cigarette. They figured you were not doing anything important. I was just listening. But actually I was hearing their confession." Barry called the soldiers "real people, down to earth people," and found that by listening he learned much about "the real inside of a boy. Just listening, whether he was bragging, or complaining, bitching, preaching without a soap box. I just listened."

The depth of their faith impressed Barry. The soldiers might not have shown it through prayer or by attending weekly Mass, but they exhibited it with their day-to-day actions. "The fact that they were night after night putting their life on the line, they were very good as far as God is concerned. Our Lord said that is the essence of life, the essence of love, to lay down your life for another. If you lay down your life, you cannot do any more."[56]

The rest period ended in early September when the regiment packed gear, donned their weaponry, and prepared for the next battle. Father Barry had witnessed much since leaving the United States, but he would learn new definitions for death and misery in the coming months. The Italian mainland—and a place called Anzio—awaited.

PART II

CHAPLAINS AT THE BATTLEFRONT

January 1943 to December 1944

"I NEVER EXPECTED TO COME OUT OF THE PHILIPPINES ALIVE"

Chaplains in the Pacific, 1943

"The Women Wept Openly"

On the other side of the world from Father Barry, Fathers Carberry and Duffy could hardly think of taking the fight to the enemy. The two priests could focus on only two matters: staying alive and helping others endure the harsh conditions of Cabanatuan, a prison camp that Father Albert Braun, O.F.M., a chaplain and friend of Carberry's, called "hell on earth."[1]

In October 1942, Father Carberry learned that he was to be among a group of one thousand prisoners transferred to the Davao Penal Colony in Mindanao, hundreds of miles to the south. Those who remained at Cabanatuan held what they jokingly referred to as a "wake" for their departing brethren, lifting glasses of medicinal alcohol with calamansi juice to honor their comrades.

On October 29 Carberry's group began the fifteen-mile walk to Manila, where they would board a transport for the ten-day voyage to Davao. The display of loyalty and sympathy exhibited by the Filipinos, who gathered along Manila's streets in support of the Americans who had fought for their nation, touched Carberry and the others with him. "The Filipinos who lined the streets looked at us silently and with compassion," wrote Army Air Force Captain William E. Dyess, one of the captives accompanying Father Carberry. "The women wept openly. Wherever we looked, people covertly were making the *V* for victory sign."[2]

The Japanese herded the prisoners aboard the *Erie Maru*, a vessel so squalid that Cabanatuan's grime paled in comparison. They placed a dozen men in quarters designed for half that number, requiring Carberry and five other companions to stand while the other half dozen slept. Lice and bedbugs inundated the prisoners, who soon sickened from the hold's smells and the gasoline fumes that rose from the storage area below. Each day on the voyage, the Japanese lowered buckets for use as bathroom facilities, their contents fusing with the vomit of seasick men to create a suffocating stench.

The ship docked on November 7 at Lasang, Mindanao, where they embarked on the fifteen-mile trek to Davao Penal Colony. Watchtowers and guard stations, buttressed by machine-gun emplacements and armed patrols walking the camp's perimeter day and night, posed frightful signs that Davao would be far worse than Cabanatuan.

Carberry remained at Davao for twenty months until, with Allied forces closing in on the Philippines from General MacArthur's Southwest Pacific route, Japanese authorities decided to move all prisoners from camps in the southern Philippines to locations farther north. On June 6, 1944, a day remembered by the world for events then unfolding in Normandy, France, the Japanese crammed Father Carberry and more than one thousand prisoners into another transport for a nineteen-day voyage to Manila. From there, the weakened men walked to Bilibid before completing their ninety-mile journey north back to Cabanatuan.

WHILE CARBERRY bounced from camp to camp, Father Duffy languished at Bilibid after being recaptured by the Japanese. Except for seven weeks in mid-1943 when he was confined at the Lipa work camp, Duffy remained in Bilibid's miserable conditions from February 1943 until December 1944. "I never expected to come out of the Philippines alive,"[3] he concluded upon seeing the horrors of Bilibid.

Resting on the northern bank of the Pasig River, Bilibid was a seventeen-acre penitentiary built by the Spaniards in 1865 to house

Filipino criminals. Filthy walls twenty feet high and four feet thick, topped with six strands of barbed wire, enclosed the cell blocks and administrative buildings. In the center of the compound stood a three-story building, the hub from which four cell blocks spread like spokes on a wheel. The Japanese used one section of the camp as a collection area for prisoners being transported to other prison camps, such as Cabanatuan to the north and the Davao Penal Colony to the south; a second part confined those prisoners considered disciplinary cases; and a third housed Father Duffy and the rest of the inmates. A hospital, the largest part of the camp, comprised the fourth section.

"Mourning and Weeping in This Vale of Tears"

The Japanese forces treated the six Notre Dame missionaries differently. After they seized control in the Philippines following Wainwright's surrender, from January 1942 until July 1944 they adopted a fairly lenient policy toward religious personnel not actively serving with the military. Since the Japanese government wanted the cooperation of the Filipino population, which was predominantly Catholic, they permitted priests, brothers, and nuns to continue their work in church-related activities and allowed the religious superiors to handle matters.

Brother Rex wrote that for two and a half years "our lives remained pretty much unchanged." The group worked in the garden, read, played basketball, and "carried on an almost normal religious life."[4] Fathers McKee and Lawyer could leave to say Mass at different churches and convents in the region, and although they knew they were being spied upon the entire time, they exercised their priestly duties without interference. They taught catechism and coached basketball with the boys of St. Rita's Hall, while Brother Theodore spent most of his time in the garden and Brother Rex, whom everyone loved for his constant smile and affable nature, organized the altar boys and coached basketball and boxing.

When a guard who had been a teacher in a small country town in Japan took out photos of his family and said he missed them, Brother Rex "assured him that I knew how he felt."[5] Another guard—nicknamed St. Louis by the internees—persisted in saying that after Japan won the war, he would live in St. Louis and cast his vote for Tojo for president.

One day Brother Rex was called to the parlor to meet an unexpected visitor. He walked in to find a Filipino man who had been fighting with a guerrilla band operating south of Manila. The guerrilla had heard that there were Holy Cross people at the Ateneo, and "he was hungry for news about Notre Dame and the various priests and religious there." He had graduated from the university a number of years before and, he told Rex, had never forgotten the motto adorning the archway at Sacred Heart, "God, Country, Notre Dame";[6] those words inspired him to greater exertions to defeat the Japanese.

Reacting to the increasingly effective opposition waged by the guerrillas and uncooperative Filipino civilians, the Japanese imposed tighter restrictions in early 1943. Sister Olivette recorded in her diary on January 15, "A warning in today's paper to enemy nationals 'to behave themselves properly in due appreciation of the generous attitude shown them by the Imperial Japanese forces.' Order to aliens to wear a red band on the arm when outside homes."[7]

With the war situation further deteriorating for the Japanese in early 1944, according to Sister Olivette, "their treatment of the religious internees began to show an ominous change." In February the Japanese arrested three Canadian nuns for aiding guerrilla forces, and in April the Japanese whisked away the superior of the Maryknoll Sisters for a nine-month stay in the feared military prison at Fort Santiago, where she endured torture and isolation while the Japanese tried to wrest information from her. "All of us feared the dread Santiago prison inside Manila, ancient torture chamber," said Sister Olivette. She added, "Things were gradually tightening up. You could feel it all around you."[8]

Meanwhile, superiors at both Notre Dame and Saint Mary's persisted in efforts to discover the fates of their religious compatriots in the Philippines. Mother Vincentia unsuccessfully sought help wherever she could, even from the archbishop of San Francisco. "We have followed every possible clue to contact our Sisters and shall continue to do so," she wrote to Sister Caecilius's mother, Mrs. William J. Roth, on February 1, 1943. "Surely before long the tide will turn and we shall be able to reach them. In the meantime we must leave them in God's keeping, knowing that in His divine plan they are fulfilling His purposes for souls."[9] Mother Vincentia expressed the possibility that Sister Caecilius's work in the Philippines might end up being more important than the labors to which she had formerly been assigned in India.

Word finally arrived in the form of a February 19, 1943, telegram from Sister Olivette, relayed through the Japanese Red Cross. "Season's greetings and to Marian Iddings [a student at Saint Mary's whose father had been interned in Manila] from Father. All well. Sister Olivette." The next day Mother Vincentia mailed a copy of the telegram to Mrs. Roth, again adding that God possessed His own plan for the religious personnel trapped in the Philippines. "As you know, we have exerted every effort to get in touch with the Sisters. We are all thanking God for this word from them." She closed with "God must have some special design in their regard. He will continue to keep and care for them."[10]

The religious in South Bend and their families throughout the United States finally knew that their loved ones were safe, at least for the moment. Severed from regular correspondence, however, families constantly worried that something ill had occurred. A telegram from Sister Caecilius to her family seven months later—the only other solid news to filter out of the islands to the mainland United States—provided some consolation when the nun reassured everyone, "We are safe and well in Manila at Assumption Convent." She asked her parents, "When you receive this please let the Sisters know that you heard from me." At a time when she would have been justified in requesting that they pray for her safety, she instead assured them that she kept them in her daily prayers and signed the telegram, "Your loving daughter, Sister Mary Caecilius."[11]

The restrictions tightened in July, one month after Father Barry entered Rome and Father Sampson parachuted into Normandy, when the Japanese moved the six Notre Dame religious from their comparatively comfortable confinement at Ateneo and Assumption Convent to Los Baños, a barbed-wire internment camp forty miles southeast of Manila at what used to be the Agricultural College of the University of the Philippines. "Trucks arrived on time," Sister Olivette wrote in her diary on July 8. "Japanese soldiers loaded our things on. Much left behind."[12]

The Filipino population again expressed their support by gathering along the road with good wishes. "When the time came for us to go," wrote Brother Rex, "there was a large crowd on hand. Many of the people came to bring us farewell gifts, despite the fierce looks of the Japanese guards. Boys from my Sanctuary Society loaded me down with cigarettes, matches, soap, cookies, and a lot of other things." Rex praised "the wonderfulness of the Filipino people" who risked the wrath of armed soldiers to lend help with food and moral encouragement, but added that once he boarded the truck, "then began one of the most hectic two days I have ever lived."[13]

Internees stepped into the back of the canvas-covered trucks for a three-mile ride from the Ateneo to Santo Tomas. As the vehicles pulled away, one of the Jesuit priests, Father McCaffrey, intoned the first notes to "Salve Regina." The famed Latin hymn, more commonly known as "Hail Holy Queen," dates to the Middle Ages and implores the aid of the Virgin Mary.

> Salve, Regina, Mater misericordiæ:
> Vita, dulcedo, et spes nostra, salve.
>
> ————
>
> *Hail, holy Queen, mother of mercy,*
> *our life, our sweetness, and our hope.*

Others joined Father McCaffrey as the Ateneo faded in the background, the Latin words wafting out from the convoy and filling the countryside with the plea:

> Ad te clamamus, exsules filii Hevae.
> Ad te suspiramus, gementes et flentes,
> in hac lacrimarum valle.
>
> ————
>
> *To thee do we cry, poor banished children of Eve.*
> *To thee do we send up our sighs,*
> *mourning and weeping in this vale of tears.*

Dreading the unknown travails that waited, the congregation of religious emitted a powerful plea as the trucks bounded along the road:

> Eia, ergo, Advocata nostra,
> illos tuos misericordes oculos ad nos converte.
> Et Jesum, benedictum fructum ventris tui,
> nobis, post hoc exsilium ostende.
>
> ————
>
> *Turn then, O most gracious Advocate,*
> *thine eyes of mercy towards us.*

And after this, our exile,
show unto us the blessed fruit of thy womb, Jesus.

O clemens! O pia! O dulcis Virgo Maria!
___

O clement! O loving! O sweet Virgin Mary![14]

Upon their arrival at Santo Tomas, a large internment camp in Manila, the group joined five hundred other Americans, mostly Protestant ministers and their families. The guards herded them into a gymnasium, where they spent a miserable night on the floor, alternately trying to sleep and swatting throngs of mosquitoes.

Lights interrupted their fitful slumber around 3:00 a.m. The religious devoured a breakfast of watery coffee, a duck egg, and a corn muffin served by internees of the camp, and within two hours they were back aboard the trucks for the journey to a train station. "It was pathetic to see the older people and the children, after a night such as the one described above, being shoved around," wrote Brother Rex. "However, there was nothing that could be done about it."[15]

The trucks transported them to the local train station for the forty-mile ride to the Los Baños depot. When the group stepped off the train at the depot, guards lined up and counted the prisoners before trucks conveyed them to the camp. While Brother Rex described their initial night inside Los Baños as one that "will long be remembered by all who were there," Sister Olivette focused on the pleasant change of scenery. "Beautiful location here in the mountains with Laguna de Bay in distance," she recorded in her diary on July 9. "Barracks very good considering."[16]

She would make few additional positive comments regarding the camp's facilities over the next eight months.

"Standard Dress Was a Pair of Shorts—Period"

Whether in Cabanatuan, Bilibid, Davao, or Los Baños, the living quarters varied only in degrees of discomfort. In Los Baños, the wooden barracks rested in a field of weeds. Housing ninety-six people each, the structures, stretching a football field long and thirty feet wide, had bamboo walls and thatched roofs. The Japanese had divided each into sixteen cubicles holding six mosquito-netted planks serving as beds. Although five-foot-high partitions separated the cubicles, no one enjoyed any privacy. An open washroom contained toilets and showers, but the flow of water rarely rose above a trickle. A single light bulb offered the only illumination, and a wood-burning stove provided heat to cook the meager fare distributed by their captors.

The Japanese divided Los Baños into two parts. The 1,500 civilians and their families lived in an area they referred to as Hell's Half Acre, while the religious resided in a separate section the civilians called Vatican City. Brothers Theodore and Rex and Fathers Lawyer and McKee lived in one barracks with a group of Jesuit priests (next door, unfortunately, to a building that housed prostitutes for the Japanese guards), while the nuns resided in their own barracks.

Harsh schedules matched the brutal settings in which the prisoners lived. One barracks served as the chapel where the religious and many of the six hundred Catholic men, women, and children—mainly nonmilitary workers and their families who had been trapped when war flared—began each day with an early Mass before roll call. A clanging bell from one of the guard towers awoke the internees each morning at 6:00 a.m. People shuffled outside to stand in formation in front of their barracks and remained standing until the guards were satisfied that everyone had been accounted for. After roll call and a meager breakfast, the religious performed their tasks, whether it was working in the gardens, tutoring other inmates, or cutting wood for their stoves. Brother Theodore tilled a garden, Brother Rex prepared meals in the kitchen, Fathers Lawyer and McKee gathered vegetables, and Sisters Olivette and Caecilius tended to patients in the infirmary.

Incarceration forced the priests and religious to don garb they never would have considered before the war. The two Holy Cross nuns continued to wear white habits but substituted stiff paper for the usual starched white flutes under the cloth of their headdresses. In the early months the men wore white pants, T-shirts, and shoes, but they cut the pants into shorts when the fabric began fraying. Eventually, wrote Brother Rex, shirts "went out of vogue" from overuse and "the shoes were saved for our release. Standard dress was a pair of shorts— period."[17] Lacking razor blades, the men, civilian and religious alike, soon sprouted beards and moustaches.

In their separate camps, Carberry, Duffy, and the six religious faced futures in which their existence depended, in large measure, on the whims of the camp commandant and guards. They had to adapt to an alien world in which every move was controlled by an enemy who cared little whether they lived or died.

In Cabanatuan, under the camp commander Lieutenant Colonel Shigeji Mori, Carberry and his fellow inmates had to gather for roll call twice each day, avoid approaching the fence line, salute or bow to every Japanese, and follow a host of other regulations that worsened as their confinement continued. To forestall attempts at escape, Mori divided the prisoners into groups of ten and vowed that should one man try to flee, the other nine would be shot.

The prisoners nicknamed every guard based on the soldier's looks or actions. At Bilibid, Captain Bligh and Pig-face were excessively cruel guards who relished punishing internees. At Davao, internees learned to keep their distance from Lieutenant Yoshimasa Hozumi, an officer who beat them so often that they handed him the moniker "The Crown Prince of Swat."

"The Talk of Food Became So Constant"

From their first day of confinement, the captives subsisted on a diet that was little more than protracted starvation. The daily fare of rice gruel and soup at Cabanatuan was in reality tepid water with a vegetable or tiny scrap of meat tossed in. At Los Baños, breakfast was one cup of rice gruel—a menu that would be repeated at noon lunch and 6:00 p.m. dinner. Bilibid's daily ration amounted to approximately ten to twelve ounces of cooked rice, heavily infested with weevils and rat droppings. Father Duffy initially hesitated to eat the repulsive mixture but, having no option other than death, soon choked down the meal. Father McKee supplemented it with improvised cheese made from fermented coconut, bits of grass, and deep-fried banana skins. Others fried the grubs they found beneath the barracks, which McKee called "gritty, but deliciously fatty worms."[18]

"Our situation is desperate," wrote Lieutenant Commander Thomas H. Hayes, the camp's chief of surgery, in his secret diary at

Bilibid on October 31, 1943. "A Red Cross shipment would certainly help." He described Thanksgiving Day the next month as "just another wasted day out of my life in old Bilibid. Menu—dry rice." Camp inmates ghoulishly joked that their food allotment would not keep a bird alive, and in desperation they scrounged for other edible items. "It's open season on cats and rats," Hayes added in April 1944. "The prisoners kill and eat them. We are eating everything and anything."[19]

Food supplies worsened in October 1944, shortly before MacArthur's landings in the islands. The Japanese at Los Baños reduced prisoners' meals to two a day. "If you can imagine getting just one ladel [*sic*] full of what we call lugao," Sister Caecilius later explained, "which is 2/10 rice and 8/10 water for breakfast and the same am't for supper with what here they call stew but such stew you would never recognize it. It was colored water with maybe a few pieces of some green weeds and if you were lucky maybe a piece of the skin of a pig. The piece about the size of your thumb."[20]

Despite the hardships, conditions were about to worsen. "We thought things bad then," wrote Brother Rex, "later we found out how wrong we were." He was referring to the months from December 1944 until February 1945, which camp inmates labeled the starving time. In Rex's barracks, the group repeatedly used the same coffee grounds, with the product weakening each time until the concoction was little more than yellow water. Some people cut down papaya trees, skinned and boiled the pulp until it was soft, and chewed on the substance for nourishment, but every short-term remedy lacked the substance to maintain weight and the nutrients to ward off disease. People lost an average of thirty pounds during this time.

Inmates adopted all sorts of measures to obtain additional food. In Los Baños, Father McKee and Brother Theodore traded their wristwatches for extra rice or beans. Those possessing a little money from before the war's start could purchase bananas, coconuts, eggs, and coffee from the Japanese (though the internees later learned that the food came from supplies originally earmarked for them). However, supplies dwindled and prices soared—at one point, Brother Rex saw people paying five dollars for an egg—once the U.S. military severed supply lines to the islands. "Soon, though, nothing came in and no one had to worry about this matter,"[21] he wrote.

Smuggling food into camp under the noses of the guards was a risk worth taking. At Cabanatuan, men laboring on work details outside the camp picked up fruits and vegetables and hid them under their clothing, or arranged for friendly Filipinos to smuggle in food and medicine. Father Buddenbroch, a German Catholic priest who had been in Manila for two decades, came and went freely because, as a German, he was an ally of the Japanese. He sewed large pockets inside his cassock, where he sequestered and sneaked into camp medicine, money, and Mass wine and wafers.

Filipino merchants near Bilibid smuggled in food, and other locals concealed peanuts, sugar, limes, shoes, clothing, and other essential items to share whenever the Japanese permitted them entry. Some civilians risked the guards' wrath by tossing over the barbed-wire walls molasses mixed with ground coconut, a delicacy treasured by each inmate, and Filipino Catholic priests organized smuggling operations.

A Filipino woman named Lulu Reyes repeatedly imperiled her life to deliver Rosaries, prayer books, food, and supplies to Father Duffy, which made the priest a popular figure about Bilibid. Duffy stifled a smile when he figured out why the number of prisoners who wanted to convert to Catholicism suddenly spiked. "Son," he whispered to one man who asked to convert, "you don't want to be a Catholic. You're just hungry."[22]

Father Duffy appreciated the help provided to him and other captives by the courageous Filipinos. He praised "their loyalty to America, their unselfish sacrifices, their passive resistance, their harassing resistance in the face of certain death, their constant fidelity, their daring in attempting to bring aid to American P.O.W.s," and heralded "the hundreds of their race who had their heads lopped off by the invaders for their devotion to the Americans." He claimed that "their valour and the unequaled bravery of their womanhood, in the face of the most desperate odds, should endear them forever to all Americans. They as a people never lost hope. They felt the shame and the pain of the American incarceration more than we did and whenever they met any of us, there was always a friendly 'V' and the familiar salutation, 'It won't be long now.'"[23]

Any prisoner smuggling food faced swift, ruthless punishment. One night at Cabanatuan, guards grabbed five men who were caught accepting food from Filipinos through the barbed-wire fence that surrounded the grounds. Lieutenant Colonel Mori ordered the five tied to stakes outside the camp where, for forty-eight hours, without food or water, they sweltered in the blazing sun by day and shivered in the darkness at night. Finally, the Japanese ended their misery with a bullet to the head. Mori ordered other internees to bury the quintet on the spot.

As the war unfolded, guards paid more attention to people seeking extra food. A civilian at Los Baños, Pat Hill, slipped under the wire one night to snatch a pig from outside, but the guards detected him as he returned and shot him in the back and chest. A Japanese officer, Lieutenant Sadaki Konishi, took perverse pleasure in catching internees sneaking food into Los Baños. When guards shot George Louis, a civilian worker, for approaching too close to the fence line in an attempt to get outside, Konishi refused to let the physician treat him. Louis lay there for two hours, growing weaker as his blood coursed onto the dirt, until Konishi ordered a guard to shoot the civilian in the head.

The International Red Cross attempted to ameliorate conditions with Red Cross food packages, but the Japanese released them sporadically and only after first taking food and cigarettes for themselves. The parcels still supplemented the miserable food portions distributed in the camps and often meant the difference between life and death.

"No Christmas present I can ever get will thrill me as much," wrote Captain Dyess at Cabanatuan. Father Carberry and his companions traded items with one another—sugar for cigarettes, saltines for evaporated milk—while others cried as they opened packages which "undoubtedly saved our lives,"[24] especially when the camp commandant subsequently reduced their daily rations in light of the packages.

The desire for adequate food tormented the inmates. "Many a night I spent in bed, my mouth watering, thinking of ham sandwiches and malted milks and other delicacies," wrote Brother Rex. "The talk of food became so constant that we agreed not to discuss the matter with one another."[25] At one point at Los Baños, the nuns pretended to hold a grand picnic. Sisters Olivette and Caecilius fried their rice into a cake-like substance and, with a few friends, laughed and joked as they consumed their mock dessert.

Reduced to living in such a quagmire, some hoarded what little food they had or abandoned their principles to obtain extra food and boost their odds for survival. "It's a constant fight against personal self-ishness," Lieutenant Commander Hayes wrote in his diary of such an occurrence at Bilibid in the fall of 1943. "A continual battle against in-dividuals who would sacrifice their comrades for personal gain."[26]

Guards were not alone in swiping food. Father Carberry confided to Lieutenant Colonel Leslie F. Zimmerman, the senior Protestant chaplain at Cabanatuan, that he knew of a third chaplain who retained items intended for others. "Carberry," Zimmerman wrote in his diary on October 9, 1942, "says he has proof that Talbot has had money given to him by the padre from Manila that has been sent to patients, and if they are dead, Talbot has used it for himself."[27] Zimmerman put an end to it, but the incident showed Carberry that under extreme duress, some people will do things they would never think of doing under nor-mal circumstances.

When a nun at Los Baños lifted vegetables from a garden belong-ing to the camp physician, thinking no one would object as they were intended for the hospital patients, the doctor, who was revered among the inmates, demanded she be "tried" by the camp court. For days everyone gossiped about the trial, some people siding with the beloved doctor while others supported the nun. When the man selected as judge asked the physician to identify the nun who supposedly stole his vegetables, the doctor scrutinized the group of nuns in the crowd, threw up his hands, and said, "They all look alike to me. I can't tell one from another."[28] With that the judge dismissed the case, sending away everyone but the doctor with smiles, either at the hilarious ending or from the fact that, at least for a time, their minds had been diverted from the miseries of camp life.

Others, especially parents who sacrificed their meals so that their children could eat more, impressed the Notre Dame religious with their compassion and love. Father Duffy credited his priestly training in helping him survive travails that defeated others. He and the other Notre Dame priests and religious were better prepared for the condi-tions because of the discipline demanded by their training and vows. They had sacrificed much, and their pledge of obedience required them to accept without complaint the stations and tasks handed them by su-periors. "The greatest loss was not among the older men who had learned self discipline the hard way," Father Duffy explained, but among those "who refused to discipline themselves to eating the harsh prison camp fare of rice and grass soups."[29]

"Low Marks in Deaths Today; Only Three"

Deplorable conditions and lack of nutrition in every camp assailed weakened captives and made them vulnerable to sickness. In Bilibid, swarms of flies infested overflowing latrines and spread malaria and other diseases to the frail men and women. "Mosquitoes and flies have become impossible," Lieutenant Commander Hayes confided to his diary in the spring of 1943. "Our half-naked bodies are caked with dried mud" because strong winds blew dust over everything in the sweltering weather. Dysentery and malaria ravaged men who had been in top physical shape on December 7, 1941. Body weights plunged below the one-hundred-pound mark; Father Duffy, a tall man of hefty build, shed more than fifty pounds in camp. "Our sickbed situation is going from bad to worse,"[30] wrote Lieutenant Commander Hayes on the war's second anniversary. Sick men occupied every available cot in the infirmary, requiring some to lie down on the concrete floor.

On July 4, 1942, Hayes recorded, "Within these dingy prison barracks are crowded all the human flotsam and jetsam from Bataan and Corregidor. Filipino and American alike, side by side on the concrete deck. The mattresses they lie on are filthy, stinking and vermin-ridden." Father Duffy was a common sight among the sick and dying in the hospital, which Hayes called one of the most "heart-rending sights imaginable. The mixed smells of dirty bodies, rotting tissue, dried blood, and excrement are repulsive to every filament of the esthetic senses." The physicians did the best they could under the circumstances, but Father Duffy and the other chaplains too often had to administer Last Rites over the skeletal men. "Our job is to do all we can with the pitiful little available to us," Hayes wrote. "At best," he glumly concluded, "many will die. In this prison the war has just begun."[31]

In Los Baños, Father McKee commiserated that the camp cemetery held at least 150 dead, all from malnutrition. "The next few months in these barracks," McKee wrote, "were to be a life of starvation, death, prayer and hope."[32]

Father Duffy became all too familiar with what the doctors called "dull eyes" among the Bilibid patients; this glazed stare indicated that the person had given up and preferred death over living with hunger and privation. Father Duffy journeyed to the camp cemetery more frequently, holding funeral services for men who, had they only been given a decent diet, would have survived.

Each April the chaplains conducted a memorial service to remember those who had perished in the last year. In April 1944, for instance, Father Duffy and his fellow chaplains, Catholic and non-Catholic, assembled at the cemetery where, after a minute of silence, they called the roll of those who had succumbed. One chaplain read a psalm, and after Father Duffy recited a prayer, men placed wreaths on the graves while a private sounded taps.

In Cabanatuan, a work detail traipsed each morning to Zero Ward, the section of the camp hospital reserved for the worst cases, and then to the barracks, where the bodies of those who had died overnight had been placed outside in neat rows. They gently gathered the remains, sometimes of close friends, and carried them a mile south to the cemetery. In the early months Commandant Mori refused to allow chaplains to accompany the burial details, but in August 1942 he relented after repeated requests from senior U.S. officers in camp. Accompanied by Carberry or one of the other chaplains, the men placed the bodies in a trench, but were not permitted to cover the remains with dirt until twenty bodies filled the pit. In rainy season the uncovered bodies sometimes floated in the water, and at night wild dogs descended on the corpses.

Deaths became so common that Carberry and others noted the rare occasions when few died. "Low mark in deaths today; only three. There is much rejoicing,"[33] Chaplain Zimmerman at Cabanatuan wrote in his diary in August 1942.

"We Should Go Without Him"

Despite Lieutenant Colonel Mori's admonitions, some prisoners responded either to their soldierly call of duty, which encouraged them to make escape attempts should they be captured, or to the hunger that gnawed at their stomachs. While Carberry was at Cabanatuan, three officers failed in an escape attempt. Mori spared the nine men in their sections but gathered the camp in roll-call formation and made them watch while guards beat the three until their faces were undistinguishable masses of pulp. He then had the three shot.

In July 1944 Brother Romaine, a Canadian Holy Cross religious delirious from malaria, climbed the compound fence and wandered about the hills near Los Baños. Guards seized him and threw him in a hut surrounded by a seven-foot-high fence topped with three strands of barbed wire, but a few nights later he escaped and ran through the camp before again being detained. In early August the Japanese transferred the fifty-year-old religious to a Manila sanitarium where, according to conflicting accounts, they either bayoneted or shot him during the slaughter of civilians in that city.

One successful escape attempt at Davao forced Father Carberry to make a torturous choice between his personal desire to escape and his duty to his fellow inmates. It began in hushed nighttime meetings in the barber's shed, where ten men plotted escape possibilities. During one gathering, prisoner Sam Grashio suggested that the presence of a Catholic priest could be helpful as they fled through jungles and fields populated by devout Catholic Filipinos. Grashio recommended Father Carberry, who was in relatively decent shape and who, at age thirty-eight, was still young enough to withstand the rigors of an escape. Father Carberry's decoration for bravery during the fighting on Bataan had proven his toughness, and all assented that he would be a welcome addition.

Carberry was delighted to be included, but he struggled with the decision. Grashio and the other military were encouraged as soldiers to make escape attempts, but the priest's duty was to God, not to a military code. He had brought comfort to the prisoners in diverse ways, and Carberry wondered if he should now place his desires above those of others. He understood that should he decline the offer, continued confinement could easily lead to his death or permanent ailments. Like everyone else in camp, he longed to be free from the squalor and return to the United States and his family. He hoped to again visit the Grotto on campus or stroll by the Golden Dome. Torn by the options, Carberry reluctantly accepted their invitation.

As historian John D. Lukacs related in his book, *Escape from Davao*, the eleven refrained from sharing the news with anyone outside their group to preclude placing themselves and the other camp inmates in danger. They knew that certain individuals, weakened from the harsh regimen, were willing to share information with the Japanese in exchange for extra food. The conspirators even avoided muted conversations in the open lest someone might overhear them. Once they had escaped, the prisoners left behind in camp could justifiably claim ignorance of the plan and hopefully avoid punishment.

A Japanese guard, Lieutenant Yoshimasa Hozumi, almost foiled their plans when he appeared for a surprise inspection that nearly discovered their hidden cache of supplies. The men had stored food, medicine, and other materials in five-gallon gasoline cans and covered them with banana leaves, and Father Carberry, carrying two of those cans to the camouflaged area, was forced to hide in a nearby banana grove until Hozumi left.

A few days before their planned escape, the group gathered at the shed for a final meeting. McCoy cautioned everyone to act as normal as possible on the morning selected so as not to draw attention to themselves. He told Father Carberry to say his Mass as usual and the other men to pretend that they were going to work.

Father Carberry remained conflicted over his choice. Freedom was worth risking his life, but he continued to question whether he had the right to do so at the expense of others. He had taken solemn religious vows at his ordination in Notre Dame's Church of the Sacred Heart, and those vows admonished him that, despite discomfort and misery, he had a duty to assist those in need.

Carberry explained his quandary to Father Braun and asked what the senior chaplain might do if he faced a similar predicament. Braun answered that since the men depended on him for Mass, Confession, and a host of other religious matters, and since they found solace in his willingness to share in their suffering, he in good conscience could not leave. Braun understood Carberry's desire to flee but asked the priest if he was willing to cause added suffering to the inmates he left behind. If a priest were among those who escaped, the commandant, Major Kazuo Maeda, would most likely ban further religious services and punish those remaining in the camp with reduced rations or other restrictions, if not outright executions. Could Carberry live with that? Braun reminded the priest that his duty was to remain with the men and help them through their ordeals rather than to sate his personal desire. Carberry had all but arrived at that conclusion himself, but Braun's advice helped him decide to forgo the chance for freedom.

Shortly before dawn on Sunday, April 4, 1943, the group headed to the mess hall as usual for breakfast. When Father Carberry failed to appear, Grashio checked around camp and learned that the priest was in the infirmary. "I went there at once and found him lying in bed," said Grashio. "He told me that he hoped to go with us but that he was too weak to make the attempt now; that we should go without him."[34]

The priest had lied to his friend. Unwilling to share his decision with the ten, and fearing that they might talk him into escaping, Carberry instead pretended to be ill. He told Grashio that in his weakened condition, he would be a hindrance to them as they fled through the jungles and over the harsh terrain.

Grashio accepted Carberry's explanation and rejoined his compatriots. In a dangerous journey, the ten fled through mosquito-infested swamps to friendly Filipinos, who helped them rendezvous with a submarine that whisked them to Australia.

Their story made headlines in the United States and illuminated the tribulations faced by Carberry and the other men still subsisting in prison camps. Dyess wrote a book about their escape and told a reporter for the *New York Times* that while he and the other nine endured a rough trip, "We were always able to thank God we were anywhere except back among the Japs, subject to their barbaric cruelties, their policy of systematic starvation, and their creed of murder for captives." He added of Carberry and the others still at Davao and other camps, "If you triple my troubles and multiply the result by several thousand, you'll get a rough idea of what went on. And when you do that, bear in mind that I got out alive. Thousands of the boys didn't—and won't."[35]

"Suffering Set to Music"

The ten Davao escapees comprised the fortunate few. Those they left behind, including Father Carberry, faced months, even years, of attempting to maintain morale in the face of repeated atrocities.

Daily Mass helped many endure. Commandant Mori at first denied Carberry and the chaplains at Cabanatuan permission to say Mass or conduct religious gatherings. The edict forced them to adopt furtive methods, such as saying Mass in the latrine, where guards were less likely to burst in, or leading small groups in saying the Rosary behind a shed. They risked beatings if discovered, but Carberry accepted the hazards as part of his priestly duties in prison camp. Mori finally yielded to the persistence of Father Braun, Father Carberry, and the other chaplains and allowed each priest to celebrate one Mass a day, and two to lead the men in reciting the Rosary each evening.

At Davao, the priests awoke as early as 3:30 a.m. to say Mass because Major Maeda demanded that everyone, including the officers and the chaplains, join a work detail. The persuasive Lulu Reyes had convinced Japanese officials to allow her to bring into camp altar wine and wafers for the priests' Masses, as well as Rosaries and medals to hand out to the inmates.

Father Duffy improvised at Bilibid. His parish lacked the beautiful trappings that priests back home enjoyed, but even amid squalor and filth, he could boost the spirits of his comrades. The effervescent Duffy regaled the men with tales about his prewar life as a chaplain, his time at Notre Dame, and his friendship with Knute Rockne. "We would gather around him and he would tell us stories and jokes," recalled Army Sergeant Abie Abraham, who spent hours listening to Father Duffy and chatting about home. "He always had us laughing and we would forget our hunger and misery." Abraham often spotted Father Duffy squatting beside the beds of the ill, encouraging them to retain their hope and faith, or praying with those who were soon to die. "He was an inspiration and did a lot for the many thousands of sick Americans," said Abraham. "The sick looked up to him."[36]

Ben Steele forged a lifetime friendship with Father Duffy, who visited him often while he was incapacitated by illness. "He would stop by and talk to me every day as I was very ill for months,"[37] he later wrote. Once he regained his strength, Steele served as an altar boy for the priest, who used a lean-to against the wall for an altar. The pair continued the discussions they started in the infirmary, with Duffy encouraging Steele, a gifted amateur artist who drew to take his mind off the horrors about him, to depict the daily lives of the captives. Steele sketched on scraps of paper and anything else he could find, and soon amassed seventy charcoal scenes illustrating the men at work, standing at roll call, in the infirmary, and engaged in other activities. Worried that the Japanese might uncover and confiscate the drawings, Steele asked Father Duffy to sequester them. Each time Steele completed a sketch, the priest concealed it in the bottom of his Mass kit. The two agreed that after the war, they would collaborate on a book about their experiences, with Steele's drawings complementing Duffy's words.

Father Duffy hoped he and Steele could produce a graphic account of their camp existence that illustrated not only the atrocities, but also scenes of the human spirit overcoming barbarism by simply enduring from one day to the next.

Once the chaplains had received permission to celebrate Mass, they pushed for more. They persuaded camp commandants that recreation periods would improve the men's work performance, and consequently the internees arranged lectures and formed camp orchestras and choirs. At Cabanatuan, Mori permitted one variety show each week. The melodic notes and powerful words of songs such as "Let Me Call You Sweetheart" provided a connection with home and had a calming effect on the camp. Other songs, written by internees, emphasized their longing for freedom, for a juicy steak smothered in mushrooms, or for other comforts taken for granted at home. A group labeling itself the Mighty Cabanatuan Art Players presented "Snow White and the Seven Dwarfs" and other skits, including many that poked fun of themselves and, gently, the Japanese. Father Carberry participated in these gatherings, but his principal form of leisure came during the nightly bridge games that he and a group of officers organized.

At Father Duffy's camp, a group of inmates known as the Bilibid Players organized skits, musical performances, and other forms of entertainment. Duffy loved most shows because he saw how much the men enjoyed them, but he frowned at the risqué humor that sometimes crept in. He once complained to Hayes, who dismissed the priest's objections. "The Chaplain's comments were ridiculous," Hayes wrote in his diary on December 12, 1943. "I will admit that the humor was a little lusty, but it's humor of a kind and we need it."[38]

The weekly musical performances conducted by twenty-nine Jesuit seminarians became a highlight at Los Baños. The young men interspersed songs with humorous skits, delighting the audience with their renditions of popular tunes. They altered the words to reflect camp life and express the hope that liberation would soon arrive. The songs, which often teased the guards by using idioms and phrases the Japanese failed to understand, not only comforted the people but also became a form of passive resistance that made the internees feel that they were doing something to fight back. "They were battle songs, spirit raisers, laughter, and suffering set to music when laughter and music were invaluable gifts," claimed Sister Olivette. "In song we told our experience of where we were, what we did, how we suffered, the pangs of hunger, what we thought of our captors, how we would like to repay them, our dreams of freedom,"[39] and other topics of significance.

The words of one, sung to the tune of Irving Berlin's popular 1925 song "Always," poignantly illustrate their hopes as American military forces neared the Philippines.

A hospital is there in Leyte
Nurses everywhere in Leyte
A private room for you
Pink and white and blue
Private showers too
In Leyte, Leyte.

Flowers blooming there in Leyte
A fragrance in the air of Leyte
Swans out on the lake
Mushrooms on your steak
A chocolate layer cake
In Leyte, Leyte.[40]

Sisters Olivette and Caecilius claimed that the optimism that prevailed among most American internees, and the ability to lighten their burden through song, contributed to their survival and confounded the Japanese. "The Japanese simply couldn't understand the American spirit," said the nuns, "our ability to laugh at our troubles, to continue our community recreations, our efforts at cleanliness and order."[41]

Sporadic correspondence with home also sustained the internees. Messages ranged from the official communications informing family that their loved ones were confined in camp to the brief, penciled comments on index-size cards the Japanese sometimes allowed prisoners to mail. When Sister Olivette opened her first letter from home in late 1944, "you could hear my shout of joy from one end of the barracks to the other."[42]

"At long last we have word through the International Red Cross that you are alive, although a prisoner of war," Bishop Alter wrote to Father Duffy in May 1943. Duffy's superior in Toledo told him that each Wednesday he celebrated Mass for the diocese's chaplains "and your name is first on my list."[43] At the same time, Father William R. Arnold, the chief of chaplains, sent a similar letter to Father Carberry, expressing his relief that his priest was alive.

Mail, however, could be a double-edge sword. The welfare of family members, especially the elderly or ill, was a constant concern for the prisoners, and that their parents might not even know if they were alive in the Philippines haunted them. Brother Rex said that had he known with certainty that his family had received word of his survival, his time in Los Baños would have been easier. Father Carberry's sister, Rozella Soreghan, rushed a reply to Father Arnold's information that her brother was safe in hopes of getting word to her brother that their father, James Carberry, had died suddenly the previous August.

Commander Hayes in Bilibid longed to hear from family, but feared that information from home would deepen his melancholy. He and others were not certain how to interpret certain sentiments or half-thoughts expressed by wives or mothers. "So instead of being a help to morale," Hayes wrote, "the mail becomes a kick in the pants and does more harm than good."[44]

ALMOST FROM the start of their incarceration, when the prisoners believed that MacArthur would rush to their rescue or heard that two divisions of army infantry had landed in Luzon, rumors about the European and Pacific theaters boosted the internees' morale. The rumors were sometimes surprisingly accurate, such as in mid-November 1942 when, only two days after the U.S. Fleet turned back the Japanese in a major action off Guadalcanal, internees spoke in hushed tones about a huge naval battle won in the Pacific by their country. More often, though, rumors wildly missed the mark, such as in late 1942 when word spread that thousands of Allied aircraft were bombing Germany and forcing evacuation of their cities.

Since the Japanese had severed their access to American radio stations, the internees relied on Filipinos to smuggle in word as they brought supplies into camp. Filipinos listened to American West Coast stations over concealed radios in their homes and relayed that information by tossing over Bilibid's walls rocks with messages wrapped around them. Men on work details overheard conversations, and merchants permitted into camp brought additional war news. At Los Baños, the Japanese newspaper *Manila Shimbun* became their most reliable source of information. The articles presented only the Japanese version of events, but perceptive readers gathered enough clues to conclude that the war had turned in favor of the United States. An article might report that a squadron of Japanese aircraft had sunk an American ship but add that none of the triumphant planes returned from the mission, or might declare, whenever U.S. Marines seized an island, that the Japanese had purposely yielded the location because they no longer had any use for it. Rumors gained credibility when the Japanese cut back rations and other items for the prisoners, who took it as a sign that the war must be going poorly for their captors.

They concluded correctly. Throughout 1944, American land, sea, and air forces tightened the military noose about the Japanese, seizing Central and South Pacific island bases and forcing the Japanese to withdraw toward the Home Islands. Among those units was General MacArthur's assault group intent on liberating the Philippines and making good on the officer's vow to return.

Liberation for the Notre Dame religious was drawing closer, but would they live long enough to reap its benefits? From their prison camps Fathers Carberry and Duffy, as well as the six Holy Cross missionaries, faced a deadly race whose outcome would determine their fate. Would they survive prison camp long enough to be liberated by the forces now steamrolling across the Pacific, or would they succumb before friendly faces arrived?

CHAPTER 5

"DAILY WAS I SHELLED, NIGHTLY WAS I BOMBED"

Father Barry from Sicily to Rome

Now that the Germans had been forced out of Sicily, the Italian mainland became the next objective for Father Barry's 157th Regiment. Operation Avalanche called for a landing at Salerno, forty miles south of Naples, to gain a port through which supplies could be brought in as well as a base from which to launch additional drives up the Italian boot. General Mark W. Clark, commander of the Fifth Army of which Barry's regiment was a part, referred to the punishing warfare that awaited in Italy when he told one correspondent, "We're spitting into the lion's mouth and we know it."[1]

On September 9 the regiment landed against heavy opposition. Father Barry had just stepped into a landing craft preparing to descend to the water from the transport when an officer told him to switch to another boat. The second landing craft hung out over the transport's side with twelve soldiers, but before Barry could step into it, the chain on the front end snapped and emptied the dozen occupants, weighed down with weapons and equipment, into the water. As Father Barry watched from above, all twelve drowned. He had avoided that same fate by mere seconds.

The landing craft came under thick fire from German guns emplaced on high ground bordering the landing beach. The Germans rained down mortar shells, artillery barrages, and machine-gun fire on the regiment, which also had to thread through mines in the water to reach shore. Barry tended to fallen men lying on the beach before rushing toward a field hospital set up in the ancient Temple of Neptune, constructed by the Greeks around 470 B.C.

Later that night the Germans unleashed a counterattack that forced officers to toss cooks, clerks, and musicians from the regimental band into the fighting. With bullets smacking the ground and bombs bursting about him, Father Barry tried to focus on his tasks.

Bill Mauldin, a newspaper cartoonist who chronicled the foot soldiers' war with his unforgettable drawings of Willie and Joe at the front, accompanied the Forty-Fifth Division. He recalled the time at Salerno when he watched a Catholic chaplain, whose name he failed to obtain, celebrate Mass. In the middle of the service a German fighter plane attacked the group, sending priest and soldiers scampering for the closest foxhole to elude the bullets. The priest, noted Mauldin, leaped into a ditch a split second before bullets ripped into the mud at the ditch's edge. Once the plane disappeared, the chaplain emerged and resumed the Mass as if nothing had occurred.

While Mauldin omitted the name of the chaplain, soldiers with Father Barry recalled frequent interruptions by German aircraft at his Masses, making it possible that Mauldin had observed Father Barry. "Religious services in battle zones offer weird contrasts to bursting shells and the twisted wreckage of war. It is strange to see reverence helmeted and armored," Mauldin wrote. "I have a lot of respect for those chaplains who keep up the spirits of the combat guys. They often give the troops a pretty firm anchor to hang onto." The incident served as the inspiration for one of Mauldin's most touching cartoons. In it, he depicts a chaplain standing next to a bunker, prayer book in hand, with a quintet of soldiers listening as he ends a prayer with the words, " . . . forever, Amen. Hit the dirt."[2]

Barry's quiet courage, displayed by the unarmed priest's willingness to risk his life in battle to tend to them, inspired his boys. The soldiers around Barry appreciated his extra efforts in their behalf and realized that in Father Barry they had a chaplain who did more than just pray.

Barry proved he could ignore the bullets and shells and stand with them as only a buddy could.

"Death Would Come Like a Thief in the Night"

Once the Allied forces moved out of the Salerno area, Rome, one of the most revered spots of the world since ancient times, became their next objective. Seizing the Eternal City required a gargantuan effort involving the crossing of swollen, icy rivers, scaling hills and mountains, and advancing through mud so thick it clutched the men's boots and mired trucks and jeeps. Nature's obstacles, made worse by the pestilential rain, sleet, and snow, would have been difficult enough to conquer, but the 157th Regiment also had to eliminate the crack German divisions guarding each slope and lining the sides of every valley.

Three German defense lines stood between the 157th Regiment and Rome, one hundred miles to the north. The German commander planned to inflict as many casualties as possible on the Americans at the first line and then fall back to repeat the process at a second line before making his last stand at the Gustav Line. That formidable final barrier would force the Americans to advance through the Liri Valley, guarded by German forces entrenched in the oldest Christian monastery in the Western world, Monte Cassino. "I don't know what these Germans are taught," Barry wrote of the new round of combat, "but I do know that our troops have to blast them out of their 8 foot holes and mountain side, rock-carved caves and pill boxes."[3]

He and his boys fought through the most miserable weather and terrain offered in the European theater. Ice-clogged rivers coursed through mountain slopes so steep that men had to grab rocks and branches to keep their footing. Soldiers measured advances in yards, not miles, and reached the summit of one hill only to find another waiting to be surmounted. Rocks ripped their boots and gashed their feet. Mules bringing supplies up the tricky slopes and bearing casualties down on their return trips emitted chilling wails as they lost their footing and fell to their deaths. Bitter cold froze toes, and trench foot became commonplace in the ever-present mud and rain. From their lofty perches in the hills German snipers picked off soldiers foolish enough to remain in the open too long. Some generals wondered if it might be better to call a halt to the offensive and wait until the weather improved, but their commander, Major General Dwight D. Eisenhower, kept the offensive going. Those troops in Italy needed to keep attacking to prevent the Germans from switching divisions to France, where a June 1944 invasion was then being planned.

Father Barry visited wounded and dying soldiers in field hospitals, consoled men in foxholes who neared a breaking point, and risked death in bringing religious comfort to his boys. He climbed tricky slopes and helped carry wounded back down, and handed out medals and prayer books. "There's no fanfare over here, just a dirty, uncomfortable and dangerous campaign," Father Barry wrote to a friend, sportswriter Jim Costin of the *South Bend Tribune*. "Mountains rise straight up from the valleys and to get at the Jerries in their strong defensive positions they have to climb almost straight up the sides of the hills. Crawling and wading, sliding and marching, up mountains and down mountains, carrying a blanket and some K-rations in their packs, toting rifles, machine guns and mortars—fighting the terrible weather and terrain as well as the well-entrenched Heinies."[4]

To cut through the mountains and valleys to Rome, the Allies had to destroy a revered object: the monastery at Monte Cassino, which had been occupied and fortified by the Germans because it overlooked the quickest route into Rome. Allied forces required four months of attacks, including a February 16, 1944, bombing and artillery assault that pulverized the monastery, to crack through.

"We have fought and slaved for three months trying to get in there from above," Father Barry wrote of Monte Cassino to a priest friend who had visited the monastery before the war. "The Jerries are fighting like fanatics to keep us from taking that famous town and the road that leads to where all roads lead (Rome). Up the mount where you climbed for recreation, we have been climbing for 're-creation' of the four freedoms."[5]

Torrential rains morphed roads and fields into muddy quagmires. "Pray for less rain in sunny Italy,"[6] Father Barry commented on his monthly chaplain report for November 1943. Soldiers learned to walk with their rifles slung upside down over their shoulders to prevent water from seeping into the barrels.

Mauldin's cartoons often depicted a rain-soaked Willie and Joe pining for dry socks. Men with trench foot crawled to aid stations, but when they removed their boots, their feet swelled such that they could not slip their boots back on. After sleeping in the mud, men ached and suffered from congested chests. "It was miserable!" said Sergeant Stigliani of E Company, 157th Regiment. "Rain, sleet, snow, and mud, lots of mud! We'd walk until our boots were caked with mud, and then fling our feet out to get the mud off and hit the other guys. We'd have mud fights, like kids. Father Barry would have faced the same situations as us, caked boots and everything."[7]

Father Barry claimed that all he needed was a pair of skis to operate in the miserable conditions, which featured mud he joked was only a foot deep. "Greetings from sunny (?) Italy," he wrote to Costin. "The sun may be shining somewhere, but over here we've been fighting this war for the past month in mud up to our knees from the constant rains." Ever the sports enthusiast, Barry compared the climate to major-league baseball hurler Johnny Vander Meer of the Cincinnati Reds, known for erratic extremes in his performances:

> When it's good it is very good, and when it's bad it's awful. All through June in Africa and July and August in Sicily we didn't have a drop of rain. It was so dry that the dust from the roads would powder your face and clothes and give you a ghost-like appearance. Along about the latter part of September after we had hit the mainland around the Salerno sector and started pushing north, the rains finally came. They not only came, but they stayed, and now every time you dive into your foxhole it is necessary to wear a life preserver, because if the shellfire doesn't get you, the depth of the water in the hole might.[8]

Barry shared the horror of artillery barrages that terrorized the soldiers. It is easy to forget that chaplains mirrored the men they tended, and as humans, they succumbed to the same fear, anger, envy, and doubt that assailed those soldiers. Describing the experience of German artillery fire to Father Steiner, he wrote, "When you are crouched against a thick wall while the air splits and the earth quakes there is one and only one thing to do: pray boys, pray."[9] He admitted he was never afraid of dying, but the merciless barrages, during which hardened soldiers had been known to crumble, terrified everyone. Nighttime barrages—a favorite of the Germans because, even if they failed to hit an American, they at least disrupted sleep—were worse. In the darkness a soldier was left alone with his emotions.

According to Mauldin, enemy artillery, especially the hated German 88mm anti-tank and antiaircraft artillery gun, "is the sound of terror of every dogface." He explained that a soldier could spend hours strengthening and masking his position, only to be killed by a shell fired from a gun standing miles away. A German sniper needed to see his target, but a "shell is just as likely to hit the good soldier who is under cover as the dumb one who is standing on top of a knoll."[10]

Like the soldier who stifles his terror and rushes the enemy, bayoneted rifle in hand, Barry moved from foxhole to foxhole under fire, Bible and spiritual comfort his weapons of choice. He risked his life for the same reason soldiers and sailors risked theirs: his buddies needed him. He might not share drinks with them during their sparse breaks from the front, and he certainly would forgo visits to some of the shadier spots frequented by the men, but he was every bit as much a buddy as their fellow fighters.

"Shells never seemed to get on his nerves," said Lieutenant Stemmons of Father Barry. Unlike some of Stemmons's own soldiers, Barry "never worried about being hit. All that had a calming effect on the men. In combat he moved around all the time. He'd go to the aid station where the wounded were, and then he'd be at the front under fire. He never asked which units we were from, he just kept moving around. We knew he'd be in the line of fire." Stemmons explained that Barry even went beyond his priestly duties to help at the front. "If we needed equipment or ammo, he'd go get it for us under fire. That wasn't the job of the chaplain."[11]

Barry's wartime letters to Father Steiner and others contained added poignancy during the Italian campaign, where nature and the enemy conspired to create near intolerable conditions. Barry used his letters as therapy, as his way of combating war itself. The letters became his link to all that was not war—to Notre Dame, to friends, to football, to laughs and civilization. In his letters he escaped, however briefly, the horrors he faced on a daily basis. They became his refuge, just as he was the refuge for those boys he served.

In one letter to Art, a Holy Cross friend, in which he tried to describe artillery barrages, Barry told the priest to dig a hole no bigger than a grave and consider it his "bedroom, parlor and bath." He then asked his friend to imagine someone tossing bricks at him day and night for two weeks amid deafening explosions and noises, and remain in it while torrential rainstorms filled the hole with a minimum of two inches of water. "Reading this over, Art," Barry glumly concluded, "I feel foolish trying to make you feel what the kids go through. When all is said and done, you must live it, and get it in your blood and bones, and then you know from experience and not from 'extras.'"[12]

Barry wrote to Father Steiner about spending the previous night in a town blasted by German artillery from midnight to 3:00 a.m. The shells poured in without pause, and each one seemed to be coming straight for him. Barry explained that he could do nothing but squat deeper in his hole, which would do little to save him from a direct hit, and pray. "Our Lord told us Death would come like a thief in the night, quiet-like. He descended last night on this community like a cyclone, hitting the roads like a head-on collision of Big Four. You wonder if you are the next to be called. It is a strange feeling like a man being buried alive. I have learned one thing and that is nothing counts but God. And in this game of flip-life and sudden death the Presence of God is the supreme consolation. How often have the lads told me the same thing."[13]

As he advised his boys, Barry leaned on his faith to take him through the travails of combat. God and religion forged his anchor, and in the direst moments he clasped them tighter. "We all live so close to death that in this game, the Mass and the sacraments are all that matter," he wrote to a Holy Cross friend. "My listening ear reminds me of the state in which most of these boys live. Every last one of us fears death day and night, and no matter how much shelling we have been under, each new barrage brings new fear. However, one thing I have learned: there is no sweetness like the sugar of a clean soul."

Even though he endured horrors on a daily basis, Barry would be nowhere else, for in combat, artillery barrages and all, was precisely where he was most needed. "All my lads realize the same truth. In spite of the physical hardships we all must suffer, I honestly thank God I can be with these courageous kids."[14]

As usual, even in describing life-threatening conditions, Barry could not refrain from turning to that impish humor for which he was famous at Notre Dame. Singling out one advantage of the artillery barrages, he told Father Steiner, "I'm told prostate trouble comes after 40. I have not seen the disturber yet. Shelling however seems to relax the piping."[15]

"Christmas Found Me on the Front Lines"

"Well, Art, my feet are stone cold and besides, it's time for me to visit the lads in the front lines," Father Barry wrote to a Holy Cross associate. "The time is 10 p.m., the night is dark, the Jerries are shelling again, so wish me luck and continue to pray for Yours truly, Joe."[16]

All through the Sicilian and Italian campaigns, Father Barry could most often be found at the front, surrounded by fighting and killing. He sometimes left for the aid stations to the rear to tend to the wounded and dying gathered there, but he preferred to be with his young soldiers where they most needed him, as they met the enemy face-to-face in mortal combat. The risks were great—more chaplain casualties occurred in Italy than anywhere else in the war—but he shrugged aside the hazards to be with the soldiers to whom he had ministered since training.

"I must move more carefully lest Jerry decides that my neck would make a nice target," he wrote to an associate, but his willingness to endure the shelling and bombs, machine guns and mortars, endeared him to the soldiers, who were far more likely to divulge their fears and concerns to a chaplain who had shared those same battlefield experiences. Barry became a charter member of what Mauldin labeled "The Benevolent and Protective Brotherhood of Them What Has Been Shot At," making him not simply a chaplain, but one of them. He looked after 1,500 soldiers, "to spit and polish spiritually, as we say in the language of the infantry," in the process bathing as infrequently as did his boys, which Mauldin joked was "twice during the summer and not quite as often in the winter."[17]

Barry was in his element at the front, among the privates and corporals who comprised the youngest group of soldiers fighting the war, partly because he found those boys to be refreshingly honest and straightforward. He harbored no resentment toward officers, but the privates and corporals wanted nothing more than to take the next hill, move on to the next mission, and end the war. As most were resigned to the fact that they would be either killed or wounded, Father Barry learned to be an excellent listener so those infantrymen would feel free to unburden themselves on topics ranging from officers good and bad to females decent and not to their innermost fears.

He loved that if a soldier—or a chaplain—failed to do his job, his boys called him out. "I found the kids nakedly honest," he later said. "If they knew a guy was dogging it, they would make no bones about it. They would say, 'You bastard. You knew that you were supposed to be there, and you were not.'" Barry told the interviewer that in such an incident, the men would say, "I will be a son of a bitch if I will take a trip with you again."[18]

A paralyzing thought for a wounded or dying soldier was of lying alone on the battlefield, left to contend with his fears while fighting to stay alive. Cognizant of that, Barry ran, stooped, or crawled to reach a boy prone on the ground and bring him the peace of knowing that someone was there with him. One glance at the kindly face of Father Barry, called Father Joe or Padre by his boys, helped ease a wounded soldier's anxieties or a dying soldier's terrors.

Of all his duties, Barry considered the administration of Last Rites his most important. Whether on the battlefield or in an aid station, he wanted to be with his boys at the moment of death. With so many soldiers under his care, he could not possibly have fulfilled that wish, but he made every effort to do so. "After 54 years, I can still see Father Barry administering last rites to soldiers in the field while enemy shells exploded all around him," wrote Albert R. Panebianco, a soldier in the Forty-Fifth Infantry Division. "He was a dedicated priest and I will never forget him."[19]

On one occasion Barry talked with a soldier who, due to go into battle in a few hours, feared that "this might be my last night." The soldier confided that he accepted fear as part of his task but wondered if he would control his panic and still perform when it counted.

Barry knew better than try to convince the soldier that, no matter how many Germans fired at him or how many mortar shells erupted nearby, he would come through alive, as both he and the boy knew that the priest would only be "talking through your helmet." Instead, Barry gently asked if he wanted to go to Confession and inquired if there was anything the priest could do for him. The boy had one request. Above all, he told Barry, he had wanted to be a good soldier, for his men, his family, his country, and his God, and if he died, would Barry please tell his family that he had been a good soldier. During combat later that night, German fire cut down the youth. Father Barry rushed to him, cradled the mortally wounded boy in his arms, and with explosions and combat nearly drowning out his words, whispered into the dying boy's ear, "Remember how we talked last night. Here it is. And I can say you were a good soldier."[20]

Father Barry never grew accustomed to the process following the death of one of his boys. Barry retrieved the dog tags and, if possible, fingerprinted the man for identification. He then covered the body and, if time permitted, waited until a burial crew arrived, but he usually had to hasten to another wounded man. When the fighting ended, he collected the deceased soldier's personal effects for transmission to his family, an excruciating task as they usually included photographs of mothers, wives, or children who would soon receive word of their loved one's death. At the burial, Barry conducted the service appropriate to the soldier's religion—Catholic, Protestant, or Jewish—but if the remains provided no hint of the man's religious affiliation, he conducted both a Catholic and Protestant service at the gravesite.

Father Barry wished he could avoid the next anguishing step: writing letters to parents and loved ones. He penned hundreds of such notes, often at the behest of a dying soldier who asked the priest to inform his mother or wife that he loved her. Barry attempted to personalize these letters, which he understood would have a life-altering impact on parents or widows. Above all, he made certain that they knew that their son had died with a priest at his side.

"I wrote to so many. You could write what they wanted to know more than anything else, 'I wonder if there was a priest with my boy.'" Barry explained in an interview. "And that is the only reason I wrote," he said. "'I just want you to know for your own consolation that I was with your son the night he died.'"[21]

A May 1944 letter from Margaret Ahern to Father Steiner illustrated how important that knowledge, or in this case, lack of that knowledge, was to family back home. Her son, Thomas C. Ahern, had written regularly every week and a half since leaving for overseas, but the letters had suddenly stopped three months earlier. An attempt to obtain information from the Red Cross failed, and, she wrote, "We would not be so concerned except for the fact that two of the boys who were with him in Italy have been seriously injured, and up to this writing, the parents have not been officially notified by the Government." The two families had, however, received letters informing them of their sons' safety, one from the soldier himself while he recovered in an evacuation hospital and the other from a nurse, but as yet the Aherns had heard nothing from Thomas.

She explained to Father Steiner that their son had written a friend about his chaplain, "telling how wonderful he was, and mentioned the fact that he had formerly taught at Notre Dame before entering the Service." She wondered if Steiner might know the chaplain's identity so she could write to him. "This Chaplain knew my son personally, I understand, and I am quite sure if I could only contact him, he could give us some recent information as to my son's welfare when he last saw him."[22] Father Steiner sent Barry's military address to Mrs. Ahern but never learned if the mother and chaplain connected.

Father Barry took each death personally, for he had eaten meals with the soldiers, counseled them, laughed and cried with them. He would have agreed with Mauldin's moving words about his buddies from the Forty-Fifth Infantry Division who had died in Italy: "When you lose a friend you have an overpowering desire to go back home and yell in everybody's ear, 'This guy was killed fighting for you. Don't forget him—ever. Keep him in your mind when you wake up in the morning and when you go to bed at night. Don't think of him as the statistic which changes 38,788 casualties to 38,789. Think of him as a guy who wanted to live every bit as much as you do.'"[23]

Barry eventually found the delicate balance he needed in wartime of placing death in its proper perspective. For every boy who perished, another ten required his services, and Father Barry could not afford to linger over the loss of one of his charges. "You have no time for grief," he explained in an interview. "These things day after day and night after night, they keep coming in one form or another. I cannot remember a time when I even cried. You could not, because that would be the first step of going haywire. And I have seen a small number of priests who when they got in a tight situation, they just fell apart. When you fall apart you cannot do any good for any one." He added that he was in so many actions, "you would not last if you gave in."[24]

To celebrate Mass for his boys, Barry improvised on a daily basis, holding the service one day in a barn and the next out in the field. In

"Daily Was I Shelled, Nightly Was I Bombed" 133

one letter he mentioned using as altars the fronts of jeeps, the backs of trucks, and the tops of wooden crates. He said Mass wearing altar vestments or, if the situation stipulated, only his uniform. He conducted services in dry river beds, atop snow-covered mountains, and in schoolhouses and cowsheds. He consecrated wine and hosts in rain, sun, and darkness, and told Father Steiner that once "so thick and deep was the mud that I found it almost impossible to turn for the Dominus vobiscum." German shells and bombs interrupted more than a handful of Masses, forcing Barry and his congregations to seek shelter. At one Mass he was about to begin a prayer "when all hell broke loose from the skies. The Mass was over under present conditions"; on other occasions bullets from German snipers drove everyone to shelter. He said of another incident, "vestments and all I dove into a nearby shell hole." Father Barry shrugged off these risks whenever reporters asked if he had ever said Mass while under fire. If a newspaperman persisted, Barry reluctantly acceded but, not always successfully, requested that the reporter omit that part. One *South Bend Tribune* reporter quoted Father Barry as saying, "Oh, sure, we were fired upon by snipers during celebration of Mass, but don't mention that. That has been told before."[25]

Sergeant Stigliani attended one of Father Barry's Masses celebrated in a grove of fig trees in southern Italy. "You try to pick a spot for Mass that had some camouflage," said Stigliani. "The hood of a Jeep was the altar, and Father Barry placed a blanket over it for his chalice and items. All of us soldiers sat on our helmets." Barry had intoned the opening words to the Mass when "we heard motors. Three planes, British planes that had made a mistake, came down firing at us and we all scattered." Stigliani dashed up a hill and jumped into a haystack. "I don't know why, because hay can't stop bullets, but anything is better than nothing. The planes didn't hit anyone, but they sure scared us! There was already another guy in there, just two guys trying not to get hit. Lo and behold it was Father Barry. Afterward, he couldn't find his glasses, and although we all looked around for them, he never did find them. He told me later it took two to three months for him to get replacement glasses."[26]

The soldiers appreciated Barry's efforts to bring the benefits of Mass and Communion under the most difficult circumstances. One corporal wrote his mother that, "If the folks back home could see the harrowing conditions and the awful places where our chaplains have to offer Mass they would be more grateful for our nice parish churches and not kick so much when the pastor reminds them these need to be heated and lighted and that takes a lota dough." A second soldier remarked that he enjoyed attending services because "when I'm at the service I can forget about everything and imagine I'm home again."[27] Father Barry provided not only spiritual comfort, but also a crucial link to family and home that sustained many soldiers as they headed into combat.

One of the boys asked Father Barry to say a Mass of thanksgiving in his behalf. When Barry asked the reason, the soldier answered that he had been stringing wire along a mountainside. "When he finished he moved down the trail," wrote Barry. "Three minutes after a shell hit right where he moved from." The soldier's faith, which illustrated that the young men facing "death day and night" find their "greatest protection in the strong arm of Our Lord,"[28] touched the priest.

Staff Sergeant Michael J. Jaskovich claimed that Father Barry did more than bring the Sacraments to his soldiers—he helped the unit perform under fire. Jaskovich was so proud of the record his men compiled and of Father Barry's role in it that he took the time to write Father Steiner at Notre Dame. The sergeant heaped praise on the 157th Regiment and added, "Much credit goes to our regimental Catholic Chaplain who made it possible for us to receive the holy sacraments on many fronts and under fire." Besides the Sacraments, Barry brought peace to war-torn fields and hills, sometimes in surreal ways. "On a cold December day," added Jaskovich, "Father Barry climbed a wet slippery hill that we were holding in the Apennines Mts. in Italy. The area was under constant enemy artillery fire but during the thirty-minute service not a single shell came our way. This is only one of many instances."[29]

Christmas 1943 was especially moving to Father Barry. As usual, powerful emotions flowed at a time when everyone thought of home, loved ones, and peace on earth. Barry counseled more soldiers than normal that December, dealing with young boys whose bodies were in Italy but whose minds were back home.

While he extended optimistic greetings that season to Costin—"A Merry Christmas to you, Jim, and let's hope the New Year is a happy one and brings peace on earth"—he turned down an invitation for Christmas dinner that most would have been delighted to accept. The regiment's commanding officer asked Barry to accompany him to dine with General Clark and other dignitaries who were visiting the front lines. Barry politely declined, preferring to deliver Christmas mail and boxes to his boys rather than dine with a general. On Christmas and New Year's Eve he conducted services for each battalion. "Christmas found me on the front lines, all right, not at mess but at Mass," he wrote to his friend Father Hope. Similar to the Holy Family, who welcomed Jesus in a stable, Barry celebrated in a humble location. "To keep the spirit and to provide protection from Jerries' machine guns, we had Mass in a mountain cave."[30]

Staff Sergeant Jaskovich was one of those who attended one of Father Barry's Christmas Eve Masses. He had just completed months of bitter combat, during which he had seen buddies die or drag themselves from battlefields with torn limbs. He had endured hunger, cold, and exhaustion for so long that he forgot what a break and rest felt like. But on that Christmas Eve in December 1943, he found a few moments respite from the madness raging about him. He found quiet. He found God.

He remembered it as a "cold and dreary day" during which the regiment held defensive positions against German artillery and gunfire, but one also marked with a sudden, and in his mind, near miraculous occurrence. "At midnight for fully two minutes there was a reverential silence. Not a shell was heard, there was a short respite from a living hell, church bells rang in the distance, in each fox-hole a silent prayer was said, there was temporary peace."[31]

On the holiest of nights, in a desolate mountain cave, Father Barry celebrated Christmas Eve Mass surrounded by soldiers from the 157th Regiment rather than join a famous general for a sumptuous dinner. The moment epitomized why Barry had volunteered for the front lines, for it was there, where danger was highest, where he and his boys dodged bullets and bombs and tried to smother fear and terror, that he brought to every scared soldier that peace on earth represented by the baby whose birth he now celebrated.

"He Preached by Example"

In many ways, Father Barry was a father figure to the soldiers. That he constantly referred to them as "my boys" or "my lads" shows that to him they were more than mere infantrymen. They were family. He understood their ways and empathized with their emotions, even when couched in rougher language than Barry had been accustomed to. "These kids really lead a rough life and consequently get in the habit of using rough language," he explained to Father Hope. "They do not like to display their belief; not that they are ashamed—but you know how lads are. I know how they feel inside, because I make it my business to know. I also know how they feel about the 'gang', so I operate according to circumstances."[32]

Above all, he understood the sacrifices these young men endured to defeat their country's enemies and restore order to a chaotic world. In conveying that thought to Costin Barry again reverted to one of his favorite worlds, the sports arena. "As a sportsman, Jim, you've seen many outstanding feats of agility, strength and courage displayed on the gridiron, on the diamond and on other fields of sport, but you'll never see the likes of what these kids go through over here and still remember how to grin." He told his friend that it was neither Costin, nor the people back home, nor himself who would achieve victory, for that moment would belong to a select group: his boys. "When the war is over it will have been won by these men who are worn thin and gaunt from living in cold, wet weather, and from fatigue; the guys who keep pushing forward, always forward, and always dreaming of the warm, soft bed back home and the life that will be his again when he returns."[33]

That young kids could exhibit such bravery humbled Father Barry. He was at times embarrassed that he could not do more, and he asked of himself years later, "What kind of a hero can a chaplain be if he does not even have a weapon?" Despite those qualms, he loved being with the soldiers and claimed that "those were the happiest years I spent in the priesthood"[34] because he worked with such courageous young men.

Those young boys would vehemently dismiss Barry's concerns that he could not be a hero, for he disproved that every day. Many considered his actions proof of a greater bravery because, unlike them, he charged onto the battlefield without a weapon. "Barry was what we called with admiration a 'foxhole chaplain,'" said Private First Class Caudle of C Company. Some chaplains tended to linger at aid stations or spend most of their time in the rear, but never Father Barry. If Mauldin had created a priestly counterpart to match his beloved infantrymen, Willie and Joe, it would have been Barry, a chaplain who tended to the privates and corporals in the thick of the fighting. "When we slowed down a bit, he'd get guys together and have a service," said Caudle, but far too often German artillery or aircraft intruded. "He would be giving a sermon, and here comes shells. Everyone dives for cover, for a foxhole, and then when the bombing stopped, Barry resumed his service."[35]

They admired Barry because he was one of them. He shared every hardship tossed at the soldiers—the enemy, the elements, the lack of food and decent quarters, and everything else. "Absolutely he would have experienced everything the soldiers did," said Lieutenant Stemmons. The officer could tell that his men had bonded with Father Barry because the soldiers kidded around with the priest like they did with each other. Only someone who had earned their trust would be so honored. "They'd tease him, 'You don't have to worry about being hit because you're too small. They can't hit you.' Everybody was his friend. He preached by example, and did what he should instead of just saying it. He was the chaplain, but he didn't act like he was any better than anyone else."

Stemmons recalled how on more than one occasion he and others relied on Barry while the bullets were flying, and not always for spiritual aid. "When we were under fire, if we wanted to get information to another unit, we'd sometimes say, 'Father Barry will be along soon, and we'll give him the information and he'll pass it along,'" for the priest never remained long in one spot before dashing to another part of the battlefield to see who needed him. "We knew he'd be with us soon, we didn't know when, but we knew he would. And we also knew he'd be leaving us soon for other units. He was always on the move." If a soldier wondered about a buddy he had not seen in a few hours, he would shout to Barry, "Hey, I haven't seen Joe in a long time. Can you find out?" And, said Stemmons, "We knew Father Barry would find out."[36]

Barry's reputation as one of the most beloved chaplains reached Father Steiner and Barry's fellow chaplains. From his office at the Military Ordinariate in New York, Bishop O'Hara told Steiner that Barry was held in higher esteem than almost any chaplain in the service. In his letters to other Holy Cross priests working in the military, Steiner heaped praise on their compatriot in Italy. "We get marvelous reports about Father Barry," he wrote to Father Harrington, still serving as a chaplain with the Army Air Corps in India. "He has been in the thick of it for over a year. Many boys are writing in about him, saying he is 'tops.'" To Father Edward Fitzgerald, stationed with the Fifty-Third Troop Carrier Wing in England, Steiner added, "His experiences are most interesting. The constant danger they are in, makes the boys very serious, and eager to get all the spiritual consolation they can get. It is very evident from his letters that Fr. Barry is giving it to them, and that he is always with them, even at the fronts. May God direct and preserve him."[37]

A FEW lighthearted moments broke through the gloom of battle for Barry and his boys. The Italians of the towns the regiment liberated as they moved north toward Rome greeted Barry and the Forty-Fifth with wild celebrations, including meals of pasta and wine. "I have had some good times sitting in their kitchens, surrounded by spaghetti and vino, finished off by Italian songs," Barry wrote Father Hope. He called the home-cooked fare "quite a welcome change" to rations "wrapped up in tin," and communicated with the Italians with a mixture of "a little Latin, a little French, and a little Italian."

He found disheartening the extreme poverty and hunger that afflicted many, including young boys wearing little more than rags, but was proud of the generosity exhibited by his lads. "The troops are generous and share what they can. They [Italians] come in the mess line with buckets, cans, boxes, anything that does not leak. In the evening, the lads will visit their humble homes and sing and chat and laugh." For a time his men adopted an orphaned fourteen-year-old boy named Marino, "so he is now part of the family."[38] Nicknamed Mac, the teen washed their tin dishes and hung around until the regiment had to leave for its next objective.

The jubilant greetings from Italian citizens contrasted with some of the news from back home, where people griped about food rationing and factory workers struck for higher pay and improved conditions. Men on the front lines, who had sacrificed in blood, scoffed at hearing about meatless meals and worn-out tires in the United States. They asked how people would like it if soldiers struck for even a brief period of time. "A lot of people aren't very smart when they write to a soldier," wrote Mauldin. "They complain about the gasoline shortage, or worry him or anger him in a hundred different ways which directly affect his efficiency and morale."[39]

Those letters made Barry's task more difficult, for he now had to counsel irate boys who complained that while they faced German bullets, family and acquaintances back home griped about food shortages. Barry asked Staff Sergeant Jaskovich to send Father Steiner the poem Jaskovich wrote while in Italy, which pointed out the selfishness exhibited by some on the home front. One stanza stated:

We'll take your rationing of meat
And your rationing of booze,
We'll pay ten times your taxes,
to be in your shoes.[40]

Father Barry's experiences in Italy and throughout the war altered his outlook. Matters that had seemed important before his service no longer occupied such prominence, and he doubted that he would be the same priest after the war that he was before. "I fear I'm going to be very impatient when I return to the States and hear complaints about domestic troubles, low wages, sore arms and stiff necks."[41]

Most of the news from home, however, proved welcome. Father Barry shared with the regiment the issues mailed by Costin of the *South Bend Tribune*, which carried frequent articles about Notre Dame. Even though the papers were two months old by the time they reached Barry, he and the troops loved reading the funnies and sports section. "Your column is a morale builder to a lot of the boys in this outfit," Barry wrote to Costin, "for quite a few call Indiana home." He begged him to "keep the sports dope flowing this way. . . . We'll do our best to complete all the unfinished business on this end in a hurry."[42]

Football was Father Barry's preference. He unabashedly spread the news Father Steiner relayed about the university's thrashing of Michigan. "After giving Pittsburgh and Georgia Tech sound drubbings, the team took Michigan last Saturday 35 to 12 before 86,000 people. This was the largest crowd Michigan ever had in its stadium." Steiner explained that even a Detroit newspaper, which could be counted on to support Michigan, said, "Notre Dame outclassed, outplayed, and outmaneuvered Michigan."[43]

Barry read in *Stars and Stripes*, the newspaper published for soldiers, that following those victories 99 of 101 sports writers picked the Irish as the number-one team in the nation. "That's the kind of news that keeps my morale up . . . up . . . up for Notre Dame," he wrote to Steiner. "Here in the Army you get a cross-section of the feeling for Notre Dame. Believe me feeling is high. Kids that never came within a thousand miles of the Golden Dome talk about her gridiron victories like a certain Jim Costin writes about the ND-Ohio game."[44]

Chatter about football and national rankings gave Father Barry a break from the war. Even better was the period of rest the regiment received in January 1944. They would need it, as Father Barry and his boys were about to be part of the hell that was Anzio, a place Barry termed "a bad dream."[45]

"Sliding on His Belly through the Mud . . . Came Father Joe"

In early January 1944 French troops relieved the Forty-Fifth Division so the Americans could leave the mountains for a rest and training area near Naples. This was the first extended break Barry and the soldiers had received in more than four months, a time that left the 157th Regiment with almost 1,000 dead or missing, 2,550 wounded, and another 61 taken prisoner. The men enjoyed a USO show featuring actor Humphrey Bogart and comedian Joe E. Brown, regained weight and health, and tried to forget that they would soon again have to march back to the battlefield.

With the Allied advance toward Rome stalling in the mountains against the German troops dug in along the Gustav Line, strategists planned an amphibious assault that skirted those defenses to land at the ancient city of Anzio, the emperor Nero's birthplace forty miles south of Rome. They hoped to force the Germans to retreat northward to avoid being trapped, thereby weakening their remaining forces along the Gustav Line. The plan was sound, but as most of the landing craft had already been sent to England in preparation for the upcoming Normandy assault, only two divisions could be initially sent in.

The divisions landed on January 22. While they achieved surprise, the commanding general foolishly ordered his troops to dig in on the beaches and prepare for an expected counterattack instead of advancing as far inland as he could before the enemy had a chance to regroup. Two days later Barry's regiment landed and took their positions at the western side of the line, with the Germans to their front and the Tyrrhenian

Sea to their rear, operating in an area where, as war correspondent Ernie Pyle described it, every sector became the front line.

Father Barry could have remained a mile or so behind the lines, but he was, as usual, at the front. "The lads who take rations, water and ammo up must do it at night to avoid machine gun fire," he explained to Father Steiner. "They were having a rough time of it so that night I got my driver and jeep and started out about midnight to see the fire works." While moving along a road where he could as easily have run into German units as his own, he came upon seven soldiers sitting in two jeeps. "The lads were so frightened that they could hardly speak." One asked in astonishment, "Padre, what are you doing up here?" The soldiers explained that in the dark they had taken a wrong road and got lost. A German tank spotted them "and let the kids have both barrels. One shell blew the trailer skyward. Water cans burst, K-rations were in splinters. Another shell hit five feet in front of the jeep. They hit the ground—a shell would strike close, lift them three feet in the air and down they would come. Now the miracle is this," Barry told Steiner, "no one got a scratch. Not one."

Their comments moved the chaplain. One boy said that "the Sacred Heart protected me," while a second told Barry, "I said a prayer to my guardian angel—I'm glad he works nights too." A third joked that only the good die young, and since they were twenty-one, they must be too old to die. "No one in the States knows what these kids go thru," he added. "The faith and the trust of these kids is wonderful."[46]

Three nights later Father Barry learned that one unit had suffered heavy casualties, so "I started out to get the bodies of five of my lads that were killed." He and his driver, accompanied by another vehicle, met some British troops whose truck was mired in the mud. The second vehicle continued up the road, but Barry and his driver, unfamiliar with the path, "decided to remain put—hoping our lead truck would come back—it did not. The kids came up just in time to get right in the middle of a Heinie counterattack—on they came yelling, cussing, blasting away." Those soldiers eventually evaded the Germans and returned to friendly lines, "safe but plenty frightened." Thinking that Father Barry had either been captured or killed, they "were very pleased to see me saying Mass in the woods the next morning."[47]

A thundering February 16 German bombardment preceded a massive counterattack the Germans hoped would split the Allied lines, shatter their beachhead, and shove them back into the sea. The fighting broke into hundreds of individual clashes, including hand-to-hand combat with fixed bayonets and German tanks firing point-blank into American lines. With shells creeping in deadly precision toward Barry's position, the priest prayed to God that he be spared, not for selfish reasons, but because he needed to minister to his boys. Thinking they might not make it, "we huddled against a wall and prayed, prayed, prayed," said Barry. The innate compulsion to live tugged at him to remain where he was, but his desire to help his boys overrode that concern. Feeling useless and cut off from men who needed him, Father Barry ran toward the thickest fighting. "I realized that I must go out to help retrieve my boys who had been killed and to comfort the wounded and frightened."[48]

One soldier who survived the barrage recalled, "We huddled and tried to sink into the ground—shells raining down on us. No one dared lift his head above the slit trench. Men were wounded, some screaming in pain, some paralyzed by fear. But sliding on his belly through the mud of the trench we had dug came Father Joe, coming to assist the wounded, to comfort the terrified boys, to bless the dead."[49]

The Germans broke the line at a handful of locations, forcing the regiment's officers to call artillery fire on their own positions in a desperate move to halt the attack. The division eventually deflected the counterattack, but not before absorbing horrific casualties. One company had only 68 of 165 men left, and the division counted 400 killed, 2,000 wounded, and another 1,000 missing in action, most likely taken captive.

At Anzio Barry operated in a precarious arena. With the Germans holding the high ground behind the beaches and enjoying a view of every American position, Barry scurried from trench to foxhole in what the soldiers called the "Anzio slouch," keeping low to the ground to offer as small a target as possible. Soldiers who wished they were Barry's diminutive size joked with the priest about the advantage he held.

"Anzio was unique," wrote Mauldin. The beachhead contained an entire infantry corps, a British division, and artillery and special units. No one could seek sanctuary, for "there was no place in the entire beachhead where enemy shells couldn't seek you out." Throughout the day mammoth shells from two German guns nicknamed "Anzio Annie" and "Anzio Express" destroyed equipment and pulverized American foxholes and trenches. In the daylight hours German fighters strafed their lines, while at night the soldiers camouflaged their foxholes against the "popcorn man," enemy pilots who dropped "hundreds of little butterfly bombs down on your head." Mauldin wrote that "it was a constant hellish nightmare, . . . and it lasted for five months."[50]

Father Barry was every bit as important as the ammunition handler who rushed supplies to the soldiers. He daily talked with men whose hatred of the enemy grew each time they lost a buddy or screamed in fright during an artillery barrage, yet Barry hoped that he could keep love and charity alive against this backdrop of hatred and anger. He believed it to be the only way that, once the carnage ended, his boys could return to their families as whole as possible.

"On the Anzio beach-head where a person couldn't stick his head above ground in the day-time," wrote Staff Sergeant Jaskovich, "Fr. Barry crawled through canals and drainage ditches to bring us spiritual encouragement. More than ever before in our lives, we needed courage, pitting the perishable body against formidable engines of indestructible steel. More formidable than steel, however, is the immortal soul of man."[51]

Barry, who had proven his courage in Sicily, gained added esteem at Anzio, where he loved to joke that his Masses were celebrated in an open-air cathedral and his office was any hole in the ground. As usual, though, he placed the praise on his boys. "Night after night I see things and listen to stories that would make your heart bleed," he wrote to Father Steiner, "and yet they always have some humorous things to say." He admitted that he had survived an action that killed or maimed hundreds of soldiers, but he was more thankful for his troops than for himself. "Three times I swam to foreign shores, daily was I shelled, nightly was I bombed. Forty times save one have I been scared to death, but like Paul I can say too, 'Deus providebit [God will provide].' I thank God I'm able to serve these wonderful self sacrificing American boys."[52]

The misery at Anzio ended on May 23 with a massive Allied attack against the German lines. After four days of combat, the Germans retreated, allowing the Allied troops to break out of their beachhead and advance inland. One soldier claimed that leaving the beaches of Anzio was like being freed from what he heard a Nazi concentration camp must be like.

He and Father Barry would eventually learn how inadequate a comparison that statement was.

"Only God Knows Why I Came Out Alive"

Upon leaving Anzio, the regiment set out for one of the world's most ancient and revered places, the Eternal City, Rome. "After five months of hell on Anzio beach we finally pushed thru, but not without a hard and rough fight," Barry wrote to fellow Holy Cross priest Father W. P. Corcoran on June 4. "For two days we were pinned in a ravine—the Krauts were looking down our throats. Shells weighing 500 lbs were hurled at us. I am one of the few lucky ones. Why we were not all killed God alone knows."[53]

Barry knew that many newspapers back home had been critical of the American senior command for what they considered a tepid, snail-like breakout through Anzio's defenses and on toward Rome, but the priest considered that view ignorant of the skillful defense offered by the Germans in Italy's severe terrain. He wrote Father Steiner that maybe the people back home thought they were too slow in moving on to Rome, "but you should see the high mountains, the concrete pill boxes, the flock of tanks, the stuff thrown in our path. Last night we had an air raid. Flares were dropped. Black night was turned into a high June noon. The Heinie zoomed in and dropped their eggs—and not too far from our dugouts—and just when we were cooking a can of coffee. After the raid and Jerry went home we had our coffee and sugar and canned milk just to celebrate."[54]

He claimed the fighting was as rigorous as any yet offered and that "I shall never forget the heroic deeds I saw performed by our American lads as they fought over the historic roads of Caesars." He chuckled when, as the regiment neared Rome, many of the soldiers asked him about the pope. "To hear my kids talk, you would think all I had to do was to go up to the front door, knock, and say, 'Is the Pope in?'"[55]

Barry hoped to see the pope but doubted someone of his low rank would gain either the time or the chance to enter Vatican City. It was moot anyway unless they successfully entered Rome, and until then he was satisfied with other "luxuries." "Took a bath yesterday in a horse trough," he wrote to Father Corcoran. "Have seen no Roman baths yet."[56]

By June 4 parts of the division reached the southern edges of Rome and secured a bridge over the Tiber River. The next day units pursued the retreating enemy and completed the seizure of the first Axis capital, leaving Berlin and Tokyo to conquer.

"At long last we entered the City Eternal and concluded 272 days of combat," wrote a weary Barry to Father Steiner. He had every right to be proud of his boys, as they had, since landing in Sicily, been in near-continuous combat for the last eleven months. Entering Rome capped their accomplishments, and, as he wrote to his friend Patricia Brehmer, "we have the great distinction of being the first troops that ever came in to take Rome as liberators and not as conquerors."[57]

Their elation heightened when, only days after entering Rome, Barry and the regiment learned of the June 6 Normandy landings. The thought that separate Allied forces, one in Italy and now a second in France, would be applying pressure on the Germans made some wonder if they might be home for Christmas.

In the meantime, Barry and the Forty-Fifth Division turned tourist. Each soldier received a forty-eight-hour pass to visit the Colosseum, St. Peter's, the Circus Maximus, and other popular spots.

Father Barry's hopes of seeing the pope materialized when he stood among thousands of soldiers in St. Peter's Square as Pope Pius XII addressed the throng. That, however, was only a warm-up for a second visit arranged for Barry and sixty-three other chaplains by Bishop O'Hara and other officials at the Military Ordinariate in New York. "The highlight of our visit was the audience with the Holy Father," he wrote to Father Steiner. "For ten minutes the Holy Father talked about the work that was done and about the work left to be done."[58]

As Barry listened, Pope Pius XII spoke of his pride in the deeds of the chaplains in front of him. "Just now," said the pope, "in this tragic hour of human history, called from the regular life of the parish or from the calm of retirement of the student or professor, you have been caught up in the maelstrom of war and thrown into the perils of battle and the temptations of a soldier's life. No ordinary shepherds of souls are needed here. Your Bishops and religious Superiors know how immediately important and how arduous is this apostolate and they have given their best for it." He added, "You are Our Joy and Our Crown.

You have hurried with eager, unselfish zeal in pursuit of souls"[59] thrown into the storm of war.

After speaking to the group, the pope spent a moment with each chaplain, asking his name and his hometown. When a Benedictine chaplain began to cry, the pope said loudly enough that every chaplain could hear his words, "I know that many of your young men are no longer living and that is why you are crying, but you . . . are doing more for your Order than you could ever do in a lifetime in the monastery."[60]

When Pope Pius XII moved to Father Barry and learned that he was from Notre Dame, he smiled and replied, "It is very beautiful. I was there you know."[61] They shared a few words before the pope moved to the next chaplain, but Barry was touched that the highest official of the Catholic faith had uttered such eloquent words to him and the group. In combat a chaplain has no time to dwell on the significance of his actions, but to have the spiritual leader of the church express such sentiments underscored the importance of Barry's work. He left the Vatican convinced that the work now at hand would be the most important of his life, and that this must be the ultimate of what Christ wanted a priest to be.

After his audience with the pope, Barry and another priest prayed at the tombs of Saints Peter, John, Paul, and Aloysius, visited the block on which Saint Paul was beheaded, and celebrated Mass in the catacombs. Receiving extra leave time, he and three others traveled to Malta, Cairo, Tel Aviv, and Jerusalem, where he paused at the garden of Gethsemane, celebrated Mass atop Calvary, prayed at Jesus's tomb, visited Bethlehem, fished in the Sea of Galilee, traveled to the mountain where Christ was tempted, walked along the route of the Stations of the Cross, and stood where Jesus ascended to heaven. As he told Father Steiner, they "saw the place in which Our Lord was tried and mocked, the spot on which He fell as He carried His cross, and last but not least we visited the humble home in Nazareth in which the Holy Family spent so many years." Father Barry's first lengthy respite from the war so rejuvenated him, spiritually and physically, that he told Father Steiner, "All in all we had ten full days, days that will live with me forever."[62]

His break ended amid rumors that the regiment would once again be engaging the Germans. Some soldiers assumed they would continue to drive up the Italian peninsula and hit the Germans from the south while their compatriots broke out of Normandy and raced across France, but no one knew for certain. Father Barry hoped that "we might be eating our Christmas dinner in the land of the free and the home of the Dealers of things old and new," but, figuring that he would likely miss another December 25 at Notre Dame, he focused on gaining weight for whatever awaited, even swapping cigarettes for food to add a few pounds.

"Only God knows why I came out alive while so many wonderful lads sleep the sleep of peace," he wrote to Father Steiner. He doubted that his good fortune would continue, but he would not let it deflect him from being at the one place he was most needed: the battlefield. "I'm a little grayer . . . somewhat thinner . . . but just as mean as ever," he joked with Brehmer. Turning serious, he then added, "Do pray for me and for all my gallant lads."[63]

Father Barry would need not just Brehmer's prayers, but also the thoughts of everyone at Notre Dame. He and the 157th Regiment had completed a rigorous test in the mountains and valleys of Italy, but more waited in France and Germany.

IN THE MEANTIME, one of his Notre Dame colleagues had joined a group of paratroopers and jumped into Normandy to commence the colossal June 6 D-Day landings. June 1944 would be a memorable month indeed for Father Francis L. Sampson.

CHAPTER 6

"FACE TO FACE WITH THE REALISM, THE TRAGEDY, AND THE HORROR OF THE WAR"

Father Sampson at D-Day

While Father Barry and the 157th Infantry Regiment neared Rome, Father Sampson prepared to jump into Normandy with the 501st Parachute Infantry Regiment as part of the enormous Allied assault against Hitler's forces on the European mainland. The operation had been much anticipated since September 1939, when the German military swept across Poland and plunged the continent into warfare. As June 1944 neared, the 501st joined other units at assembly sites sprinkled along England's eastern and southern coastlines, ready to fly or churn across the narrow English Channel and commence what the Supreme Commander, Allied Expeditionary Forces, Major General Dwight D. Eisenhower, termed the Great Crusade to free Europe of Nazi tyranny.

"Their Sons Had Been Well Prepared for Death"

Father Sampson had looked to this moment since January 1944, when he and the paratroopers boarded the transport U.S.S. *George W. Goethals*.

Howling winds and sheets of rain buffeted the ship during the transatlantic voyage to England. Attendance at Sampson's Masses increased, and each day he heard confessions for two hours to accommodate the men leaving home to fight for their country.

After the transport pulled into Glasgow, Scotland, the soldiers boarded trains that whisked them to a tented training camp near Newbury, England, a city of fifty thousand standing sixty miles west of London. For the next half year the Newbury area would be their home as the men trained for the invasion and, in their time off, became familiar with the British countryside and its inhabitants. Father Sampson found the citizens of Newbury friendly but was surprised that the city showed little evidence of the catastrophic bombings that beset London and other metropolitan areas during the infamous Blitz of 1940–1941.

Calisthenics, running, long-distance marches, and other activities shook the seas out of their legs. Under the watchful eye of the division commander, Major General Maxwell D. Taylor, parachute jumps formed a crucial part of the preparation. Two major exercises, codenamed Beaver and Tiger, required the men to jump from trucks and spread out to capture causeway bridges, while the more realistic Exercise Eagle in mid-May, when Sampson and the paratroopers leaped from aircraft, served as a dress rehearsal for the June invasion.

As he described in his book, *Look Out Below!*, Sampson found that the cold, drizzly English weather hampered the exercises, making the field problems more hazardous than those back in the States. Whereas the warmer North Carolina climate had produced a thicker atmosphere that filled the chutes and made jumping comparatively easy, and the sandy soil helped absorb the shock of hitting a hard surface, the thinner English atmosphere led to faster descents, and the men landed on rocky terrain dissected by fences and hedgerows. Sampson's visits to men in the hospital with broken legs or bad backs quadrupled compared to the numbers recorded in North Carolina.

Sampson incurred the wrath of his regimental commanding officer, the hard-nosed Colonel Johnson, during one night exercise. After parachuting, Sampson's group was to make its way toward the village of Lambourn a few miles northwest of Newbury, establish a roadblock, and wait a few hours before "attacking" the village. After the men set up the roadblock, the weary priest nodded off. A short time later a hand lightly smacked his chin, and he awoke to find Colonel Johnson glaring down from above. "Chaplain," Johnson barked from between clenched teeth, "in combat you would have been a dead duck by now."[1] Only Sampson's rank as chaplain saved him from worse punishment. Johnson intended to lead a crack regiment into combat, one that could withstand the fury certain to be thrown at them by the German Army, and this incident showed Sampson that whether a paratrooper was priest or private, he had best be ready.

Since 1939, when Hitler tossed Europe into war, Sampson had heard about the hardships endured by the British citizens. A glance at each day's newspaper headlines offered bounteous proof of the sorrow and suffering that Europe's families accepted on a daily basis, but it was not until he and his regiment observed it firsthand that they began to grasp its severity.

General Eisenhower concluded that the majority of the Normandy assault troops pouring from American training camps and ports remained shockingly ignorant of how the British had suffered. Eisenhower, who had driven through the worst of the bombed sections of London and observed the destruction, thought that his men would benefit from a similar experience. "Most were mentally unprepared for the realities of war—especially as waged by the Nazis," Eisenhower contended. "Others believed that the tales of British sacrifice had been exaggerated. Still others failed to recognize the difficulties of the task ahead."[2] Eisenhower consequently ordered a series of educational programs to explain the war's history and asked each commander to organize tours through devastated areas.

Eisenhower's tactics worked. A paratrooper with an accompanying regiment, Sergeant Donald Malarkey, walked London's streets and chatted with residents to learn of the London Blitz and other aspects of the war. It was only then that "the idea of war started becoming more real than it was back in the States. We started hearing the people's stories of the bombings in London; even in the rural areas, where people weren't huddling in subways, the British people were weary."[3]

As an indication that this war had engulfed the world, Father Sampson saw soldiers from Canada, South Africa, New Zealand, and other countries. He noticed the lack of young British males, many of whom were in the Far East fighting Japan, and each neighborhood block, with the charred remains of once-splendid buildings, reminded him of the cost this war had already exacted.

Training camp offered its own challenges, but in London Sampson surveyed the damage, heard the air-raid signals, and walked among the ruins of recently bombed buildings. Drill sergeants in boot camp had tried to warn the recruits, "but the first sight of London and the first experience of an air raid while there," Sampson wrote, "brought us face to face with the realism, the tragedy, and the horror of war. Here was not just a newspaper account."[4]

Besides visiting London, Father Sampson spent time at the Saint Gabriel's Home for Children, an orphanage seven miles north of Newbury operated by the Franciscan Missionaries of Mary, where he worked with boys and girls orphaned by the war. He and twenty-five other Catholic chaplains in the area also held monthly meetings at the orphanage to discuss common problems, such as how to best improve the men's morale, how to prod more into receiving the Sacraments, and how to navigate the confusing myriad of forms the chaplains had to fill out for everything from soldiers' life insurance to monthly chaplain reports.

To Sampson's delight, one of those chaplains happened to be a Holy Cross priest from Notre Dame, Father Edward Fitzgerald, C.S.C. Thirty-eight years old when the war started, Father Fitzgerald joined the army's chaplain corps as a first lieutenant in 1941. Unlike Father Barry, the taciturn chaplain who only wanted to serve his boys, Father Fitzgerald carried a martial demeanor to war. Three days before the end of 1941, he wrote to Father Steiner that he did not mind where he would be posted because "it won't make much difference since there's a big job to be done." He added that while Geneva Conference rules banned the use of firearms for chaplains and medical personnel, he would not let technicalities halt him from doing whatever he needed to defend himself in the savage war. He informed Steiner that "from what we read I guess the rules don't apply to this war. So yours truly is fully determined to get a little practice in on the range just in case the Japs or the Germans fail to see that little cross we wear."[5]

After a request to be relieved of what he considered unfulfilling administrative duties, in April 1944 Fitzgerald joined the Fifty-Third Troop Carrier Wing in England, a unit of lumbering air transports earmarked to ferry soldiers to Normandy. Long hours of training occupied Fitzgerald's days and nights, including three practice missions over the

English countryside. He said Mass for other airborne units lacking a Catholic chaplain, earning their gratitude at each stop. "The men have responded beautifully and the results, thank God, are more than gratifying," he wrote to Steiner on April 10, less than two months before the scheduled assault. He could tell his superior little, mainly because he knew nothing beyond what concerned his work as a chaplain, but promised that he and the soldiers "are working hard on the invasion plans and awaiting the 'green light' to move over on the continent."[6]

He and Sampson enjoyed the meetings held at the orphanage. "We discussed many of our problems and the good sisters put on a grand meal,"[7] Fitzgerald wrote to Father Steiner. Prominent among those problems was adultery. The war had ripped men from homes, many for the first time, and now in England, the temptations provided by British women proved more irresistible than some could handle. A comforting feminine touch was just the medicine for long, exhausting marches or the uncertainty of dealing with life in a foreign land.

Others came to see the chaplain after they learned that their wives had been unfaithful back home. Hardest of all were the "Dear John" letters sent by former girlfriends or wives informing a paratrooper that they had met someone else and wanted to break off the relationship or file for a divorce. The love of husband and wife, the crucial fabric holding families together, unraveled before their eyes. "This war is costing our country far more than just the lives of our young men,"[8] wrote one chaplain stationed not far from Sampson.

Before the unit lifted off from British airfields and flew toward combat, Sampson had urged his paratroopers to take advantage of the ten-thousand-dollar government life insurance policy offered to each soldier. He explained that husbands needed to take care of their wives and children, and that sons must think of mothers and fathers, so that, should anything happen, their loved ones would at least be relieved of financial difficulties during an arduous period.

After participating in morning and afternoon jumps and exercises, Sampson spent most evenings counseling his paratroopers. It was apparent that the men of the highly skilled unit were ready to fight, but he worried about their spiritual and psychological preparation. He learned to be a skilled listener, as he found that "when men live together for long periods of time, they get to speaking their innermost thoughts, their secret desires, their fears, their anxieties, their unanswered questions about religion, their sense of confusion about life's meaning and its basic problems."[9]

The pace heightened as April turned to May and the Normandy landings drew closer. Rumors of impending action reduced the usual banter and joking that marks any large group of men away from home, and soldiers took more seriously the stories culled from the veterans of North Africa or Sicily who had seen battle. Armed guards prevented anyone from entering or leaving the tented camps, lest word of the invasion sneak out, a restriction that produced a concomitant rise in Mass attendance. In the Fifty-Third Troop Carrier Wing, Father Fitzgerald was likewise busy providing, as he wrote, "religious services for airborne troops in areas where Catholic chaplains were not available."[10]

As landing day drew nearer, Sampson's superiors arranged for him to fly to multiple airfields to hear confessions. For three days Sampson gave absolution to hundreds of men, and he asked each penitent to put his name in a box next to his tent as they entered so that he could make certain that they later received Holy Communion. The day before departing for Normandy, Sampson spent one hour delivering Communion at each of the two Masses he held for those men so that, he recalled, "I could later write with certainty to the parents of men who did not return from Normandy that their sons had been well prepared for death."[11]

Sampson then looked to his own spiritual welfare. The priest knew that, as he was soon to be in one of the deadliest assaults of the war, he might become a casualty, so he wanted to be as prepared for death as were those men he had just seen. He and another Catholic chaplain, Father Maternowski, heard each other's confession, wished one another good fortune, and then returned to their units.

The invasion was initially set to begin on June 5, but overcast skies and heavy rains and winds forced General Eisenhower to reconsider, especially in light of what Sampson's 101st Airborne and other paratrooper units would face. Eisenhower met with his meteorologists to receive updates about the deteriorating weather and weighed whether he should postpone the airborne assault and throw the invasion off schedule, or risk disaster to maintain that timetable. Should the invasion proceed as scheduled and fail, "then I would carry to my grave the unbearable burden of a conscience justly accusing me of the stupid, blind sacrifice of thousands of the flower of our youth."[12] On June 4, Eisenhower postponed D-Day twenty-four hours, disappointing Sampson and the paratroopers, who figured that they would have to cross the channel into France sooner or later and might as well get it over with now.

Late on June 4 meteorologists informed Eisenhower that a break in the weather might permit the attack to proceed on June 6, but that overcast skies would be an issue, especially for the airborne units. The next morning Eisenhower consulted his commanders, listened to their opinions, and then said, "Well, we'll go!" Knowing he had just made a decision that, at best, would cost many American lives and, at worst, could result in the war's greatest calamity for Allied forces, Eisenhower murmured to his staff, "I hope to God I know what I'm doing."[13]

Before leaving for Normandy, Colonel Johnson delivered the fiery talk to Sampson and the paratroopers in which he drew his Bowie knife and vowed that before the day ended, it would be stuck in a Nazi belly. Father Sampson, more interested in the men's religious well-being than their martial attitude, viewed matters differently. A chaplain, he wrote, "is more interested in what is going on inside men than in what is going on outside them. To him the souls of men are even more involved in combat than their bodies; their spiritual resources are more vital to real success than any material factors. The eternal life of a man is as much at stake there as his physical life, and the sacraments of Penance and the Holy Eucharist were healing the wounds of his soul while blood plasma, penicillin, and the sulfa drugs were healing the wounds of his body."[14]

Upon receiving the go order, Sampson visited the paratroopers he would accompany for the brief flight across the channel. He found that each man understood the risks of jumping in the overcast, rainy conditions, and that they approved of Eisenhower's decision. After muttering a few encouraging words, Father Sampson leaned back and silently waited for the most momentous day of his life to begin.

"The Tracer Bullets Alone Made It Look Like the Fourth of July"
Father Sampson on D-Day

The Normandy plans involved dangerous, demanding tasks for Sampson's 501st Parachute Infantry Regiment. Five hours before the main invasion armada arrived, aircraft would drop the paratroopers to the east and west of Carentan, a vital link in Normandy between the Utah and Omaha Beaches earmarked for assault by U.S. infantry. Once the troops landed, they were to seize crucial canal locks and destroy bridges over the Douve River to hamper German efforts to move reinforcements to the beaches.

In the hours before his airborne troops were to take off, Eisenhower issued to his forces his Order of the Day. "Soldiers, Sailors and Airmen of the Allied Expeditionary Forces!" Eisenhower started. "You are about to embark upon the Great Crusade, toward which we have striven these many months. The eyes of the world are upon you. The hopes and prayers of liberty-loving people everywhere march with you."[15]

Neither Father Sampson nor any other Americans involved in the invasion, with the exception of a handful of top aides and senior commanders, knew that Eisenhower had also composed another message, one he hoped he would never have to broadcast. This message would be handed out should the Germans prevent Eisenhower's units from gaining a foothold on the mainland and force him to withdraw.

While men at the airfield synchronized their watches and blackened their faces with charcoal, Sampson gave general absolution to the Catholic paratroopers. He then checked his equipment. His load would not be as heavy as that of some paratroopers, who packed as much as one hundred pounds of ammunition and gear, but the sixty-six pounds he carried were hardly inconsequential. Two parachutes, his Mass kit, an extra uniform and boots, first aid equipment, a canteen, K-rations for a fast meal, blood plasma for the wounded, and a life preserver made him glad that he was in the best shape of his life. Instead of a weapon, Sampson lugged extra plasma, a doctor's field kit, and comic books and murder mysteries for the troops.

Shortly before 11:00 p.m. on June 5, the men boarded the C-47 transport aircraft aligned at airfields at Merryfield and Welford for the short trip across the English Channel. Like most of the paratroopers weighed down with their equipment, Sampson struggled to board the craft. Some men needed the help of comrades behind to climb into the plane's hold. Once inside, the men sat in sticks of ten each with their backs to the fuselage, facing ten men on the other side of the cramped plane. They were, Sampson noticed, so close that their knees almost touched.

Now in the aircraft, Sampson led the paratroopers in prayer. He only had a few moments to hold their attention before the men's thoughts turned inward to ready themselves for battle. The quiet that encompassed his group, broken only by the drone of the aircraft's engines, stood in stark contrast to the deafening noise of battle that was soon to unfold on and behind France's beaches.

The short trip covering the one hundred air miles between their airfield and drop zone ended quickly. As the plane neared its objective, Sampson gathered his thoughts: "It was hard to believe that we were now only seconds away from the enemy and that within an hour some of us would be dead."

The dead would include some of those 150,000 men below. More than 4,000 Allied ships, aided by 3,500 heavy bombers and 5,000 fighter planes, transported the troops to Normandy's shores on June 6. Before those infantry stepped into landing craft and headed toward the five invasion beaches, Sampson and his group would already be operating behind German lines. Some would undoubtedly be dead.

As soon as Sampson's plane left the channel and crossed over the German-controlled beaches, hundreds of enemy antiaircraft shells peppered the sky. Planes to Sampson's right and left battled through the thick blanket, and numerous bullets punctured his aircraft's thin skin, wounding some of the paratroopers aboard. As strong winds buffeted the plane, the jumpmaster, who directed each man when to parachute from the aircraft, ordered Sampson's group to stand and attach their hooks to the line strung inside. When the green light indicating "go" lit, the paratroopers stepped up to the cabin door and leaped into a predawn darkness eerily illuminated by shells and plane explosions. Until the moment they left the aircraft, Sampson and his companions hoped that they might catch the Germans by surprise, but one look quickly dispelled that notion. German antiaircraft fire so filled the sky that "the tracer bullets alone made it look like the Fourth of July."

When Sampson jumped from the transport, then only five hundred feet from the ground, the prop blast and a stiff wind buffeted him about as if he were a toy. Finally, after what seemed minutes to Father Sampson but were actually only seconds, his parachute snapped open and, with a hefty jerk, stabilized his descent. Sampson dangled from the end of his parachute strings as colorful tracer shells screamed by. Here in the sky, before he touched down and started helping the para- troopers, he was on his own. As it seemed that every German machine gunner below aimed directly at the priest, he collapsed part of his chute to speed his fall, but mostly the powerless chaplain relied on faith and good fortune to safely alight on French soil.

Fortunately, less than one minute after leaping from the plane, Sampson hit ground without suffering a scratch from German tracers. Because he had jumped from such a low altitude, the impact of his hard landing in the middle of a stream left black and blue marks on his legs and arms. Struggling to remain above water, he had to cut away the bags containing his Mass kit and first aid kit to avoid drowning. Strong winds blew the chaplain downstream until, reaching shallower water, he was able to stand and, after ten minutes of labor, collapse his canopy and free himself from the parachute. Exhausted but fueled by the adrenaline coursing through his body, Sampson hurried back to where he had first hit the water to recover his Mass kit. After five or six dives beneath the surface, Father Sampson finally located it "by pure luck."[16]

Ready now to begin his work, Sampson oriented himself and found that he was several miles from target. The sky above had become an action-filled canopy of low-flying planes trailing white chutes that flut- tered into heavy German fire. The rat-a-tat-tat of machine guns joined the drone of American aircraft engines to produce a deadly symphony.

Sampson helped his clerk, an army corporal, out of his parachute, and the pair rushed to a nearby hedgerow as a flame-enveloped aircraft plunged directly toward them. Cowering low to the ground, the two waited for an explosion they feared they would not survive, but the plane crashed one hundred yards away in an impact so strong that it hurled plane and body parts over them.

Sampson and his clerk, who had lost his weapon in the drop, looked around for friendly forces. One of those men, Corporal George Koski- maki, expressed how everyone still breathing then felt: "I lay there per- fectly still for a moment—listening," he said, "and I thanked God for my safe deliverance."[17]

June 6, 1944, known as D-Day to the world ever since, was off to a halting start for Father Sampson.

"I Held His Head in My Arm"

The pace quickened almost immediately, with the area around a French farmhouse providing more drama and danger over the next twenty-four hours than Sampson wished. As he related in *Look Out Below!*, Sampson and his assistant wound their way to the farmhouse, where another twenty-five paratroopers, all either injured from the jump or wounded by German fire after landing, had taken refuge. A chaplain from another regiment, a Protestant minister by the name of McGee, was already on the scene, offering medical and spiritual aid to the group with the assistance of the French farmer, his wife, and a young daughter.

Sampson had just begun to lend a hand when a mortar shell struck the house and killed the French woman and her daughter. Sampson knelt to anoint the two, at which point the farmer threw himself on the bodies of his loved ones and sobbed uncontrollably. "When I put my hand on his shoulder, he jumped up, his hands and face smeared with the blood of his loved ones, and went yelling down the road shaking his fists in the direction of the Germans."

Figuring that the Germans would soon attempt to seize the farmhouse, which rested on high ground, and lacking enough men to defend the location, the paratroopers able to walk prepared to leave. They asked Sampson to accompany them, but the priest answered that he and a corpsman would remain with the fourteen seriously wounded men.

Sampson and the corpsman were unarmed and stranded in the middle of German-controlled territory with fourteen incapacitated soldiers. Should the Germans appear, as seemed likely, Sampson would find himself, at best, a prisoner of war before the invasion was a day old. Sampson took down a crucifix from the farmhouse wall and, thinking it might be a comfort, handed it to a soldier grievously wounded by a German hand grenade. He then crafted a white flag from a sheet and hung it outside the door, hoping that the Germans would respect the cloth as a symbol of nonresistance.

Father Sampson moved from soldier to soldier, doing what he could with the sparse medical supplies from his first aid kit. Sensing that the paratrooper suffering from grenade wounds was about to die, Sampson squatted beside him, held him in his arms, and whispered a prayer as the man expired. The soldier was "clutching the crucifix I had taken down from the wall. It was a peaceful and holy death. All the boys joined in prayers for him."[18]

Sampson administered Last Rites to several other men, each of whom impressed the priest with their calm. "I was always amazed how calmly they took death," Sampson said. "I was overwhelmed by the almost serenity [*sic*] of kids with serious wounds."[19]

A noise interrupted Sampson's treatment of the paratroopers. Sampson peered outside a window to see a group of German soldiers setting up a machine gun in the front yard. Trusting in the white flag and his chaplain insignia to keep him from harm, Sampson slowly exited the farmhouse, but had crossed only a few yards when a German soldier stuck a rifle in the priest's stomach. He ignored Sampson's entreaties that the house contained only wounded and dying men, and when another German came over, they shoved Sampson toward a road a quarter mile away and pinned him against a hedgerow. When the pair raised their rifles and aimed at the priest, Sampson, certain he was about to die, tried to recite the words to the Act of Contrition, but in his fright could only recall the grace before meals.

With the soldiers about to pull their triggers, two shots shattered the stillness. A German noncommissioned officer hurried down the road, issued a stern order to the two soldiers, and told Sampson to follow him. When Sampson identified himself as a Catholic chaplain, the German snapped to attention, bowed, saluted the priest, and pointed to a Catholic religious medal pinned to his uniform. He took Sampson to another officer, and when queried Sampson explained that he was tending to the wounded soldiers in his role as chaplain. The officer allowed Sampson to return to the farmhouse and added that a German doctor would arrive in a day or so to help. The officer cautioned Sampson, however, that the priest would endanger the entire group if he shielded anyone but the wounded.

Around midnight a four-hour German artillery barrage shook the farmhouse. Sampson huddled low to the floor and prayed that the shells would spare them, but two hours later a salvo collapsed a portion of the house onto two wounded men lying on the kitchen floor.

"Father Sampson!" shouted one of the wounded. Sampson rushed toward the kitchen, but before he could reach the soldier part of the ceiling crashed down on the boy. "I held his head in my arm and cleared away debris till I could touch his chest," said Sampson. "His heart pumped very hard for about one minute and then stopped." Sampson took a few seconds to pray over the soldier, and then dug in the debris to locate the other paratrooper. By the time he found him, however, he was dead.

In the heat of the action, Sampson had little time to process what had just transpired. As the shelling intensified, Sampson calmed the men's nerves by asking each to take a turn in leading the group in the Lord's Prayer. After the first few had done so, two wounded began arguing over whether to use the shorter Catholic version or the longer Protestant prayer with the doxology. Sampson smiled at the absurdity of such a debate occurring in the midst of heavy shelling and told everyone they could recite whichever version they preferred. His advice doused the argument, and with the words of the Lord's Prayer clearly audible amid the explosions, Sampson noticed that "praying together seemed to calm the men."

When the artillery barrage briefly ceased, Sampson spotted a lit flashlight that had been blown out of the farmhouse. Fearing the object would draw further fire, he ran out to retrieve it, but as he bent over to pick it up Sampson saw a German soldier lying in a creek a few feet away. He inched over to do what he could for the enemy soldier, but as Sampson lifted him into his arms, the German groaned a few times and died. The Catholic chaplain from Notre Dame, wearing an American uniform, gave absolution to a German soldier dying in a French creek. He hastened back to the farmhouse, where a few moments later a German bullet entered through a window, grazed his leg, and briefly set his pants afire.

Father Sampson had been in combat only one day, but he had already administered the Last Rites to numerous soldiers, held two American soldiers in his arms as they died, been taken captive and then saved from execution, been struck by a bullet, and given absolution to a man who, had he been healthy, might have attempted to kill him. No training—military, religious, or otherwise—had prepared him for this, but Sampson believed that in those tumultuous twenty-four hours he had brought more succor and hope to men in troubling moments than he had in many years.

Dawn ended the artillery barrage, but Sampson feared that daylight would bring additional German forces. Instead, an American officer had crept up on the farmhouse and was about to toss grenades into the building when he heard American voices inside. The officer later told Sampson that he had intended to destroy the house because he suspected that it sheltered a group of German soldiers.

Before he left the area, Sampson gazed at the bullet-riddled farmhouse, the chewed land, and the shattered tree trunks, a scene more apt for Dante's *Inferno* than for a French pastoral. "Dead Germans lay in the fields and in the roads and in the ditches, and bloated cows and mules were lying on their backs with legs sticking grotesquely in the air."[20]

Colonel Johnson thought enough of his chaplain's D-Day exploits that he later submitted Sampson's name for the Medal of Honor. Superiors agreed that the priest had displayed inordinate courage, but insufficient for them to grant the military's highest honor. Instead, they awarded Sampson the Distinguished Service Cross.

While Sampson had been occupied at the farmhouse, Colonel Johnson had organized his scattered forces and, by nightfall, secured the locations designated for his paratroopers. D-Day, a momentous day for Sampson, for the paratroopers, and for the world, was over.

"Confession and Communion Are the Greatest Comfort"

As historic as was June 6, it was merely the beginning of a year that would challenge Father Sampson in every conceivable manner. Until the war ended, he endured the physical exhaustion of working under fire at the front lines, the mental struggle over whether he would perform his duties in the heat of battle or shirk his responsibilities, and doubts about whether he made a significant spiritual contribution to young soldiers facing the most extreme crisis of their lives.

After his one-day ordeal at the farmhouse, Father Sampson joined Colonel Johnson and his paratroopers as they moved toward the city of Carentan to attack German positions on high ground. They encountered significant resistance on June 7, crossing a stream and swampland while artillery barrages, sniper fire, and tank guns roared at them from the flanks. At a place aptly nicknamed Hell's Corners, Colonel Johnson and his men finally vanquished the German defenders to seize their objective.

Captain Joseph D. Barry during the Italian campaign. Photograph courtesy of the 45th Infantry Division Museum, Oklahoma City, Oklahoma.

Starting in Sicily, and then in Italy, France, and Germany, Father Barry said Mass wherever he could when at the front. Here he distributes Holy Communion to some of the members of the 157th Regiment in Italy. Father Barry wrote on the back of the photograph, "Mass in the field at the front!" Photograph courtesy of the Holy Cross Archives, University of Notre Dame.

Father Barry during one of his infrequent breaks in Italy. On the back of the photograph, he wrote, "The mileage is beginning to manifest itself on my mug. I trust a good rest and some hot meals will erase some of the war made grooves from the cheeks." He signed it, "Somewhere in Italy, Summer 1944." Photograph courtesy of the Holy Cross Archives, University of Notre Dame.

Father Barry says Mass in an Italian field after the bitter fighting at Anzio. "A Mass of Thanksgiving after returning from battle," he wrote on the back. "These gallant lads are a credit to their faith." He signed it, "Somewhere in Italy, spring, 1944." Photograph courtesy of the Holy Cross Archives, University of Notre Dame.

The *45th Division News* profiled the popular chaplain. Photograph courtesy of the Holy Cross Archives, University of Notre Dame.

The Notre Dame chaplains laboring around the globe during the war maintained their connection with Notre Dame through the many letters mailed to their superior at the university, Father Thomas A. Steiner. Photograph courtesy of the Holy Cross Archives, University of Notre Dame.

Father Barry *(middle)* stands with two other chaplains, identified only as Chaplain Morris *(left)* and Chaplain Carney *(right)*, outside his dugout on Anzio Beach. Photograph courtesy of the 45th Infantry Division Museum, Oklahoma City, Oklahoma.

Along the road to Rome in the spring of 1944. On the back, Father Barry wrote, "Late in May, 1944, on the push towards Rome. At this Italian home we set up an aid station. Gave the kids caramelli, tobacco to Pa, coffee to Ma, and then we were invited to a spaghetti dinner." Photograph courtesy of the Holy Cross Archives, University of Notre Dame.

Father Barry found scenes such as this when he walked to the railroad yard at Dachau. Bodies lay in every boxcar. Photograph courtesy of the 45th Infantry Division Museum, Oklahoma City, Oklahoma.

Father Barry *(not pictured)* stood face-to-face with ultimate evil when he scanned the yard at Dachau. Photograph courtesy of the 45th Infantry Division Museum, Oklahoma City, Oklahoma.

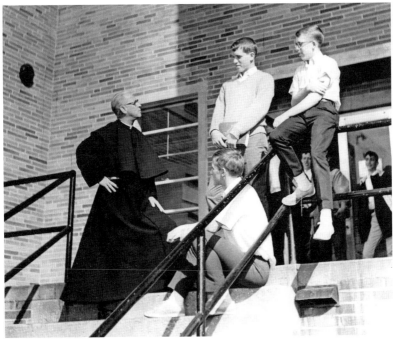

In this 1966 photograph, Father Barry talks with some of the students—his postwar "boys"—he counseled at Archbishop Hoban High School in Akron, Ohio. Photograph courtesy of the Holy Cross Archives, University of Notre Dame.

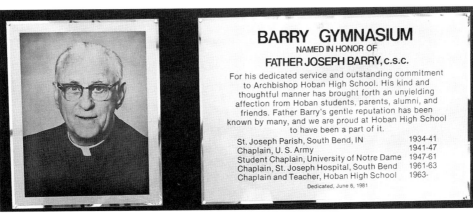

BARRY GYMNASIUM
NAMED IN HONOR OF
FATHER JOSEPH BARRY, c.s.c.

For his dedicated service and outstanding commitment to Archbishop Hoban High School. His kind and thoughtful manner has brought forth an unyielding affection from Hoban students, parents, alumni, and friends. Father Barry's gentle reputation has been known by many, and we are proud at Hoban High School to have been a part of it.

St. Joseph Parish, South Bend, IN	1934-41
Chaplain, U. S. Army	1941-47
Student Chaplain, University of Notre Dame	1947-61
Chaplain, St. Joseph Hospital, South Bend	1961-63
Chaplain and Teacher, Hoban High School	1963-

Dedicated, June 6, 1981

Father Barry's "boys" in the Forty-Fifth Infantry Division were not the only ones to shower him with affection. In recognition of his outstanding work counseling students at Archbishop Hoban High School in Akron, Ohio, the school dedicated a new gymnasium named after the priest. Photographs from the author's collection.

Father Barry's final resting spot, at his beloved University of Notre Dame campus. Photograph from the author's collection.

Father Francis L. Sampson during training to become a paratrooper at Camp Barkeley, Texas. He later jumped into Normandy on D-Day with the 101st Airborne Division. Photograph courtesy of the Army Chaplain Corps Museum, Fort Jackson, South Carolina.

Following combat in Normandy in June 1944, Father Francis L. Sampson recites Last Rites over some of the paratroopers killed in the bitter fighting. Photograph #111-SC-190490 from the National Archives and Records Administration, College Park, Maryland.

Photograph of Father Francis L. Sampson taken by his German captors before he entered prison camp. After the war he became a close friend of Father Theodore M. Hesburgh and for a time headed the university's ROTC program. Photograph courtesy of the Army Chaplain Corps Museum, Fort Jackson, South Carolina.

Following the war, both Fathers Francis L. Sampson *(front row right)* and Father Edmund J. Murray *(back row right)* maintained their ties with the military. They are pictured here with members of the Veterans of Foreign Wars. Photograph courtesy of the Holy Cross Archives, University of Notre Dame.

After completing graduate studies at the university in 1931, Father Richard E. Carberry traveled to the Philippines as an army chaplain. Trapped in the Bataan Peninsula after the war started, he endured the torments of the Death March and three years in prison camps before boarding the Hell Ships for transport to Japan. Photograph #GDEV-11-12-01 from the University of Notre Dame Archives, Notre Dame, Indiana.

Father John E. Duffy, class of 1923, from the Diocese of Toledo, Ohio, was proud of his long career as an army chaplain. Like Father Carberry, he was captured in the Philippines and languished in prison camps until war's end. Photograph courtesy of the Army Chaplain Corps Museum, Fort Jackson, South Carolina.

From 1934 to 1937 Father Duffy was posted as an army chaplain in the Philippines, where he worked with the military as well as Filipino congregations. He is here pictured in the Philippines with an unidentified Filipino officer. Photograph courtesy of the Diocese of Toledo Archives, Toledo, Ohio.

His thin frame showing the effects of his years in prison camps, Father Duffy *(middle)* is interviewed at Kunming, China, after the war ended. He returned to Ohio, where he became pastor of Our Lady of Lourdes Parish in New London. Photograph courtesy of the Diocese of Toledo Archives, Toledo, Ohio.

NATIONALITY	NUMBER OF IMMIGRANTS OF RECORD		QUOTA NUMBERS AVAILABLE		QUOTA NO. REQUESTED	
	Preference	Non-preference	Preference	Non-preference	Preference	Non-preference

Radio Message

This is Father John E Duffy, Chaplain (Major) U.S. Army, formerly Chaplain First Philippine Corps; for my Bishop, Most Rev Karl J. Alter, D.D. 2544 Parkwood Ave, Toledo, Ohio. U.S.A. Thanks for Your Excellencies and the priests greetings received Feb 20th 44. Evidently the Japanese informed the States I was a prisoner immediately as it was eight months after Bataan's fall I came into their hands, as I was abandoned for dead, rescued and nursed by natives. For over a year I have been Catholic Chaplain at Hospital for Military Prisoners, and have been able to say Mass daily. The Japanese obtained a Mass kit for me and each month obtain altar breads and wine, as well as Rosaries, Prayer-books, medals and religious literature. Last Easter and Christmas special decorations. I am well. if you send anything tinned food will be preferred. Best wishes to Your Excellency, Msgr Boeskin, my brother priests and people

Father John E Duffy
Chaplain (Major) U.S. Army
formerly Chaplain 1st Philippine Corps

American Consul

During his confinement, in late 1944 or early 1945, Father Duffy was allowed to send the above radio broadcast to the United States. The words were censored by the Japanese so Father Duffy could not divulge the harsh conditions he and the other prisoners endured. Photograph courtesy of the Diocese of Toledo Archives, Toledo, Ohio.

Sister Mary Olivette *(left)* and Sister Mary Caecilius *(right)* in late 1941 before their departure from Saint Mary's College for the trip across the Pacific. Photograph from the Archives, Congregation of the Sisters of the Holy Cross, Notre Dame, Indiana.

Sister Mary Olivette *(far left)*, stands with two other sisters in the prison yard in New Bilibid in late 1944 or early 1945. Photograph from the Archives, Congregation of the Sisters of the Holy Cross, Notre Dame, Indiana.

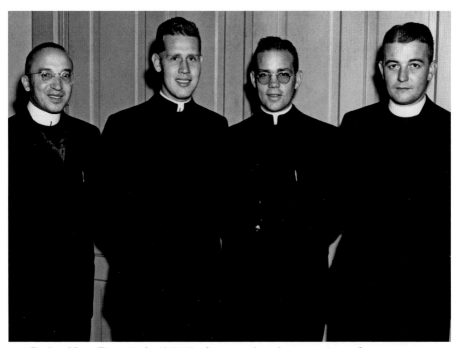

Back at Notre Dame in April 1945, after more than three years in confinement, are *(left to right)* Brother Theodore Kapes, Brother Rex Hennel, Father Jerome Lawyer, and Father Robert McKee. Photograph #GDIS-18-33-01 from the University of Notre Dame Archives, Notre Dame, Indiana.

Two pages from Sister Olivette's diary record events of late 1941 and early 1942. Photograph from the Archives, Congregation of the Sisters of the Holy Cross, Notre Dame, Indiana.

Sister Mary Olivette *(middle)* and Sister Mary Caecilius *(second from right)* aboard the U.S.S. *Eberle* upon their arrival in the United States in early May 1945. Photograph from the Archives, Congregation of the Sisters of the Holy Cross, Notre Dame, Indiana.

Father Edward R. Fitzgerald's chaplain identification card was typical of what every chaplain received upon entering the military. Photograph courtesy of the Holy Cross Archives, University of Notre Dame.

Father Edward R. Fitzgerald says Easter Sunday Mass in Iceland in 1943. He subsequently participated in the Normandy invasion with the Fifty-Third Troop Carrier Wing. Photograph courtesy of the Holy Cross Archives, University of Notre Dame.

Father Thomas P. Jones worked with wounded and dying soldiers in the U.S. Army 315th General Hospital Battalion in England. Photograph courtesy of the Holy Cross Archives, University of Notre Dame.

Father Edmund J. Murray saw fierce combat in Europe with the U.S. Army 104th Infantry Division. He maintained a deep love for the military for the rest of his life. Photograph courtesy of the Holy Cross Archives, University of Notre Dame.

Father Maurice E. Powers works in his Berlin office after the war. He witnessed the collapse of the German military while with the U.S. Army 101st Mechanized Cavalry. Photograph courtesy of the Holy Cross Archives, University of Notre Dame.

Before he headed to the Pacific with the Fourth Marine Division, Father John M. Dupuis *(second from left)* stopped by the movie set where Bing Crosby was filming *Going My Way*. From left to right stand a chaplain named Brophy, Father Dupuis, a chaplain identified as Driscoll, Bing Crosby in his priestly garb for the film, fellow Holy Cross chaplain Father Patrick R. Duffy, and a chaplain identified as Finnegan. Photograph courtesy of the Holy Cross Archives, University of Notre Dame.

Father John M. Dupuis hears confessions from a line of marines during the fighting at Saipan in the Mariana Islands. He wrote on the back of the photograph, "After the island was secured, the Confessional line-up. A letter from home in my pocket." Photograph courtesy of the Holy Cross Archives, University of Notre Dame.

Father John M. Dupuis celebrates Mass on Saipan following the bitter battle. "Saipan, one of the islands the 4th Marine Division took," he wrote on the photograph's back. "Front lines not too far away. Sunday it is peaceful but only a few days before men were dying." Photograph courtesy of the Holy Cross Archives, University of Notre Dame.

Father Francis J. Boland stands aboard his troop transport, U.S.S. *Highlands*. From that ship he witnessed some of the most severe combat of the Pacific at Iwo Jima and Okinawa, including kamikaze attacks. Photograph #GDIS-41-99-01 from the University of Notre Dame Archives, Notre Dame, Indiana.

Father Boland's U.S.S. *Highlands* in the Pacific. Photograph #NH-98837 courtesy of the Naval History & Heritage Command.

Father Thomas E. Hewitt, seen here in 1943, was stationed in New Caledonia, New Guinea, and the Philippines with the U.S. Army 125th Infantry Division before reaching Japan, where he stood at the ruins of Hiroshima. Photograph courtesy of the Holy Cross Archives, University of Notre Dame.

Father Henry Heintskill saw action in both the European and Pacific Theaters aboard the escort carrier U.S.S. *Tulagi*. He witnessed the terrifying results of kamikaze attacks in the Philippines in early 1945 before the carrier steamed north to Iwo Jima and Okinawa. Photograph courtesy of the Holy Cross Archives, University of Notre Dame.

Father Henry Heintskill's ship, U.S.S. *Tulagi,* on her way from New York to Casablanca in June 1944, her deck loaded with army fighters for use in the Allied assault of German-held France. The destroyer U.S.S. *Marsh* (DE-699) is alongside. Photograph #80-G-364378 from the National Archives and Records Administration, College Park, Maryland.

Father Henry Heintskill encountered one of the war's most terrifying weapons when kamikazes attacked during the January 1945 landings in Lingayen Gulf. Here, on January 6, a kamikaze approaches the cruiser U.S.S. *Louisville*, a ship not far from Heintskill's *Tulagi*, only moments before smashing into the cruiser. Photograph #80-G-342368 courtesy of the National Archives and Records Administration, College Park, Maryland.

Father Norman Johnson was stationed with the Fourth Cargo Combat Group in the China–Burma–India Theater. Here he says Mass before a large gathering of his soldiers. Photograph courtesy of the Holy Cross Archives, University of Notre Dame.

Father James E. Norton in 1943 at the U.S. Navy Chaplain Training School, William and Mary College, Williamsburg, Virginia. Photograph courtesy of the Holy Cross Archives, University of Notre Dame.

Father James E. Norton using native transportation to visit one of the islands in the Ulithi Atoll in the Caroline Islands. He was stationed with the Marine Aircraft Group 45 but often ministered to the civilian islanders. Photograph courtesy of the Holy Cross Archives, University of Notre Dame.

Father James E. Norton tended to the needs of the local civilians as well as those of his military units. On the back of this photograph of an altar on Fassarai Island, Ulithi Atoll, Father Norton wrote, "Altar in native chapel. Statues, holy pictures, etc., had been treasured by the natives and preserved during the Japanese occupation. The Catholic 'Padrea' had been excluded from the atoll for more than five years yet the Catholic Faith of these devout people had not suffered." Photograph courtesy of the Holy Cross Archives, University of Notre Dame.

Father Norton celebrates January 1945 Mass for islanders in the Western Carolines. Photograph courtesy of the Holy Cross Archives, University of Notre Dame.

In September 1945, only weeks after the war with Japan ended, Father James E. Norton *(far left)* sits with Japanese officers on Yap Island in the Carolines. He wrote on the back of the photograph, "A strange meal—with Jap officers in the middle of the jungle and in the heart of the Jap Headquarters country." Photograph courtesy of the Holy Cross Archives, University of Notre Dame.

Father Francis D. Bridenstine celebrates a Sunday Mass service in 1945 for servicemen on Enubuj Island, Kwajalein Atoll, Marshall Islands. Photograph #SC-400265 from the National Archives and Records Administration, College Park, Maryland.

Father John J. Burke *(far right, head visible above the cloth cross)* says Mass in August 1945 aboard the U.S.S. *Pennsylvania* in Buckner Bay, Okinawa. A survivor of the attack at Pearl Harbor, the ship would be one of the last American vessels to suffer a hit from Japanese aircraft. "Sunday Mass on fo'c'sle—quarterdeck awash," wrote Father Burke on the back of the photograph. Photograph courtesy of the Holy Cross Archives, University of Notre Dame.

On August 12, 1945, the U.S.S. *Pennsylvania* rests low in the water after being struck by a torpedo from a Japanese torpedo plane. With a salvage tug alongside, hoses pump water from the damaged areas below. Photograph #80-G-490327 courtesy of the National Archives and Records Administration, College Park, Maryland.

Father John J. Burke conducts the burial ceremony for some of the twenty sailors of the U.S.S. *Pennsylvania* killed by the August 12, 1945, torpedo strike. "This picture of first four [bodies] recovered—one a Catholic," he wrote on the back of the photograph. "Tomorrow will be declared peace. Tomorrow is the end of the war, thank God." Photograph courtesy of the Holy Cross Archives, University of Notre Dame.

Father Theodore M. Hesburgh's hopes of being a navy chaplain during the war never materialized, but he contributed by coauthoring a series of religious pamphlets written for servicemen. Here he is seen after the war, accepting a document from a naval officer following a midshipman cruise. Photograph #GPHS 1/05 from the University of Notre Dame Archives, Notre Dame, Indiana.

Sampson noticed that in this action, the first major battle in which he participated, the paratroopers' morale improved as the risks increased. "In the thick of things there seems actually to be a zest for battle that makes it as interesting as a big traditional football game,"[21] he wrote later. He hoped that in the coming days, undoubtedly to be painted with bloodshed and death, he could measure up as to those men.

The next day the paratroopers forced the Germans to retreat from Saint-Côme-du-Mont. Three days later, after crossing the Douve and preparing for the final assault into Carentan, the 501st Regiment drove the Germans off Hill 30 in an assault highlighted by Sergeant Frederick "Fritz" Niland's grenade attack against a German machine-gun nest. The regiment subsequently entered and secured Carentan. For its actions, the regiment was later awarded a Presidential Unit Citation, an honor that recognized the efforts of an entire group over those of a single individual.

Since the airborne landings six days earlier, whenever Father Sampson came across a dead body, American or German, Catholic, Protestant, or Jewish, he stopped and said a prayer on the boy's behalf. He celebrated Mass wherever he could, setting up improvised altars in bombed-out structures or open fields and, like his counterpart in Italy, Father Barry, becoming accustomed to using the hoods of jeeps as makeshift altars. During one Mass, German artillery shells exploded in a nearby field, hurling rocks and pieces of turf over Sampson's head. He turned to tell the men to seek shelter, only to find that they had already disappeared.

From the start, Father Sampson found his time as a chaplain rewarding. "Combat truly was a perfect laboratory for a priest's study and work," he wrote. "There human nature was exposed for dissection and analysis. All the artificialities and superficialities of civilian life were cut away. There remained nothing but bedrock character, or sometimes, unfortunately, the almost total lack of character. Family position, social status, money, influence—these were mighty useless assets at the front."

He also learned that, except for the small handful of men he considered "thugs and ex-criminals," who preferred complaining about everything and going absent without leave, and the conspicuously courageous leaders, such as Colonel Johnson, he could never predict which man would perform extraordinary deeds in battle. He found that it was often the quiet soldier everyone overlooked in training who surprised his buddies, while at other times the paratrooper everyone guessed would be a tiger on the battlefield proved to be precisely the opposite. "In the test of battle," he wrote, "the ex-floorwalker sometimes succeeds where the professional soldier may fail; the former prizefighter may run, leaving his buddy, a lad who never got away from his mother's apron strings, to hold the position."

Father Sampson concluded that the men who carried strong religious convictions into battle seemed more disciplined and composed. In the turbulent conditions in which they found themselves, their faith provided something solid, something familiar, to clutch. Sampson noted that even non-Catholics sometimes expressed the desire to possess the calmness with which his deeply religious Catholic paratroopers approached battle. "Confession and Communion are the greatest comfort to our men at the front, and non-Catholics observed with open envy our Catholics receiving the sacraments."[22] On more than a few occasions, Sampson waited for the soldier kneeling next to him to begin reciting how long it had been since he last went to Confession, only to discover that the soldier was not Catholic. The man sought the same consolation that his Catholic buddies received after confessing to Father Sampson.

Father Sampson spent much time in aid stations, helping both American and German soldiers wounded in the Normandy invasion and aftermath. In what was becoming an all-too-familiar part of his day, he administered Last Rites, somber moments that were offset by the lack of hatred between the American and German wounded, soldiers who a few hours earlier had been trying to kill each other. He estimated that 60 percent of the German captives were Catholics, mostly from Bavaria, who freely made the Sign of the Cross whenever Sampson took out his stole to hear confession.

In an aid station jammed with dying and grievously wounded soldiers, Sampson witnessed a moment of empathy that restored his hope that despite the widespread miseries then afflicting the world, good might yet prevail. As he moved from cot to cot, he glanced across at a wounded German soldier lying in a cot next to an American soldier, who moaned in pain from severe head injuries. The German slowly rose and gently arranged a blanket under his enemy's head. Sampson believed that Americans back home, so often embroiled in petty arguments and feuds, could learn a lesson from soldiers who had "a great compassion for each other" and wondered why world leaders "can't have more common sense."[23]

Those instances paled in comparison to the times when he buried the dead, which offered grim evidence that the compassion shown by the German soldier in the aid station could do little to halt the avalanche of killing and maiming yet to come. A few days after the June 6 landings, Sampson visited the division cemetery to administer Last Rites to the still-unburied paratroopers who had given their lives for their country. Instead of a handful, as he expected, Sampson gazed at several hundred shrouded bodies lying in a French field, many of them paratroopers with whom he had only the week before chatted and joked.

"I was shocked to find so many of my faithful boys among the dead," wrote Sampson. "It didn't seem possible that these young men who had been so confident a week before, whose hands I had shaken before we boarded the planes, who had confessed and received Holy Communion on the eve of D-Day, who had wise-cracked that 'no Nazi bullet has my name on it'—it just didn't seem possible that they were in eternity now."[24]

As hard as it was for Sampson to administer Last Rites to so many young men, writing letters to their loved ones proved more strenuous. He attempted to personalize each note, but what could he say to the families of paratroopers he had not known? He found that the greatest comfort he could lend was assuring families that their loved one had received the Sacraments before lifting off from British airfields for the invasion.

Among the most difficult moments for Sampson was the experience of Sergeant Fritz Niland, decorated for his bravery on June 12 at Hill 30. The youngest of four boys and two girls, Fritz came from a family that boasted a long military heritage. His father, Michael, had fought as a Rough Rider with Theodore Roosevelt in Cuba during the 1898 Spanish–American War, and his three older brothers had already joined the service. When Fritz learned during an interlude in combat that his brother Robert had been killed, he asked Father Sampson to help him locate the body at one of the cemeteries dotting the fields. They spent an entire day searching for Robert's remains before Sampson finally spotted the name *Niland* on a grave marker. Unaware that Fritz had a second brother in Normandy, and thinking the news would come as a relief, Sampson called out to Fritz, "The only Niland here is a Preston Niland."[25]

Indeed, within one torturous week of D-Day, all three of Fritz's brothers had become casualties. Technical Sergeant Robert Niland, so ferocious a fighter that his fellow paratroopers in the 502nd Parachute Infantry Regiment called him "Bob the Beast," was killed in heavy fighting at Neuville-au-Plain on D-Day. Second Lieutenant Preston Niland of the 22nd Infantry Regiment, 4th Division, was killed in June 7 fighting northwest of Utah Beach. And Fritz's oldest brother, Technical Sergeant Edward Niland, a gunner on an Air Corps bomber, had been shot down over Burma on May 16 and was missing in action.

Sampson immediately started paperwork to arrange a transfer home for Fritz. The four had not been posted to the same unit (unlike the five Sullivan brothers who perished in the Pacific aboard the cruiser U.S.S. *Juneau* in late 1942), but Sampson figured he would have little difficulty obtaining Fritz's release. When approval arrived in late summer, with accompanying orders to serve as a member of the military police in Buffalo, Fritz objected.

"No," he said to Sampson. "I'm staying here with my boys."

"Well, you can bring that up with General Eisenhower or the President," replied Sampson, "but you're going home."[26]

The Niland story became one of many that director Steven Spielberg used to fashion his film *Saving Private Ryan*. No unit searched behind enemy lines for Niland, as the movie suggested, but Father Sampson's aid, especially in managing the paperwork, helped save Fritz. Fritz later learned that Edward had escaped from a Japanese prison camp and had made his way safely to British lines. After the war, Fritz graduated from Georgetown University and opened a practice in oral surgery.

Whether it was through Mass, Holy Communion, Confession, or simply lending an ear, Father Sampson and his fellow chaplains stood as beacons pointing the way to a better world. They offered hope for the future and gave others something to hold onto. Each time a frightened paratrooper glanced toward Father Sampson or an exhausted captive spotted Father Carberry, he remembered that better times awaited and gained an inner strength he could never have obtained from drill sergeants or Silver Star recipients.

THREE DAYS before the end of June, the Eighty-Third Infantry Division relieved the paratroopers. Sampson and his unit remained in France until mid-July, when they returned to England for a brief rest and to begin training for their next assignment.

At the same time, Father Fitzgerald worked from his base in England, shuttling to and from Omaha Beach to bring replacement chaplain supplies to priests laboring on the battlefronts and to accompany the wounded on their way to hospitals in England. Sampson and Fitzgerald had been among the first American chaplains to touch French soil, but as American forces neared Germany, more chaplains would be asked to minister to the men, including priests from Notre Dame. Together, they took front-row seats for the collapse of Nazi tyranny and, in the process, witnessed Hitler's most horrific excesses.

IN THE MEANTIME, American land, sea, and air power chipped away at Japanese dominance in the Pacific. Notre Dame chaplains accompanied these forces, too, as they embarked upon a two-pronged path toward Tokyo. One path led straight to the Philippines, where Father Duffy, Father Carberry, and the Notre Dame missionaries waited patiently for rescue.

CHAPTER 7

"OUR CHAPLAINS ARE BECOMING MORE SCATTERED EVERY WEEK"

Chaplains in the Pacific, 1944

While Father Duffy and the other Notre Dame religious tried to stay alive in prison camps, the U.S. military had been busy in the Pacific. The navy registered a major mid-1942 triumph at Midway, where its torpedo planes and dive bombers sank four Japanese aircraft carriers, while later that same year a combined marine, navy, and army force swept onto Guadalcanal in the South Pacific's Solomon Islands. After months of hard fighting they took control of Guadalcanal, while forces under General MacArthur landed in New Guinea, to Australia's north, to begin an arduous campaign across thick jungle terrain.

The next year, other units embarked upon a Central Pacific path toward Tokyo that required them to subdue a line of Japanese island bastions sprinkled over five thousand miles of the ocean. Marines had waged a successful, but bloody, beginning at Tarawa in the Gilbert Islands in November 1943, but savage combat awaited in the Marshall Islands and the Marianas before considering the leap to Okinawa and on to the Japanese mainland. Those island bases, each bristling with trenches, machine-gun pillboxes, and well-armed infantry, caused some military planners to conclude that a decade of killing and dying might elapse before the Stars and Stripes flew over the Japanese capital.

The Notre Dame religious in the Philippines could do nothing but wait and rely on their dwindling strength, morally as well as physically, to face the daily tribulations of prison camp. Each day they remained in Japanese hands drained part of the reservoir of optimism that kept hope alive, and each week they subsisted on watery gruel further sapped their energy.

Liberation inched closer as 1944 dawned. In February a massive task force approached the twin islands of Roi and Namur in the Marshall Island chain, three thousand miles from Bilibid and Cabanatuan. Included in that combined marine and navy assemblage was marine chaplain Father John M. Dupuis, C.S.C.

"Ring Side Seat to the Final Shelling and Bombing"

Unlike Father Barry, who participated in extended campaigns across much of the European continent, Father Dupuis saw war in minuscule. His fights, which asked U.S. Marines to wrest island garrisons from foes determined to die while inflicting gruesome casualties on the invaders, lasted days or weeks instead of months. Still, his brief encounters in combat matched the brutality of what his Notre Dame counterpart witnessed in Italy.

The struggle to seize Tarawa in November 1943 had been a grim foreshadowing of Pacific combat. Over a period of seventy-six hours, on an isle barely two miles long and seven hundred yards at its widest—less than half the size of New York City's Central Park—six thousand American marines and Japanese soldiers died. The marines absorbed twice as many casualties seizing tiny Tarawa as had the infantry units on Sicily, where Father Barry received his initiation into battle.

Born September 18, 1908, in Sault Ste. Marie in Michigan's Upper Peninsula, John Dupuis graduated from Notre Dame in 1931, four years after joining the Congregation of Holy Cross. After religious studies in Washington, DC, he was ordained at the university's Church of the Sacred Heart in 1935. He did one year of parish work in South Bend before returning to Notre Dame, where he taught philosophy and served as assistant prefect of discipline. When war erupted, he requested permission to enter the navy as a chaplain, a wish that was granted when he was appointed in April 1943 with the rank of lieutenant, junior grade, and posted to the newly formed Fourth Marine Division.

To prepare for combat, for half a year Father Dupuis and the Fourth climbed the rugged hills of expansive Camp Pendleton in California before concluding with a large amphibious maneuver at San Clemente Island. Dupuis worked with a headquarters and service company of 270 officers and men, of whom 74 were Catholic. He wrote Father Steiner in the fall of 1943 that his labors with the marines in training had deflated a myth held by many—that servicemen become more religious. He claimed that the contact he had with the men "doesn't bear that notion out at all" and concluded that, at least while in the United States, most of the Catholics in the company "are Catholics in name only." Mass attendance rose during training, but once the maneuvers terminated, "they just quit going."[1] Dupuis's initial months as a chaplain fell short of expectations and compared unfavorably with his accomplishments in parish work and at Notre Dame, but he hoped that once overseas, his work would have more meaning.

Dupuis could at least enjoy himself before the inevitable ocean voyage to the far reaches of the Pacific. During one break, he and another navy chaplain from Notre Dame, Father Patrick R. Duffy, C.S.C., visited the Hollywood movie set where Bing Crosby, in his role as Father O'Malley, was filming *Going My Way*. In a photograph taken with the famous singer and actor, while the chaplains stood in military uniform, Crosby was ironically the only person wearing priestly garb.

Like his fellow chaplains from the university, Dupuis frequently referred to Notre Dame and its football team in correspondence. Six days after Notre Dame defeated the University of Michigan, 35–12 in October 1943, Father Steiner wrote Dupuis that despite the war, on campus "the great interest right now is football." Steiner added, with satisfaction, that the game "was sweet music to our ears," and that the *Detroit Free Press* "ran a whole column on the front page" extolling Notre Dame's dominance of the Michigan squad. Two months later, after Coach Leahy's boys ran off nine consecutive victories, the undefeated Irish succumbed to the Great Lakes Navy team, 14–9, to record their only blemish for the season. Though the team was unanimously named the national champion, the solitary loss bothered the chaplain. In the game's aftermath Dupuis wrote to Steiner, "it certainly was a tough break for Notre Dame. The luck of the Irish finally gave out.

I hate to think of it." With the football season concluded, he admitted, Saturdays "are a little empty now."[2]

Dupuis had little time to commiserate about football, for within a few weeks he and the Fourth Division were on their way to the Central Pacific and the outfit's first taste of combat. Kwajalein, the world's largest atoll, sat in the middle of the Marshall Islands 2,600 miles southwest of Pearl Harbor. At the northern end of the string of isles comprising Kwajalein were the twin isles of Roi and Namur, while the isle of Kwajalein, namesake for the entire atoll, rested at the southern end. The U.S. military wanted to seize the pair to deny the Japanese use of four large airstrips, smash a huge gap in the enemy's outer defense line, and advance American power closer to Japan and to the day when American bombers could, from island bases, reach the Japanese Home Islands.

American military intelligence predicted a bloody encounter for Dupuis and his marines. The Japanese had controlled Kwajalein for a quarter of a century, during which they constructed sturdy defenses, installed machine-gun pillboxes, and mined the approaches. Concerned that appalling casualty numbers would alarm the public, top American military commanders leaked information to the press so the home front could be prepared for a repeat of Tarawa.

In the Pacific, Japanese officials ordered the commander at Kwajalein, Rear Admiral Monzo Akiyama, to fight to the death to delay the United States. "When the last moment comes, I shall die bravely and honorably,"[3] one Japanese soldier wrote in his diary after learning of his fate.

The Fourth Division left San Diego on January 13, 1944, for the eighteen-day voyage. Once the California coastline receded, the number of men asking to see Father Dupuis mounted. As the transports inched toward battle, questions about combat superseded thoughts of families and girlfriends. Young marines not long out of high school asked what combat would be like. Some feared that when bullets and mortar shells rained down they would freeze in terror instead of being there for their buddies, and husbands wondered if they would ever again see their wives.

Dupuis faced queries he would never have heard on campus. Some marines asked about the morality of taking another man's life, even if it occurred in combat. Others were anxious that the horrors of combat would permanently alter their personalities or lead to postwar issues. Dupuis reminded the men that God would never condemn anyone for defending family and country and assured them that they could lean on their faith both in combat and after the war. Even the men who had no need to see Dupuis appreciated the priest's presence and took comfort in the knowledge that when the bullets flew and the bombs burst, Dupuis would be at their side.

When he was not counseling marines, Dupuis walked around the transport, offering encouragement. He celebrated Mass every afternoon and heard confessions for at least seventy-five minutes each evening. "Sometimes I heard for close to three hours," Dupuis wrote to Father Steiner. "Oh, the boys want to get all straightened out before they go over the side of the ship."[4]

The armada of eleven aircraft carriers, nineteen battleships and cruisers, sixty-three destroyers, and twelve destroyer escorts drew within sight of its destination on the last day of January. Battleships and cruisers formed offshore, swerved their big guns toward tiny Roi, and arced shell after shell toward the island. Explosions, smoke, and dust nearly shrouded Roi from view, convincing some marines that few Japanese would be alive to contest the landing.

"My the Navy hit those islands with everything it had," wrote Dupuis of the bombardment. "Roi and Namur were completely demolished. The destruction was terrible." He added that the naval bombardment had commenced two days before, when "The giant ships of the Navy poured their sixteen inch shells onto Roi and Namur; the cruisers their eight and six inch shells, and the destroyers their fives. The air force went into action and dropped their five hundred, one thousand and two thousand pound bombs. Everything was completely demolished. How anyone could have lived through all of that fire is beyond me. It was literally hell."

The bombardment continued as the Twenty-Third Marine Regiment and Father Dupuis landed at Roi on February 1. "We circled around in the lagoon before the islands before we received word to go in," wrote Dupuis. "It was ring side seat to the final shelling and bombing which took place that morning. It was awful."

When the bombardment ceased and the landing craft turned toward the beaches shortly after 2:00 p.m., the marines encountered little opposition. Before they arrived, the Japanese had pulled most of their defenders to Namur, where Rear Admiral Akiyama would make his last stand.

"No opposition on our island at all," wrote Dupuis, "and save for a few snipers in pill boxes, everything was practically secured." For the next few days the marines traversed Roi to eliminate the few Japanese soldiers who remained, but mostly they encountered grisly images of the bombardment's effects. "The mopping up process took several days though. A few Japs were still hiding out. They would live down in tunnels which crisscrossed the islands and pop up during the night. As a matter of fact they had to live down there with rottening [*sic*] Jap bodies. How they did it I don't know."

The marines hitting nearby Namur faced tougher opposition from Akiyama's defenders, who mounted withering fire at the intruders from their trenches and pillboxes until their positions were overwhelmed. The fierce fighting continued into the night, when the Japanese charged marine lines in a desperate *banzai* attack that killed and wounded many, including Private First Class Stephen Hopkins, the eighteen-year-old son of Franklin Roosevelt's adviser, Harry Hopkins.

"The islands were a mess," wrote Dupuis. "Pill boxes demolished, gun emplacements blown to smithereens, the guns twisted and bent, palm trees blown into the ocean yards away or sheared in half like match sticks cut in two with a razor." He was surprised that, even with the brevity of the battle, grime covered every participant. "Dust and dirt. It was everywhere: in your eyes, ears, hair. It caked your skin, filled the pores of your body. You ate it with your rations, drank it with your water. But you never got used to it."

Although the assault failed to match the bloodbath at Tarawa, 313 marines died and 502 were wounded securing Roi-Namur. More than 3,000 Japanese bodies littered the isles, presenting Dupuis with his first images of the physical toll exacted by combat. In the aftermath, however, he was more concerned with the mental levy on young men who had to reconcile the brutality in which they had just been involved with the moral precepts that instructed them not to kill. Disconsolate marines who lost buddies needed counseling, while others returned to the ships with grievous wounds, requiring Dupuis to sit at their side. "You have already read what the Marines did in the Pacific, that is, the fourth division,"[5] he wrote to Father Steiner, referring to the newspaper accounts describing the horrible cost exacted on his congregation.

Their sacrifices placed U.S. forces halfway from Hawaii to the Mariana Island chain, the anchor solidifying the next Japanese defense line in the Pacific. Once they seized the Marianas, including the key islands of Saipan and Tinian, they would stand only 1,500 miles from Tokyo, a distance from which they could employ the new B-29 Superfortress bombers to reduce the Japanese capital and other crucial installations. "The war situation has assumed unprecedented seriousness," intoned one Japanese broadcaster over Radio Tokyo. "The tempo of enemy operations indicates that the attacking forces are already pressing upon our mainland."[6]

Those forces, Dupuis understood, would include his Fourth Marine Division. After Roi, the unit was sent to a secure area to begin training for the next operation. Besides talking with the men, visiting the wounded, and hearing confessions, he was inundated with military forms relating to his work. He confided to Father Steiner that he had to complete paperwork "for the Military Ordinariate, for the Secretary of the Navy, for the corps chaplain, for Workman, for Public Relations, for Fitness Reports, for this and for that. If I never see another form in my life it will be too soon for me." Even the accountant at Notre Dame sent him "a lot of forms to fill out" relating to his expenses, and Dupuis wondered if, as he was so busy ministering to the marines, he might receive an exemption from detailing those. "And now he wants to know how much I spend for food, for clothing, for this and for that," Dupuis wrote of the accountant. "Would think I was a pastor of Saint Joseph's Church [in South Bend] or something. Put a buz-buz in his ear to lay off."[7]

Steiner intervened with the accountant and made certain to let his comrade know how vital Dupuis's work was. In doing so, Steiner foreshadowed what Dupuis and other chaplains would face at war's end. "You young men are passing through experiences that will remain with you the rest of your lives," he wrote to the marine chaplain. "In years to come they will be nothing short of night-mares to you. The consolation and encouragement you have, is that you are doing God's work. The souls you bring back to God will ever be solicitors and intercessors for you at eternal High Court."[8]

Dupuis had no idea where he and the division might be sent next; he told Steiner that the priest back at Notre Dame probably knew as much about matters as he did in the Central Pacific. "You will read about our operations in the papers," he wrote to Father Steiner in late April. "I can say no more. That isn't much, is it? But as a matter of fact you know as much as I do about it."[9]

Within six weeks Dupuis would have his answer. After the Fourth Division had completed training, it again embarked on troop transports for an ocean voyage to yet another of the Pacific's islands. Saipan in the Marianas was nothing like tiny Roi, he would learn.

"Our Uniform Day after Day Continues to Be Sweat Soaked Khaki"
To the Philippines

While Father Barry in Italy and Father Sampson in Normandy advanced toward Germany, and while Father Dupuis approached Saipan, other Notre Dame associates accompanied seaborne units as they battled their way across the Pacific toward the vast Philippine archipelago, home to not only thousands of Japanese aircraft, tanks, and infantry, but also Americans incarcerated since the war's early days. They experienced a different aspect of chaplaincy service than their prisoner-of-war compatriots, but whether stationed aboard an aircraft carrier or posted to an island base, they provided labor similar to that being offered in Cabanatuan or Bilibid.

"Our chaplains are becoming more scattered every week," wrote Father Steiner to Chaplain Thomas E. Hewitt of the increasing number of Holy Cross priests serving in the military. "Fathers Johnson, Boland, Norton and Heintskill are all on the alert or already gone. They move them out quickly these days."[10] Father Steiner's efforts to free as many priests as possible to become chaplains while still meeting the requirements of his order showed results as 1944 unfolded. More chaplains from Notre Dame flooded to Europe and the Pacific, all eager to reach the front lines.

"I am looking forward with considerable enthusiasm to this new duty," wrote Father Francis J. Boland to Father Steiner of his posting as a navy chaplain to the attack transport U.S.S. *Highlands* (APA-119). "From what I can learn it will be somewhat hazardous as these troop ships take the men to immediate scenes of action. However, there is a tremendous opportunity for wonderful work and I am hoping to give satisfactory performance."[11]

His Holy Cross comrade Father Henry Heintskill boarded the escort carrier U.S.S. *Tulagi* (CVE-72), in Vancouver, Washington, similarly impatient to reach the battle zone. "So here I am aboard, and like a good many other men on the ship, looking forward to the first taste of salt water." He told Father Steiner that in addition to his duties as chaplain, which entailed daily Mass, Confession, and a general service for all faiths, he served as the ship's librarian and as the welfare officer, which involved handling significant sums of money—"I'm not too sure I'll like that." He enjoyed, however, the many chances he had to confer with his charges, who sought his counsel for problems ranging from homesickness to divorce, from the longing to again hold a girl in his arms at a dance to the loss of loved ones. "You can imagine how many boys have come in to moan on my shoulder," he told Steiner.

Before the new vessel, commissioned in late December 1943, settled into Pacific combat, it first completed an uneventful round trip from California to Pearl Harbor, ferrying aircraft and military personnel on their way to the war zone more than two thousand miles to Hawaii's west. Upon returning to the mainland, Heintskill wrote in early 1944 that, "There hasn't been too much to remind us of war—everything is so calm it's almost like a pleasure cruise." The tranquility had everyone guessing where they might be headed, which reminded Heintskill of those days each year at Notre Dame when every priest anxiously awaited word of his next assignment. "I guess human nature is the same everywhere. We always want to know just a little bit ahead of time what's going to happen next."

Heintskill had received newspaper clippings and letters heralding Father Barry's exploits in Europe and Father Dupuis's achievements in the Pacific, and confessed to Father Steiner that, "I must admit I feel rather envious. Here we are still peaceably fighting the war in the comparative comfort of the fighting *Tulagi*. By this time we had all thought we would be in the thick of it—but now it looks pretty far off." He explained that the pilots were especially eager to see combat, "and as for myself I guess it's partly curiosity and partly a feeling that a touch of the real thing will bring around some of these Catholic boys of mine."[12]

Heintskill's initiation into combat finally occurred in August 1944, when army infantry units, including that of his friend Father Barry, landed in southern France as part of Operation Dragoon. While the army mounted a southern route through France toward Germany to complement the path Father Sampson's division staged out of Normandy, Heintskill's carrier, which had arrived in Mediterranean waters the month before, stood offshore to provide air support for Barry's regiment and their compatriots as they advanced inland.

"This is not exactly the evening before the battle, but it is pretty close to it," he wrote to Steiner in the days before the operation. "It's hard when you're so close to the uncertainness of danger to analyze your feelings. Naturally I'm very proud to be a part of it all—and especially to be with this crew of ours. Come what will I know that they will do a splendid job. I feel too, very grateful to you for having made it possible for me to be here right now. I don't think I would have wanted to miss this for anything in the world."[13]

Unlike Barry or Dupuis, who operated on the front lines with the land units, Heintskill remained aboard the carrier to continue his work among the sailors and aviators. "After several months of piddling around we are finally out on a real job," he wrote to Father Steiner. "Most of the men aboard know now what it is to keep long hours and do work that is on the hard side." He explained that as arduous as their tasks were, they shrank in comparison to what Barry and his soldiers endured fighting on land. "Up to the present we've been in no great danger, and it begins to look very much as though even when we go into the big thing there won't be too much trouble. Submarines—our biggest concern are generally wary of us—and it seems that there are not too many enemy planes on the prowl."[14]

In thirteen days of combat off the French coast, *Tulagi*'s aviators flew more than five hundred missions, in which they shot down six German aircraft and destroyed twenty-three locomotives, forty-eight vehicles, two ammunition dumps, and twenty-two fuel tanks. With the exception of three fliers who were shot down—two of whom reached friendly lines and returned to the ship—the carrier's crew escaped without injury.

Heintskill worried about extracurricular activities when his men enjoyed liberty in Algeria and Alexandria, Egypt. What he considered "the moral corruption of many of the port towns" shocked the priest. He thought of contests and activities aboard ship to keep the men out of trouble ashore, but he fought an uphill battle. "I think that if the military would take just half the money they stick into prophylaxis propaganda and use it to buy some trucks to take the men on swimming parties and so on," he complained to Father Steiner, "they wouldn't have a quarter of the trouble they do have." Heintskill wrote that people back home would be shocked at the decadent behavior ignored by the army and navy, and that he feared that the services "are going to send back to the States after this war is over a morally corrupt youth."

He delivered a Sunday sermon "to both the Catholic and to the Protestant men" in which he "blasted away on immoral recreation." He was heartened when a dozen men thanked him afterward "for letting them have it straight from the shoulder," but when the sermon failed to slow the alarming practices, he turned to a simpler remedy—beer. "One reason for it was that we carried quite a supply of American beer, and as soon as we would dock we'd organize a swimming party with free beer. All but a very few of the men preferred the beach and beer to going into town, drinking doped liquor and winding up in trouble. I've found it's a lot easier to provide the men with decent recreation than to preach about bad recreation."[15]

Having completed the operation off France, in September the *Tulagi* crossed the Atlantic for an overhaul in Norfolk, Virginia. Three weeks later the ship passed through the Panama Canal and entered the Pacific. Still distant from the combat zone, Heintskill lacked enough hours in his days to complete every task. A yeoman typed his chaplain's reports and other correspondence, set up the altar, and served at Mass, but Heintskill needed every minute to minister to the crew of more than eight hundred men.

"Right now we are bouncing around on the Pacific—it's early in the evening but almost everyone is in bed," he wrote to Steiner in November. "They've been up since four and have been at flight or battle stations almost continuously. This gives every indication of being a good bit tougher than the Mediterranean."

He at times questioned if he had accomplished anything consequential, as so few men attended daily Mass, but "just when one begins to feel discouraged and wonders whether he couldn't be doing more good someplace else, the good Lord sends encouragement."[16] One evening a group of officers, heatedly debating philosophical issues, asked Heintskill how he would answer the question of man's purpose on Earth. Heintskill joined the discussion, and while he believed he failed to make an impression, a few days later one of the sailors asked if he could begin instructions into the Catholic faith.

Heintskill awakened each day "almost as early as we did back at Notre Dame. At sea we always beat the sun up—sun up then finds all the men at their battle stations ready for action." From dawn to dusk, in port or at sea, Heintskill tended to the "dozen little things that fill the day. Sometimes almost the entire day goes by without my getting topside for some sun and air."[17]

Anchoring the day was Heintskill's celebration of the Mass and Protestant general services. For the 137 Catholics aboard, half of whom attended regularly, he held two Masses on Sundays in one of the wardrooms and a daily Mass in the small cubicle he used as an office. He hoped that as they approached the battle zone in the far western Pacific, with its heightened risk of death or injury, more would attend Mass and receive the Sacraments. "I think that what we really need is something that would give the men a good scare," he wrote to Steiner.

After being disheartened when only one sailor showed up for the Stations of the Cross, Heintskill related to Steiner, "It's funny that these Catholic boys kick like anything when they don't have a Catholic priest aboard—and when they do get one they're no models of Catholic Action." However, he better understood the crew's dynamics when a sailor "explained it to me by saying that they feel if they have a Catholic priest aboard it's all right—he'll be around when they really need him. I hope they're right."

Heintskill's sense of humor helped him navigate the more trying moments. In one letter to Steiner, he joked that he delivered a sermon that knocked the attendees out of their pews. He had just started his second Mass one Sunday when rough seas rocked the carrier from side to side. Heintskill continued his prayers, but "about half way thru the Mass the ship took a terrific lurch; I reached out for the chalice to steady it, and just then out of the corner of my eye I saw a half dozen men go skidding along the deck right past the altar. As I found out later on the roll had completely unseated them. That I imagine is as close as I'll ever come to unseating a congregation."

Heintskill appreciated what he termed the "roses among the thorns," the naval aviators who surprised him with their "sincere Catholicity." Most attended Mass, "and even a temperature of 110 degrees—which seems to be the normal temperature for my office these days—doesn't discourage them." Winter or summer, all days in the South Pacific seemed like the middle of July, transforming altar vestments into an onerous burden. "Our uniform day after day continues to be sweat soaked khaki," he remarked. He joked about seeing so many of the crew walking around in "Boy Scout shorts, sacrificing dignity for comfort."

He regretted his inability while in port to visit all of the destroyer crews who served aboard ships the navy deemed too small to require a chaplain. He told Father Steiner that he had held Mass once "for the boys aboard some of the tin cans," many of whom had been constantly at sea and therefore unable to attend a Mass. "You can imagine how glad they were to get to Confession and receive Holy Communion."

Heintskill filtered among the crew to make himself more visible, and every sailor knew that the chaplain's office remained open for private consultations, day and night. Far from home and loved ones, sailors brought their problems to the one person they thought could help while maintaining confidentiality. Homesickness, girlfriends, fear of approaching battle, lack of shore leave, fights with shipmates, disheartening news from home—all were subjects Heintskill faced in a normal day. So hectic were his days that Heintskill could not always complete letters he started to Father Steiner because of the constant interruptions. "In the last four minutes a half dozen fellows have been in my office," he remarked to Steiner.

Mail, and the lack of it, topped the list of grievances with which Heintskill contended. Sailors who received unwelcome news from home, such as a girlfriend breaking off a relationship or a family illness, sought out Heintskill to unburden their souls. "This time we have been without mail for a good long while," he wrote to Steiner in late 1944. "Each day you could see the faces of the crew grow longer and longer."[18]

Men entered and exited Heintskill's office like a carousel, making the priest one of the most knowledgeable men aboard ship. He heard every rumor and listened to all the complaints. Officers sought him out when they could not determine how to handle a recalcitrant sailor, and sailors stormed into his quarters to vent their wrath about overbearing officers. More than anyone, Heintskill monitored the crew's pulse and could, without offering specifics or breaking confidentiality, provide insights at the skipper's request.

Heintskill's experience as a chaplain at sea often mirrored that of Fathers Barry and Sampson on land, but he also carried responsibilities unique to the navy. As the entertainment officer for the crew, Heintskill arranged for movies, sporting contests—boxing matches were especially popular—musical performances, and sightseeing jaunts when in port. He managed the ship's library and offered educational lectures, and he made it a point to teach educationally deficient sailors how to read and write.

Once they reached the western Pacific and the escort carrier's flight operations took up all available space, Heintskill and the crew turned to other forms of entertainment. He once joined sailors who had bunched at the carrier's fantail, the rear portion of the vessel, to watch a group of men being transferred to another ship by breeches buoy, a life preserver, fitted with a sling similar to a pair of short pants, that carried men from ship to ship via a rope and pulley system. As each man strapped into the buoy, sailors laughed and placed wagers on whether the man would reach his destination wet or dry. Most hoped that "the lines would suddenly slacken and give the rider a dunking," wrote Heintskill. "No such luck, but everyone was satisfied because there were a couple of near-dunkings. You can see there's not an awful lot to keep the boys amused."[19]

As the *Tulagi* steamed farther west and closer to the Japanese, the lighthearted mood turned somber. With the military now well supplied with goods from home-front factories and shipyards, Heintskill and his shipmates faced nearly constant action. "Our job now isn't one of trying to evade the Jap—now we go out where we think we will find him, and keep on hunting for him," he wrote to Father Steiner. "It's dead-serious work and all the men realize it. But there is little tension among either officers or men."

Whenever general quarters sounded each man to his battle station, Heintskill rushed to his post in the sick bay, where his task was to calm the wounded and tend to the dying. He had the skipper's approval to move about the carrier, should the situation demand it, but he primarily worked with the ship's doctor. "Last week half of each of our days was spent at our battle stations," he wrote in April 1944. The doctor assembled a first aid kit for Heintskill so that, should the ship sustain battle damage, he could go topside and treat the wounded. Along with the kit, the physician gave Heintskill a speedy tutorial in how to use its contents and how to administer morphine for pain. "The first aid kit is a swell excuse to move about at will—and since we are short-handed as far as corpsmen go the doc is very glad to have an extra kit in use."

Although Heintskill sporadically visited Hawaii and other gorgeous locations, he rarely set foot on the Pacific isles of lore, featuring blue lagoons, sumptuous beaches, and palm trees. Instead he saw places the navy had already bombarded from an offshore perch or the dour anchorages used by the U.S. fleet for fueling and resupply, locales the priest described as clumps of coral rock sparsely dotted with palm trees and so small he could walk around them "in a half hour." Some were so flat that he could stand in the water on one side and look across the isle to see the water on the other side. "It's almost unbelievable to think of the value these little hunks of land have acquired," he wrote, and yet he recognized the deep significance of every island. "No man would give a shovelful of Indiana dirt for a dozen of them—and yet to get them it was worth the lives of many men."

He was, however, impressed with the emerging power of the navy. He labored in the midst of war, where death or injury were daily possibilities, but felt secure in being part of the floating armadas that plied the Pacific. "Out this way there have been times when looking out toward the horizon you'd see what seemed to be the skyline of San Francisco harbor," he wrote in December 1944. "But it was not skyscrapers we were looking at but the masts and superstructures of ships. Looking at something like that makes you realize that no matter how fantastic news stories of our superiority and success may seem, they are true."[20]

"Bloody Business in a Concentrated Dose"
Dupuis and Others

As Heintskill's *Tulagi* operated at sea, other Notre Dame chaplains in the Pacific served with units that converged on the Japanese by land. Ordained in 1937, thirty-five-year-old Father Francis D. Bridenstine, C. S. C., traveled with the army's Seventh Division. The unit had participated in so many major Pacific operations that Bridenstine found it difficult to keep Steiner informed. "This outfit to which I belong has been moving right along. As soon as we finish one operation we start preparing for another. Between operations I have all I can do to prepare the men, new and old, for what is to follow."

He accompanied the Seventh Division during its operations in the frigid Aleutians, where Father Kmiecik was posted, during the speedy assault at sultry Kwajalein in the Central Pacific, and again in the November 1944 landings in the Philippines, where General MacArthur took his first step toward making good his pledge to return and liberate the Filipinos from Japanese rule. "They have all been interesting but tough operations,"[21] he wrote to Father Steiner.

They would become deadlier as American forces dislodged the Japanese in the Philippines, where Fathers Carberry and Duffy, and the six Notre Dame missionaries, were incarcerated. The Japanese were not about to easily yield control in those islands, whose resources were sorely needed to fuel ships and supply armies. The fighting would again intensify for Bridenstine and every American soldier or sailor as combat swerved north toward Japan. They would first have to eliminate the enemy from a succession of island fortresses before forcing the Japanese to surrender with a massive invasion of the Japanese Home Islands, a terrifying assault that every military strategist predicted would be a bloodbath.

IN JUNE 1944 Father Dupuis rejoined his marines as they engaged in savage combat on Saipan in the Mariana Islands. The Japanese defended every yard and hill, forcing the marines and their army comrades to wrest enemy soldiers out of trenches and hillside caves with mortars, flame-throwing tanks, machine guns, and bayonets. Each time Dupuis celebrated Mass on Saipan at a makeshift altar, he became a tempting target for Japanese snipers. Swarms of flies from decomposing Japanese bodies forced him to cover his chalice and quickly elevate the host.

"The first five days were really busy," he wrote to Father Steiner of his work at an evacuation center in the days following the June landings. "Wounded and more wounded. This bloody business [is] in a concentrated dose, and frankly that concentrated stuff starts to get you down. A relief when our station began to receive a mere dribble of wounded."

Dupuis ate rations from tin cans and forgot what it was like to take a shower or wear a clean uniform. He celebrated with the marines as American antiaircraft fire brought down enemy bombers. "One night I saw our AA knock down two of those Japs out of the sky. It is a sight I will not forget for a long while. You could hear the cheers go up all over the island from the front lines down to the beach. But they came again."

During lulls, Dupuis consoled the wounded, took charge of the personal effects of the dead, and sat on a crate of ammunition beside a palm tree to hear the confessions of a long line of marines. "Things are quiet of a sort on Saipan. Boys are resting up for what is to come." He told Steiner that he bunked in a place already familiar to the home front for its savagery. "In following the war on Saipan you probably read of bloody hill 500 with its many caves." In that two-day action, his Fourth Division marines seized a strategic position from the Japanese by charging uphill into thick fire and engaging in hand-to-hand combat. He said that his bunk was then in one of those caves facing the ocean on the east side of the island. "Beautiful view from here. A few weeks ago it was hell."[22]

After completing the Saipan operation, Father Dupuis enjoyed a breather at one of the back areas that served as a training ground for future assaults and as rest and recreation for the troops. He enjoyed hot showers and decent food and recharged his batteries. During a troop singalong, which included the tune "When Irish Eyes Are Smiling," Dupuis wrote to Father Steiner that "all I could think of was the band marching on the field between the halves of the football games." After reading a *South Bend Tribune* article heralding Father Barry's achievements in Europe, he commented to Steiner that their Holy Cross associate was "A little man with a big heart."[23]

WHILE FATHER Dupuis served with the men at the front lines, in the Pacific other chaplains from Notre Dame ministered to troops stationed behind the active combat zone. Most preferred to be at the front, but soldiers and sailors posted to airfields and naval supply ports, hundreds if not thousands of miles from the fighting, required chaplains.

When Father Joseph Corcoran, a chaplain with the army's Thirty-Second Infantry Regiment, accompanied the soldiers to a small Hawaiian island for training after they finished combat at Attu in the Aleutians, he claimed he was standing on an island "which even Eleanor did not find." He referred to the widely publicized Pacific travels of the nation's first lady, Eleanor Roosevelt, who visited troops stationed at locales ranging from Hawaii to Guadalcanal. He said Masses for the troops in training camps and recuperating in hospitals, ran into Father Bridenstine, and reveled whenever he could enjoy a sip of cool water. "And I am not kidding when I say that that tasted better than a regular Christmas dinner back in the states."

Corcoran briefly served as the post chaplain in Hawaii, which he described as "quite a change after having been so long in the field." He told Father Steiner that he felt more like a parish priest, celebrating three Masses on Sunday, a morning weekday Mass, a Wednesday night Novena, and a Saturday Rosary and benediction followed by two hours of Confession.

Other than the sultry Pacific weather, Corcoran felt like he was back at campus because he met so many military who had graduated from Notre Dame. He attended a meeting of the Notre Dame Club, which gathered once a month to exchange news and swap tales of campus, mostly revolving around the football team. "Those meetings are a great help to all of us and enjoyed very much," he explained.

As much as he enjoyed his time behind the front lines, Father Corcoran longed to return to combat, where soldiers in mortal peril needed him more than did the troops on breaks. Besides, he noted, the Hawaiian sojourn had added a few excess pounds to his frame: "It might be a good thing [to return to combat]. If I stay here much longer I'll settle down and grow fat like a permanent Pastor."[24]

"The 'Jeep Ridin Padre'"

Four thousand miles southwest of Hawaii, in New Caledonia off Australia's northeast coast, Father Thomas Hewitt attended another Notre Dame gathering. Assigned as chaplain on the island, Hewitt celebrated Mass, had supper, and shared news from home with the SOPAC (South Pacific) Notre Dame Club. "The evening was complete with song and story of Notre Dame," he wrote to Steiner.

Like every chaplain, Hewitt explained, he "must be everything from a Master of Ceremonies to a good ball player." He traveled so often about the island, used as both training and rest facilities for troops and headquarters for senior navy commanders, that the troops nicknamed him the "Jeep Ridin Padre." Each day he heard confessions and celebrated Mass for a different unit. When holding services for Protestants, Hewitt asked them to select their songs, and he chose as subjects for his sermons only those areas in which Protestants and Catholics agreed. When conducting services for Jewish troops, he focused entirely on Old Testament themes.

Hewitt credited his Holy Cross training, especially his involvement in conducting religious retreats about the nation, with helping him convey meaningful messages to the soldiers, including one service attended by two thousand men. He asked Father Steiner to urge everyone on campus to keep him and his soldiers in their prayers, which Hewitt contended meant a great deal. "You know the cost out here. Nothing grips these fellows so dramatically as the simple statement that all of you are down on your knees for them when they are trying to stand on their feet."

Later in the war Father Hewitt moved to the thick jungle terrain of Dutch New Guinea, north of Australia. While his location remained behind the front lines, he related to Steiner that "the jungle is a mass of twisted, tapering tentacles of vines which seem to form a barrier around this prison of parrots, strange beaked birds who inhabit this natural zoo." He added that the jungle "is alive with alarming noises at night. The eeriest squeals, animal calls and sudden noises rise in a symphony that can raise goose pimples on a healthy body."

Two of nature's smallest creatures posed Hewitt's largest dilemma. He described New Guinea as "a land of crawling, slippery, slimy, slender spidery insects. The fearsome black widow seems to thrive in the dampness." He mentioned that ants swarmed everywhere: "They crawl into ones[*sic*] clothes. At night the regions of ones bed does not possess immunity."[25]

THIRTY-THREE YEARS old when the war started, navy chaplain Father Patrick Duffy, ironically, rarely boarded a ship. He instead worked with naval units stationed in the bases and repair facilities at Nouméa, New Caledonia, where Father Hewitt was posted for a time, and two thousand miles further northwest at Emirau, an island one degree below the equator, north of New Guinea.

He arrived in Nouméa in late 1943 to serve with a construction battalion unit, a force comprised largely of civil engineers who worked with the heavy equipment required to build airfields and other military installations. He also ministered to Catholics in units that loaded and unloaded ships, men in the ammunition depot who "pass the ammunition on to Bougainville and to other points in the direction of Tokyo," the military police who guarded the ammunition, and the receiving station that processed sailors newly arrived from the United States or from ships that had been sunk.

"These construction guys are great guys and have done marvelous, almost miraculous jobs in this war. Their work (and mine with them now) is not spectacular, there is little bang-bang and cowboy-and-Indian stuff about it." Father Duffy claimed that "these CBs will run a bulldozer behind Jap lines, build roads, and have been known to throw up the blade as a protection and bulldoze the machine gun net [sic]. They are older than the average man in service and most have been in the building game—electricians, plumbers, carpenters, welders."

A tepid reception at first disappointed him, but he later learned that the men were only waiting to see if he resembled the chaplain he replaced, a dour, arrogant Protestant minister whose sermons focused on sin and damnation. Larger crowds began attending his services when they assessed Duffy as down to earth, including sailors who repeatedly appeared at Duffy's 5:30 a.m. Mass. "Pretty strong faith, don't you think?" he asked Father Steiner. Duffy lived in a Quonset hut but enjoyed the small chapel constructed by the men. Behind the altar hung a navy flag in blue and gold, but to Duffy it represented the university's similar colors. "Have to ring in N.D. somehow."

Duffy shifted to jungle terrain in the spring of 1944 when he accompanied the marines on a mission to dislodge Japanese soldiers remaining on Emirau. "I am sitting in my tent in the jungle, noises quite alienated from the twin lakes in my ears—if you know what I mean [the two small lakes on Notre Dame's northwest side]—and all to the accompaniment of a mournful, pitiless rain." As he now worked in an advanced unit, he informed Steiner, "Can't say any more 'less the chattering buck-teeth of the little yellow fellows start chattering." He asked Steiner to excuse the poor handwriting, but "I am writing on a desk that is my knee. It is pouring rain in the jungles of the S. Pacific." He asked Steiner for his prayers and remarked that one thought kept him going through the travails: "my dream objective is the sanctuary of old Notre Dame!"

At a small island near Emirau, each Wednesday Duffy conducted a Novena and benediction. Fridays, after the base movie had ended, he held the Stations of the Cross in the tiny chapel. Although the Japanese occupied Rabaul and Kavieng not far away, American air and carrier raids had neutralized them by this time and they posed little threat. "We have Japs on three sides of us but the poor saps can't do anything about it—just 'take it.'"

One of his principal duties as chaplain at a naval base was to contact each ship that steamed into the harbor, especially those that would soon be leaving for combat, to inquire whether they had any religious needs. "For many it is their last chance before the battle," he explained, and he went to great pains to accommodate those men. "All this and the equator too add up to a life a bit different from stateside."

However, it was not so different that Notre Dame was far from his mind. He commiserated when on November 4, 1944, the navy squad handily defeated his Irish, 32–13, mainly because at navy-dominated Emirau no one let him forget it. "There was little respite for me Monday when the Navy-ND score came in. So I made believe I had never heard of N.D. and insisted that I was a Navy officer! But then they wanted to know why I never dragged the Navy into my sermons as I do N.D."[26] Father Duffy endured considerable teasing, but soldiers and sailors at war do not tease men they do not respect.

Their high regard for Duffy also appeared in the letter Ensign Charles Varnak mailed to Father Steiner. The junior officer was so impressed with Father Duffy that he collected $750 from his companions at the torpedo boat base as a donation to the Holy Cross's Bengal Missions in India, frequently mentioned by Father Duffy. He enclosed the money order in a letter with effusive praise for Father Duffy. "I'm quite positive that nearly all the boys, after returning to civilian life, will long remember the work our Catholic priests are doing in this war and will never forget those who remain out here to carry on their mission work," Varnak wrote to Steiner. "We also feel very grateful for having such a fine chaplain in Father Duffy. He really is doing a marvelous job here. He travels from one part of the island to another where he either has Mass or other Devotions throughout the week. The fellows are supplied with good reading material and small store articles through his efforts. And he is as Catholic and Irish as his name."[27]

"Someday They Would Come to Help"
Events in Los Baños

While Father Duffy and other Pacific chaplains lent support to their units, the Notre Dame missionaries in Los Baños attributed their survival to two factors: their faith and the community spirit that came from being confined together. "As we look back over those days," Sister Caecilius wrote to her grandmother, "we wonder how we ever survived them but we realize that if God had not given us the grace we could never have lived through them."[28] Brother Rex claimed that his strong faith in God helped him endure the endless days of deprivation and abuse, while all stated that the religious groups and the civilians developed a unity from sharing the same hardships.

Catholics in camp attended daily Mass in the barracks chapel, which the missionaries called St. Joseph's Cathedral. The priests rationed the meager wine supply allowed into camp by using an eyedropper to put fifteen drops of wine into each chalice. Nuns plucked bugs from flour before making Communion hosts, which the priests then broke into smaller pieces to distribute to communicants. Daily benediction in the late afternoon, followed by recitation of the Rosary and Litany of the Saints, maintained a semblance of normalcy for religious so abruptly wrenched from routine. "It wasn't like home," wrote Brother Rex, "but one of the greatest consolations in the camp was the chapel where we could go and talk things over when the going got tough."[29]

Spirits rose in September 1944 when erroneous rumors that Germany had capitulated raced through camp. Two weeks later Sister Olivette wrote in her diary that "Gen. MacArthur is close to Philippines,"[30] and in late September aerial bombings of Japanese facilities in the area began, a moment they had awaited since those bleak days of December 1941.

The internees had become accustomed to the Japanese fighter aircraft that conducted training flights in the skies above Manila, but when they followed a group of planes attacking on September 21, some spotted white stars on the wings of the planes, indicating that the aircraft were American. Father McKee watched planes fill the sky and drop bombs near Manila. Nurses rushed to the hospital balcony to obtain a better view as American Hellcat fighters dueled with Japanese

Zeroes amid antiaircraft shell bursts. "All of us were laughing, crying, and dancing around in juvenile giddiness," wrote nurse Dorothy Danner of the electric moment. "Wave after wave of American planes seen on their way to & from Manila," recorded Sister Olivette of the spectacle. "We could hear the bombing even at this distance 35 miles away."[31]

Lacking airfields in the Philippines, the short-range American fighters could only have lifted off from aircraft carriers off the coast. The planes' appearance indicated that their day of liberation was at hand. "60 beautiful American planes flew over our way with a gorgeous blue sky & perfect white cloud banks for a background," she wrote the next month. "No opposition from enemy planes. Many more flew to the S.east [*sic*] in the distance."[32]

They witnessed the preparatory attacks for MacArthur's October 20 amphibious assault of Leyte, an island almost four hundred miles southeast of Manila. The general had assembled land and sea forces that, after securing a beachhead on Leyte, would sweep northward up the Philippines and chase the Japanese out of the islands. The campaign promised to be long and difficult, as the Japanese would adopt every measure to retain the Philippines and their vast natural resources, but at least American soldiers would be operating on the same ground as the prisoners. It would be only a matter of time until they reached Los Baños and other camps, including Cabanatuan with Father Carberry and Bilibid with Father Duffy, and freed the captives.

American fighters and bombers sliced through the skies in the following days, sometimes roaring close to Los Baños. The priests and nuns held up empty plates and waved at the planes to let the aviators know they were American, and their airborne countrymen dipped their wings in recognition of the message. "Someday they would come to help, for sure,"[33] thought Father McKee.

The elation dampened when the Japanese, irate over the bombings, adopted harsher measures against the prisoners. They erected a double row of barbed wire about the camp and slashed an already inadequate diet to almost nothing. Within days "the regime of starving started," wrote Sisters Olivette and Caecilius. "We were eventually reduced to a handful of rice a day."[34]

They heard through friendly Filipinos of MacArthur's October 20 landing, causing Sister Olivette that day to underline the welcome news in her diary. Three days later she added, "General MacArthur broadcast to Filipinos to stay off main highways & away from coastal cities!"[35] She, along with the other internees, rejoiced over the following weeks as news filtered in of an impressive U.S. naval victory at Leyte Gulf and northward progress by MacArthur's infantry. Hopefully, the day of liberation for which everyone had prayed would soon arrive.

It had to, for the alternative was something no one wanted to ponder. Many of the weaker internees, especially among the young and the old, were perilously close to death. Beriberi and dysentery swept through every barracks, felling as many as 80 percent at Los Baños and claiming a death a day. Sisters Olivette and Caecilius, lacking medicine, could do little more than wipe foreheads and whisper encouragement. Brother Rex noticed that by the first week of 1945, "the processions each evening to the cemetery became regular occasions."[36]

They pushed to the back of their minds the unspoken thought that they were pawns in a deadly military race. Could they hold on until American forces rescued them, or would they perish before that day of delivery? Each day their rescue was delayed could mean the difference between living and dying.

As THOSE rescue forces converged on the Philippines to begin the campaign to free the Filipinos from almost three years of Japanese rule, Fathers Corcoran and Bridenstine accompanied their units, both working with regiments of the Seventh Infantry Division, for the October landings. "This last one was the worst of the lot," Bridenstine explained to Father Steiner about the assault at Leyte Island in the Philippines. "I spent a little better than a week up front and during that time I believe I gave out better than three thousand Communions. I also managed to say several Masses for the troops while we were still under fire. They were the first Masses they had heard on this operation. For some unknown reason I am to receive the Bronze Star for meritorious service. Personally, I think they are making a mistake." (Father Corcoran would also receive a Bronze Star for his work with the troops.) Bridenstine then mentioned that two Notre Dame graduates had been killed in the fighting: "They were both fine men and carried Notre Dame's spirit with them."[37]

U.S. naval forces registered a decisive victory over the Japanese in the October 1944 Battle of Leyte Gulf, after which MacArthur's land units started moving up the Philippine Islands toward Manila and the prison camps holding Father Duffy, Father Carberry, and the six Notre Dame missionaries. Should the march continue unabated, American forces would be at the gates of Los Baños, Cabanatuan, and Bilibid within a few months.

"The Providence of God Gave Us Consolation When We Most Needed It"
Christmas 1944

Christmas 1944 brought bittersweet emotions for the Notre Dame chaplains serving in the Pacific. The deep religious significance of the season inspired them, but they could not help but notice the contrasts in celebrating the birth of the Prince of Peace in the midst of daily killing and maiming. This season contradicted their experience of Christmases past.

"It does not seem at all like Christmas out here both because of the warm weather and the war atmosphere," Father Boland commiserated with Father Steiner from his perch aboard the troop transport *Highlands*. Father Dupuis, fresh from the battlefield, was thankful to be celebrating Christmas at a back base, not for himself "but for the kids themselves. It is going to be hard for them away from home and out of the States. I rather think there will be many a homesick Marine this coming Christmas." He told Father Steiner that he would be preaching to 1,500 marines at a Midnight Mass held in an outdoor theater.

In New Caledonia, Father Hewitt began hearing confessions ninety minutes before Midnight Mass was to commence in a large park, but due to the overwhelming numbers he continued until Communion time arrived. He then helped distribute "hundreds upon hundreds of Holy Communion."

In the vast anchorage at Ulithi in the Caroline Islands, 1,500 miles southeast of the Philippines, Father Heintskill experienced a much quieter Christmas Eve. After hearing confessions for three hours, he walked the deck of the escort carrier *Tulagi*, alone with his thoughts as a warm breeze gently fanned his face. He stared across the miles of water housing ships in every direction, each vessel blacked out to avoid detection by the occasional Japanese bomber that sneaked in. "I feel right now that peace which comes to every priest in knowing that to him God has given the power to reconcile the souls of weak human beings."

As he continued his tranquil stroll, a lookout extended a warm Christmas greeting. Then, in the quiet, Heintskill heard two other sailors humming "Silent Night." In a Christmas Eve letter to Father Steiner, he mentioned that the humming was "terribly off key but with feeling. You somehow feel that tonight our lookouts are not the best in the world. Somehow you feel that even though they're looking up toward the sky their eyes are staring off into the blackness back toward their homes."

Like the attention of the sailors around him, his thoughts wafted homeward. "Somehow up here in the night it seems so very much like home. There's no snow—but the night is the same—the stars are the same that the folks back home can see."

Not forgetting the Holy Cross brethren trapped in prison camps, Heintskill informed Steiner, "Before long I hope to send you word personally from Father Gerry Lawyer and Bob McKee. That is, if they're on hand to welcome us."[38]

IN LOS BAÑOS, Sister Olivette recorded in her diary on December 13 that three rumors had rejuvenated everyone's spirits: that Red Cross food parcels had arrived, that Red Cross personnel would soon distribute them to the internees, and that three thousand packages from home were about to be handed out. "Buoyed our hopes up," she wrote, "but all proved false." Eight days later—a day she described as "Truly 'the darkest day'"[39]—the Japanese commandant announced that no relief supplies would be distributed to the internees.

As Christmas 1944 drew nearer, Danner noticed that people in Los Baños, about to spend their third Christmas as prisoners of the Japanese, severed from family, friends, and American military forces, became more depressed than usual. On Christmas Eve afternoon the Jesuit seminarians staged a special holiday program of songs and skits that helped cut through the melancholy. Most of the camp joined the religious in crooning both lighthearted tunes that produced laughter and sentimental favorites that led to tears. Not surprisingly, a song about food, set to the tune of Bing Crosby's popular "White Christmas," became an instant hit:

I'm dreaming of a fudge sundae
that's in a store in Baltimore!
Where the fountain glistens
and Daddy listens
when children say, "I'll have some more."

I'm dreaming of a ham sandwich
with every mongo bean I bite,
and when I'm not sleeping at night,
I pretend I'm choosing rye or white!

Another, sung to the tune of "She'll Be Coming 'Round the Mountain," also mentioned food, but added lyrics that expressed their greatest Christmas wish.

They'll be bringin' Christmas candy when they come.
They'll be bringin' Christmas candy when they come.
They'll be bringin' Christmas candy
and the chocolates will be dandy.
Oh, the chocolates will be dandy when they come.

And we will be free forever when they come.
Oh we will be free forever when they come.
And in spite of all our labors,
we'll be glad that we were neighbors.
We'll be glad that we've been neighbors when they come.[40]

Even more powerful was the Midnight Mass held in the barracks chapel, which almost as many non-Catholics as Catholics attended. "In its simplicity, the altar was beautiful in the candlelight," Danner wrote. The Nativity scene featured the Holy Family and shepherds sculpted from sand by one of the Holy Cross brothers, and while the priests concelebrated the Mass, the nuns led the multifaith congregation in Christmas carols and Mass songs. "So the Providence of God gave us consolation when we most needed it,"[41] wrote Sister Olivette.

That Midnight Mass of 1944 cast an indelible impression on Brother Rex. His family was thousands of miles away, Notre Dame stood in a different hemisphere, and he lacked the simplest necessities, but he was overjoyed by what he termed the happiest Christmas Day of his life. "Sitting quietly before the Blessed Sacrament with the whole of my possessions on me—a pair of shorts and a pair of wooden sandals—I fully realized I had all that I needed."[42]

Danner choked back tears as the Mass continued. She had witnessed horrors in her time at Los Baños, but the brutality of prison life now paled next to the simple beauty of a priest chanting Latin prayers to honor the birth of an infant who had started life in similar substandard surroundings. "This celebration of the birth of Christ," she recalled, "would turn out to be the most meaningful I would ever know."[43]

"That First Night in the Hold . . . Was Madness"
Duffy and Carberry to Transports

Fathers Carberry and Duffy could not say the same, as their situations had altered for the worse. Two weeks after Father Sampson parachuted into Normandy, a large group of prisoners arrived in Bilibid, "looking like the wrath of Mars"[44] according to Father Duffy. One of those ragged captives was Father Carberry, part of the contingent being transferred from Davao in Mindanao.

With the American military conducting its steady and decisive march across the Pacific, the Japanese began rushing prisoners out of the islands to prevent the loss of this valuable source of free labor for their war machine. If the situation deteriorated further, they also planned to use those prisoners as bargaining chips to obtain more amenable terms in a peace treaty. Their primary concern, though, was that if the United States successfully invaded the Philippines and freed the prisoners, the captives would form a damning pool of witnesses able to testify to the horrid treatment administered in the camps.[45]

The thought of moving more than one thousand miles to the north, farther from American forces, alarmed the prisoners. In distant Japan they would face additional months, possibly years, of incarceration. Many doubted that they possessed the strength to endure the extra tribulation. Help was on the way in the Pacific, but would Father Duffy, Father Carberry, and the six missionaries confined in the Philippines survive until friendly forces reached them?

"The drafts are leaving here as fast as the Japanese can put them together,"[46] wrote Lieutenant Commander Hayes in Bilibid. Additional groups left in the fall, especially after MacArthur's troops landed on Leyte in October.

"Japs in utter confusion,"[47] Father Duffy wrote at the appearance of the first American air attack in their vicinity. His hopes of remaining in the Philippines ended when the Japanese ordered the senior U.S. officer in camp to prepare two groups for shipment out of the country.

On the morning of December 13, the Japanese assembled the dispirited internees, including Fathers Duffy and Carberry, for the walk from Bilibid to the docks, where the prisoners would board a transport for the journey to Japan. Father Duffy handed his precious American flag, which had helped him endure beatings, starvation, and every other rigor of prison camp since 1942, to a chaplain who was being left behind, with instructions to send the flag to his niece in Ohio should that man survive the war. As a chaplain, Father Duffy was permitted to keep his Mass kit, which still concealed Ben Steele's drawings of camp life.

Once the 1,619 prisoners gathered, Lieutenant Junsaburo Toshino and his interpreter, Shusuke Wada, a pair that had gained notoriety for cruelty, led the prisoners out of Bilibid. With guards posted on either side, the Americans shuffled along dusty roads and through Manila streets. Filipinos, many in tears, lined the route, offering silent support for the Americans and surreptitiously flashing the V for victory. Duffy's first sight of the devastation in the city, once a jewel of the Philippines but now reduced to rubble, stunned the priest, and as he neared the docks he saw the masts of sunken ships protruding from the waters of Manila Bay.

There the transport *Oryoku Maru*—a prewar passenger vessel fresh from delivering a shipment of horses to the Philippines—waited at anchor for its next cargo. While 2,000 Japanese women and children filtered into relatively decent quarters on deck, the prisoners descended into the darkness of one of three manure-littered holds below. Duffy entered Hold No. 2 amidships along with Lieutenant Commander Hayes, other chaplains, and 250 men.

The ship left Manila Bay in late afternoon and headed northward along the Luzon coast. The men confined in the three holds cried for air to ease the odor of manure, sweat, and urine. "You are disturbing the Japanese women and children," Wada shouted into the holds. "If you do not shut up I will order the guards to shoot into the hold!"[48] When some of the men continued to wail in the intolerable heat, Wada slammed the hatch shut.

At twilight the guards lowered slop buckets and food containers to the famished men below, but in the darkness many prisoners could not distinguish between the two pails. Screams intensified as men lost their composure, frightening others in the suffocating hold.

Prisoners labeled the transports that moved prisoners from the Philippines to Japan "Hell Ships" because of the unspeakable conditions. "That first night in the hold of the *Oryoku Maru* in Manila Harbor there was madness,"[49] said one of the prisoners. During that traumatic time, men gasped for air in temperatures that soared past one hundred and ten degrees. Men fought for scraps of food. To allay their thirst, some scratched themselves or the man next to them to drink blood, or licked condensation from the sides of the hold. While Duffy's hold enjoyed greater discipline under Hayes's firm guidance, the other two holds dissolved into chaos. By morning, fifty men had perished below decks of the *Oryoku Maru*.

On the morning of December 14, planes from the aircraft carriers U.S.S. *Hornet* and U.S.S. *Hancock* attacked the ship, now in Subic Bay fifty miles northwest of Manila. The aviators, unaware of the contents of the vessel, swooped down on the *Oryoku Maru* and other ships, spraying the prisoner transport with bomb shrapnel and bullets that killed Japanese civilians on deck and punctured Duffy's hold so near the priest that a piece of shrapnel "caved in my hat but did not even scratch my head."[50]

American aircraft from the *Hornet* returned the next morning and landed seven hits on the *Oryoku Maru*, killing two hundred prisoners. When the ship subsequently ran aground in Subic Bay one mile from shore, the Japanese removed all the women and children and then forced the prisoners to jump over the side and swim for shore. Father Duffy joined the throngs on deck, grateful to be free of the vile hold, but petrified that American aircraft would kill him before he hit the water. "We waved our arms," recalled Father Duffy. "They realized then that we were Americans. The planes dipped their wings and flew off. That deck was a shambles. We had to get off. I helped a chap named Cummings swim to shore."[51]

Duffy and other prisoners tossed into the water anything that could buoy those who could not swim. They then stripped to their underwear and leaped overboard. In their weakened condition, many struggled in the waters, but a gasping Duffy reached shore, where Japanese soldiers herded him and everyone else onto a tennis court surrounded by a fifteen-foot-high fence. In abandoning the ship Father Duffy lost everything he brought with him, including his altar vestments, his Mass kit, and Ben Steele's drawings.

The captives spent five days at the court, where some died from exposure or wounds suffered in the aircraft attack. Father Duffy buried six men in the bomb craters dotting the court, and one glance around convinced him that this quintet was only the beginning. One spigot provided a meager source of water for the 1,200 survivors, who had to subsist on four tablespoons of uncooked rice per day.

On Christmas Eve, while the six Notre Dame missionaries celebrated Midnight Mass in Los Baños, Father Heintskill quietly walked the decks of the escort carrier *Tulagi*, and Father Barry huddled for warmth in a snow-covered foxhole in Germany, the Japanese moved Duffy's group by truck and train from the court to a port city on Lingayen Gulf in northern Luzon. On Christmas morning, more tired and hungry than at any time since the Death March two and a half years before, Father Duffy stumbled into a trade school building, uncertain of his future. "No Mass. No clothes. Only food in three days a canteen cup of rice and camoties per man,"[52] he later wrote of Christmas Day 1944.

BACK AT the Notre Dame campus, Father Steiner and his Holy Cross brethren celebrated Christmas with Midnight Mass in the Church of the Sacred Heart, a building resplendent with religious paintings, icons, and statues. As people entered the cathedral, some passed beneath the inscription "God, Country, Notre Dame," carved onto a door's arch to honor the graduates and students killed in World War I. Father Steiner's thoughts were not merely for the young Notre Dame men who as soldiers had perished in this subsequent world war, but also for the university's chaplains and religious.

"I am afraid the people in this country have been too optimistic about the whole war," he wrote to Father Heintskill that Christmas season. "There have been some bad upsets on the European continent this last week. This alone should sober our people, and bring home to them the seriousness of it all. I am very much afraid that we have still much to see and experience in both Europe and Asia. Peace is farther away than most people think."[53]

Steiner had reason to be glum. While the nation's military continued to spiral the Japanese backwards toward Tokyo, in Europe Hitler launched a Christmas offensive that had American forces in disarray. In the midst of the attack stood Father Sampson and the 101st Airborne. For all the wrong reasons, the "Paratrooper Padre" experienced a Christmas for the ages.

CHAPTER 8

"HOPE MR. HITLER GOES UNDERGROUND BEFORE WINTER"

Chaplains in Europe to the End of 1944

Military developments set the foundation for Father Sampson's notable Christmas. He and the men of the 501st Parachute Infantry Regiment first spent three months in England, where they alternated leave time with extensive training for their next assignment.

Now that the paratroopers had been in action, Father Sampson counseled men struggling over their part in combat and how it affected them and their families. Some asked if they had committed a mortal sin in killing a human being. Others wanted to know how to temper the hatred they felt toward the enemy for killing their buddies, or how to deal with the fear that all too often suffocated them.

A few, like twenty-six-year-old Lieutenant John W. Ell, a devout Catholic from Pennsylvania, hoped to find the proper words to assuage his parents' concerns over their son's safety. In a letter home, Lieutenant Ell mentioned that in combat, "one is never out from under the shadow of the Old Reaper." He added that he had lost many of his buddies and had on more than one occasion barely escaped death, and he attributed his good fortune to "your constant prayer, Mother."

Ell, who knew and admired Father Sampson, then mentioned his worries over how, should he die, the news of his death would affect his parents. "Now then, Mother and Father, understand this, can you receive news of my death with composure? And resignation?" He said that his death would be "much harder on you than it would be on me" but hoped they would not let it become so overbearing that it kept them from living complete lives. He assured them that, having experienced combat with the 501st Parachute Infantry Regiment, he was "battlewise now, know the tricks, and exercise constant vigilance,"[1] and hoped that if he should not survive what remained of the war, they would accept the news and carry on.

"Row after Row of White Crosses"

Their time away from the battlefront ended in September. British Field Marshal Bernard Law Montgomery, who had gained fame for his exploits in North Africa against German Field Marshal Erwin Rommel, the renowned Desert Fox, promoted an elaborate offensive thrust deep into Holland to outflank German defensive lines and establish a base from which to plunge deep into Germany itself. Called Market Garden, his plan required American paratrooper units, including Sampson's, to jump into Holland on September 17, 1944, and seize a succession of bridges across key rivers and canals along a sixty-mile route from Allied positions in Belgium to the Dutch town of Arnhem. Those troops would have to hold those bridges until British armored and motorized forces dashed along the corridor thus created and relieved them. Sampson's regiment was assigned to seize and defend the southernmost bridges spanning the Aa River and Willems Canal, part of a fifteen-mile stretch of road nicknamed Hell's Highway.

The 501st again faced the difficult task of leaping into enemy-held territory, risking attack from every direction. They had successfully utilized the technique at Normandy, but would they repeat their triumph in Holland where, closer to the German border, the enemy was likely to fight with more determination?

Father Sampson prepared for his second combat jump in much the same fashion as his first. The day before his regiment left England, and again lacking time to hear everyone's confession, he gave general absolution, handed out Communion to a long line of men, and shook hands with each paratrooper as he left the hangar to board his aircraft. Many of the soldiers, after shaking Sampson's hand, knelt and asked for the chaplain's blessing.

Late in the morning of September 17, plane engines sparked to life and lumbered down runways. Two hours later they arrived over Holland, where the thick antiaircraft fire that had welcomed them in Normandy was conspicuously absent. When Sampson leaped into the daylight to begin his descent, his chute only partially opened, causing him to drop faster and with less control than normal. Sampson shouted a warning to the paratrooper below him and attempted to nudge his chute sideways, but instead landed on top of the man's chute. Lying flat for a moment, Father Sampson slipped off before the second soldier's chute also collapsed. As he plummeted toward earth, the chaplain frantically pulled at the strings, trying to entice air into his canopy before he smashed into the ground. Finally, less than one hundred feet from a violent death, his parachute ballooned with air and safely deposited the frantic priest in four feet of water in a moat surrounding Heeswijk Castle. In a grim repeat of Normandy, Sampson struggled to extricate himself from his chute before he drowned.

Sampson's paratroopers teased the chaplain on his apparent love of wet landings. A Baptist chaplain with a nearby unit joked that Sampson's twin dunkings proved his fondness for immersions and suggested that he had chosen the wrong religion.

Within three hours the paratroopers had seized the bridges across the canal and river, taking fifty prisoners in the process. However, blind luck favored the Germans as two panzer divisions, ordered to the area for rest before the attack, and two infantry divisions had been inadvertently positioned to halt the Allied drive.

Ordered to hold Hell's Highway until Allied armor advanced toward them from the south, Sampson's regiment repelled bitter German attacks around Eindhoven, Son, and Veghel. In the fighting near Eindhoven, a German tank shell cut down Lieutenant Ell, who had written the moving letter to his parents, and a mortar shell killed Colonel Johnson, the beloved no-nonsense commander who had led the regiment since training camp in the United States. As he was being taken to the aid station the mortally wounded Johnson, who had purposely crafted an image of being a hard-nosed, profanity-laden leader, sounded more like Father Sampson when he said to another officer, "Take care of my boys."[2]

To reach as many of the two thousand men spread along Hell's Highway, Father Sampson raced along the roads and paths on a captured German motorcycle. He made quite a spectacle darting here and there, ignoring the risk of capture or death to bring God to his men.

Humor sometimes blossomed from the danger. When a Dutch priest asked Father Sampson how many Masses he celebrated each day, he replied, "One." The Dutch priest smiled and explained that twelve different paratroopers had approached him with the same story—that their chaplain, Father Sampson, had sent them to obtain wine from the Dutch priest for Mass. Both priests laughed at the ingenuity of the soldiers' ruse.

Sampson became the butt of additional laughter the week following the November 11, 1944, football contest pitting his Irish against the vaunted Army squad. Army, who boasted some of the top collegiate talent, steamrolled their opponents on their way to an undefeated season that ended with a national championship. When Army handed the then 5–1 Irish their worst defeat of the year with a 59–0 shutout, the paratroopers missed no opportunity to tease their chaplain.

Unfortunately for the Allied side, Montgomery's ambitious plan collapsed. When some of the units involved failed to seize their objectives, and with additional German divisions pouring into the area, the American–British line crumbled, forcing Eisenhower to order a withdrawal. He would have to find another route into Germany.

Before the regiment departed Holland, Father Sampson conducted a memorial ceremony at the cemetery for the men who died during the operation. After reciting a few prayers, he gazed out at the white crosses and Stars of David that encompassed him and saw before him the bloody price his men had paid. "It is really shocking," Sampson wrote, "when you look upon row after row of white crosses, each one representing a young man you knew so well, so full of life before, so anxious to get home to his loved ones and they so anxious to see him again, and now . . . they lie here in Holland."[3] One cross marked Lieutenant Ell's final resting spot.

Father Sampson would see more deaths before the war ended. He was about to experience December combat in Belgium, where a place called Bastogne garnered world headlines.

"I'm Sorry I Got You into This Mess"

While the paratroopers recuperated from the ordeal in Holland and prepared for their next assignment, Sampson caught up on paperwork. Topping his list was the hardest item: writing letters to the families of the soldiers who had died in Holland. What words of condolence could he offer to help salve the anguish of mothers and fathers mourning the loss of their son? Still, as he tried to accompany his soldiers in the hour of their direst need, he now also attempted to convey, if only by long distance, his support for their parents in their worst hour.

In addition to the letters, Mass, and other religious duties, Sampson welcomed the new paratroopers sent in to replace the many who had died or been severely wounded in Holland. Most of the current men had lost buddies in the fighting and would keep their distance until those arrivals earned their trust under fire, but Sampson kept tabs on the new paratroopers to make their transition easier.

One of those newcomers was Leon A. Jedziniak, a twenty-one-year-old medic from Connecticut. With the other new arrivals, he listened as Lieutenant Colonel Julian J. Ewell, Colonel Johnson's replacement, ran through a list of procedures. When Ewell introduced Father Sampson, he had a little fun with the priest's parachute landings. "In Alabama he lit in the Chattahoochee [River]; in England he lit in a lake; in Normandy he lit in a creek; in Holland he lit in the canal." Then, as smiles broadened and a few laughed, Ewell ended, "And I guess, if he ever jumps in the Sahara Desert, he will land in a puddle left by some cockeyed camel."[4]

Hopefully there would be no need for further paratroop drops. News of a July 20 assassination attempt on Adolf Hitler, combined with the steady advances through France, led some to think the war could be over by Christmas. Others, who believed the skilled German armed forces would not easily yield ground, scoffed at such optimism. "Hope Mr. Hitler goes underground before winter," wrote Sampson's Normandy compatriot Father Gerald Fitzgerald to Father Steiner in October, "but I have my fingers crossed on that. Give the devil his due—they are fighting courageously are they not?"[5]

The rumbles of war called Sampson back to the front all too soon. He had just dropped onto his cot after writing a few more letters to parents when, at 2:00 a.m. on December 16, the assistant adjutant, Lieutenant Lawrence Critchell, awakened him with the news that a massive German offensive was, as another chaplain put it, "chopping great holes"[6] in American lines strung through the Ardennes Forest in Belgium. The paratroopers had been ordered to rush to the strategic town of Bastogne and buttress the faltering lines. Should Bastogne fall, the German offensive could succeed and shatter hopes of an Allied victory any time soon.

Newcomers like Jedziniak had no time to adjust to the battlefield. An officer shouted to the scared and inexperienced medic, "Saddle up, we've got to go to Bastogne."[7] The unit moved out with such haste that Father Sampson again lacked the time to hear individual confessions. He celebrated a fast Mass and then visited each company as it was gathering to pull out to assemble the Catholics, give general absolution, and distribute Communion. Sampson also checked on Jedziniak and the other new arrivals who were about to head into combat for the first time.

The paratroopers loaded into trucks for the overnight dash to Bastogne. As supplies for their next assignment had not yet reached the division, the paratroopers lacked winter uniforms and sufficient ammunition and food. "Some guys went [into combat] with just a bayonet or a trench knife," recalled Jedziniak. "That was it."

They arrived during the night of December 18 to 19 and dug in around Bastogne, only to be informed that they were all but surrounded by the advancing German military. Atrocious weather conditions, with heavy snow and frigid temperatures, hampered operations. "You dug a foxhole, got in it, and in the morning woke up with two feet of snow on top of you," said Jedziniak. The troops had "no galoshes, no gloves, no jackets, no nothing. Your boots are all wet, frozen. If you want to walk, you bang that boot against a tree, get the ice off."[8]

Fighting off the worst conditions he had seen as a chaplain, Father Sampson traipsed from foxhole to foxhole, asking if he could be of comfort, religious or any other way, to the young paratroopers shivering where they squatted. He also checked in at the regimental aid station set up in the chapel of a seminary, where the first of what would become a stream of wounded had been quartered.

Under the trying circumstances, which demanded that the paratroopers halt a skilled enemy in harsh weather, Father Sampson confronted a new phenomenon. Combat fatigue, where a soldier reached the end of his endurance and was no longer able to perform in battle, soared around Bastogne. Men quaked under the frequent artillery barrages and cried out when mortar shells crashed only feet away. Father Sampson came across one paratrooper, who had often volunteered for dangerous patrols and had earlier knocked out a tank with a bazooka, lying in his foxhole, quivering and sobbing. The man had to be evacuated for his own good as well as the welfare of the men around him, who could be unnerved by the cries of a buddy who had repeatedly proven his mettle under fire. "There was nothing wrong with the boy's courage," said Sampson, "he had plenty of it, more than most men; but combat exhaustion had made him useless to the regiment."[9]

Private First Class Richard V. Bostwick had just dug in when artillery fire and bullets forced everyone to duck back. "Suddenly," said Bostwick, "I was startled when, through all of this, comes a Catholic priest, crawling on his hands and knees." Father Sampson almost landed on top of the young paratrooper as he scrambled for cover, but looked around, asked the private if he were a Catholic, and wondered if he wanted Sampson to hear his confession. "A most unusual place to hear my confession. What guts!"[10]

On another occasion a soldier informed Sampson that a wounded soldier lying in a culvert by the railroad tracks a few hundred yards away was pleading for a priest. Sampson and Jedziniak followed him to the scene to find a German tank standing between them and the wounded paratrooper. The three skirted the area and climbed a fence, but drew the attention of the tank's machine gunner, who sprayed bullets about the three. "He was firing at Father Sampson, myself and the kid," said Jedziniak, who had earlier exchanged his medic's helmet for a regulation one because the Red Cross stamped on it made him a choice target for German snipers. "The kid got hit in the arm, but Father Sampson and I dove over the bank."[11]

They leaped into a ditch along the tracks, where Sampson and Jedziniak left their wounded companion and scurried on to assist the paratrooper for whom they had come. Keeping low to the ground, they reached the man but were now pinned down by crossfire. When Jedziniak told Sampson that the soldier would not survive his wounds, the chaplain knelt beside the wounded paratrooper, heard his confession, and anointed him. They stayed low and waited until the tank departed, at which time, despite heavy German fire, they dragged the mortally stricken soldier to an aid station.

Five days before Christmas, an officer informed Sampson that the Germans had ambushed a group of paratroopers out on patrol and that their bullet-riddled bodies lay two miles to the north. Hoping that some might yet be alive, Sampson and his driver, Private Adams, drove their jeep to the area. Sampson and Adams steered to the site along a road littered with German dead, but as they reached the hill's crest, an unwelcome surprise awaited. "I drive my jeep over the hill and was immediately surrounded by Germans," said Sampson. "There were hundreds of them in this area and a large mechanized German column moving up on the road." When an armored car pointed its gun at them, Sampson said to Adams, "Stop the jeep, Adams. I'm sorry I got you into this mess."

"That's O.K., Father,"[12] replied Adams as German soldiers stepped toward the pair. Soldiers confiscated Sampson's chalice and wristwatch as souvenirs but returned them when an officer threatened to discipline them. Sampson could easily have gone without the wristwatch, but a chalice, given by family at the time of a priest's first Mass, is any cleric's most valued item.

The Germans moved their prisoners a few miles from the front lines in a captured American half-track. Separated from the regiment and friendly forces, Sampson and Adams hoped that their captors would follow the rules of war over the proper treatment of prisoners. As Sampson related in his book, they were moved east for two weeks, each day traveling farther from American units while passing long lines of German soldiers and vehicles pouring toward Bastogne. Many Catholic German soldiers pulled out pictures of their children and chatted with the priest about their families.

When they reached Luxembourg, the Germans confined Sampson and Adams with another group of captured Americans. An interrogator quizzed Sampson on what he knew about military matters but released the priest after a short session.

Sampson and the group of captives marched the remainder of the day and into the next morning, when the Germans allowed them to rest in a barn. However, when thirty hours had passed without food or water, Father Sampson, the sole officer of the group, asked for a meeting with the German officer in charge and demanded that they be given something to eat and drink. Whether it was because of Sampson's boldness or because he was a chaplain, the officer relented and brought in bread and water for the captives. He apologized that he could not arrange for more, but since they were still so close to the combat zone, he had difficulty providing for his own soldiers, let alone prisoners.

In the days leading up to Christmas, Father Sampson and some four hundred captives continued their weary march out of Belgium toward Germany. One evening he received a cold boiled potato and a small green apple before slumping to the floor of a small church for a few hours' sleep, and on Christmas Eve he marched until dark, without lunch or dinner. His jubilation when American P-40 fighter aircraft strafed German vehicles along the road to Belgium soon dissolved into fear that the action might prod angry guards to take vengeance on the prisoners.

After walking across Luxembourg, on Christmas Day Sampson's group, now comprising almost eight hundred, including high-ranking officers, entered the German town of Prüm. Guards herded them into a large auditorium, adorned with photographs of Hitler and other Nazi leaders, where they consumed a Christmas dinner of half a boiled turnip, half slice of bread, and a cup of warm water.

When the disappointed captives appeared ready to riot due to the primitive treatment, Father Sampson, convinced that any resistance from the weakened prisoners would be met with gunfire and death, suggested to the American colonel in charge that a brief Christmas service might quell the emotions. After leading the men in singing "Silent Night," Father Sampson recited a prayer and then spoke for fifteen minutes, reminding the now-hushed captives that even in the midst of their predicament, Christ was with them.

The day after Christmas offered more of the same, with the Americans marching all day on only a single piece of bread. After covering twenty miles to Gerolstein, where they joined seven hundred other captives, the men collapsed for the night in a bombed-out factory building. In the darkness American bombing killed forty prisoners resting in a different part of town, but Father Sampson's group was unharmed.

A new threat now arose from the enraged citizens of Gerolstein, who had lost family members and watched many of their structures collapse in flames. Guards escorted some of the prisoners out of the factory to help the residents battle the fires, and when these men returned they related tales of the harsh treatment by those German civilians.

The following night American fighters again attacked, killing another eleven prisoners with machine-gun fire. The next morning the prisoners received a cup of soup each, a fifth of a loaf of bread, two inches of liverwurst, and the warning that the food had to last them two days. "Gerolstein will always remain in my mind as a town of misery for both Germans and Americans," Sampson wrote in his book.

The next two days repeated their miseries, with the men plodding slowly but steadily along as guards paced alongside. Whenever American aircraft swooped low, the prisoners waved to the pilots, who dipped their wings in recognition, but no one counted on any relief this far behind front lines. They dreaded arriving in towns immediately after an American bombing run out of concern that they would suffer the residents' wrath, a point illustrated when, at one location, a civilian rushed out with a shovel and smacked Father Sampson in his buttocks.

As Sampson related in *Look Out Below!*, they next stopped at the village of Boz, where this time friendly inhabitants fed them potato soup, sandwiches, and hot ersatz coffee. When villagers learned that Sampson was a priest, they explained that their Catholic pastor had admonished them that, as Christians, they had a duty to do all they could for the prisoners. Father Sampson never forgot the oasis of kindness and compassion he experienced at Boz.

After the group passed through Koblenz, a major metropolitan center that had been heavily bombed by American and British bombers, German guards stopped them for the night at Bad Ems. The residents there refused to feed the captives or offer quarters for the night, even declaring animal stables off limits.

The next day the forlorn column continued twelve miles to Limburg, where an air raid forced the townspeople and prisoners into concrete shelters. Even though he was their captive, Sampson took compassion on the elderly men and women and the throngs of frightened children, who were victims of terror as much as he was. "The look on these poor people's faces," he wrote in his book, "was enough to soften even our own bitterness into something like sympathy and compassion. They regarded us with neither fear nor hatred; nor did it seem to occur to them to enjoy seeing us subjected to a bombing from our own planes. One of the pilots in our group told me that had he been able to really envision the misery suffered by the poor people of the towns he bombed, he would never have been able to do it. In a plane, he said, all seemed so impersonal."[13]

After walking more than 150 miles in ten days, groups of sixty prisoners stepped into boxcars built to hold forty men. For six days the captives sweated in the confining cars without food or water. They alternately stood and sat because lack of space did not allow everyone to sit at the same time. Father Sampson conducted a New Year's Day service in the boxcar, and once more he empathized with an enemy he realized endured their own tribulations. From that time on, Christmas and New Year's carried more meaning for a priest who before the war thought he fully understood every nuance of the birth of Jesus.

The train continued through Berlin and onward to the north. Six days later, famished and exhausted, the men arrived at Neubrandenburg, a city along the lake Tollensesee in northeastern Germany renowned since medieval times. From there, the weak and undernourished men, eating snow for sustenance, stumbled along the four-mile trek to their home for the indeterminate future: Stalag II-A. Like the Notre Dame religious confined in the Pacific, Father Sampson was a prisoner of the enemy.

"The Good Little Priest Has Been a Real Chaplain"

While Father Sampson disappeared into prison camp, south of Bastogne the chaplain who had seen almost continuous combat since arriving off North Africa prepared for his fourth amphibious landing. In mid-August Father Barry added the landings in southern France to Sicily, Salerno, and Anzio. The only rest for his division, according to cartoonist Bill Mauldin, "seemed to come when they were waiting for boats to carry them to other lands where the language was different but the war was the same."[14]

Barry's routine from Sicily to southern France varied little. He gathered religious items to hand out to soldiers, made certain he had his Mass kit, and visited as many soldiers as time allowed. The young men smirked when an obviously uncomfortable Father Barry delivered to every company, one by one, a talk about avoiding one of the ills of war as they wound through France. "One day the company was assembled to hear a talk by our chaplain, Father Barry. As I recall, he did all services, Catholic and Protestant and others," said Private First Class William F. Lyford of G Company. "His talk was concerning girls setting up for business in the corn field. He explained how unsanitary it was, among other things."[15]

Early in the morning of August 15, landing day in southern France, men aboard the ships awoke at 2:00 a.m. for breakfast. Afterward, many in Father Barry's vessel filtered toward the ship's hold for a scheduled 4:00 a.m. Mass. By 3:30, according to Sergeant Thomas Riordan, the large hold was packed with "GIs sitting on tanks, jeeps, trucks, boxes of ammunition and rations," eager to pray with Father Barry and receive Communion. Immediately before Mass, Father Barry asked if someone could serve as altar boy. Riordan hesitated, but when no one else volunteered he raised his hand.

"Father, I can serve, but I don't know all the Latin responses," he said to Barry.

"That's OK, soldier," the priest replied. "I'll answer the ones you can't."[16]

The landings, with British prime minister Winston Churchill observing through field glasses from a destroyer offshore, met little resistance. "At daybreak on the 15th of August, the Feast of the Assumption, we hit the southern coast of France and have been moving rapidly toward the German frontier ever since," Barry wrote in a report to the Military Ordinariate. The unit traveled northward through towns and cities nestled in breathtaking surroundings, receiving such a warm welcome as liberators that the soldiers labeled it the Champagne Campaign. Young women kissed soldiers and tossed flowers as the infantry marched through the streets, and families offered food or wine. "The scenery all through the French Alps is truly breathtaking," wrote Father Barry. "The people treat us like kings and the men really feel like liberators here. Many of the churches in these Alpine villages are eight hundred or more years old, but have weathered the years with great dignity."[17]

As the regiment pushed on, Father Barry, as he had in Italy, often took extraordinary steps for his boys. When he received a request from a soldier's mother asking if the priest could obtain a cake for her son's nineteenth birthday, Barry scrambled to fulfill her wish. "There we were up in the front lines in France, and I hadn't the slightest idea how I was going to get that cake," he explained. "But, it was the boy's first birthday away from home and I wanted to carry out that mother's request." After making inquiries among the local population, Barry finally located a woman who agreed to bake the dessert, and "we had a birthday party with a cake complete with candles."[18]

Father Steiner received another home-front letter praising Barry. Marian Ficco wrote to the Notre Dame superior that his son, Daniel A. Ficco, was missing in action in France, and he wondered if Steiner, as one of Barry's fellow Holy Cross priests, could put him in contact with the chaplain. Uncertainty over their son's safety weighed heavily on the family's minds, and could Father Barry possibly lighten the burden? Their son, Ficco explained, was a "good friend of Father. He mentioned his name in all his letters, telling us the wonderful work he was doing on the battlefront [and] that he was one of the best."[19]

Barry's compassion extended to the enemy as well. During a visit to a military cemetery, an officer told him that a prisoner detail digging graves had asked to see a priest. Barry walked over to the ragged collection, most of whom were Polish, and spent time with them as if they were part of his own regiment.

Steiner was proud of every chaplain who worked on the front lines, daily risking death to bring God to the servicemen, but he had a soft spot for Father Barry. "We are much pleased to know from one who has been there that our little Father Barry has been doing great work," Steiner wrote to Staff Sergeant Jaskovich. "We have heard from other sources that the good little priest has been a real Chaplain, and real father and companion to the fighting men."[20] Barry's work with the boys up front gained sufficient notice that in September 1944 a South Bend radio station aired a program dramatizing his actions overseas.

German opposition stiffened as the regiment moved north through France toward Germany. Thick forests in the Vosges Mountains offered choice spots to ambush unwary Americans, snipers picked off soldiers, and mortar shells crashing among the trees whipped razor-sharp shrapnel and branches onto the men.

During one action in ice and rain, Robert Donohue of E Company, 157th Infantry Regiment, became separated from his squad. Under fire from a German machine gun, Donohue lost his helmet when he tripped over the bushy undergrowth as he rushed for cover. He crawled back to friendly lines that night and had just started up an embankment onto a muddy road when a three-quarter-ton command car suddenly stopped next to him. "Soldier, where is your helmet?" asked someone from inside. Before Donohue could respond, a hand thrust a helmet through the canvas side flaps and the man inside said, "Here, take this one."

Donohue gladly accepted the helmet from his unidentified donor, but was perplexed the next morning when his buddies began teasing him. "Unknown to me," said Donohue, "my new helmet had a bright silver cross on center front for all to see and wonder about."[21] He made a few inquiries and learned that Father Barry, his regimental chaplain, had given it to him. Donohue removed the silver cross and kept the helmet, grateful for the priest's thoughtfulness.

Barry's 1944 Christmas, spent with his regiment in snow-covered foxholes, lacked the splendor of Christmases past, but it packed more emotion. Not only had the costly fighting in the Vosges spiked a rise in battle fatigue, but the soldiers also had to cope with being away from loved ones for a second consecutive Christmas. Father Barry recorded more instances of self-inflicted wounds and desertions than ever and spoke often to the men about leaning on their faith to help them through the adversity.

The holiday ceremony helped bring a little of home to the men. On Christmas Eve, the local pastor offered his church, choir, and organist to Barry so that he and his soldiers could enjoy Mass as they had celebrated it in normal times. The pastor even asked his parishioners to remain home so that there would be enough room in the church for Barry's soldiers. For one of the few times since he had left the United States, Father Barry said Mass accompanied by the singing of Latin chants and Christmas carols. The ceremony, he proudly reported, drew so many of his boys that some had to stand along the sides and back because the pews were full.

That December he wrote to his friend Patricia Brehmer that, despite what she and others back home read in the newspapers, those articles "do not tell half the story because you must be up front to get it and very few [correspondents] are there since [Ernie] Pyle took off for the States." He agreed that rationing and shortages back home caused hardships, but asked, "Do say an earnest prayer for the boys fighting along this western front. The boys have a word for it—'plenty rough.' From the looks of things right now our Christmas will be a 'scary' one. These Heinies are fighting mad now that we are fighting in their homeland, in spite of the baloney of one Mr. Hitler."[22]

Sergeant Daniel Dougherty recalled a talk that Father Barry, whom he called "the beloved chaplain of their regiment," delivered to a group of soldiers at the time. "It was the night before we were to go to the line, and we were ordered to assemble in the school house in town. It was dark inside, so I couldn't see him, but I could hear Father Barry loud and clear. He didn't mention religion or God, but told us not to desert. Apparently some men had gone AWOL and someone must have asked Father Barry to talk to us."[23]

It might be simple to conclude that, since Father Barry was a chaplain, his religious fervor made him impervious to the pain and suffering about him, but every horrid condition that afflicted the soldiers afflicted Father Barry as well. He shivered when they shivered; he trod wearily along dusty roads in Sicily and muddy quagmires in Italy; he shrank from the sounds and explosions of the dreaded German artillery barrage; he felt the same emotions that poured out of his boys in confidential chats. He brought comforting words to soldiers on the brink of battle fatigue, but they came from a human being staring into the same abyss. That human element was a crucial reason why Father Barry became so valuable to his boys. He was one of them, not simply a man of prayer, but a human experiencing the same joys and sorrows as they did.

He had a right to be wary of the dangers, for the army chaplain ranks suffered a larger percentage of casualties than any other military branch except the infantry on the front lines and the Army Air Corps. More than one hundred chaplains, including twenty-five Catholic priests, died in the performance of their duties, and nearly three hundred others suffered wounds. Catholic chaplains registered a high rate of casualties because, like Father Barry, they believed that their place was with the dying to administer Last Rites, and the dying were most often in the thick of the fighting. "The mortality rate of chaplains in the combat zones has been extremely high," groaned one Protestant chaplain in words that would be seconded by Father Barry, "and there aren't enough new men to go around."[24]

"I Should Like to Be Attached to an Active Unit"
Other Chaplains

Other priests volunteered to bolster the chaplain ranks in Europe, but not all received combat assignments. Among them were nine of Father Barry's comrades from Notre Dame, three of whom already served at the front. Thirty-seven-year-old Father Edmund J. Murray's love of all things Irish—his father and his mother, a McMahon, were both Irish, and he taught Irish history at Notre Dame—was matched only by his love of country and his devotion to God. He arrived in Europe in August 1944 with the army's 104th Infantry Division in time to participate in the fall combat in France and Belgium, deadly preludes to the fierce fighting his unit would see in the coming months once they crossed into Germany.

After working in England with his men in the Fifty-Third Troop Carrier Wing, where he attended meetings with Father Sampson preparatory to the D-Day landings, Father Edward Fitzgerald crossed to Italy with the unit as part of the same invasion into southern France that involved Father Barry. He was constantly on the move, providing, as he explained, religious services for paratroopers "located in various fields covering about a 75-mile radius."[25] With the wing absorbed as part of the First Allied Airborne Army, the unit saw action in Holland and Belgium not far from where Father Sampson parachuted into northern Europe and was subsequently captured.

Father John T. McGee met Father Sampson in Belgium, but unlike the rest of his Irish cohort, the native of Canada served as a chaplain with the Canadian Army. He wrote to Father Steiner that while Murray's outfit had not yet been in battle when the two met, "I imagine they will get a taste of what it is like before the Winter is over." He added that he and his men "have been in the thick of things without a rest since Caen [France]" and that Belgium was "a land of water and swamps and dykes, a very dismal country, where it seems to rain every day, or at least part of every day." As far as he could tell, any home-front optimism that the war would soon end was displaced. "I don't know how things look from where you are," he wrote to Father Steiner, "but from here it does not look as if things will end soon." Although McGee had been on the move every day, dealing with the life-and-death issues that faced a chaplain in the combat zone, he found time to inquire about the university's football squad. "We are having very beautiful fall weather," he wrote in October from Belgium, "and naturally everyone is interested in the progress of the football team—so far it has done well."[26]

Others entered the chaplain corps but never reached the front lines. McGee's fellow Canadian Father John Biger longed to be overseas with his compatriot, but instead he languished at military installations in Canada. He informed Father Steiner, "I doubt whether I shall be sent overseas, even though I have a few extra languages at my command, because seniority [in Canada] is a dominating factor in selecting Chaplains." He believed he was helping the soldiers under his care but commiserated that they stood an ocean away from the front lines. He longed for combat, "where contact with the boys would really mean something. This station belongs to the permanent force, has every facility and comfort and it seems a shame that we younger men who are anxious to rough it with the boys must stay here."[27]

Father Steiner tried to console the Holy Cross priest by responding that not every chaplain would minister in the midst of combat. Vast numbers of soldiers and sailors labored behind the lines, and those men needed the services of chaplains like any other soldier. Duty behind the lines, Father Steiner wrote, "is part of a Chaplain's experience, so you priests must steel yourselves and take it. The greatest consolation for you is that you are bringing faith and religion to the men, and only the heavenly ledger will reveal the great good that you have done."[28]

Father Steiner frequently answered queries from chaplains who had yet to go anywhere near the front lines. They wanted to be with the combat units, but while they might not gain the attention that frontline chaplains in Europe and the Pacific received, their vital work helped prepare men on their way to combat or soften the pain of being away from loved ones.

Father Theodore Hesburgh was one of those priests who pestered Father Steiner, in his case to serve as a navy chaplain. He hoped to be posted to an aircraft carrier, where he would tend to a large group of military aboard ships earmarked for combat. However, Father Steiner, who recognized a rising star in Father Hesburgh, both for the university and for the Holy Cross Congregation, declined his request. He ordered Hesburgh to first obtain his doctorate at Catholic University in Washington, DC, after which the two would discuss his entry into the military. After receiving his doctorate in March 1945, Hesburgh wrote Steiner that his cousin had helped him arrange a spot in the navy's chaplain class at William and Mary, but Steiner again turned him down and told him to report to Notre Dame to instruct naval midshipmen at the university.

Hesburgh could at least take comfort in knowing that during his stay in Washington, DC, he had helped his country's fighting personnel by collaborating with a handful of priests in writing guidance books for men and women in the military. Three million copies of one pamphlet, *For God and Country*, were distributed throughout the armed forces, and Hesburgh estimated that the combined total of all the publications fell between six and seven million. "Judging from the incredible amount of mail they generated," he wrote, "I would think hundreds of thousands of lives were affected."[29]

Other chaplains joined Hesburgh in never reaching the combat zone. Father Robert W. Woodward served as regimental and harbor defense chaplain, a post responsible for the forces defending the homeland from an attack. This included troops stationed in Bermuda, the Bahamas, Cuba, Newfoundland, Labrador, Greenland, Iceland, and the United States proper. Father George Welsh worked with soldiers freshly evacuated from the battlefield and recuperating in military hospitals in Northern Ireland and France, while Father Clement Kane did the same with wounded veterans who had been transported to hospitals in the United States.

Father Maurice E. Powers would not be denied his chance to join the troops overseas, however. He started his barrage of queries as early as December 22, 1941, fifteen days after the attack at Pearl Harbor, when he asked the Bureau of Chaplains for information about becoming a chaplain. The thirty-six-year-old native of Massachusetts earned a degree in philosophy from Notre Dame before teaching full time at the university, where he also directed the glee club. He explained to the bureau, "I am very much interested in assisting the thousands of boys of my Roman Catholic Faith to have the facilities many of them wish during the present conflict."

He finally received permission in August 1943 and was sent to the Harvard Chaplain School, but by late 1944 he had yet to leave the country. He followed the military's progress in both theaters and feared that the war might terminate before he had the opportunity to serve at the front, as were his associates Father Barry and Father Sampson.

In November he poured out his anguish in a powerful letter to the chief of chaplains. "Having been in this country for almost one year, assigned to two different units, neither of which will probably ever see foreign service, so I am told by a superior ranking officer, I should like to make a request. Because I am very healthy, very active athletically, meaning I am in good physical condition, and because my commanding officers have told me several times that they appreciate my work, I should like to translate all my zeal and energy to serving men overseas. I should like to be attached to an active unit in the Pacific." He added that to serve the men, he was willing "to go through the fiercest, most dire conditions," and that ministering to troops in combat would be the ultimate form of service he could ever render, to God, to his country, and to the military. "Coming from a university where I am a religious priest in the Order of the Holy Cross Fathers, the University of Notre Dame, I should like to have the privilege of knowing that I have been with a fighting unit."[30] Father Powers was ultimately granted his wish, and he would soon know what it was like to be a frontline chaplain. That knowledge would offer more than he expected.

Notre Dame chaplains in the Pacific experienced the same. They encountered, however, a different form of hell as they converged on the Philippines and moved closer to their captive Notre Dame religious.

PART III

ONWARD TO VICTORY

January 1945 to Present

CHAPTER 9

"I HAD THE DEVIL SCARED OUT OF ME MANY A TIME"

Closing In on Japan

Father Henry Heintskill's hell came from the sky. After operating off the coast of France for the June 1944 landings, the priest's escort carrier, the U.S.S. *Tulagi*, was among the hundreds of ships participating in the elaborate assault on the Philippines. Since the Japanese could ill afford to lose control of the islands and their vital natural resources, American military strategists concluded they would employ every weapon in their arsenal, including aircraft, to halt MacArthur's return.

A succession of four major operations ensued from October 1944 to January 1945, led by the October 25 Battle of Leyte Gulf in the Philippines. That widespread clash, in which the United States handed the Japanese a resounding defeat, brought the first organized kamikaze assault of the war. The Japanese suicide planes, which often approached under the radar, crashed into five escort carriers and sparked eruptions that tossed troops and aircraft hundreds of feet into the air. Unfortunately, the sight of mangled ships and burning men would soon become common. The terrifying tactic reappeared as MacArthur's forces commenced the three-stage advance up the Philippines, landing troops at Ormoc Bay and Mindoro along the island's west coast before depositing infantry at Lingayen Gulf, 120 miles above Manila.

"I'm well and still in one piece," wrote Seaman First Class Tom Fern of the destroyer U.S.S. *Laffey* to his mother on December 13 after witnessing kamikazes transform nearby ships into infernos. "Still can stand on my two feet, but what I've seen in the past week makes a fellow wonder—am I next? I've never felt the need for prayers as much as I have in the past weeks."[1]

Father Heintskill first surveyed evidence of the aerial carnage in early January 1945 at Lingayen Gulf, the fourth and final stage, when his ship steamed near another escort carrier still aflame from a hit by a suicide plane. When two days later three kamikazes approached *Tulagi*'s formation, the escort carrier's deck antiaircraft gun crews helped splash two planes before the third smacked into the cruiser U.S.S. *Louisville*. During the Lingayen Gulf landings, the carrier's gun crews repelled three air attacks, with one plane coming close astern of Father Heintskill's carrier before swerving toward a different target, while another kamikaze crashed into the flight deck of the escort carrier immediately ahead of *Tulagi*.

When Father Heintskill first joined the ship, another Catholic chaplain admonished him, only half joking, that to date no escort carrier with a Catholic chaplain aboard had been struck by the suicide planes, and that he had best not spoil that record. Heintskill was happy to oblige, but stood ready to offer comfort to badly wounded or dying sailors should the worst occur. "We're thankful that we missed it," he wrote to Father Steiner after the Lingayen operation had ended, "but at the same time you can't help but feel a little bit down. It's tough to stand by and see some other ship take it, and know that the Catholics aboard are without a priest. It's one of those things that just has to be."

Heintskill wrote that while the carrier came through the Lingayen landings "very nicely," during the more than five hundred sorties flown in support of the infantry ashore they lost three aviators, one of whom was a Catholic. He added, "I'm pretty sure that he was ready because the day before he had been to confession and Holy Communion."[2]

In the fighting's aftermath, Heintskill turned to more routine matters, many having little to do with his religious duties. According to his annual chaplain report, his schedule was "necessarily determined by the conditions of the forward area."[3] As the ship's welfare officer, he obtained supplies for recreation and entertainment of the crew and arranged athletic competitions when conditions permitted. He assisted the ship's doctor, and as the insurance officer he helped the crew apply for insurance and select beneficiaries. He managed the small collection of books and magazines in the ship's library, twice each month coedited the carrier's newsletter, and supervised and helped prepare menus for the wardroom mess. In his role as assistant public relations officer, Heintskill gathered material about the ship and the crew for release to local newspapers, and in 1945 alone wrote more than two hundred newspaper articles for hometown publications. On top of that, during one four-month stretch he conducted an hour-long class each weekday in elementary reading and writing for crew lacking those skills.

Father Heintskill never allowed those added duties to overshadow his main motive for being aboard the *Tulagi*. He celebrated Mass each day—twice on Sundays—immediately after the end of dawn general quarters (all hands to battle stations), after which he visited sick bay to check on the progress of the men confined there. Sailors could see him during his regular office hours in the afternoon and evening, but Heintskill was also available around the clock should the men need him for any reason. He conducted Novena services each Tuesday evening, and he scheduled confessions every Saturday evening and Sunday morning, although rarely a day passed that someone did not seek him out for that purpose. When the ship was at anchor, Heintskill visited ships lacking a Catholic chaplain to say Mass and hear confessions. As the sole chaplain aboard *Tulagi*, Father Heintskill also scheduled religious services for non-Catholic officers and enlisted. He held Latter Day Saints services every Tuesday afternoon and a Jewish ceremony each Friday evening.

During Lent, Heintskill checked with the supply officer to ensure that the menu offered a meatless selection on Ash Wednesday, Good Friday, and Holy Saturday, so "we have a menu for those days that our boys can eat with a clear conscience." Since the carrier operated for long stretches at sea, Heintskill discovered that meatless meals were the least of his problems. Some sailors never adjusted to the "dehydrated spuds, weevily bread, and suspicious food," while others devoured anything in sight. Heintskill wrote that some of the crew teased the men who declined to eat "bread because it had bugs in it as pansy waists. Last night we had our first fresh vegetable in over a month; lettuce and potatoes really are good we've learned."

The hectic Philippine invasion timetable kept the ship busy every moment, mainly in lending air support to the infantry fighting on land. "We are continuing to stay out here," he informed Steiner, "moving in with each successive invasion. The only ships that are being relieved at all are those which take injuries—so as long as we are still floating we can expect to be right out here."[4]

Heintskill figured that he would remain at sea for a while. After completing the Philippine landings, his ship moved north toward Tokyo as part of a campaign that would undoubtedly terminate with bloody landings against the Japanese Home Islands. No one could predict how many months—or years—that might take.

"The Wandering Chaplain"

Before U.S. forces could reach Japan, key island obstacles north of the Philippines had to be removed. The invasion of Iwo Jima, where U.S. Marines absorbed horrendous casualties before raising a flag atop Mount Suribachi, as memorialized in granite in Washington, DC, began in February 1945. Two months later, grim ground combat and swarms of kamikaze aircraft in Okinawa provided frightful hints of what lay in store for U.S. forces when they eventually invade the Home Islands.

Three Notre Dame chaplains served at Iwo Jima, two aboard offshore ships and one on the island. Father Henry Heintskill had continued north to Iwo Jima with the *Tulagi*, where the carrier provided air support for the marines. With war intensifying as American power swept toward Japan, attendance at Heintskill's Masses tripled and additional men appeared for recitation of the Rosary and other prayer services.

In his spare moments Heintskill wrote letters "to the mother and wife of every Catholic man aboard." He assured each that their son or husband had received the Sacraments and that he would be with their loved one through the coming months, and he accommodated the sailors who asked him to include certain messages to their mothers. "It's surprising how many of the boys came in," he wrote to Steiner, "to have me tell their mothers that they received Holy Communion on Easter Sunday." He told Steiner he wished he could divulge more, but military censorship imposed tight restrictions on what he could write. "There's a good deal I would like to write, but can't. My health is excellent; climbing up and down ship's ladders gives me a fair amount of exercise, but at times I'd like to get out and play a good game of softball."[5]

Heintskill's Notre Dame compatriot Father Francis J. Boland experienced on February 19—D-Day at Iwo Jima—a morning unlike any other. As he watched his first Pacific landing from the ship's bridge, he marveled at the elaborate military production converging on the heretofore unknown island. The waters between his transport, the U.S.S. *Highlands,* and shore teemed with marine-laden landing craft, and battleships and cruisers plowed every inch of the landing areas with a thundering bombardment. "It was a very impressive sight to see so many warships surrounding the island and blasting away at it with their big guns," he wrote to Father Steiner. "We were about four miles from shore which seemed at the time close enough."

A bright sky and calm seas—the sole day out of the ensuing week that lacked heavy fog and rough waters—blessed the invaders. He told Steiner that "If the landings had been made on any of the subsequent days of that week, it is very doubtful as to whether the Marines could have taken the island," and most likely "the massacre of the Marines would have been almost complete."

Even with temperate weather, the marines waded into carnage. Japanese defenders, anchored by their guns and entrenchments on Mount Suribachi, decimated marine ranks with sheets of bullets and mortar shells. Boland told Father Steiner, "To me it is miraculous that they ever got by the Jap gunfire from Mount Suribachi, the high hill at the south end of the island, where all the landings were made."

Father Boland watched from his post aboard *Highlands* until the afternoon, when the first casualties from the island arrived at the transport. Boland had tried to prepare himself for this moment, but nothing could steel him for the stream of broken, mutilated bodies that flowed from Iwo Jima to his ship.

Father Boland moved from marine to marine, lending soothing words and providing a benediction. He lingered longer over those he knew were about to die, giving Extreme Unction to the Catholic marines and whispering a prayer over Protestant and Jewish marines. He stifled tears and the urge to regurgitate; as he told Steiner, "Needless to say the sight of so many boys with hands and legs shot off, in some instances heads practically crashed in and innumerable wounds from Jap mortar fire, was sickening to see. *Time* Magazine was right in stating that the Marines met with the most violent death possible."[6]

In the following days, wounded and dying marines poured onto Boland's transport, as if a deadly funnel connected the *Highlands* with Iwo Jima. Two days after the landing, a pair of Japanese kamikazes battled through thick antiaircraft fire to smash into the escort carrier U.S.S. *Bismarck Sea* (CVE-95), stationed off Iwo Jima not far from where Father Heintskill's *Tulagi* would soon operate. The resulting explosions sank the vessel, taking more than 300 crew to their deaths. Destroyers and destroyer escorts retrieved 600 survivors, 158 of whom were taken to *Highlands*, where Father Boland and the crew tended to the oil-covered, exhausted men. Many, Father Boland noticed, had been hideously scalded. His own ship, he also speculated, could be just as easily transformed into an inferno at any moment.

Highlands left Iwo Jima on February 25 to transport the wounded to Saipan hospitals before continuing to a rest area at Espiritu Santo in the New Hebrides, southeast of Guadalcanal. "We have had some interesting experiences since leaving Pearl Harbor on January 27," he wrote to Steiner. He explained that after moving to the western Pacific in a great convoy that stopped at Eniwetok and Saipan, he arrived off the island. "Iwo Jima was our target and I am sure that you have read in detail of the terrible battle fought there." He added that, "Iwo Jima was my first taste of war at first hand although we had several attacks from submarines at earlier dates."

He related the sad news that First Lieutenant Jack Chevigny, a star running back for Knute Rockne, had been killed the first day at Iwo Jima. Boland had seen Chevigny a few times at Pearl Harbor, and the athlete "was in fine spirits and wonderful physical condition."[7] Boland knew of a handful of other Notre Dame graduates who had been on the island but lacked information on their welfare.

Meanwhile, on shore, so many marine casualties flooded aid stations set up near the landing beaches that Father Dupuis, the veteran chaplain from Roi and Saipan combat, found little time to break away to be with the advancing units. He soon realized, however, that on this finger of an island capped by Mount Suribachi, wherever a soldier or a chaplain stood, he was at the front.

Dupuis and the Fourth Pioneer Battalion worked on Iwo Jima's beaches for nearly three weeks, providing support for the landing forces while operating from the beach areas. Until marine patrols eliminated every Japanese gun on Mount Suribachi, Dupuis was never safe from the enemy mortar barrages and snipers.

Father Steiner and the rest of the Holy Cross community at Notre Dame avidly followed the Pacific developments. "We had heard that you were on the Island where the fighting was the fiercest yet. Naturally we were worried about you," Steiner wrote to Dupuis in April. "The headlines of the daily press gave us sufficient information about the horribleness of it all."[8]

Once Iwo Jima was secured, Father Dupuis informed Steiner that he was happy to be out of the fighting, and that while he emerged from Iwo Jima without a scratch, "I had the devil scared out of me many a time." He explained that as the fighting had terminated, he had turned to other chaplain duties. He celebrated Requiem Mass for the deceased members of his Pioneer Battalion and then focused on writing letters of condolence to parents and widows. Like every chaplain, he struggled to find the right words to console people who had just learned of a loved one's death, but trusted the instincts he had developed through his years in ministry to guide his thoughts. Dupuis also notified Steiner that he was being detached from the Fourth Pioneer Battalion to a different unit in need of priests and so signed his letter, "The Wandering Chaplain."[9]

FATHER HEINTSKILL and *Tulagi* remained off Iwo Jima until the end of February, providing support for the marines ashore. In March Heintskill told Steiner that the *Tulagi* crew had avoided injury at Iwo Jima, "including all of our pilots who had the toughest end of the job as far as we were concerned." He explained that he already saw one benefit emerging from the island battle: confidence. Even though talk of another big operation dominated ship scuttlebutt—Okinawa was then less than one month in the future—"the attitude of our crew and officers is now a lot different—they know now what to expect; they know that every time we go into these jobs there's a pretty good chance of not coming out of it; but they are all quite sure too that they've learned a lot of mistakes of others."[10]

IN RESPONDING to his chaplains, Father Steiner used much the same phrasing as he did to Father Dupuis after Iwo Jima. He reminded them that everyone on campus kept them in their prayers and that Masses were being offered in their behalf. "Now that you are back in safety [from Iwo Jima]," he told Dupuis, "it will be best for you to forget as much as you can the terrible activities on the Island. Let us hope that you may never have to face any more battles of this kind."[11]

Father Steiner's sentiments were noble but unrealistic. Okinawa's suicide planes and the subsequent invasion of the Japanese Home Islands, with their casualties and destruction, loomed.

"Hope Rose Higher and Higher as We Starved"
The Missionaries at Los Baños

Death and sorrow were precisely what the six Notre Dame missionaries held captive at Los Baños were trying to evade. They had been confined in different prison camps since 1942, living without hint of relief, while their food situation deteriorated and men and women succumbed. The October 1944 troop landings under General Douglas MacArthur boosted spirits, but hard fighting across 450 miles lay between MacArthur's forces and their freedom.

The prisoners received a welcome surprise on New Year's Eve when American aircraft, which had until then been bombing and strafing Japanese targets miles from the camp, swooped low over Los Baños. "Seven dark blue planes flew over the camp and strafed an objective just north of us," Sister Olivette scribbled in her diary. "So low we could see the numbers in white on right wing."[12]

The internees thrilled at the sight of their American military hammering the enemy. "Again the bombers and fighters in beautiful formation to pick up our spirits," Sister Olivette recorded, while Brother Rex added that the increased sightings made everyone realize that "war was coming our way." Father Lawyer did not learn until later that among the crew of one of the planes that flew over Los Baños was his brother, a sibling who was, as he wrote to Father Steiner, "so near yet so far away."[13]

Another harbinger of optimism occurred in early January 1945 with the news of a massive American landing less than 150 miles away in Lingayen Gulf on Luzon's northern shore. Aircraft dropped leaflets bearing MacArthur's vow to return, and with friendly units closing the gap, liberation seemed closer.

Even the most pessimistic among them admitted that freedom might be near when, early in the morning of January 7, the camp's guards suddenly disappeared. The noise of their departure awakened Sister Olivette. "Father Burns S. J. saw us out and came over with the news. The Japanese are leaving!"

The prisoners renamed Los Baños "Camp Freedom" and greeted the new day with an action they had long awaited. "At dawn the American flag was raised and now we're waiting for our boys! 3 meals!"[14] wrote Sister Olivette. The sight of their nation's flag billowing in the morning breeze enthralled the religious, who during the past three years had often doubted that they would again cast eyes on the flag. Fearing that their open display of the Stars and Stripes in a war zone might draw Japanese reprisals on the camp, the flag remained hoisted for only a few moments before being lowered.

Sisters Caecilius and Olivette turned on the concealed radio and, for the first time since their seizure, listened to the voice of their president, Franklin Roosevelt. Inmates foraged for food, and friendly Filipinos arrived with clothing, bread, meat, fruit, eggs, and other luxuries many had not seen since their incarceration. Men and women unabashedly cried at the thought that American forces might soon be near. Fearing that the Japanese might return, the Central Committee, a group of internees tasked with helping maintain control in the camp, scoured the countryside for food and increased the daily allowance to three meals a day. In addition, each internee received five pounds of rice to use in an emergency.

The increased food rations helped save lives when the guards returned on January 13 and, angered by MacArthur's advances in the Philippines, imposed a harsher regimen than before. "At 2:45 a.m. awakened by a voice announcing, 'The Commandant, Konizi, and all his staff have returned,'" wrote a morose Sister Olivette. When the Japanese, who explained that they had been away from camp on a secret mission, ordered the internees to stay clear from all sentry boxes and to remain in their barracks until ordered, she concluded, "They're back!!!" According to Brother Rex, when the Japanese returned "there was more unpleasantness between internee and guard; in general, the Japanese reflected the attitude that if it was going to be tough for them, we had no right to expect it any easier."[15]

The guards' sour demeanor and an increase in barracks searches hinted that the race between Japanese guards intent on killing them and American soldiers rushing to their rescue had tightened alarmingly. "There was a sinister manifestation of a growing hostility in the mood of the enemy," wrote Sister Olivette. "Rumors of eleventh hour vengeance were in the air. They were said to have boasted that the Americans would find nothing when they returned."[16]

By early February rations had been so reduced that nurse Dorothy Danner claimed it was "suicidal for a rat, snake, or a snail to venture into our camp, much less a stray dog." Medical supplies dwindled as diseases spread, resulting in so many deaths that crews had difficulty making enough coffins and garnering the strength to dig the graves. The daily appearances by American planes on their way to bomb Japanese targets helped, but was it all in vain? "Hope rose higher and higher as we starved,"[17] Father McKee wrote later.

The daily pressure of wondering whether that day would bring massacre or freedom chipped away at their depleted reservoirs of strength. "At about 6:40 a.m. a close shot was heard—one of the internees who had been out during the night was shot on returning—only wounded however," Sister Olivette wrote on January 28. "No priest was permitted to see him. He was taken outside the gate and a little after 8 executed by order commandant. Planes above very active probably made them nervous. More stringent regulations esp. during air raid—off the road, stay in barracks. Roll call twice a day 7–7:30 a.m. & 6–6:30 p.m."

Three days later she recorded, "Food rations definitely lower and lowering daily. Physical condition of internees poor. Beri-beri in greater or less degree common condition." Sister Olivette became so desperate for nourishment that one day she entered the chapel and "bit into the wooden pews" out of hunger, a moment she described as "the lowest point" of her three years of captivity. Father Lawyer later wrote, "We were gradually starving to death—so weak we could hardly stand. Then, too, we didn't know what those Japs would do in their desperations."[18] In his deepest desperation, he relied on prayer to the "Dear Blessed Lady" to sustain him.

Emotions daily swerved from one extreme to the other. Between February 15 and 19, Sister Olivette recorded the deaths of four people from beriberi—a disease caused from vitamin deficiencies that leads to heart and circulatory problems, nerve damage, loss of muscle strength, and death—interspersed with references to friendly aircraft crossing the sky. On February 8 she wrote, "Between 2 & 3 p.m. two planes flew so low & circled over the camp that some could even see the pilot. The nearest we have seen our planes since 1941." Nine days later, as MacArthur's units drove the Japanese from Manila, she added, "2 planes flew very low—just over top of barracks. This p.m. a warning to stay in our cubicles when planes go over & to remain calm if we hear shots nearby. All afternoon sounds of gunfire after several days of comparative calm."

Accompanying the imminent fall of Manila was news of the slaughter of almost one hundred thousand Filipinos, another indicator of what the Japanese planned for Los Baños. Impatient with the lack of progress, Sister Olivette scribbled on February 19, "The rumored arrival of our troops today did not take place, so the rumor today is that they are coming slowly [underline hers] from Calumjat. As someone said it must be on tip toe."[19]

Desperation prevailed by February 20. People died at the rate of one every day, and the food supply, inadequate even in the best of times, had diminished to one bowl of watery soup per person each day. "Daily we were burying the dead from starvation," wrote Father Lawyer. "Normal walking ability was nowhere to be seen. The Japanese were acting queerer than usual. We didn't know what was going to happen."[20] Each evening, reminiscent of their visits to the Grotto at Notre Dame, the religious and others recited the Rosary and a litany as part of a three-day exposition of the Blessed Sacrament and continuous recitation of the Rosary.

The sounds of U.S. artillery blasting Japanese lines drew louder, but that ironically heightened the apprehension inside Los Baños. Might the proximity of American troops force their captors' hands? In addition to the reductions in their food allotment and the emplacement of additional machine guns, guards now began digging a trench that, to most internees, served only one purpose: a mass grave.

The religious prepared themselves for the worst. "As American power increased, enemy vigilance and brutality mounted," recalled Sister Olivette. "Rumors of eleventh hour vengeance were rife. Daily we were lined up for enemy inspection with the threat of shooting made realistic by lesser evidences of revenge. Each morning, prepared for death, we went forth to undergo inspection." When a few religious from other orders were killed by guards, the Notre Dame group was certain "that a similar fate might be ours any day."[21]

BELIEVING HE stood on the verge of a catastrophe that could include the execution of hundreds, if not thousands, of Americans, on January's final day MacArthur ordered his commanders to race to Manila as quickly as possible and free the internees at Santo Tomas and other prisoner-of-war camps. He had reason for trepidation, as the Japanese planned to institute a program of mass extermination. An August 1, 1944, document uncovered after the war outlined the measures that camp commandants were to take if their camps were about to fall to approaching American forces: "Whether they [prisoners] are destroyed individually or in groups, or however it is done, with mass bombing, poisonous smoke, poisons, drowning, decapitation, or what, dispose of them as the situation dictates." The document ended with the menacing statement, "In any case it is the aim not to allow the escape of a single one, to annihilate them all, and not to leave any traces."[22]

"And Here They Were—Our Own American Men, with a Notre Dame Man among Them"
Missionaries Rescued

On February 21 the Japanese issued each inmate a can of unhusked rice and warned them that this was to be their food for the next two days. The following evening, Father McKee spotted a group of American fighters bombing and strafing Japanese locations northwest of Los Baños, but whereas prior attacks lasted a few minutes, these stretched on for half an hour. He hoped it might be a harbinger of their immediate rescue.

McKee was correct. On that same day MacArthur received a message from Colonel W. C. Price, the chief of staff in charge of guerrilla operations, that reliable sources informed him that the Japanese had already scheduled the massacre of every man, woman, and child inside Los Baños within the next few days. The information, combined with military intelligence unearthing the existence of a few thousand Japanese soldiers in the mountains four hours to the west of the camp, prodded MacArthur into implementing a hurried rescue operation. Military planners drew up a risky plan that required the elite Army Rangers to parachute twenty-five miles behind enemy lines into territory occupied by nine thousand Japanese troops. MacArthur understood the hazards, but he was convinced that if he delayed, the Americans inside Los Baños would be executed before he arrived.

On the night of February 22, an army reconnaissance platoon canoed across Laguna de Bay near Los Baños and rendezvoused with guerrilla forces. At the same time, fifty-four troop-laden amtracs moved into position, an infantry battalion manned defensive positions along a highway leading into camp, and nine C-47 transports lifted into the air at Nichols Field in Manila, loaded with paratroopers ready to jump into the camp.

Early the next morning, soldiers from the amtracs established a roadblock to prevent Japanese reinforcements from reaching Los Baños, while the infantry battalion staged a diversion to draw attention from the camp. At 7:00 a.m. Fathers McKee and Lawyer were standing next to Father Charles Taylor when "suddenly our lives were completely changed." The three glanced up at the sound of planes approaching from the north, but coming in lower than previous aircraft. The fuselage of one bore, in large white letters, the message "RESCUE," and in seconds, according to McKee, "we saw something that caused us to shout with the first real feeling of hope in months. From beneath the nine planes were over 100 parachutes floating earthward. Americans! At last we were to be delivered from the hands of our benevolent guardians." As the sky teemed with paratroopers descending toward the camp, an incredulous Lawyer asked McKee, "Bob, do you see what I see?" Sisters Caecilius and Olivette watched the parachutes and believed God had sent them their deliverers, much as Moses had delivered the Jews out of Egypt. "We had called to Heaven for help," they wrote after the war, "and it was from the heavens that help came to us." They added, "There were our boys, 150 of them, like angels out of the blue. There was wild excitement and screams of joy."[23]

"I Had the Devil Scared Out of Me Many a Time"   235

The paratroopers descended with guns blazing. As soon as they touched down, some U.S. soldiers formed a protective ring about the prisoners while others charged the Japanese. The missionaries and their military cordon raced to the barracks for shelter, where they began reciting the Rosary—"You could hear the constant murmuring of Hail Marys," recalled Father Lawyer—and hugging the floor to avoid the storm of bullets that cut through the bamboo walls and splintered their bedsteads. One bullet knocked a tin cup out of a nun's hand, and a cleric nearby wished he were an earthworm so he could lie closer to the floor. Sister Olivette turned toward Father Scanlon, a priest huddling on the floor near her, expecting him to bless everyone, but he remained silent. "You know," she murmured to the priest as bullets snapped into cots, "better bless us, give us absolution, Father!"[24]

Filipino guerrillas rushed out of the underbrush to join the paratroopers in eliminating guards at sentry stations and in making certain that every building was clear of Japanese. Within minutes of the landing, more than two hundred Japanese bodies lay about the camp. Amtracs moved in to whisk the prisoners to safety, while soldiers hurried toward the barracks to lead them out. Brother Rex finally let himself believe that rescue was at hand when he heard familiar American phrases. "The first news we had that our men were inside the camp," he said, "came when we heard some honest-to-goodness 'cussing,' done with real American finish. We felt better then."[25]

Sister Olivette was huddled with other nuns in her barracks when a Japanese soldier burst in. An American paratrooper simultaneously crept up from behind, winked at the nuns, and gunned down the guard. Sister Olivette wrote to her sister two days later that the paratroopers had arrived just in time, "or else by now I would have been only a memory."[26]

Danner and the other civilian nurses were equally elated at the spectacle. After years of hardship and death, it seemed they were soon to be free. That is, if the soldiers could escort them though enemy-held territory to American lines and safety. "Magnificent, healthy American soldiers emerged from the amtrac, down the lowered ramp," wrote Danner of the happy moment. As the nurses choked back tears, "our heroes had come in their camouflaged uniforms, pockets bulging with hand grenades, cartridge clips, K-rations."[27]

Sister Olivette muttered prayers of thanks and awaited instructions from the Americans. "It was all unreal, but beautifully unreal. We had seen it in imagination and hope a hundred times—the arrival of help in the uniform of our country. And here they were—our own American men, with a Notre Dame man among them."[28]

That Notre Dame man was First Lieutenant John F. Finneran, class of 1933. Through the years of confinement, the missionaries had maintained hope in part because of their attachment to the university. Memories of the Grotto and the Log Chapel, the Church of the Sacred Heart and the Golden Dome formed an unassailable attachment between the missionaries and Notre Dame. Now, one of the university's graduates was here to free them. He and other soldiers handed out Hershey bars as they began to collect the internees.

Finneran and his companions told everyone to gather a few items and hurry from the barracks to Laguna de Bay, where other amtracs waited to ferry them across to safety. When Brother Theodore had difficulty deciding which items to leave behind, Lawyer took him by the arm and led him out. "It was pathetic to see Teddy leaving," wrote Brother Rex of the departure, "for he was a broken man"[29] over leaving the possessions to which he had so fiercely clung during his long years of incarceration. Father McKee grabbed four prayer books, sermon notes, and a pen and stepped away from the barracks, pausing only briefly to look back as soldiers set fire to what had been his home for the last year.

Sisters Olivette and Caecilius walked together to the amtracs. "Everybody was carrying a suitcase to take care of whatever," Sister Olivette said later. "You know, after having been without anything, you hold onto things." Soldiers and sturdier internees carried on cots those too weak to walk to the amtracs, while the stronger men, women, and children, bundles under their arms, stumbled out of Los Baños.

As the pair walked the short distance, Sister Olivette gazed at the camp that had been her home since the previous July. "Barracks burning. J's liquidated,"[30] she bluntly wrote in her diary. Not far away, the decapitated body of Lieutenant Konishi lay on the ground as Filipino guerrillas searched his pockets for anything of value.

When McKee asked a soldier why they had to rush out of a camp that had been cleared of enemy troops, the paratrooper replied that a Japanese battalion stationed not far away was fast closing in on Los

Baños. As if on cue, artillery shells exploded and Japanese soldiers appeared a few minutes later, just as the last amtrac churned out of Los Baños.

Amtracs evacuated the bed patients, children, women (including most of the nuns), and the casualties from the raid—two dead and three wounded soldiers—while the four Notre Dame priests and brothers joined the rest for the one-and-a-half-mile walk to the lake. That distance might normally have been unattainable for the weakened internees, but adrenaline and joy breathed renewed energy into people on the cusp of freedom.

Father McKee and Brother Theodore split a can of corned beef to gain additional strength for the walk, but they had to pause briefly every twenty yards to catch their breath. A Filipino woman emerged from a house along the route to offer them a steaming dish of rice, which McKee claimed was "a real banquet, one of the most tasty meals I have ever eaten." Brother Rex was equally amazed at the eggs, bananas, and coconuts the Filipinos shared. He prayed "that God rewarded these good people for all that they had done for us."[31] Paratroopers also shared their rations with the famished internees, who eagerly devoured their first food from America since the early days of the war.

The column of exhausted but elated internees—which included two other Notre Dame alumni, civilians Michael J. Adrian, class of 1925, and Anthony L. Alsobrook, who spent three years at the university in the 1920s—gradually neared the lake, where McKee and Brother Theodore reunited with Father Lawyer and Brother Rex. Some of the nurses burst into laughter when they spotted a nun sitting in an amtrac bearing the nickname "Impatient Virgin" painted on the side.[32]

The prisoners' fragile bodies slowed the winding procession from Los Baños to the lake. One soldier noticed Sister Caecilius struggling with her bags and made a quick trade—he bore her items to the amtrac while she carried his weapon. Gunfire from the handful of paratroopers serving as a rear guard kept the pursuing Japanese at a distance but reminded the group that they had no time to waste. "Our hats go off to these boys," said McKee. "If we had realized that we were being snatched out of Jap territory instead of the territory being invaded and captured by U.S. troops we might have been quite nervous and hysterical. Thank God we didn't know the truth."[33]

When shells splashed in the lake, soldiers calmed the prisoners by explaining that they came from American guns tasked with keeping the Japanese away. McKee only learned after the war that the paratroopers had lied and, had they tarried even one hour longer, the Japanese would have overtaken them.

Sister Olivette's suitcase, containing her diary and missal, almost sank to the lake's bottom when a priest helping her into the amtrac dropped it, but he retrieved it before it disappeared. Protected by American fighter aircraft, amtracs hurried the first group of bedraggled inmates away. Others, including the six missionaries, rested for an hour beneath a coconut tree while the vehicles deposited the first group safely on the other side of the lake and returned to retrieve the rest.

With the last of the prisoners safely collected, paratroopers in the amtracs barked orders to huddle low, as everyone was within range of enemy rifle fire, and turned the vehicles' machine guns on the fast-closing enemy to shield their passengers. After two hours the amtracs reached the northwest shore of Laguna de Bay near a town identified in the accounts as Cubio. There the former internees stepped into army trucks waiting to transport them to newly liberated Bilibid Prison, a haunt familiar to Fathers Duffy and Carberry. "We were a weary, grimy pack of happy people,"[34] wrote Father McKee.

As the trucks and ambulances drove to Bilibid, Filipinos lined the roads, cheering the Americans and shouting "Victory!" In late afternoon the crowd entered the gates to the once-infamous prison and gazed through tear-clogged eyes at proof of its liberation: "As we drove through the gates we saw a big American flag on a pole welcoming us home," wrote Father McKee. "In a way we were home, secure from the fears and anxieties of three years and three months under the Japanese. For us the war was suddenly over on this day which will live in our memories, February 23, 1945, the day on which the Lord answered our prayers to His Mother by sending the Eleventh Airborne troopers to snatch us home." Brother Rex described their arrival as "one similar to Our Lord's triumphal entry into Jerusalem. People stood on the road and waved signs of welcome to us and the American troops. Huge banners were spread across the roads, welcoming the Americans back again."[35]

Awaiting their arrival were twenty-three American and Filipino doctors, assisted by six Filipino nurses and twelve Red Cross workers.

Now safe, the Los Baños group enjoyed hot soup and coffee provided by the Red Cross, a meal later supplemented with canned meats, fruits, and vegetables. The famished first group devoured so large a portion of the food supply that the army had to open a second kitchen to feed the second group. "Across Laguna de Bay to beach near Santa Rosa," Sister Olivette hastily recorded in her diary, "then to New Bilibid. First group here at 11:18 a.m. last group about 4 p.m. & all soldiers & baggage by 7 p.m." She later added in a letter to her superior at Saint Mary's, "By 7:00 p.m. we were all here, even to the last soldier. . . . We were real refugees fleeing from those burning barracks with a few things we could gather up quickly. We'll be lucky to have a handkerchief when we leave the Philippines."[36]

"Food—Food—Good American Food"

The missionaries awoke early the next morning, their first as free people in more than three years, hating to waste a moment of their newfound freedom. "Mass of Thanksgiving 6 a.m.," Sister Olivette put in her diary that day. "Breakfast cereal, milk, sugar [underline hers] fruit. Letters! 3 from the girls."[37] After breakfast, which took two hours to serve a line of hungry people that stretched three blocks long, the army issued razors to every male so they could shave the flowing beards and long hair that had become trademarks of their incarceration. Afterward the former internees failed to recognize some of their freshly shaven friends.

The Red Cross also provided clothing and other essential items. McKee met Lieutenant Finneran and two other soldiers from Notre Dame who had helped in the rescue. Joined by the two Notre Dame civilians, the group held a reunion to discuss campus news. Brother Rex wrote that, while enjoying sandwiches and drinks, "we were brought up to date on the latest happenings of the football team and the other things around school,"[38] including what they recalled of different university professors.

After the successful raid, Lieutenant Finneran penciled a note to Father Steiner on a grimy sheet of paper he carried with his battle gear. "Recently I had occasion to say hello to Fr. Jerome Lawyer, Fr. Robert McKee, Brother Rex, Brother Theodore," he wrote. "They were imprisoned and liberated by the 51st paratroopers." Finneran added, "Please excuse the dirt of this note Father, but it is being written in combat," and concluded, "You will probably hear from your clerics shortly."[39]

Newspaper correspondents from the *New York Times, Chicago Tribune*, and other publications swarmed the arrivals to relay their stories to home-front readers. The *Tribune's* correspondent, Walter Simmons, sent word to his publisher in Chicago, Robert R. McCormick, who wrote to Father Steiner on February 27, "In a recent dispatch from our correspondent in Manila, mention is made that the Rev. Jerome Lawyer, C.S.C. asks that word be sent to you regarding the wellbeing of himself and the brothers mentioned in the story who were rescued by American troops."[40] He included a copy of Simmons's article, which specifically referred to Fathers Lawyer and McKee and Brother Theodore, but omitted any mention of Brother Rex or the two nuns.

The nation celebrated the rescue of the Los Baños group. Articles in the *New York Times* in late February heralded the "Skyborne troops, infantrymen and Filipino guerrillas" who snatched the prisoners from Los Baños "after killing the entire Japanese guard contingent of 243." The newspaper explained that the troops "struck in the early morning darkness, taking the enemy completely off guard and rescuing every man, woman and child in the camp." The articles quoted General MacArthur as saying, "Nothing could be more satisfying to a soldier's heart than this rescue. I am deeply grateful. God was certainly with us today." He added, "A number of Catholic priests and nuns were included. All had suffered unbelievable indignities and dangers."[41]

The missionaries wasted no time penning long letters to their families. "Yesterday we were heroically and dramatically rescued from the Los Baños Internment camp and brought here 17 miles south of Manila," Father Lawyer opened his February 24 letter to his parents. He added, "Just allow me to thank those God-sent American troops and Philippine Guerillas [*sic*]. They did a marvelous job even tho we were kept flat on our stomachs during the battle." Thinking of the image of the Virgin Mary that rests atop the Dome at Notre Dame, he credited "our Dear Blessed Lady" for bringing him and the others out of their travails. He told his parents not to worry about him, as "our new camp here is wonderful. Food—food—good American food—bread—believe it or not, sugar—meat. O God, what a difference from starvation. All of us are gaining strength and in a few weeks we will all be normal." Recognizing that the years in captivity had altered him, he explained, "The future is unknown to us—but I am sure of one thing—when I leave the Philippines I will be a very sad man." He wrote that if it were up to him, he would remain in the Philippines to work among the wonderful Catholics who populated the islands, "but I have a vow of obedience." He continued, "You may hear from Lieut. Finnerman [sic] one of the parachutists who rescued us. He is a N.D. man '33,"[42] and added that one of their number, Brother Romaine, had been killed.

Father McKee told his family, "What a physical and mental relief to be under the Stars and Stripes again, and not to have any more nightmares about food and protection. . . . I want to forget most of it." He thought that the army treatment would help in that area. He referred to shaving "for first time since last July 8th—feel like a new man." He reported that he had enjoyed three pieces of meat for supper—"What a treat!"—and added, "Today we get our first bread in about three years—I can't wait."[43]

Sister Olivette opened her February 24 letter to her family, "By this time you have heard of our spectacular rescue from Los Baños where we were interned. In the morning at 7 A.M. Parachutists came for us—we were moved out across the lake in amphibious tanks, and by 7 P.M. we were well fed and in a safe place well away from the enemy and from the fighting areas."[44]

She added in a subsequent letter, "You can imagine seeing those paratroops drop out of those planes—150 of them—not realizing we were the object of their jump until the bullets started whizzing, and we saw our boys, American soldiers!! breaking through the fences, running across the fields and down the hills." In early March she informed her younger sister, Marjorie, "We don't know from day to day what will happen to us. We know we will be repatriated but when and how we don't worry about because we are eating three meals a day and that is the momentous thing now after months of hunger. The Army is taking wonderful care of us." She reassured her sister that she was daily growing stronger. "Our first taste of American food was given us by the boys from their own ration boxes—my they were wonderful, so kind and patient. We can't say enough in their praise." Even better was that each morning, aircraft dropped more supplies via parachute into their camp. "It is very exciting to see them fly over and great parachutes (red, white, blue, green & yellow) open up and ease down with boxes of food for us."[45]

The welcome news that their missionaries were in safe hands raced about the Notre Dame campus. The school's alumni magazine began an account of their ordeal, "This is the story which came to Notre Dame in March: a story of seven Notre Dame men, six prisoners of war, and one who led them to their freedom." The article quoted Father Lawyer as saying that once they met paratrooper Lieutenant Finneran among the rescue party, "From that moment it didn't take long to establish an N.D. club here." Finneran expressed his relief that the operation had unfolded so smoothly, saying, "That slip-up did not occur—thank God!—the attack coordinated to perfection—and we killed 243 guards and militia, with a loss of two of our men and not one of the internees." The officer expressed his pride that the university played such a prominent role in the story. "It seemed—and still does—so hard to believe that we could be brought together—many thousands of miles from home—by that common bond, Notre Dame."[46]

After alerting their families, the Notre Dame missionaries sent word to their superiors. Father Lawyer informed Father Steiner that although they preferred to either remain in the Philippines to continue their work in the Manila area or to resume their travels to India, they were making preparations to return to the United States. He mentioned that everyone in the group was gradually regaining their health, but that Brother Theodore had lost sight in one eye, was totally deaf in one ear, and had impaired hearing in the other. "He was pretty weak in camp but now is putting on a lot of weight. Father McKee is getting over beri-beri. Think cure for this is food & he is getting plenty of that. Bro Rex & I lost considerable weight & acquired the usual weakness in the legs as everyone else in camp." He added that a normal diet would restore most to normal, "except for Bro. Theodore who the doctor says will need an operation to regain the sight of his eye." Lawyer boasted that "We have had several N.D. meetings here in camp" and heaped praise on Lieutenant Finneran, calling him "a great fellow. Keeps us supplied with extra food, fruit, etc. Great company & a good Catholic boy."

While he was initially disappointed in being blocked from reaching his mission station in India, Lawyer eventually realized that he and the others probably did more good in the Philippines than they could have achieved anywhere else, confirming their earlier suspicions that their wartime detention by the Japanese might hand them a ministry that none had expected. "We have enjoyed our stay in the P.I. & have been able to do a lot of ministry work—more here, we believe, than in India." They were not certain what the future held, he said, but "we are content to rest up & take it easy until we are loaded out of here." In closing, he thanked his fellow Holy Cross priests and brothers for helping them emerge from the travails of the past three years: "We are all grateful for the prayers of the community in our behalf. We went thru a lot—had some narrow escapes—all thru the power of prayer."[47]

In a March 9 letter to Father Steiner, Brother Theodore explained that his right eye went blind due to the absence of "fish, eggs & milk" and "other necessary foods," and vitamins would hopefully correct the condition. "Otherwise I am in perfect health and would love to continue the journey to Bengal, India from here," he added. He guessed that they would all soon return to the United States aboard troop transports, which he feared might end his chances of working in India, but he thanked the Lord that they had been removed from Manila, thus avoiding the mass slaughter that occurred there when the Japanese retreated from the pursuing Americans. He cautioned Father Steiner, though, that the group was not yet safe: "The danger, however, is not yet over. There are still Japanese snipers in parts of the Philippines. There is the danger of ocean travel because of Japanese submarines or floating mines. With so many people massacred in these parts an epidemic of some kind may also follow. We still need your prayers for our safety."[48]

Two days after the rescue, Sister Olivette sent a letter to her superior, Mother M. Rose Elizabeth, through the Red Cross, writing, "For the first time we can really feel satisfied that you will receive this message. None of yours have come through to us. I have received several from my family but not before November of '44." She added that "both of us are well and safe, thank God! A little bit thinner physically and much sturdier spiritually as a result of our experiences." After learning the good news, Mother Elizabeth announced that the community was offering two days of prayer "in thanksgiving to God for His care of the Sisters and for their miraculous escape. We are looking forward to having them back with us before too long."[49]

Father Steiner was relieved to receive the news but allowed his anger to surface. "They will have some hair-raising and aggravating stories to tell," Steiner wrote to Father Edward Fitzgerald. "Japs are not human, so it irks one to hear the stories of their cruelty. We are inclined to believe that the Marines are not handling them in any kid glove fashion." He explained to Father Fitzgerald that the missionaries "had to move fast before the Japs could catch up with them. It was in a way miraculous, because any slip-up or any delay meant death to the whole outfit. Brother Romaine from Canada was shot by the Japs. He was in a hospital, but the skunks came along and killed everybody."[50]

"The Sight of the Dome Made Us Realize That We Were Really Home"
The Missionaries Return

After two weeks the two priests and two brothers, along with other single men, boarded trucks that took them to Nichols Field, where planes waited to fly them to Leyte to join a troop ship bound for home. Once aloft, the pilot circled Manila, giving Brother Rex a last look "of the place that had been our home for the past three years" and a chance to ponder a trove of memories, some good, most not, for the voyage home. Once in Leyte, the army issued clothing, "and we were able to be clothed decently for the first time in a long while."

The four remained in Leyte for about two weeks before, according to Brother Rex, "with a tremendous cheer from the internees and the troops aboard, we set sail for Hawaii." It took an evasive route south toward New Guinea to avoid Japanese submarines still operating around the island. The lengthy voyage gave everyone time to regain weight and strength, as well as to think about being home, a place, Brother Rex wrote, "where we could go in a room, shut the door, and have the privacy we had been denied for over three years."[51] Three weeks later the four steamed beneath the Golden Gate Bridge and into San Francisco, where a group of Jesuits met them, provided temporary quarters, and helped them obtain suits, hats, and overcoats at a navy store.

On April 18, three and a half years after they departed for the Pacific, the men stepped off a train in South Bend and drove to campus. Father Steiner, accompanied by the university president, Father Hugh

O'Donnell, C.S.C., thought the group looked "very well, and in fact well fed. Evidently they have gotten sufficient food since their liberation." He added, though, "these poor men have been in another world for four years."[52]

However, all was now well as the quartet cast eyes on the familiar sights of Notre Dame. "The drive down Notre Dame Avenue and the sight of the Dome made us realize that we were really home," wrote Brother Rex. "Our reception was a royal one to be sure." A *South Bend Tribune* reporter wrote that the four men strained their necks trying to catch a glimpse of the Blessed Virgin statue atop the Dome, and "when they finally discerned the figure through the trees as they neared campus, they knew that they had reached the haven which they had sought since the Japanese overtook them in Manila while they were on their way to missionary work in India."[53] Father Lawyer gave credit for his survival to the Blessed Virgin, to whom he had constantly prayed for strength, as well as to the innumerable Rosaries recited by fellow members of the congregation at the Grotto.

The war and its torments had receded, but the priests and brothers who had endured those exacting years would for the remainder of their lives bear the mental scars and physical ailments inflicted by their time in Japanese prison camps. For now, they gave thanks in being home, for returning to their Holy Cross brethren and for, as Father McKee wrote, being "back at Notre Dame."[54]

SISTERS OLIVETTE and Caecilius followed soon after. Nine days before the four male missionaries returned to Notre Dame, the troop transport U.S.S. *Admiral E. W. Eberle* (AP-123) anchored in Manila Bay and commenced boarding the nuns, 2,439 civilians, and 162 military and Red Cross personnel. "These civilians are principally American and United Nations citizens," recorded the ship's war diary, "who had been interned or stranded in the Philippine Islands since their capture by the Japanese."[55]

The next day the ship, accompanied by the welcome sight of three American destroyer escorts, departed Manila Bay and turned south on a course for Leyte Island. "Sailed about 9:00 p.m.," Sister Olivette wrote in her diary. "Passed to south of Corregidor & while passing had a 'General Quarters' drill which means passengers lay below—go to bunks and sailors man their battle stations. This followed by 'Abandon

Ship' drill—hastening to our life boat station. 'Darken ship' at sunset means early to bed 7 to 7. Life belts must be worn at all times."[56]

After anchoring in San Pedro Bay on Leyte Island, the transport, now accompanied by two destroyer escorts, left the Philippines on April 15 for the transpacific voyage home. The destroyers remained with the transport for eight days and then, just to the west of the Marshall Islands, left as scheduled while the *Eberle* "proceeded independently."

Most passengers used the time to eat hearty food and relax in the sun, but tragedy struck halfway to Pearl Harbor, on April 25, when thirteen-year-old Mary Louise Reynolds, after surviving her three years in the Philippines, died as the result of a brain tumor. According to the ship's war diary, "Due to the climactic conditions and impractibility [*sic*] of preserving the body, burial at sea was determined upon and final Catholic rites were conducted in her behalf by Father O'Bierne, S.J." Following a simple and moving ceremony for someone so young, "the body was committed to the deep."[57]

After a brief stop in Hawaii, on April 27 the *Eberle* embarked on the final leg to the West Coast. Five days later the nuns and their companions spotted the mainland for the first time since November 1941 as the transport approached Los Angeles. With a Coast Guard band performing "California, Here I Come," the transport pulled in and debarked the passengers. Red Cross personnel waited to assist them in arranging food, lodging, and transportation home.

Two weeks after their four male comrades had arrived, Sisters Olivette and Caecilius stepped onto mainland U.S. soil. A train whisked them to Chicago, where the mother general welcomed them back and accompanied them on the car ride to Saint Mary's.

The faculty and students arranged a warm greeting for the returning duo. "Saint Mary's went all out in gala welcome to the youthful and intrepid pair of Holy Cross nursing Sisters," proclaimed an article in the school's publication *Holy Cross Courier*. It praised them as being people "who brought home fresh laurels for their services to American nationals and other prisoners of the Japanese, won in harrowing experiences that add new lustre to the time-honored Holy Cross nursing tradition."[58]

When the car turned into the main entrance at Saint Mary's, a long road coursing along a peaceful, tree-lined avenue, students, faculty, and other college workers stood along both sides, cheering and singing "God Bless America." Sisters Olivette and Caecilius, now back on their familiar campus and among hosts of friends, were overwhelmed by the powerful moment. "The happiest moment of it all was when our car turned in at Saint Mary's gate Monday afternoon," said Sister Caecilius. "We never dreamed of anything like that procession and formal reception. That moment was worth all the tortures and the waiting we had endured."[59]

The welcome ended in church for Solemn Benediction, followed by a formal reception and picnic. College seniors in caps and gowns sang patriotic and festive songs as the crowd extended its greetings to the nuns.

The six Notre Dame missionaries were home.

"A Procession of Death"
On the Hell Ships to Japan

Father Duffy was not so fortunate. After a miserable Christmas in confinement at a port city on Lingayen Gulf in northern Luzon, on December 27 Duffy and the more than 1,200 prisoners were marched to one of two transports for shipment to prison camps in Japan. Squalid conditions in both ships rivaled the harsh treatment of the past three years and claimed the lives of twenty-one men during the ten-day trip to Takao Bay, Taiwan.

Upon their arrival the Japanese herded every prisoner, including Duffy and Carberry, into one of the two transports, the *Enoura Maru*. Three days later, American aircraft attacked the ship, killing men in the hold on both sides of Duffy when explosions sprayed shredded metal over the tightly packed captives and collapsed steel girders onto others. Shrapnel hit Duffy, feeling like hot irons puncturing his head and body, and obliterated the face of the man near him.

Duffy later explained to Bishop Karl J. Alter, his religious superior in Toledo, Ohio, that he "was able immediately after to administer the Sacraments to the dying and wounded and aid in the straightening out of the gorriest [*sic*] mess I ever expect to see. For three days no one could get out of this hold and the Japs would give us no medical aid.

Most of the wounded could have been saved if we could have secured proper medical aid, but that's too gruesome a story."[60]

Father William Cummings tried to calm the men by leading them in prayer, but other clerics were too grievously injured to assist. On January 11, two days after the bombing, Father Henry Stober succumbed from having his left leg blown off, and Father Duffy administered Last Rites to Father Matthias E. Zerfas, an associate with whom he had worked in Bataan before and during the Death March.

For three days Duffy remained in the hold, choking from the odors emitted by the decomposing bodies of the dead and trying to block out the moans of the wounded or dying. Conditions so rapidly deteriorated that when two Japanese corpsmen boarded the transport intent on helping the wounded, they abruptly retreated at their first sight of the mangled limbs, blood, and excrement. Finally, on January 13, the Japanese moved the survivors from the *Enoura Maru* to the cramped holds of another transport, the *Brazil Maru*.

The *Brazil Maru* pulled out of the bay January 14 for the voyage to Japan. "The conditions in these prison ships defy description,"[61] Father Duffy explained in a subsequent report. Temperatures plunged as the ship continued north, forcing the scantily clad men to huddle together for warmth. Men closest to the blasts of frigid air coming from the air vents succumbed first, with others perishing from starvation or illness during the sixteen-day trip. The death toll reached forty a day, keeping Father Duffy and the handful of chaplains occupied and forcing the living to stack their deceased comrades against the transport's bulkheads.

More of Duffy's religious companions perished. Father Frank Mc-Manus died from wounds he had suffered earlier, and Father Thomas Scecina, who had administered Last Rites to the bayoneted Father Duffy during the Death March, also succumbed in the miserable hold, anointed by Father Duffy. The already weakened Father Cummings, who each evening delivered a sermon and led the men in prayer, became so ill from dysentery that he could no longer stand. To conduct his brief services, other prisoners had to prop him up. Cummings died soon after, and Japanese guards tossed his body into the Yellow Sea as the ship turned east toward Japan.

Many mornings Father Duffy and another chaplain conducted joint funeral services over the dead. In two January weeks, more than five hundred were buried at sea between Taiwan and Japan. One, in particular, carried more emotion for the priest from Notre Dame. On January 26, the kindly Father Carberry succumbed to wounds, starvation, and illness. He might have survived the war, had he joined the group that escaped from Davao in April 1943, but instead he committed himself to the religious needs of the inmates. While the ten who fled returned safely to the United States, he endured disease and malnutrition in order to serve where he was needed. Now, as Carberry died, Father Duffy knelt beside him and administered the Last Rites. The two had worked in the Philippines before the Japanese invasion, survived the Death March and various prison camps, and rode the Hell Ships together, and now they prayed together as one comforted the other during his final moments.

The *Brazil Maru* arrived in Moji, Japan, a large port city on the Shimonoseki Strait separating the Home Islands of Kyushu from Honshu, on January 30. Of the 1,619 prisoners who left the Philippines, only 400 survived what Duffy called "a procession of death."[62] Duffy and Taylor were the sole survivors among the fourteen chaplains. Trucks transported the men to various prison camps on Kyushu, the southernmost of the Home Islands.

Father Duffy first went to Omuta Camp 17 on Kyushu. "Men were beaten to death and others froze to death as a result of general sadistic treatment," the U.S. Judge Advocate General's Office stated of Omuta after the war. There, the Japanese placed Duffy in a hospital because of blood poisoning in his feet, a condition that kept the priest hovering near death for three weeks. "Close as I was to death, I was kept alive by the Christian's fighting faith. I fought grimly every hour, praying to God to spare me and give me strength." As he recovered, the priest asked other men to carry him to patients soon to die so he could administer Last Rites, a ritual that had become depressingly common in the waning days of the war. "I did what I could for each regardless of his faith," he explained later, "and a look of ineffable peace came to the face of many a tortured soul in that last bitter hour on earth."[63] In the first such ceremony conducted at Omuta, on Easter Sunday, two officers stood on each side of Father Duffy and held him upright at the altar so he could celebrate Mass. After honoring the holy occasion, he collapsed from exhaustion.

Near the end of April 1945, three long years after the Death March, the Japanese moved the ailing Father Duffy to a camp in Mukden, a frigid Manchurian town on the edge of the Gobi Desert. He reunited with some of the generals and colonels he had known in Manila before Pearl Harbor, but Duffy had lost so much weight that they at first did not recognize their old friend. The camp physician, Dr. Mark G. Herbst, described Father Duffy as little more than a bony scarecrow in baggy pants and doubted the priest would long survive in the harsh conditions. But, aided by a kindly Japanese doctor, Duffy rebuilt his health to the point where he could take a more active role in camp.

Major A. C. Tisdelle, one of the officers in camp, was impressed that the priest, though obviously sick, continued with his religious duties. "Father Duffy was more dead than alive when he got to our camp," said Tisdelle, "but he insisted on saying Mass as soon as he could stand on his feet." Other prisoners used Red Cross raisins to make wine, and cooks baked unleavened bread for hosts, which Father Duffy placed on an improvised altar consisting of a wooden table covered with towels and blankets.

Father Duffy's absence of fear of the Japanese, whom he often berated for their atrocious treatment of the prisoners, astounded Tisdelle. "He bawled out the camp interpreter every time he saw him and told him the Japs ought to be ashamed of themselves," said Tisdelle. "Even the Japs admired Father Duffy."[64]

IN EUROPE, meanwhile, another priest who had gained admiration stood face-to-face with evil incarnate. While Father Barry thought that he had seen every degradation possible, he and other chaplains, including the newly arrived Father Powers, came across vile sights in the European war's final six months, images that challenged their faith in God and their belief that, as priests, they could make a difference.

CHAPTER 10

"FACING THE INSANITY OF HIMMLER'S MADMEN"

Onward to Victory in Europe

The final stages of the European theater unfolded when Allied forces under General Eisenhower attacked along the German border, from the northernmost sector near Belgium, where Father Murray entered the line, to the southernmost near the Rhine River, more than two hundred miles away, where Father Barry's 157th Regiment battled. They eventually cracked stiff resistance to enter Germany and commence the final drive to Berlin and Nuremburg, engaging in savage combat that littered roads and fields with thousands of bodies, befouled the air with smoke and ashes, and battered once-beautiful cities, villages, and hamlets into heaps of burned-out rubble. The bitter cold and bone-chilling winds of one of Europe's worst winters assailed the units along the way. "Trench foot was prevalent," said Sergeant Dougherty of Barry's regiment, "and men were always going to the battalion aid station. Those leather boots never dried out."[1]

In a letter to Patricia Brehmer, Father Barry said his boys wearied of eating the same thing every day. They sometimes "eat but one meal and call it a day. Canned ham and eggs for breakfast (tastes nothing like it sounds). Can of cheese for dinner and corn pork loaf for supper. Dog biscuits [infantry slang for the crackers included in their ration] go with every meal. These also make excellent fire wood when we want to brew a can of synthetic coffee." He thanked her for sending a Christmas box containing shrimp, tuna, peanuts, cigarettes, cheese, cookies, and marshmallows. "Now ain't that something to have for our first picnic along the Rhine. What a contrast to corn pork loaf flavored with apple blossoms (that's what the package says)."

The regiment's soldiers considered Father Barry more than a priest. He was a buddy to whom they could let off steam about an irritating officer or share their tears over a broken heart. "Beside me sits a soldier who got a letter from a little French girl whom he met after liberating a town. He is reading aloud. I always get in on their love letters, and once in a while write them for the lads."[2]

In January fighting near Reipertswiller, the Germans nearly surrounded Father Barry and the regiment, inflicting more than 700 casualties and taking 462 prisoners. By St. Patrick's Day—occasion for celebration on the Notre Dame campus—the regiment stood along the vaunted Siegfried Line, Hitler's major system of fortifications designed to halt an enemy's advance into western Germany. Thousands of bunkers, pillboxes, and concrete pylons, protected by hundreds of miles of barbed wire, forced the regiment to destroy each position before advancing to the next. During the first months of 1945 the regiment again absorbed alarming casualties, but for Father Barry and his unit, the worst was yet to come.

"Will I Make It, Padre?"

Friends and Holy Cross brethren raved about the persuasiveness Father Maurice Powers, C.S.C., exhibited every time he delivered one of his flowery sermons or composed vivid letters to friends or his superior. Adjectives and adverbs were his trademark. The priest loved nothing more than standing before an attentive audience, clad in regal vestments, and holding men and women transfixed as he conveyed his message in a booming voice. In demeanor and desire for attention, he was the opposite of his associate, Father Barry, but he hoped he could be as helpful to his soldiers as Father Barry was to his boys.

When the war broke out, Powers had inundated superiors with letters pleading his case for being allowed to join the chaplain corps and head to the fighting zones. His persistence finally paid off with orders to join the 101st Mechanized Cavalry, a unit designated for European combat. "Father Powers is like a kid with a new toy,"[3] wrote Bishop O'Hara in New York about his companion's delight in becoming a frontline chaplain.

Powers and the 101st Mechanized Cavalry crossed the English Channel in late January 1945. From Normandy the unit moved to the front near Saarbrücken, in Germany just across the French border, forty miles west of where Father Barry and the 157th Regiment battled the Germans.

"Life has been thrilling, swift, precarious and religiously rich," he wrote to a friend. "I've watched thousands kneel at my masses aboard a transport on the blue breast of the Atlantic. We have shared the vistas of [English poet William] Wordsworth and [English author Sir Walter] Scott in the Lake Region of England, and the stone houses and pebbled streets. The Channel crossing in LST's, the push across France through Joan of Arc's Rouen, Verdun and Soissons, where we slept in the shadow of an old cathedral, down along the Marne and Moselle rivers that claim memories of blood from other decades, into the valley of the Saar under the aegis of the gallant 7th Army."[4]

On St. Patrick's Day Father Powers's mechanized unit moved into positions along the Siegfried Line; it launched an attack three days later. The troops encountered stiff resistance at Hill 283, where one officer was wounded three times trying to dislodge the enemy, but they succeeded in collapsing the opposition.

Father Powers remained near the battalion aid station to console the wounded, tend to the dying, and assist the doctors. He sat beside men blown to pieces by mortars and shells or ripped apart by land mines. He once "helped gather one of the finest soldiers into a litter; his body was riddled in three pieces." Even if men survived their wounds, Powers glimpsed for them a future filled with mental and physical ailments: "Others are broken in body and heart, twisted frames that will never walk or speak again."

Especially excruciating were those moments in the aid station when he helped frightened, dying soldiers face their final moments. Father Powers heard the same question more than he cared to, those few words that tumbled from the mouths of soldiers too damaged to comprehend their true condition, "Will I make it, Padre?" The priest who could with ease deliver stunning oratory at the Church of the Sacred Heart struggled to find the proper phrase as he held their hand, knowing "that they have 10 minutes left." He whispered a few words about their condition, gave "a hurried Absolution, the Last Sacraments, and a promise to send his ring back to Bettie or Marian." After each death, Powers moved to the next wounded man until he had reached the last, "and on we move into the next town. We must push forward."

During the days following the loss of a soldier, Powers composed the difficult letter to family. "Your boy was hit by shrapnel," he wrote on more than a few occasions. "He lingered a time and then died valiantly. He fought like an all-American tackle, ripping a line to shreds while he manned that 37mm in the turret. He loved you."[5]

Father Barry had long since earned the respect that soldiers award to chaplains who, while under fire, risked their lives to help those in need. On a cold March day Father Powers earned his. As the priest talked to the wounded at a medic station, three German shells crashed in their midst. The blasts killed four medics and a doctor who stood within ten feet of Powers, knocked unconscious one soldier and blinded another, and tossed Powers onto his clerk. "I dressed their wounds as well as I could when I regained my strength," wrote Powers, surprised that he had survived the ferocious blasts. With additional German shells screeching down, Powers dragged the injured men to a nearby house; "the next shell tore the rear porch to pieces. I thought that it was 'lights' for me too, but they raised their elevation and shot at our tanks 100 yards away."[6] He struggled to his feet, clutched two wounded men under his arms, and carried them to another aid station two miles away, where doctors were able to save the men's lives. Powers received a Bronze Star for his actions that day.

That and similar occurrences made Powers wish that people back home comprehended the perils their soldiers faced. The American public read in newspapers that their troops advanced another few miles and seized another town, and to them a battle casualty was but one more number added to the ever-lengthening list of deaths and injuries. At the aid station, however, Powers worked with the human toll that newspapers often omitted. "You read that 200 were killed and injured," he told his friend, but "we see the flower of manhood melt under German counter-attacks." He added, "In America you monotonously read: American 3rd Army advances 12 miles, takes three towns, or the

American 7th Army of General Patch spearheaded 9 miles and takes 3,000 prisoners. Over here it was different. A daily change of position, blackout driving at night as we moved 'up forward.' Sniper fire along lonesome highways, towns burning as we rolled into them to occupy, being pinned down by unknown machine gun nests. . . ."[7]

He saw the devastation suffered by both sides, with German towns obliterated by Allied air bombings and German civilians seeking shelter in ruins that once were homes festooned with decorations, family photographs, and flowers. The division entered cities to find unburied civilian casualties and the decaying bodies of horses used to convey German supplies to the front littering roads and fields. Many of the dead German soldiers, Father Powers noticed, did not look old enough to be out of high school. He remained on call day and night at the aid station, catching a moment's slumber and a K-ration wherever he could. He was so occupied that many times he went "two or three days without removing my clothing for sleep."[8]

One item shone like a beacon through the turmoil—the strong faith exhibited by many of the soldiers. "Religiously, I can vouch for my men," he wrote to his friend. "I have seen them kneel in full field equipment, dust-stained faces, weary from sleepless nights of combat. I've watched them kneel in adoration at Consecration in the rear of woodsheds, along the highway where mass was held, and in the stately churches left intact from the ravages of war."[9]

He contacted his units on the front lines every day, trying to ensure that he saw every Catholic soldier, as well as any other man who called for his help, "at least twice a week." He said Mass in fields and in forests, and handed out New Testaments and Rosaries. If soldiers appeared to be nearing the limit of their endurance, he sat with them and helped compose letters to their loved ones, hoping that his counsel would aid them in "adjusting them to battle conditions when battle fatigue seems apparent."[10]

Privates on the line loved seeing the chaplain in their midst, and officers appreciated the boost to morale he brought to their men. "Father Powers is with us for a while and is quartered in the same building," wrote Lieutenant Colonel Hubert Leonard, commanding officer of a unit in Powers's division, to his wife, Mary. Leonard usually attended the afternoon Mass Powers celebrated every day, gaining increased respect for what the Holy Cross priest achieved. "He is quite a man to have around the men; regardless of creed, all the men like him."[11]

His military superior, Colonel Charles B. McClelland, wrote in an efficiency report for Father Powers that the priest was "an outstanding officer who wins admiration, devotion, respect, and confidence from men and officers alike." He added that Father Powers was a "brilliant speaker" and that "although in some matters he is so much of an idealist as to be impractical, he is beyond doubt as great a factor in maintaining morale in this command as any one other."[12]

Father Powers accepted the recognition, but he wondered whether he was fit to perform the duties of a chaplain. He could move masses with his stirring sermons, but could he affect one soldier with a sentence when that soldier most needed it? "I have a daily duty in my own life to constantly check myself to see if I am worthy to be the chaplain of such stalwart, noble fighting men,"[13] he admitted to his friend.

That mental battle followed Father Powers throughout the war and reached into the ensuing years.

"It Hasn't Been a Boy Scout Expedition"

To the north of Fathers Barry and Powers, two other chaplains from Notre Dame operated on the front lines. Rushing into northern Germany with Canadian troops, Father John McGee faced the same tribulations that greeted every combat chaplain.

"It is quite evident that you are in the thick of things," Father Steiner wrote to McGee in March 1945. "No doubt you are much handicapped and also suffer much from the elements. Snow, rain, and icy terrain slow up everything, and also injure the health and affect the morale." Hopes that the war might end in late 1944 mounted until Hitler's offensive into Belgium halted such talk. "Several times during this last year it looked as if things might end soon," mentioned Steiner, "but this last counter-attack gave evidence of much remaining power, and so a longer conflict than we anticipated."[14]

Fifty miles to McGee's south, Father Murray and the 104th Division barreled through stout defenses toward the Rhine River in Germany, absorbing a high toll along the way. "It hasn't been a Boy Scout expedition," he informed a friend named Father Will. Three inches of snow covered the ground; "Jerry is just across the [Rhine] river and we have been throwing 88's, 105's, and 81 mortars at one another for several days. He has a public address system set up on his bank and so do we, but it is not all a battle of words."

During lulls, Murray returned to the aid station, knowing that each action would bring additional casualties who needed him. He thought that his words and prayers had a positive effect on the frightened soldiers but wished he could do more during those moments he felt useless. "I had just assisted an engineer: 2 legs blown off above the knees," he wrote to Father Will. "He came into the aid station with another kid, and while trying to remove the latter's dog-tag his brains spilled out all over my hand. He died en-route to the aid station so there was nothing the medics could have done for him."

Murray related that on another day he had just arrived at the frontlines from the aid station "when the whole countryside was lighted up—a flare from across the pond. Then all hell broke loose—machine guns, small arms fire and heavy stuff. I ducked down to the cellar. We are dishing it back right now." He avoided harm in that brief encounter, "but it only takes one bomb or one 88 to send you to heaven!" Murray had to be ever vigilant, even at the aid station a short distance behind the front lines, where German artillery could still find its mark.

One afternoon as he and his orderly drove their jeep to a larger medical clearing station fifteen miles to the rear, a land mine "blew it to bits." Murray was unharmed, but when he reached the medical station, Chaplain Paul Mussell, O.F.M., urged him to remain the night and enjoy "a nice quiet sleep here in the hospital tonight." Murray readily accepted the invitation to a night of relative calm.

His sleep was interrupted at 2:00 a.m., when he "heard the ominous buzz of the [bomb] motor—it came closer and closer." Having many times experienced those weapons at the front, he told Father Mussell to ignore the buzz bomb. "There's no danger as long as the sound of the motor is above you," he told the other chaplain. "The motor always cuts off as it plunges to earth." However, instead of shutting down its motor first, the bomb, noise and all, hit near the hospital as Murray was still talking to Mussell. "We picked the pieces of window glass (no other damage) off our bed rolls and went back to sleep!" he explained.

After that brush with death, Murray decided that whenever he left the front lines to visit a clearing hospital in the rear, instead of lingering upon completing his tasks, he would return to the front. "We are just as safe here in the cellar [the frontline location where he wrote the letter]—than 15 miles back. I'd rather hear the buildings crashing all around and above us as the artillery hits, than be caught on the 2nd story of a hospital where the buzz bombs catch you."

In his letter to Father Will, Murray vented a lament heard everywhere in the fighting zones: that people on the home front, concluding that the war was almost over now that their forces fought inside Germany, forgot about the young men who continued to die every day. Until the final bullet was fired, Murray and his soldiers could not relax. "We have several men out on patrol now. I can hear the machine gun fire that they are meeting at this moment. They won't all be back tonight or ever. But you will still be reading about the V Day Celebrations in today's or tomorrow's papers. What a laugh!"[15]

"Our Humble Prison Sanctuary"
Sampson in Camp

Father Sampson was not laughing, either, but for different reasons than his Notre Dame associate three hundred miles to the west. After the exhausting trek to Stalag II-A, one hundred miles north of Berlin, Sampson's bedraggled group shocked the captives who already lived in the camp. "These guys were in bad shape,"[16] remembered Private First Class Phil Trapani of the men, who were vomiting and suffering from diarrhea. They joined the approximately three thousand other American soldiers captured during the Battle of the Bulge.

In his account, Sampson wrote that he had lost so much weight that he could barely recognize himself when looking in a reflection. Sampson had no objections when the Germans sent him to be deloused, as it was the closest he had come to a shower in weeks, but had to choke down a bowl of cabbage soup heavily laced with worms. Many regurgitated the food, but the vile fare at least provided some sustenance. One prisoner near Sampson swallowed the concoction, looked at the priest, and said, "The only kick I have is—them worms ain't fat enough."[17]

Since Stalag II-A housed only enlisted, Sampson was designated for transfer to a nearby camp for officers. Sergeant Harry Lucas, the senior ranking enlisted American in camp, begged Father Sampson to remain as the camp lacked an American chaplain. Sampson agreed, even though conditions for officers were generally better than those for the enlisted, because he saw the benefits he could bring to Stalag II-A. When a camp doctor convinced the German commandant that Sampson was ill with double pneumonia and could not leave with the other officers, the priest became the senior American officer in the camp.

As a chaplain, Sampson enjoyed greater freedom to move about camp, which housed soldiers from many nations. Separate compounds existed for nine nationalities, plus another quarter set aside for Jewish prisoners. The Jewish captives did not yet appear subject to extra abuse, but Sampson and others worried that as the Soviet Army closed in from the east and the Americans and British from the west, conditions could drastically change.

The fare in Stalag II-A did not improve. Bread, coffee made from acorns, and soup thickened with handfuls of grass formed the main portions. When Red Cross parcels arrived in February, famished prisoners ripped open the packages, only to uncover badminton rackets, ping-pong sets, games, and football pads. They eventually received other parcels containing canned meat, powdered milk, and other items, but only after the guards had rifled through the bounty to take what they wanted. Private First Class Arnold F. Franke, a prisoner who stopped at Stalag II-A before being taken to another camp, said, "Prisoners were starving to death in those camps. All of them were sick with something."[18]

Few bothered with escape attempts, for the camp stood hundreds of miles from American lines. Besides, every inmate figured that it was only a matter of time before the Allies defeated Hitler. It made little sense to risk death by escaping when liberation might be only months away.

Like his companion priests in the Philippines, Father Sampson contended with both friendly and brutal guards. The Geek was renowned for his cruelty, while Little Adolf, a Nazi Party official who was the most hated man in camp, sported a Hitler-style moustache. Kindlier guards traded food for American cigarettes and generally treated the captives with a gentler hand.

Little Adolf, who considered Russian prisoners as little better than dogs, once asked Sampson what the priest thought of the Russians in the camp. Sampson answered, "To my mind, the Communist government and the Nazi government are two dogs of the same breed. At the moment the Nazi is the most dangerous and we'll use any help to get rid of him." Little Adolf took him to the hospital section set aside for the Russians. Dying men lay everywhere on the filthy floor, crammed in a room hardly fit for animals, while a young French priest, known about the camp for his willingness to give up his food portion to others, tended to the men, tenderly talking with the Russians and wiping grime from their faces.

When Little Adolf left, the young cleric told Sampson that a wagonload of dead was about to be moved out for burial, but that a few of the men remained alive. Sampson rushed outside as the wagon lumbered to the graveyard, the arms and legs of those prisoners clearly moving in the heap. Unfortunately, he arrived too late to halt the wagon and prevent the men from being buried alive.

On his way back, Father Sampson walked by the main gate, where a guard was searching a Russian inmate. Upon finding a concealed loaf of bread, the guard beat the Russian and slashed his neck with his bayonet, but the Russian refused to let go of the bread. "I am a priest,"[19] pled Sampson, but the guard admonished him to stay away. All he could do was kneel beside the man and say a prayer before guards dragged him away.

Father Sampson, as the official chaplain for American and British captives, used a corner of a barracks as his chapel. As he mentioned in *Look Out Below!*, he bribed the guards to obtain lumber to build an altar and scarlet blankets to use as a backdrop for a crucifix carved from wood by an Italian prisoner. Sampson fashioned Stations of the Cross from paper and crayons, and a Jewish soldier painted pictures of Mary and Saint Joseph to place on the sides of the altar. "When the light was turned on," wrote Father Sampson, "the effect was so satisfying that I doubt whether any priest ever looked upon his church with greater pleasure and joy than did I upon our humble prison sanctuary."[20]

Father Sampson celebrated Mass every day, but due to a lack of bread he could only hand out Communion on Sunday. Twice each week he held a nondenominational service for Protestants, and in an adjoining small room he heard confessions and counseled the men.

Sampson visited the camp hospital each day and administered Last Rites to an average of four soldiers each week, anointing every Catholic and holding a prayer service for the Protestants who succumbed. Afterward, guards permitted him to select eight pallbearers and an honorary group of mourners to escort the bodies from the hospital to the cemetery. The solemn procession walked between parallel rows of inmates standing at attention and saluting the deceased.

Starting in March, Sampson was able to periodically leave camp to visit American working parties. He and a German guard bicycled to their destinations along pathways that reminded Sampson of simpler times back home, when he walked the flower-lined paths on campus or knelt in prayer at the Grotto overlooking the two small lakes. With any hope, he would soon be free to once again visit Notre Dame.

"The Most Inhuman Thing That I Ever Witnessed"
Father Barry at Dachau

Before Father Barry could return to South Bend and a teaching post at the university, his regiment had to smash through German resistance. The regiment moved quickly once across the Rhine, forcing the German Army from a succession of towns and seizing hundreds of prisoners. Father Barry took as a positive the many white flags that draped the walls of buildings, indicating that, at least among the civilian sector, Germany was all but finished. In one small town, the main street held a sign proclaiming the thoroughfare as "Adolf Hitler Strasse." One of the soldiers ripped it down and hoisted in its place a cardboard sign with the designation "Frank Sinatra Strasse."[21]

By mid-April the regiment reached famed Nuremburg, the emotional center of Nazism where Hitler had delivered some of his most stirring oratory to adoring throngs. A three-day battle ended with the regiment parading through the town streets formerly accustomed to Nazi boots.

Their next destination was revered among die-hard Hitler followers as the birthplace of Nazism: Munich. Germans along the way surrendered in large numbers, figuring that at this stage of the war, with the Americans and British rushing in from the west and the Soviet Army destroying everything in its path to the east, further fighting was futile.

Barry and his boys experienced conflicting emotions. Elated that the war seemed to be in its final stage, they were yet apprehensive that they might be killed with peace only days or weeks away. Men tried to shirk patrols, and risks that earlier in the war might have been accepted without question now loomed as obstacles to their safe return home.

Before the war, the worst violence Father Barry had witnessed involved hard slides into second base on the campus baseball field. Since becoming a chaplain, however, he had confronted brutality and death on an almost daily basis. Young boys died in his arms, and others now collapsed in tears or trembled at the sound of artillery. These sights, however, paled compared to what he and the regiment stumbled across in late April.

The regiment was closing in on Munich when their drive stalled ten miles northwest of Munich at Dachau. As many as thirty-eight thousand inmates lived in the filth that was Dachau, an abandoned munitions factory transformed into the first of Hitler's concentration camps. Unlike the death camps of Auschwitz and Treblinka, the destinations for most Jews, Dachau had at first housed political opponents, German communists, Jehovah's Witnesses, homosexuals, and other "undesirables." More Jews were imprisoned there as the war unfolded, bringing the total of those confined to almost sixty-eight thousand by late April 1945, just as Father Barry's regiment neared the site.

In addition to the thirty-two barracks housing the inmates, including one set aside for cruel medical experiments, the camp contained a large section for the guards, a punishment barracks for administering torture, and a large crematorium a short distance northwest of camp. A courtyard hosted executions, and an electrified barbed-wire fence and a wall with seven guard towers cut off contact with the outside. Between 1940 and 1945, an estimated twenty-eight thousand people died in the camp or in the series of subcamps nearby.

Father Barry had feared this moment. News had circulated about the horrible scenes American troops had uncovered in the April 11 liberation of Buchenwald, and it was common knowledge that more such places existed throughout Germany. He hoped that the war would end before his boys witnessed similar haunting sights, but that was not to be.

On April 29, the Forty-Fifth Division received orders to veer from its drive toward Munich and instead head to Dachau, a place of which *Time* Magazine, in the issue following the unit's arrival, wrote, "It was the first concentration camp set up for Hitler, and its mere name was a whispered word of terror through all Germany from the earliest days of Nazi control."[22] The division was ordered to keep the inmates in camp and post guards around the location until higher authorities arrived to organize an orderly processing of whatever the division encountered.

A series of appalling images lay before Barry and his regiment. "Thunderbirds who last week still wondered why we fought the Germans and their beliefs," wrote Bill Barrett, a journalist posted with the division, "got their answer at the Dachau prison camp where death claimed victims by the carload and murder was a wholesale sadistic business."[23]

As the unit approached the camp, soldiers came upon a collection of boxcars. With rifles at the ready, they crept closer, choking as waves of stench assailed their nostrils. Inside each lay decaying bodies in grotesque forms, silent testimony to the horrors of Hitler's concentration camp system. Men covered their noses and stifled sobs as they converged on the scene. Thirty-nine boxcars held the remains of more than two thousand men, women, and children.

"The thing everyone saw first was the thirty-nine boxcars, and that set the stage for the rest of the day," said Sergeant Dougherty. "Some men were crying, they were angry." He added, "The experience of coming upon the boxcars of corpses at the Dachau Concentration Camp on 29 April 1945 will always be for us the most unforgettable event of World War II, perhaps of our lifetime. No soldier was prepared, nor was there any way to prepare, to view hundreds of stinking, emaciated bodies in the remnants of their stripped [sic] uniforms."[24]

Most of the men stood mute, incredulous at what they had uncovered. "These were emaciated, starved bodies, that were only skin and bones," wrote Private First Class John P. Lee, one of those horrified soldiers. "We had seen men in battle blown apart, burnt to death and die in many different ways, but we were not prepared for this. Tears were in everyone's eyes from the sight and the smell. Several of the dead lay there with their eyes open, a picture I will never get out of my mind. When I think back on it, it seems they were looking at us saying, 'What took you so long?'"

The images sparked anger and disgust. Men of one company cursed, looked at one another, and ran toward the camp, killing any guard they found, even those who held their hands above their heads in surrender. "Suddenly, GIs started swearing and crying with such rage:

'Let's kill every one of these bastards,' and 'Don't take any SS alive!'"
said Private Lee. "Never had I seen men so fighting mad willing to
throw caution to the wind."[25]

Father Barry was at another part of camp when these killings occurred, but he saw enough to know that "our troops sacked Dachau,
and we really sacked it, no matter what anybody says." Few soldiers felt
remorse over what they believed was justified retribution for crimes
that grossly exceeded the strictures of warfare and modern civility.
Their wrath intensified when they entered the camp and discovered
more than two hundred burned bodies inside the camp's crematorium.
"The Americans stormed through the camp with tornadic fury," described an article in the *New York Times*. "Not a stone's throw from a
trainload of corpses lay the bleeding bodies of sixteen guards shot down
as they fled."[26]

"It was horrible beyond imagining," said Chaplain Leland L. Loy,
also of the Forty-Fifth, when he saw the crematorium. "I simply could
not believe that human beings could treat each other in such a way."[27]
Few of the soldiers, overwhelmed with the sights and the stench that
pervaded the area, could eat or sleep that night, but all understood the
rage that exploded after entering Dachau.

Jubilant inmates stormed the barbed wire to greet their liberators.
Many hugged the soldiers or kissed their feet, but as Barrett noticed,
"There was hate in that crowd as well as fierce joy, hate that had sim-
mered deep inside the men for years. They had awaited this moment,
and they acted."[28] One group of Russian prisoners grabbed a guard by
the arms and legs and literally tore him to pieces, while others chased
down fellow inmates who had worked with the Germans and beat
them to death.

In an effort to evade retribution, some guards changed into prison
garb and attempted to sneak away. Most, as Father Barry witnessed,
failed. "I saw outside Dachau, prisoners lining up the guards dressed in
prison clothes, and shooting them," said Barry. Other prisoners shot or
beat to death guards wherever they found them. Barry explained, "It
was a terrible mess, confusion everywhere," and added that "the prisoners went wild, looking for the guards."[29] He did what he could to stem
the vengeance, but in the emotion of the moment he might as well have
been shouting into the wind.

"Dachau, Germany's most dreaded extermination camp, has been captured," wrote a reporter for the *New York Times* the next week, "and its surviving 32,000 tortured inmates have been freed by outraged American troops who killed or captured its brutal garrison in a furious battle."[30] Barry and chaplains from other regiments helped organize and tend to the inmates until medical aid arrived with rear echelon units. Meanwhile, the military forced German civilians living in nearby communities, who claimed they had no idea such brutalities occurred inside the camp, to walk through Dachau and witness the atrocities inflicted by the Nazi regime.

When Father Barry met an inmate who spoke English, the priest asked if the man would take him through the camp and explain what occurred in each part. "From then on it was all downhill," remarked Barry. The prisoner showed him where the guards took captives to the "showers," where instead of water, poisonous gas seeped through openings and suffocated those inside. "So they would keep pushing them in and pushing them in," explained Barry later. "When they had them all in there, they would turn on the gas. A hundred and fifty people crowded in there."

Barry had heard about the gas chambers and debated whether he wanted to confront such evil, but he believed that if anyone then in Dachau had a duty to observe the scenes, he, in his role as a religious leader, was that person. "I wanted to see them with my own eyes." When Barry and his guide arrived at the chambers, emaciated bodies lay everywhere. "They did not have a chance to move anything. The Americans came in so fast. However many bodies there were in that gas chamber, they were still there when we opened the door. The stench was such that you could not stand it long." For more than an hour the guide took Barry to different parts of Dachau and explained daily life for inmates confined amid such misery. "I think it was the most inhuman thing that I ever witnessed,"[31] said Barry later.

At that moment, Father Barry stood face-to-face with evil incarnate, the opposite of everything he had preached and practiced his entire adult life. The former altar boy had found his calling by entering the priesthood, where he devoted his life to helping others and bringing God to their lives. He had known evil, but it typically consisted of sins conveyed in the confessional box. Father Barry had listened to sinners' words, administered penance, and given them absolution.

What he saw that day in Dachau, though, screamed at him from its own sublevel of degradation. How was he to react? How does one forgive something so abhorrent? Christ taught universal love and forgiveness, but standing among the bodies of men, women, and children, some twisted in agony while others rested tranquilly, as if in sleep, Father Barry confronted the core of his religious convictions. If he were correct in thinking that man was good, how could such depravity exist? If he were incorrect, he would be admitting that the foundations of his religious beliefs were frayed at best, rotting at worst. He had entered the war to aid young men in battle but now found himself embroiled in a mental dilemma challenging his ingrained principles. His faith in man shaken, he feared he would never be the same.

Every frontline chaplain from Notre Dame, whether in Europe or the Pacific, faced similar quandaries. It was inevitable the instant they became chaplains, for from that moment on, they became men of peace laboring in spheres of violence. How were they to adjust when the two realms stood at opposite ends of the spectrum? It was as if they walked a tightrope between the two, attempting to administer the mercies of peace in the arena of war, all the while trying to maintain their balance.

For Father Barry and the others, it was a struggle that would not soon be settled.

"Come Quickly. There Is the Awfulest Sight You've Ever Seen"
Father Powers at Landsberg

A short distance north of Father Barry's position, Father Powers and the 101st Mechanized Cavalry also advanced through southern Germany as part of the U.S. Seventh Army. After smashing through the Siegfried Line, the division crossed the Rhine on March 29, Holy Thursday. "All bridges had been blown by the Krauts," Powers wrote to Maripat McCormick of Notre Dame's publicity department, "and snipers shot at us from every side."

Like every battlefield chaplain, Powers was accustomed to saying Mass in farmhouses, barns, and other locations. That Easter Sunday, Powers was celebrating Mass in a local church when Hitler's surprise weapon, a jet aircraft, "bombed and strafed the Church because they knew it was filled that Easter Sunday morning." Two bombs missed the building by eight and thirty feet respectively, but shrapnel from the explosions destroyed the altar.

As Powers and the division thrust deeper into Nazi Germany, he wrote, "We faced the dreaded SS troops."[32] They fought a series of battles with the Seventeenth Schutzstaffel (SS) Panzer Division and the SS Totenkopf Division, elite outfits comprised of some of Hitler's most devoted troops, who fought to the last man.

Father Powers spread himself thin in taking care of the Catholic soldiers in his and other units. According to his monthly chaplain report, in April he drove one thousand miles and only once stayed in the same village on consecutive nights. With the unit constantly on the move, he celebrated Mass and heard confessions whenever they paused. He said the speedy advances placed additional burdens on him, "but I well realize that the Military Mission has all priority on their time."[33]

Father Powers dodged snipers, artillery, and aircraft. He reported that in April alone he was under fire twenty-four times, including six occasions when crossfire pinned him down. He wrote that the drive through Germany, with its numerous crossings of rivers and streams at night or under a daytime smoke screen, "was perilous and precarious. My own jeep windshield was pierced several times with bullets, and yet I live."[34] He spoke of "the crossing of the Rhine on pontoon bridges, the sudden abandonment of one's jeep when jets sprayed us with steel from the sky at Tauberbischofsheim or Lauda, the mad scramble for a foxhole when 88s spread their mantle of devastation, the terrible tree bursts that killed men of my unit, the panzerfausts that riddled the flower of my combat armored unit, the sleepless nights along a highway bordering the Danube near Augsburg, and the dreaded ordeal of facing the insanity of Himmler's madmen—called SS in polite society."

On April 12 he consoled the young soldiers when President Roosevelt succumbed to a cerebral hemorrhage and died in Warm Springs, Georgia. "I saw their faces in the early morning rain when news came that our great Commander-in-Chief was dead on April 12."[35] The majority had known only one man as president, and they mourned the passing of the leader who had guided the nation out of the Great Depression and helmed the massive military endeavor to defeat Hitler in Europe and the Japanese in the Pacific.

Father Powers acted as an intermediary in a German town after the unit's interpreter was wounded and evacuated. Powers did not speak

German, but he relayed the officer's commands in Latin to the local Bürgermeister, who also spoke the ancient language. Powers could not fathom the overwhelming number of civilians who both denied that they were Nazi followers and claimed that they knew nothing of the concentration camps or other evils of the Nazi system.

Like Father Barry, Powers was most deeply moved by the men, women, and children confined in concentration camps. "Most memorable of all my days," he wrote a few days after hostilities terminated, "was not the crossing of the Rhine, nor that of watching the muddy waters of the Danube under our pontoon bridge, nor of the visit to quaint old Heidelberg, the ride through devastated Munich or my hours in Berchtesgaden on the Czech–Slovakian–Austrian border, but rather the concentration camp on the Lech River near Landsberg and Munich." Powers was waiting to cross a river bridge that had been under German fire when suddenly one of his soldiers rushed up. "Father," gasped the soldier, "see those smoldering ruins. Come quickly. There is the awfulest sight you've ever seen."

His unit had come across a satellite camp southwest of Dachau near the town of Landsberg am Lech. (Decades later it would form the central event of an episode in the ten-part television series *Band of Brothers*.) Emaciated prisoners in striped garb wandered aimlessly between rows of dilapidated barracks. Some had already killed the German guards and now scoured the countryside, looking for food and clothing. Dead and dying prisoners lay about the camp, which was enveloped in a sickening stench. Not far away, boxcars jammed with the dead rested on tracks. "I saw the unbelievable sight of hundreds of huddled nude forms still smoldering from the fires initiated the day before," wrote Father Powers. "They had been starved until their gaunt forms at death weighed less than 60 pounds in many cases."

Accompanied by an interpreter, Powers queried a trio of inmates. They informed him that they were political prisoners from across Europe—Belgium, Poland, Russia, Holland, England, Italy, Spain, and Slovakia. "We were given one crust of bread and three potatoes a week," they told the priest. "We ate grass to live." The men had lost nearly half their body mass and weighed less than eighty pounds. They told Powers of the special cases in which guards poisoned or gassed prisoners, after which their bodies were disposed of in the crematoria.

"It beggars description in words," related Father Powers. "They even spoke of the staff men in the camp who celebrated these executions by a bacchanalian orgy, using even the skulls of victims as cognac flasks. Some were made to dig their own graves, then stand on the edge, so they could fall in after being machine gunned. This is not fiction. This was told to me by two prisoners who played dead for five hours under a work bench."[36]

His unit liberated more than ten thousand prisoners from Landsberg and a handful of other concentration camps. The sights cast a pall on everything that had so far been accomplished in destroying Hitler and his Nazi regime, leading Powers to fear what they might uncover elsewhere.

"The Memory and Lesson of That Day Will Always Remain With Me"

Adjoining Powers's 101st Mechanized Cavalry, Father Barry's 157th Regiment helped secure Munich in early May. A few days later Father Barry helped rescue a Jesuit, Father Paul W. Cavanaugh, who had been confined in a prison camp at Hammelburg, fifty miles east of Frankfurt. As U.S. forces drew near the camp, German guards marched all the inmates to the southeast, away from American forces. For five wearying weeks Cavanaugh and the inmates had trudged through Bavarian towns until they drew within twenty miles of Munich. Unable to cross a river because Germans had destroyed the bridges as they retreated, the guards surrendered to an approaching American tank column, thereby freeing Cavanaugh.

The Jesuit later praised Father Barry for lifting him out of the morass. "On May 5th the Archangel Father Joe Barry drove down from Munich and brought me back with him to the many mansions which the 157th Infantry inhabit in this Paradise," he wrote after the war to Walter Kennedy in Notre Dame's publicity department. Calling himself "A liberated soul," Father Cavanaugh ended his letter by teasing, "The one shadow that mars this all but perfect happiness is that the Archangel has a C.S.C. after his name and not an S.J."[37]

Father Barry aided another prisoner of war, one whose name he had heard earlier when Marian Ficco wrote to Father Steiner inquiring about her son, Daniel. Ficco was still alive but held captive at the Moosberg prisoner-of-war camp near Nuremburg, eighteen miles north of Munich. When Ficco, whose weight had plunged from 175 pounds to 90, heard that his regiment, the 157th, had advanced to Munich, he and another prisoner crawled through a hole they made in a fence and set out for Munich to rejoin their buddies.

Ficco located his old company in the regiment, where he caught up on the news and devoured so much food that he became ill. Father Barry, however, had the unpleasant task of telling Ficco that he had to return to Moosberg until American officials processed him and he could be flown to a reclaimed American military personnel camp. "I never thought I would sneak into a prison camp," said Ficco, who drove back to Moosberg accompanied by Father Barry. He trusted the priest, though, and figured the move was for the best. "Father Barry was our 1st Battalion chaplain and another of the best," he wrote.[38]

THREE HUNDRED miles north of Fathers Barry and Powers, in late April Father Murray sat down to write a letter to Notre Dame's librarian, Paul R. Byrne. He had been through intensive combat with the 104th Infantry Division, the Timberwolves, a tenure that sparked in the priest a lifelong love for the military. Wanting to share with his friend some of his experiences, he began scribbling on division stationery bearing the motto "Nothing in Hell Can Stop the Timberwolves." He informed Byrne of the bloody fight for the city of Halle, one hundred miles southwest of Berlin, "but the city flies the Stars and Stripes now." With the division's rapid advances in April and early May, Murray admitted that "at this time things are pretty well sewed up in this theatre." He boasted that his men were close to setting a record by logging almost two hundred consecutive days at the front and informed Byrne that he had mailed to the Notre Dame library a biography of Adolf Hitler retrieved in March from the ruins of Gestapo headquarters in Cologne, a uniform "that the chief of police in [Halle] once strutted around in," a Nazi flag and brown shirt, and other items. Murray was proud that the division had "quite a few ND men"[39] but explained that he rarely had the chance to see them because the unit had been on the move so rapidly.

What Father Murray failed to include was that, for his actions in Belgium, Holland, and Germany from October 1944 to February 1945, he had been awarded a Bronze Star. The citation mentioned that Murray "rendered outstanding service to the personnel of his regiment, serving with distinction and never hesitating, because of personal danger, to give spiritual assistance to those who desired it. His actions have won the respect and admiration of the officers and men of the regiment and reflect the highest credit upon himself and the Chaplain's Corps of the United States Army."[40]

TWO HUNDRED miles northeast of Murray, Father Sampson awaited his liberation. Each night during April, after the other men were asleep, Sampson and Sergeant Lucas slipped away to the chapel, where Sampson had hidden a radio recently smuggled into camp by a friendly guard. Sampson sequestered it in his pulpit, where he thought it would be safe from the frequent searches, and the pair kept the radio's presence known to only a handful of trusted men. They took these precautions because they feared that their captors had inserted a plant among them, a German who spoke perfect English and lived as a prisoner to gather information about planned escapes and other infractions.

Sampson and Lucas figured that the Allies had drawn near when their treatment improved. Guards even looked away one Sunday when, as Sampson delivered his sermon during Mass, he leaned against the pulpit and jarred the trapdoor open, knocking the radio from its concealed berth.

On Easter Sunday, Sampson and the other Catholic chaplains concelebrated an emotional Mass in front of prisoners from all nationalities. "The memory and lesson of that day will always remain with me until the day I die,"[41] Sampson wrote. The sermon, whose message emphasized that in prison camp, no one was trapped if they shared in the love of Christ, was delivered in English, French, Polish, and Italian, and four priests needed half an hour to distribute Communion to the large gathering.

The German guards and the prisoners alike knew the war would soon end. Much of Germany lay in ruins, and Allied aircraft flew over the camp in increasing numbers, bombing and strafing targets of opportunity. Sampson and the rest of the camp feared that they would perish before freedom arrived, either at the hands of their enemy or from friendly aircraft unaware that they were bombing their own forces.

During one Allied bombing attack, Father Sampson rushed from his barracks, risking his life to aid men caught outside. The Bronze Star citation awarded for this deed stated that Sampson "rendered outstanding service to the officers and men with whom he was imprisoned." The citation explained that Sampson "went among the wounded and dying in a calm and soldierly manner, rendering final rites to those of all faiths. Chaplain Sampson was a source of courage and inspiration to those he served and his actions reflect credit upon himself and the United States Army."[42]

With liberation drawing closer, Sampson and Lucas listened to the radio for instructions from the British Broadcasting Company on what to do when the war ended. As Sampson mentioned in his book, they were told not to make any attempt to escape; that if the guards fled, the ranking officer or noncommissioned officer was to assume command; that they should paint the letters *PW* atop every barracks so friendly aircraft would not target them; and that they should fashion a huge *PW* in stones in the largest open space in camp. The BBC emphasized that there should be no violence inflicted on guards, and that any Germans surrendering to them were to be held and turned over to the liberating force.

With the Americans to the west and the Russians to the east fast closing in, German civilians evacuated Neubrandenburg. A dozen guards and the camp commandant, fearing they would be summarily executed if the Russians seized them, surrendered to Sergeant Lucas, who ordered them confined in one building. Sampson, believing that one good turn deserved another, helped two friendly German guards about to flee the camp by giving them notes for delivery to American captors explaining that the men had treated the prisoners decently.

Other prisoners warned recalcitrant guards, who had two weeks earlier segregated five Jewish prisoners, to now free the five or face reprisals. "We told the guards 'We know who you are. When the war's over, we'll get your ass,'"[43] said prisoner Michael Salome, who had been captured in Belgium. The guards quickly released the five.

Soviet planes dropped leaflets on the camp and Neubrandenburg warning of their arrival. The joy of the camp's April 28 liberation, however, turned to disgust with the Russians' treatment of both the German military and local civilians. "The events of the next few days were to be among the most terrible I have ever seen," Sampson wrote. "These Russian soldiers seemed to be wild men."[44]

Dozens of Soviet tanks smashed through the camp's barbed-wire fences and knocked down the guard towers. Some prisoners rushed from Stalag II-A to loot Neubrandenburg's homes and stores, only to be shot by the Russians, but the Americans followed the instructions delivered by Lucas and Father Sampson and remained in camp. Russian captives inside dreaded their liberation, knowing that they would be either shot for collaborating with the Germans or sent back to the front. One Russian general asked Sampson if he had any complaints about his treatment, and when the priest replied that the German doctor had provided little help, the general held out a pistol and said, "Shoot him."[45] Sampson declined the offer but had forewarning that further atrocities were to follow.

A Soviet official told the Americans that they had to remain in camp until contact was established with American forces. Each man was allowed to write a letter home. Father Sampson, however, received permission to leave to tend to prisoners confined nearby and to visit Catholic soldiers in a hospital.

Sampson could hardly believe the horrors he came across during his first visit to Neubrandenburg. He saw the bodies of several German women, some barely in their teens, who had been raped and killed. Other civilians had been hanged upside down with their throats slit, and bodies and debris littered the gutted buildings and homes. Amid the stench and gore, Father Sampson knelt beside each body to whisper a prayer.

Sampson and another priest discovered the local cleric sitting on the steps of his destroyed rectory in Neubrandenburg. Inside, his mother and his two sisters, both nuns, quaked in fear as they rested on a sofa, traumatized after being raped before their brother's eyes. The mother clutched a Rosary in her hands. On the way back to camp Sampson stopped at the site where six bodies had recently been buried. A German shepherd dog lay over one of the graves, and though Sampson tried to coax him into leaving, the dog refused to leave his master.

Units from the Eighty-Second Infantry Division liberated the camp. An American captain, part of a special group tasked with locating esteemed German scientists for relocation to the United States, persuaded Sampson to help him smuggle one man through Russian lines. At the final Soviet checkpoint, Sampson matched multiple vodka shots with the Russian commandant to gain passage, after which the American captain and German scientist helped the inebriated priest into their vehicle.

"They Knew No Glorious Drives, No Magnificent Marches"
War in Europe Ends

With General Eisenhower's May 7 announcement that the war in Europe had ended, festivities erupted in much of the world and in every American military unit not then in the Pacific. To the south, near Munich, Father Powers at last relinquished those daily concerns he had for the "mined highways under skies made perilous by swift ME 109's as they rained steel and death from the skies"[46] and from the "tree-bursting 88 shells and terrific machine-gun fire."

Personal safety was not the most important matter on his mind, though. As he accompanied an armored column of hundreds of vehicles on Germany's vaunted autobahn the night of the surrender, he watched while "thousands of once-proud Wehrmacht in stolid gray marched by dejectedly. Forlorn, defeated, they hardly raised their eyes as they filed endlessly in column to a prison cage. War was over, but we did not know it at that hour; we only knew the order: STAND BY." The violence had ended only hours earlier, but the memories would linger far into the future: "a hundred hills in flame, a dozen villages blazing, a thousand spiraling flares that lighted pathways of death, the whining terror of a 'screaming meemie' or the dread curse of a tree-bursting 88 mm."

He mostly thought of the soldiers who could not join in the revelry because they had died in one of the many actions, small and large, on the way to Germany, or because they were numbed from the disruption to their lives caused by the brutal war. "I've seen them weep when their buddies were announced as dead from sniper fire. For 91 consecutive days, I rode in column, went with them day and night, knew their fears, their lack of baths, their torn clothing, their best girls in Buffalo and Nashville and Omaha."

He added, "When the sirens sounded over the world for V-E Day, they hurled ticker tape from stone cliffs into the canyons of Wall Street; they lifted toasts of champagne along the Champs Elysees; Piccadilly Circus in London was in holiday mood; salvoes of artillery belched forth in Moscow." While the world celebrated, "I was with my men, men who fought the SS into their last redoubt and won. They said nothing. They just remembered. For some there was Hill 609; others remembered Omaha Beach, St. Lo, the Hurtgen Forest, the Colmar Pocket, Saarbrucken, Nurmberg [sic], Munich. They knew the Purple Hearts on the way; they imagined neat, white crosses where Mack and Chuck were laid. They knew no glorious drives, no magnificent marches. They know only that it was HELL all the way. They were almost silent as I walked over two miles down along that column on Hitler's arterial Autobahn."[47]

Father Powers hoped that the men he had served would not be forgotten, especially those who made the ultimate sacrifice. In a sermon delivered at a Mass celebrating peace, Powers said, "We have left behind some of our most valiant comrades." To honor their loss, he stressed a message he hoped his listeners would spread to others when they returned to family and friends back home. "Let us highly resolve that the deceased fellow-soldiers of our unit shall not have spent themselves in vain; that we dedicate ourselves to the unfinished work which lies ahead here and in America."[48]

WITH THE fighting ended, Powers remained in Germany. A platoon from his division captured top military officers, including Field Marshall Albert Kesselring and his entire staff, Hitler's secretary of agriculture and postmaster general, and the Japanese ambassador to Germany. They helped establish military government in the region, replacing the Nazi officials with military commanders until civilian administrators could be found. Powers celebrated Mass in less hectic surroundings, seeing the number of his attendees grow with each occasion. "With all this, I add, every Catholic crowds my daily Masses," he wrote to McCormick. "Wonderful fellows!"[49]

He took the time to visit the cemetery at Bensheim, Germany, where many of his men had been buried. The powerful silence and beautiful setting moved Powers, who tried to convey the emotions in one of his flowery letters home. "This May morning, in a cloud of apple blossoms along a mirror-smooth Neckar River, I drove to an American Military Cemetery to see those I knew and loved," he confided to a friend. "I found endless rows of white crosses set in perfect diagonals that stretched away endless in the morning sunlight, marking a design for eternity. Their valor is enveloped forever in silence: perhaps all too soon forgotten except by some obscure Gold Star Mother far away."[50] He hoped that wherever his ministry took him, whether back to Notre Dame or some other location, he would never forget what he owed to these young men.

Near the end of the month, Powers returned to the cemetery for a Memorial Day service in which he again used his oratorical skills to deliver a potent message. Of the men they had gathered to honor he said, "A few weeks ago he was with you, a part of that mighty machine to overcome ugly, chaotic war, a war of hardness, sweat, and grinding fear, where the whistle of death rode on the night wind, and you both saw one hundred hills aflame; a war which saw warped science labor to make men become heretics of civilization." Like those in attendance, "they had dreams, plans, and hearts that loved," but war had dramatically altered their paths. "He has bivouacked for the last time. But he has left us a heritage: 'No greater love than this: that a man lay down his life for his friends.'"

Powers ended by addressing the deceased. "Sleep on, brave men of the Cavalry whom we honor today. You have fought injustice with heroism and consecrated the soil of an alien land with your blood. You have not died for the empty praise of some orator, nor for some posthumous citation, but for the common people like your mother and mine that they might have the security and peace ensured by our Bill of Rights. Your death bestowed an obligation on us today: never to compromise what you fought so valiantly to attain. Out of fresh-made graves where you lie peacefully, we seem to hear your voices."[51]

FATHER JOSEPH Barry, the quiet chaplain who used simple words in talking about his boys, would never have delivered such a loquacious sermon, but he would have wholeheartedly agreed with every sentiment. He and his regiment also had much to celebrate. Since landing in Sicily almost two years earlier, Father Barry had tended to his boys in two continents and four countries, ending 511 days of combat in the foothills of the Bavarian Alps. "Here is where it all started," wrote the division's newspaper reporter, "the Munich beer hall, Hitler's own apartment."[52]

Nothing, however, had ended for Barry and the regiment. Hitler and his Nazi Party had fallen, but the Japanese waited in the Pacific. Everyone had heard the horror stories about the suicidal *banzai* charges and kamikaze missions. No one wanted to encounter those nightmares after facing the vaunted German military, but everyone, including Father Barry, expected it would soon happen. One platoon even renamed itself the "A & P Platoon" because they figured that as they had now completed operations in the Atlantic, they would be rushed to the Pacific.

In talking about his immediate future, Father Barry could have used the words Father Powers included in a letter home: "Perhaps it is on to Burma, China, Japan, or, perhaps, home. Whatever it may be, don't relinquish a memory prayer for my men and a Padre who needs one too."[53]

Father Barry had passed through the perdition that was Dachau. Other forms of hell beckoned on the other side of the world.

CHAPTER II

"YOU COULD HAVE HEARD MY CHEER IN NILES"

Onward to Victory in the Pacific

Father Henry Heintskill's cramped office aboard the U.S.S. *Tulagi* made Notre Dame's student dormitory rooms seem palatial. Files and records detailing his work with the almost nine hundred men of the escort carrier's crew littered the space, but fortunately, like the ship itself, the priest seemed to be in perpetual motion, hurrying out of his office to counsel a sailor here or plan a musical program there. "We've put a good bit of water behind us in these last few months," he wrote to Steiner in the aftermath of Iwo Jima, "but for all of it we haven't seen much of the land out this way. At best we see coast lines." Whenever they entered a harbor, a locale normally associated with rest and a few beers, "we are concerned about one thing; get repaired and reloaded as fast as possible." He could not claim to be in the fight every day—the Pacific Ocean was, after all, an immense body of water, and the carrier had to relocate from one landing operation to another—"but when things begin to pop they happen quickly—we pack enough activity into a couple of hours to last for several days, and to make conversation for a week."[1]

"Suicide Planes Have Caused Us Some Worry"
Action on Okinawa

Heintskill would have preferred a quieter welcome when the carrier arrived off Okinawa on April 6. As the ship took on supplies that afternoon, reports poured in that numerous enemy aircraft were approaching the island. They were the first phase of Operation *Ten Go* (Heavenly Operation), a series of kamikaze assaults designed to batter U.S. vessels off Okinawa. Except for the newest aircraft and most experienced pilots, which remained in the homeland to defend Japan's shores, the Japanese had collected every available aircraft for the operation.

The Japanese could ill afford to lose Okinawa. They boasted that in their long history the Home Islands had never been invaded, but should Okinawa fall, the door would be open for the Americans to crash their shores. The military planned to employ any measure to prevent that unthinkable event. After more than three years of war, however, they lacked the resources necessary to continue battling the United States on equal terms, so they turned to a simple equation: one aircraft, one ship. The kamikaze pilot would lose his life and plane but in the process possibly take out an entire ship and her crew.

For the U.S. military, Okinawa was merely the first step in the campaign to invade and ultimately vanquish Japan—certain to be a bloody struggle with an enemy fighting on home territory. Most military experts predicted the fighting would persist into 1947 and beyond. "There is little hope or expectation that we will return to the States this year," Father Francis Bridenstine wrote to Father Steiner a few weeks before he landed on Okinawa with the army's Seventh Infantry Division. He added, "There is still too much to do out this way."[2]

As American forces closed in on the Home Islands, a determined Japanese population, backed by squadrons of kamikazes, waited to repel the invaders. "The suicide planes have caused us some worry, because it is especially difficult to defend ships against such attacks," Steiner replied to Father Heintskill in June. "We must remember that we are not fighting ordinary human beings, but pagan barbarians. It seems that they must be killed off one by one, and the war will not end until everyone mother's son has been exterminated."[3]

That afternoon fifty kamikazes closed on Okinawa. *Tulagi* catapulted her fighters to engage the invaders, and as *Tulagi* began to turn away from shore, gunners opened fire on a suicide plane closing on the starboard quarter. Although the plane took critical damage, the pilot maintained enough control to swerve his craft and crash into a nearby landing vessel. Two more aircraft veered away from *Tulagi's* antiaircraft fire but were downed by fire from other ships.

Heintskill's carrier avoided harm, but the Japanese sank eight ships and damaged ten others in the attack, killing almost four hundred men in the process. The following days placed added burdens on *Tulagi's* aviators, who flew missions against Japanese airfields and in support of marine and army forces ashore. Father Heintskill kept busy talking with those young pilots, hearing their confessions and giving them Communion. He wrote the parents or wives of every aviator to inform them that he had administered the Sacraments to their sons.

Heintskill expressed concern to Steiner that while the pilots had so far avoided harm, "the job calls for our planes to be going night and day, with time out only when the weather closes in so tightly that we can't see the leading edge of the flight deck. It's surprising how long it's possible to keep going on that schedule." He worried about the effects of the extended strain on the pilots and noticed that the carefree, boisterous crowd that had first joined the carrier was now more focused and serious: "Our pilots aren't the eager beavers they were six months ago—they fly strictly in the groove—no horse play now. They're all very conscious of the fact that the longer they stay out here the faster their mathematical chances are of diminishing and they're taking no chances."

In his letters to Steiner, Heintskill tried to intersperse levity with the serious concerns. He claimed that the dehydrated food was not bad, and "the potatoes and carrots we're getting now are actually tasty. The concentrated fruit juices and powdered eggs still have a long way to go," but they at least supplied valuable vitamins. He told Steiner that he had been holding on to surplus money, which he figured he would need to cover replacement clothing and the travel expenses when returning to Notre Dame. "I haven't considered this a violation of poverty, but if it is contrary to your intention I will follow any plan you suggest."

The kamikaze pilots reinforced Heintskill's conclusion that he had seen enough of war. He longed to return home to see his parents, "But the more I think of it the less I like being relieved by a Protestant chaplain," not because of the replacement's faith, but because Heintskill had made significant gains with a once-reluctant crew he believed still needed a Catholic chaplain. When he arrived, "there was a good deal of suspicion and prejudice to break down first and that takes a good deal of time,"[4] but he patiently waited until the men had a chance to assess his actions. The reluctance gradually diminished to the extent that he now held nightly sessions with a group of pilots who peppered him with questions about the Catholic faith.

Steiner commended Heintskill for his work with the aviators and, above all, for writing the many letters to mothers and wives, who needed tending almost as much as did their sons or husbands at war. Steiner understood that the letters took valuable time from looking after the *Tulagi* crew, "but the consolation that these letters bring is certainly worth the effort. Mothers know that they may never again see their boys, but if they are certain that they have been taken care of spiritually, their sorrow will be much assuaged by that knowledge, in case something does happen to their dear sons. You Chaplains do not fully realize the fruitful Apostolic work you are doing. May God bless you for it."[5]

ON OKINAWA, Father Corcoran needed God's blessings, too. He had already experienced more than his fill of bitter clashes and patrols while serving with the Thirty-Second Infantry Regiment of the army's Seventh Infantry Division. He had accompanied the unit during its operations in the Aleutians and at Kwajalein in the Marshall Islands.

Before the April 1, 1945, Okinawa landings, Corcoran hoped to return to Notre Dame for a chance to regroup from his twenty-three months in the Pacific. In early March, however, he wrote to Father Steiner that the break would "have to be put off for some time to come." He visited Hawaii in between operations, during which he attended a gathering of Notre Dame alumni who met regularly to catch up on news of the university and of each other. At one meeting they even welcomed Notre Dame head football coach Frank Leahy, who shared information about the football team and other university matters. Before long, though, Corcoran knew he would "be heading for something more active." He would not know the destination until the unit had boarded ship and left the islands, "and, of course, I could not tell you now even if I did know."⁶

Steiner was accustomed to his priests' inability to be specific about locations and missions, but he could at least share with other priests the information that Father Barry was alive and still in Europe, or that Father Dupuis had witnessed the bloody fighting at Iwo Jima. He also shared his sentiments about the conflict's progress: "The war seems to be getting hot at all spots," he confided to Corcoran in March, before the European fighting ended. "No one dreamed that the Germans could hold out this long. It seems almost impossible for them to continue much longer. As for the Japs, they are going to have to be hunted down one at a time. This may take years. We have them pretty well on the run, but there are still a lot of them left, and scattered over a wide area."⁷

On Okinawa, the regiment so often mounted swift attacks against Japanese defenders entrenched in interlocked cave complexes that it earned the nickname "Spearhead." Flame-throwing tanks and aircraft dropping napalm bombs supported the regiment, incinerating hosts of Japanese who preferred to die at their posts rather than surrender. "We have seen our share of land mines and booby traps and we still see snipers brought in every day," Father Corcoran wrote to Steiner. "And there is seldom a night goes by that we do not have visitors in the air."⁸

Corcoran informed Steiner that he lived a Spartan existence on Okinawa. "I have had one bath in a couple of weeks. And that out of a helmet." K-rations with the soldiers provided his meals, making him long for "one of Brother Egbert's meals" back at Notre Dame. He shared a tent with a Jewish officer, a Baptist doctor from Georgia, and an Irishman from the east. The Baptist doctor, Corcoran wrote, "is very good at midnight requisition. So whatever is to be had, we get. Yesterday he picked up a chicken right from under a Navy Commander's tent. It really tasted wonderful."

In his letter to Steiner, Corcoran included a photograph of him saying Mass on Ie Shima, an island off Okinawa where famed news correspondent Ernie Pyle had been killed. He also apologized for the messiness of his letter, but explained that the typewriter given him was so ancient that it "must be a vet from the last war" and he had typed the letter while sitting on a cot with the typewriter resting on a wooden crate. "This is the some [sic] total of my office."⁹

"You and Father Dupuis Have Seen Some Real War"
Father Boland at Okinawa

Aboard a vessel off Okinawa, Father Boland was about to experience firsthand the death and mayhem brought from the sky by suicide craft. The priest was fresh from the Iwo Jima campaign, where his transport, the U.S.S. *Highlands*, brought troops and supplies to the volcanic island and evacuated the wounded. After depositing the wounded at Saipan, *Highlands* began a 2,500-mile journey south of the equator to pick up troops and equipment earmarked for the next operation. The ten-day trip, free from death and injury, brought a welcome breather to the crew. They organized the navy's traditional Neptunus Rex ceremonies, in which crew who had never crossed the equator were initiated by those who had, and stopped overnight in the Solomons, the location, as Boland put it, "of the famous Guadalcanal," before continuing south-ward to the New Hebrides. "The trip down to Espiritu was long and hot and we were all happy to arrive there," he informed Father Steiner.

After ten days in Espiritu Santo, on Palm Sunday the transport began the long journey north to Okinawa. On April 9 the ship an-chored near the island, where they commenced preparations for ferry-ing troops from the army's Twenty-Seventh Division to seize Tsuken Jima, a small island off Okinawa's eastern coast. Intelligence estimated that since fewer than one hundred Japanese defended the island, as Bo-land put it, "the operation would be over in a few hours, a day at most."

Early in the morning of April 10, *Highlands* anchored off Tsuken Jima to disgorge the infantry. Flares turned the predawn darkness into day, and flashes from mammoth naval batteries conducting the prelan-ding bombardment of the beaches propelled hundreds of arcing salvos shoreward.

The troops began leaving for shore at 7:00 a.m., and from his perch on the transport, Boland saw immediately that the operation would be no cakewalk. "We could see the shells from the Jap shore batteries and mortars splashing in the water around our boats as they approached the beaches," he informed Steiner. "There were many Jap snipers on the is-land and machine gunners with extraordinary accuracy of aim. They were camouflaged so perfectly that our troops could not discover where the gunfire was coming from and that was the story most of the time for the two days it took to capture the island."

Matters worsened during the night. "Many of the boys said afterwards that they had never lived through such a night," Boland wrote to Steiner. They claimed as much because of "the usual Jap night infiltration. They threw hand grenades into the foxholes and a number of boys were killed and wounded seriously during the night and had to lay where they were until daybreak. It was an absolute rule that no soldier was allowed to move from his position during the hours of darkness, not even the medics."

Highlands again took on casualties, receiving seventy-nine soldiers who, even as they left Tsuken Jima, drew fire from enemy snipers. "Needless to say, our boys were glad to get off that island. Most of them were pretty glum and sullen over the experience and the general opinion was that the Japs had been greatly underestimated."

Once again Father Boland wound through the injured, lending words of comfort and holding the hands of young soldiers teetering between life and death. "Five died on this ship. One of the Jap snipers was particularly accurate and shot several of our boys through the head, in some cases right in the middle of the forehead."

In the aftermath, Father Boland's anger erupted over home-front coverage of combat, which focused on major operations while ignoring minor ones. He hated to see lesser skirmishes, such as the landing at Tsuken Jima, relegated to the backwaters, for those men, too, placed their lives on the line. When soldiers died, whether while storming the Normandy beaches in Europe, in battling the enemy at Guadalcanal, or on a little island off Okinawa, they sacrificed their dreams for the future and deserved to be recognized. "All in all, it was a costly little operation, although the news reports represented it as trifling," he vented to Father Steiner. "Some of the boys who got killed were out here for over three years and this presumably was to be their last invasion. For them and their families, the price was pretty high."

On the morning of April 12 the *Highlands* raised anchor off Tsuken Jima, steamed around the southern tip of Okinawa, and turned up the west coast to the port city of Naha, "around which a great battle was raging." Shortly after the transport had departed, a massive Japanese air raid hit ships in the Tsuken Jima area, but off Naha Boland now witnessed the impact of the American military might produced in home-front factories. "The bay was literally filled with ships of all kinds, from big battle wagons down to the smallest type of craft. There was a continuous barrage from the warships on the city of Naha and the coastal inhabitants. It was a beautiful spring afternoon and it seemed a pity to see so much destruction going on."

The afternoon turned deadly when, before *Highlands* reached her anchorage, "Jap planes were on the attack." Boland watched intently as planes dove at ships. Antiaircraft guns splashed one kamikaze, but another barely missed the stern of a nearby ship "as the pilot was making a suicide attempt. This was our introduction to Naha and Okinawa. It was evident that we were in for some hectic days and indications were not wrong."

The next two days brought more of the same, with the call to general quarters frequently sending men to their stations. Boland counseled as many men as possible on the transport, believing that even a moment's visit with the young sailors boosted their spirits. Even soldiers and sailors who had paid only cursory notice to religion credited chaplains with bringing calm to chaotic situations, and Catholics who rarely attended Boland's Masses admitted they liked having the priest around.

Boland faced an issue with which every chaplain struggled. While he brought solace to his crew, he had no one in whom he could confide his own fears and doubts. The sailors leaned on him during troubling times, but who among the crew could sympathize with Boland's problems? He might occasionally share concerns with an officer, whose age might be closer to Boland's forty-nine years than that of the teenagers he nurtured, but only another chaplain could understand Boland's responsibilities, problems, and pressures, and aboard *Highlands* he was the sole chaplain.

The kamikazes swept in again on Friday, April 13, "in great numbers." General quarters sounded three times during that night, calling Boland and the crew to their stations from 7:00 p.m. to 10:00 p.m., again from 11:30 p.m. to 1:00 a.m., and finally from 3:15 a.m. to daybreak. "It was really quite a night," Boland wrote.

Father Boland followed the progress ashore, which he described as "very intense and our troops do not seem to have made any great progress in the last few weeks." Navy vessels provided what help they could, as "gunfire from our warships keeps going day and night," and he watched each night as flares shot skyward by ships or dropped by aircraft turned the darkness about Naha into daylight "to prevent Jap infiltration into our lines and to furnish a better target for our Navy guns. The brightness from these great flares, with usually three or four in the sky at the same time, is truly amazing."

Whenever possible a boat took Boland for visits around the harbor so that he could celebrate Mass and hear confessions aboard ships lacking a Catholic chaplain. "I have been extremely busy," he wrote to Steiner, "since at present I am the only Catholic Chaplain serving over twenty ships and numerous small craft. I have four or five Masses on Sunday, going to various ships, and I try to make a different one each week day for Mass and Confessions."

Other kamikazes appeared in force Sunday evening, when Boland witnessed what he called "the most exciting spectacle that we have yet seen." The evening, "a perfectly beautiful, warm, calm evening with a marvelous sunset in prospect," was interrupted when "radar showed Jap planes were on the way. Some suiciders had succeeded in getting through our outer line of air defenses and were out for the kill." Sailors raced to stations and manned antiaircraft guns. Every ship in the harbor, joined by antiaircraft guns ashore, filled the sky with shells and tracers that stitched a deadly pattern in the dark. "The noise was deafening," wrote Boland of the display.

Boland saw three kamikazes fall to American gunfire, with two smacking into land and the third into the water. "It was an amazing sight to see one of them hit in mid air and spiral down in flames, causing a great explosion when it landed on the shore. Shortly after, another was shot down, hitting the shore, and then a third came tumbling out of the skies and landed in the water near a ship, making a great splash."

Gunners successfully deflected that first attack, but more kamikazes returned shortly after dark "with great fury. Again, all of the ships in the harbor from the big battle wagons to the smallest craft, opened up with their guns and the scene was almost indescribable. The whole sky was literally aflame with tracer bullets and exploding shells." The firing inched closer to *Highlands* until the explosions burst directly over their heads, forcing Boland and everyone to seek cover from the deadly shrapnel that rained down on their deck. "A shell from one of our own ships, a short round, exploded on our after well deck, but fortunately nobody was seriously hurt. You can easily imagine that it was quite a relief when we finally got the word to secure from general quarters that night."

The next day Boland's thoughts turned from kamikazes to the army units leaving the transport for action ashore. He had visited as many Catholic soldiers as time permitted and saw how they "really hated to go into the battle for Naha just a day or two after coming from their invasion of Tsuken." He wished he could accompany them, but the transport was also taking on another group of one hundred wounded from Naha that required his services. Like most chaplains, Boland had too few hours in each day to handle the responsibilities that cried for his attention.

In midmorning, just as they were getting underway for "a distant, safer port," general quarters again called the crew to stations. More than two hundred Japanese aircraft winged toward Okinawa, where they attacked multiple ships. Fortunately for Boland and the *Highlands*, most of the kamikazes focused on shipping to the north instead of targeting the twenty-four slow-moving transports, which would have been easier marks. American fighter aircraft downed one plane in a vicious dogfight forward of the ship, which "caused a tremendous splash in the water. His bombs exploded when he hit the surface, pitching up tons of water in a great geyser-like stream, some five hundred feet into the air." Boland wrote, "We all felt much relieved a couple of hours later when we secured from general quarters. It would have been a little rough to get hit and sunk with nearly a hundred helpless casualties aboard."[10]

As *Highlands* again pulled away from Okinawa to transport the casualties to military hospitals on Saipan, 1,300 miles to the southeast, Father Boland comforted the wounded, wrote letters for them to their families, and administered Last Rites to more young men than he wished. After transferring the wounded at Saipan, *Highlands* continued south to Ulithi and then west to the Philippines. There, Boland and the crew joined other ships and land forces in preparing for something no one wanted to face: an invasion of the Japanese Home Islands that every military strategist expected would produce nightmarish casualties.

Back at Notre Dame, Father Steiner offered what comfort he could in his letters. After reading Boland's powerful correspondence, he replied, "You and Father Dupuis have seen some real war. You have witnessed slaughter and destruction that has never occurred before in the history of war. We thank God that both of you have come through so far without a scratch."[11]

Should the United States need to invade Japan itself, though, no one, whether private, sergeant, colonel, or chaplain, could expect to enjoy continued good fortune.

"Did He Get the Last Sacraments, Father?"

One priest had seen little of the war. The university's prefect of discipline, Father John J. Burke, had been hounding Father Steiner for permission to become a chaplain, but his requests fell on deaf ears until the war's third year. After finally obtaining approval, forty-year-old Burke graduated from the Navy Chaplain School at the College of William and Mary in July 1944. By that time, Fathers Duffy and Carberry had been in Philippine prison camps for almost three years, Father Barry had dodged bullets and shells in Sicily, Italy, and southern France, and Father Sampson had parachuted into Normandy. Burke realized that he was a latecomer to the war, but he hoped to make an impact before the conflict ended.

The next month Burke arrived at his first post, the National Naval Medical Center at the Naval Hospital in Bethesda, Maryland. Disappointed at not being rushed to the active areas in the western Pacific, he was at least happy to spend his days counseling patients newly back from the Pacific, many of whom related harrowing tales of combat on land and at sea. "Although I had always thought of the Navy Chaplain in a thundering atmosphere of strong guns going booming, of battleships and destroyers bouncing on the heavy seas, and of snipers and mortars and heavy artillery of Marine jungle warfare, and never in terms of a modern up-to-date hospital like this one," Father Burke wrote to Bishop O'Hara in the Military Ordinariate in September 1944, "I am resigned and content to serve out, to the best of my unmilitary ability, this tour of duty here."

The patients' physical and mental ailments foreshadowed what the priest might encounter should he reach the combat zone. He told Bishop O'Hara of a 1941 Notre Dame graduate who was commanding a group of transports at Normandy when his ship hit a mine and "was blown sky high. Both his legs broken and knees shattered. The right leg is paralyzed and gangrene has already eaten up the toes, the sole of the foot and a spot on his ankle, the size of a silver dollar. When he recovers sufficiently from the operation on his left elbow, also broken & shattered, they will amputate and adjust the right leg. He is in good spirits. I see him daily and of course fan the breeze about N.D. & the boys." His duties took a heavy toll on the priest as he made the rounds. "The physical and mental condition of many of the boys and yes of many of these waves [women in the navy], makes for tears in the heart."[12]

After nine months in Bethesda, Father Burke received his wish when the navy stationed him aboard the U.S.S. *Pennsylvania* (BB-38), a venerable battleship and survivor of Pearl Harbor that had already participated in eleven different operations from the Aleutian Islands to the Philippines. "The boys call the *Penny* 'Old Falling Apart,'" stated the ship's *Summary of War Service*, "because she turns out such a volume of gunfire you'd think she was falling to pieces."[13] If the battleship continued her stellar record, Burke was about to be involved in plenty of action.

"It is quite obvious that I have seen nothing of war," he wrote to Father Steiner in May 1945; "anxious as I am to get out there, those whose chests are decorated with ribbons and stars would just as soon remain here until the thing's over." The veteran members of the crew had seen their fill of war. They dreaded returning to the combat areas where fighting was likely to last for at least another year or two, a time heavily dominated by Japan's most recent weapon—"They don't like those suicide planes!" Burke hoped that the ship's array of antiaircraft guns could keep kamikazes and torpedo planes away from his new home. "I am anxious to notice my first reaction to the guns—over 150 of them. This ship is just built for guns, as you know. She has had some narrow escapes in acquiring the fine record she has."[14]

Burke was unprepared for the volume and noise of the firing when the battleships headed to sea for gunnery and antiaircraft drills. He received permission to select his own battle station, which gave him the freedom to "get to where I hope I may never be needed," but "when she rapid-fires you think all hell has broken loose and she shivers me timbers," he wrote to Steiner. "We have undergone simulated air attacks—and they are beautiful, so long as they are simulated. But God bless & forgive us if they ever really come at us in groups of sixty or more—some are bound to get through the anti-aircraft barrage."

Father Burke was disappointed with "the religious health of my flock." Sparse crowds attended his daily and Sunday Masses, and faith did not seem important to the men while they operated off the coast of the United States, thousands of miles from the fighting areas. "The atmosphere is saturated with profanity. A two-star admiral addressed the officers assembled when we were at San Diego and I never heard fouler language. He Goddamned everything & everyone—those who 'sat on their lazy ass on the beach etc.,' then he concluded with a 'God bless you.' He approved of the assumed condition that each of us had a blonde or three brunettes on the beach—we needed that for relaxation. I wonder what the proportion will be when he gets another star!"

He concluded that matters would not improve as long as they remained safe in the United States, but "perhaps when we get closer to the brink of the abyss the boys will come to daily Mass and at least weekly Communion." Until then, or until the war ended, "I am trying to make the most of this experience and I shall be very happy to return to the paradise that is Notre Dame."

In July, with American carrier aircraft already pounding the Home Islands, the battleship left San Francisco for the voyage first to Pearl Harbor and then to the battle zone. "I just returned to my room from the quarter-deck after passing under the Golden Gate bridge," he wrote to Steiner, "getting a last look at the Bay and the buildings on the hills of San Francisco." In addition to the crew, they were transporting almost one thousand sailors to Pearl Harbor, seventy-six carloads of ammunition, one and a half million gallons of fuel oil, tons of equipment, and more rations than he ever thought he would see. "A battlewagon is a monster with an elastic & seemingly limitless capacity," he wrote, and "I wonder how we stay up on the ocean and make 20 knots!" He wished he had been sent to the war sooner, but "at long last we are on our way, and what the future holds the good Lord only knows."[15]

During the trip, when the ship's officers formed a betting pool predicting the exact date of the war's end, Burke selected August 15, a choice his betting mates considered foolish. The war, in their minds, would certainly last longer than one month. Sailors on deck and officers in the bridge talked of the peace overtures Japan had supposedly relayed to the United States, but most still expected the war to stretch into 1946 at least.

After the brief stop in Hawaii, the battleship continued west, where training maneuvers to prepare for the bloody invasion of the Home

Islands were already underway. That final titanic clash fought in Japan proper would end the war, but who among the soldiers and sailors would survive the inevitable waves of kamikazes and *banzai* charges that an invasion of Japan would bring?

Father Burke maintained a diary to record his thoughts while aboard the battleship. Most comments referred to training exercises or religious services, but on August 9, as the ship neared Okinawa, he entered two words about a moment that changed everyone's lives: "Atomic Bomb!"[16]

The two atom bombs that demolished Hiroshima and Nagasaki in early August thrust peace prospects front and center. The men felt relatively safe operating in Okinawan waters, four hundred miles south of the Home Islands, but until the war had officially ended, crew still had to man guns and maintain watches.

Father Burke tried to keep their minds focused. In a Sunday sermon, he told his attendees that they remained "in dangerous waters" and that one of his functions as their chaplain was to write to the parents of those who died. "I recalled the obvious: that we were sitting on a keg of dynamite [the battleship's vast stores of ammunition], that we were allowed Holy Communion without the fast because we were in danger of death because of submarines, of aerial attack, of sea attack." He cautioned them that should disaster strike, he might be unable to reach them, and emphasized that every man needed to make certain beforehand that he had confessed his sins and received Communion. Burke mentioned that what their wives and mothers wanted to hear in those letters was "not that he died heroically in the defense of his country, not that he earned the Silver Star or the Congressional Medal because of his heroism in death, but rather: 'Did he get the last Sacraments, Father? Did he go to Mass & Communion frequently?'"[17] He hoped that, even in what might be the final days of the war, they would take care of their religious needs.

"Water Everywhere. Can't Get to Men"

Burke's words proved prophetic. As the ship lay at anchor in Buckner Bay, Okinawa, on August 12, a Japanese torpedo plane slipped through American defenses and launched a torpedo that struck the aft portion of the battleship, punching a twenty-foot hole in the stern. The explosion rattled the warship and gushed water into compartments below decks, causing the *Pennsylvania* to settle by the stern and trapping men, many already dead, at their stations.

Repair parties brought the flooding under control, but as their work ended, Father Burke's began. "I gave General Absolution just as soon as I recovered my wits after the explosion of the torpedo," he later wrote. He strove to reach the injured and dying men in the aft sections, but the waters kept him at bay. "Up all night," he entered in his diary that night. "Water everywhere. Can't get to men." He hoped that at least some had heeded his words and gone to Confession and received Communion but he figured that the vast majority probably had not, and the thought that Catholic sailors might be dying without a priest to administer Last Rites haunted Burke. Some, he knew, already lay motionless in their watery grave. When repair parties brought up five bodies, Burke arranged a makeshift funeral and recorded, "Burial service on fo'csle [forecastle], 1 Cath, 4 Prots,"[18] in his diary.

Twenty men died and another ten were wounded in the attack. "Thank God, thank God, neither the big fish nor the blast got quite to our powder magazines," he wrote to Father Steiner, "otherwise the community would be less one weak member who would not be buried in the cemetery at N.D." Once the crew pumped out the remaining water, the ship would head to Guam for repairs and then "I hope to USA."[19]

Burke confessed his distress that he had been unable to battle through the waters to be at the side of those twenty men in their final moments. "God forgive me for my weak power of suasion," he wrote in reference to the sermon he had earlier delivered. He wished he shared Father Powers's gift of swaying crowds with his oratory. "I even emphasized the probability, which alas became the certainty, that I might not physically be able to reach them with the Holy Oils. I have prayed and am confident that at least they had a moment of perfect contrition, which thank God I had thoroughly explained to them one Sunday."[20]

He conducted a general worship service for all faiths the day after the attack, and wrote to Steiner, "Thank God the war is over. We are still in Zebra condition [men at battle stations], however, with guns manned and on the alert—don't trust 'em. Besides we're still a sitting duck."[21]

On August 14 the battleship's crew gathered on the forecastle to attend the burial service for the bodies so far retrieved. Father Burke stood at the table serving as altar, complete in his altar vestments, with the flag-draped coffins between him and the surviving crew. Following that ceremony, Burke accompanied this first group of bodies—some remained trapped below—for burial at the American cemetery on Okinawa.

Burke was so preoccupied with trying to determine which crew members had been killed, collecting their personal belongings, and writing letters to parents or wives that he had neither the time nor the energy to fully celebrate the news everyone in the world had long awaited—peace. A trio of words in his diary on August 15 refer to the moment: "End of war."[22] The loss of shipmates only three days earlier overshadowed the happy event.

According to the ship's war summary, when the *Pennsylvania*'s skipper, Captain W. M. Moses, informed the crew about the surrender, "there was no hilarious rejoicing. Instead there was a minute of utter silence as the men, weary from three nights' work to save the ship, paid homage to their shipmates who had given their lives so very near the end."[23]

Father Burke was about to consecrate the host during a Mass celebrating the Assumption of the Blessed Virgin when an announcement over the loudspeaker brought the joyous news. He asked the sailors in attendance for a moment of silent prayer, and then turned back to the altar and whispered, "Hoc est enim Corpus Meum," Latin words meaning, "For this is my Body."

Even after the ship was able to depart on August 27—"Leaving in morning. Hurrah!" he wrote in his diary—repair parties were still recovering additional dead. "3 more bodies," he wrote on September 9. "Burial 8 men,"[24] he added the next day.

A bit of levity returned when officers reminded the priest about his July prediction that the war would end on August 15. When the officers asked how he had chosen the exact day, Burke answered that as war had erupted in the Philippines on December 8, the feast of the Immaculate Conception (December 7 in Pearl Harbor on the other side of the International Date Line), he decided to select another holy day. August 15, the feast of the Assumption of Mary into heaven, seemed an apt choice.

IN THE Philippines, the August 15 announcement halted the training in which Father Boland's *Highlands* was involved for the looming assault into the Japanese Home Islands, but crews remained vigilant until surrender ceremonies made the war's termination official. The end of the war "has brought a great relief to the men out here in the Pacific," Boland wrote to Steiner, "although the tension of the past few years still remains to a considerable degree."[25] Boland took advantage of the calm to say three Masses each afternoon, one each on three different ships anchored nearby, and hear confessions.

AT CLARK Field near Manila, not far from Boland, Father Hewitt and a group of officers listened to the morning news summary from a daily radio broadcast from back home. Ever since the atom bombs had incinerated Hiroshima and Nagasaki, the men had debated about the timing of the Japanese surrender. "Suddenly it came," wrote Hewitt of the announcement from President Harry Truman that Japan had accepted his peace proposals. The group paused, as if in disbelief; "Then pandemonium broke loose."

Hewitt had vowed that he would mark the day by ringing a church bell. He hurried to the parish church, climbed the bell tower, and interrupted a Mass below by fulfilling his pledge. "I watched soldiers pause in their walking; mechanics hovering about the planes stood up to stare at the church tower. Peace came to us with almost the suddenness of the Pearl Harbor attack. In the camp area men rushed up to grab my hand saying, 'Father, do you realize what this means to me? I am going to see my wife and child!'"

That evening Hewitt offered a Solemn Military Mass of Thanksgiving for victory and peace. "If I was back at Notre Dame," the jubilant priest wrote Father Steiner, "you could have heard my cheer in Niles, Mich. [a city ten miles north of the campus]."[26]

"God Bless You in Your Present Sorrow"

Father Burke could have used some cheerful words, as he was about to contact the families of the men who perished in the attack on the *Pennsylvania*. The first letters from anxious parents and loved ones to Father Burke arrived within three weeks, all seeking the same information. Is my son alive? Has he been killed? If injured, is it serious? Orn Catherine Rawls had heard nothing from her son, Coxswain Floyd L. Rawls, since the incident. Rawls had regularly sent her letters, but once they suddenly halted, she wrote, "I'm so worried I can't eat or sleep." She asked him to investigate and "wire me at my expense."[27] Fortunately for Mrs. Rawls, her son survived, but her anguish was typical of what all parents and loved ones endured in the absence of specific information.

J. P. McGlone of Wisconsin was not as blessed. She received a notice that her son, Quartermaster Second Class John A. McGlone, was reported as missing, but had heard nothing more since August 12. She asked Father Burke if her son "was one of those trapped in the navigation department? If so, would there be any possible hope that he might have been rescued?" The distraught mother, a Catholic, added, "We were gratified to learn that there was a Catholic Chaplain aboard."[28]

Alvena Olges had been unable to obtain information about her brother, Seaman First Class Bernard J. Olges, also reported missing. She worried because newspaper accounts had stated that most of the casualties had occurred near her brother's station. "Personally I have no hope for his safety," she wrote, "but would like for you to tell me anything you can." She informed Father Burke that Bernard was "a good Catholic boy and I'm sure has confided in you," and that, "he has a wife and two small daughters who needed him so badly at home. His wife still has some hope of his safety but I cannot feel that he had a chance." She ended the lengthy letter by mentioning that she had five brothers in the military, one of whom had been killed the prior year, and that, "all this had been very hard on my parents who are in poor health, especially my mother."[29]

Father Burke had to mail twenty responses to the United States in which he relayed, with dignity and compassion, information about the loss of a loved one. Even though it would have simplified his task, he refrained from sending form letters. Instead, he wrote similar paragraphs to open and end each letter, but inserted personal information in the main portion. "God bless you in your present sorrow," Father Burke began each letter. "As the Catholic Chaplain aboard the U.S.S. *Pennsylvania* I want to assure you that your son [here he inserted their first name] received Catholic Burial. The Holy Sacrifice of the Mass was offered several times for the repose of his soul."

Father Burke continued by explaining, "On the morning of August 14th, in the presence of the Captain, the officers, and the crew I conducted the burial service for all our dead shipmates on the forecastle of this ship. His body was buried in the grave blessed by me in the Army, Navy, and Marine Cemetery No. 2, on Guam. Nothing was lacking in the honor and respect due to this young hero of our beloved Country."[30]

Rather than delve too deeply into the precise manner of death, which might have been excruciating for loved ones to read, he told every parent that their son had perished immediately from the concussion of the torpedo's explosion and that their loved one had felt no pain. To the father of eighteen-year-old Seaman Second Class John B. Roemer, Father Burke wrote that their son was the first recovered of the twenty "who were killed during these last tragic days of the war. I was present when the doctor examined his body. It was whole and entire with no visible wounds. He was killed instantly by concussion from the terrible explosion of the torpedo." He included a photograph of the burial service conducted on the forecastle and added that "not a day has passed but John and his shipmates have been remembered in the Holy Mass every morning. God rest his soul and bless you his sorrowful parents."[31]

At this point in the letter he added personal information that offered complimentary comments about the soldier. To Angeline Ortbals of Ferndale, Michigan, whose son, nineteen-year-old Seaman First Class Robert J. Ortbals, had died, he reported that Robert's division chief said, "He had a heart of gold" and went out of his way to help his shipmates.

"Your husband had an enviable reputation aboard this ship," he wrote to Margaret Olges, the widow of Seaman Olges. "He was the kind of man that stands like a rock amidst the waves of trials and difficulties." To the parents of twenty-one-year-old Quartermaster Third Class Thomas F. Quealy Jr. he wrote that their son "was a gentleman" and his "character was true gold which shone brilliantly in an atmosphere that demands character." He mentioned to the parents of Seaman Roemer that while John had only been on board a short time, he had been developing into an efficient man, "eager to learn and with a sense of responsibility." He added, "I feel that a boy so young must very soon, if not already, be enjoying the eternal happiness of heaven which is beyond human description and to which, in God's mercy we all look forward."[32]

Father Burke ended all letters in similar fashion, noting that the deceased had recently attended Mass and received Communion and had, as far as he knew, led a religious life. In closing, he wrote, "It is impossible for me to express anything that will lessen the sorrow which you must endure. You have returned to God your beloved son on your Country's Altar of Sacrifice. In this supreme sacrifice your son is most like our Divine Savior; and you, I trust, most like his Blessed Mother. God bless you with the humble and Christian spirit of resignation to His Divine Will. Please call upon me if there is anything further I can do."[33]

Burke realized that he could offer only minor consolation, mainly about the good reputations of these men and their religious observances, but worried that he had not adequately comforted the families. He still wondered whether he had made an impact with the sermon in which he urged the attendees to be cognizant of the dangers they faced, and in which he emphasized that one day he might have to write their parents and answer whether they attended Mass and received the Sacraments regularly. Had he, with these twenty letters, accomplished his task? "Then the fatal torpedo," he wrote to Father Steiner, opening his soul to his superior, "and I tearfully and sadly confess I was unable to definitely and frankly answer that question in the letters of sympathy I had to write."[34] It was a concern that Father Barry or any of the other combat chaplains would have understood.

He learned from subsequent letters that the loved ones had appreciated his efforts. Ortbals thanked him for his "comforting letter" and wrote, "You can't know how much we appreciate hearing from you." She explained that the family had received many letters of sympathy, "but Father, none of them mean as much to us, as your promise to remember Robert and his shipmates in your daily offering of the Holy Mass." The grieving mother was proud that officers and shipmates so highly regarded their son, who "was a credit to his country and to us," and added, "My husband and I have suffered a great shock in losing our son we loved so much, but God will see us through, for the sake of our five younger children and an older son, Leo, who is in the Army."[35]

The McGlones were consoled "that John had received a Catholic burial" and was buried on land instead of at sea, where they could never recover the remains. "It was also a comfort to know that John didn't suffer in his death," they wrote, and they trusted that John had taken advantage of having a Catholic chaplain to receive Communion "and was ready to go." His mother enclosed five dollars and asked Father Burke to celebrate a Requiem High Mass for John and his deceased shipmates. Mrs. Frank Daniels, whose nineteen-year-old son, Quartermaster Third Class Clyde W. Cox, was among the dead, thanked Father Burke for his letter and wrote, "He was one of the swellest kids in the whole world. Our house will never be like it was when he was home."[36]

THREE DAYS after the Japanese torpedo struck Burke's *Pennsylvania*, a different aerial event brightened another Notre Dame priest's day. At long last, Father Duffy's liberation was at hand.

CHAPTER 12

"I HAVE SEEN MY SHARE OF BLOOD, DEATH, MUD, HUNGER AND COLD"

Home

Sixteen United States paratroopers following close on the heels of friendly Russian forces liberated Father Duffy. He joined his Protestant minister friend Reverend Taylor in conducting a thanksgiving service a few hours later. In his sermon, Taylor said they were all humbled to have their prayers for deliverance answered "and in that humility must commit ourselves to rebuilding a world where such a war can never again occur. We're going back to our families soon. Let's go back with love in our hearts and His work in our hands. Let's tell the world what God did in Cabanatuan, Bilibid, O'Donnell, Fukuoka 22, and Hoten. This is not the end but the beginning. Let's turn the world right side up—for God and for our country."[1] Father Duffy then closed the service by leading attendees in the Lord's Prayer.

After a period of resting, eating decent food, and focusing on his health, Father Duffy turned to correspondence with people back home. Telegrams from the American Red Cross had already alerted Duffy's superior in Toledo, the Most Reverend Karl J. Alter, that Duffy had been freed and would soon be on his way to the United States, but the priest now wanted to provide additional information. In a long letter to Bishop Alter written eight days after his liberation, Father Duffy provided further details about his condition. "At last we are free and by God's mercy, alive. I'm one of the few survivors of a trip in which we rode four ships to get to Japan, one of the two chaplains and the only priest out of the nine who were originally aboard." He explained that he was still slow in moving around, mainly due to feet swollen from beriberi, but expected to return home on the first plane out. "Henceforth, Alcatraz will hold no terror for the survivors of Bataan and Corregidor. All of us who have survived know God has been very good and are most grateful, tho many has been the day in the past when death would have been a merciful end to temporal suffering." Referring to man's ability to triumph over evil, proof of which Duffy had seen since his capture in 1942, he added, "It is difficult to understand the wonderful and mysterious works of God but He certainly looks after His own."[2]

Father Duffy had changed in the last three years. Before the war, he had enjoyed the company of generals and colonels, politicians and bigwigs, especially Generals MacArthur and Wainwright. After enduring months of pain, torture, and misery, and after administering Last Rites to many individuals, including his fellow alumnus Father Carberry, Duffy was more attuned to the attributes and needs of people he might have overlooked earlier in his career. Duffy's Pacific ordeal had strengthened his faith, and he now shared an affinity with Father Barry, the priest who had focused on serving his "boys."

THE ATOM bombs had made the invasion of the Japanese Home Islands unnecessary. When Father Boland's ship, the *Highlands*, lifted anchor in the Philippines on August 25 and set course for Japan, he and the crew left as victors and occupiers instead of invaders.

During the trip he wrote to Father Steiner that he would soon be in Tokyo Bay, where he would send Steiner "greetings from the Nipps [*sic*] capital." They expected to dock on September 2 at Yokohama in Tokyo Bay, where they would have a front-row seat to that day's surrender ceremonies. "It should be a very interesting sight with so many ships present. They are taking no chances and we will enter the bay at general quarters. We have thirty transports in our group alone and are heavily escorted."[3]

As expected, *Highlands* arrived in Tokyo Bay on V-J Day and landed elements of the First Cavalry Division for occupation duty. After unloading her cargo, two days later *Highlands* steamed out of the bay, now resplendent with ships of all sizes, for the voyage back to the Philippines. The ship made additional supply runs to Okinawa and Japan before departing for the United States, where ship and crew arrived on November 2.

Boland left behind one of his Holy Cross associates. Father Hewitt, who had served in New Caledonia, New Guinea, the Philippines, and now Japan, volunteered to remain in that defeated country with the occupation forces. The priest at first feared an unfriendly welcome from Japanese civilians, but after Emperor Hirohito urged them to lay down their arms and accept defeat, Hewitt moved about unhindered.

One place in particular must have left a lasting imprint on Father Hewitt. The twisted building frames and leveled structures of Hiroshima, a city of 350,000 residents now reduced to ashes, covered the landscape for miles. Just as Father Barry had stared at Dachau and failed to find the words to convey his emotions, Father Hewitt now stood silent before Hiroshima. The priests confronted two of the most devastating instruments of the war, the concentration camps and the first atom bomb, and wondered if hopes for a better mankind had dissipated in vapor, as had so many lives in the ovens of Dachau and in the atomic annihilation of Hiroshima. If the world were to improve, both mused, more was needed than the same weary remedies and temporary fixtures. People would have to exhibit the goodness and decency that Father Duffy saw in Bilibid and the Holy Cross missionaries witnessed in Los Baños. They would have to imitate the valor of Father Sampson's paratroopers leaping into the Normandy darkness and the unselfishness of Barry's 157th Infantry Regiment as it battled the Germans in Sicily, at Anzio, and through France. Anything less was bound to lead to a repetition of depravities.

They had dashed to war eager to serve their fellow man, but they returned pessimistic that the war had helped create a better world.

"I Was Contented to Lie in Bed All Day"

Most Notre Dame chaplains had seen enough of war and looked forward to again being on campus and celebrating Mass in undamaged churches instead of barns and fields. "I need not tell you that I am most eager to get back," Father Barry wrote to Father Steiner shortly after the Japanese asked for peace. "I believe I have seen my share of blood, death, mud, hunger and cold." Resting with his regiment in a military camp in France, Barry eagerly awaited the transports that would "take us back to home sweet home."[4]

Father Barry had every right to be excited about returning home as quickly as possible. His regiment had been overseas for more than two years, during which it had participated in twenty-three major battles and countless skirmishes and patrols. Barry was there the entire time. Other than a few days between operations and a few extended breaks in Rome and other locales, Barry had been on the front lines with his boys, taking care of their spiritual needs while forgoing his own. He had endured bombings, machine-gun fire, mortar shells, artillery barrages, and aerial attacks. He had exerted every ounce of effort in calming petrified soldiers before attacks and comforting grievously wounded boys after attacks. Their anguish and suffering had become his, and other than a few seconds of peace snatched in a foxhole or a half-destroyed structure, Barry had had no support of his own beyond his correspondence with Father Steiner, an ocean away.

The transatlantic crossing handed Father Barry time to unwind. He remained with his boys, but ecstatic survivors about to reunite with family and friends had replaced the frightened youth of 1943. Too many, Father Barry perceived, would require postwar medical and psychological assistance. On the expansive waters of the Atlantic, now free from the U-boat peril that had threatened their initial crossing two years before, the priest could relax.

Barry arrived in Boston with the regiment in early September 1945. Fittingly, he there joined the Notre Dame football squad, fresh from administering a 34–0 thrashing of Dartmouth, for the train ride back to Notre Dame. A few relaxing days on the rails, during which Father Barry laughed and kidded with Notre Dame personnel and football players, ended at South Bend's train station, where university luminaries provided a warm homecoming. "Local Priest Modestly Returns as War Hero"[5] proclaimed the headline in the *South Bend Tribune* on October 22. For the first time since leaving the United States, Father Barry could reunite with friends at Notre Dame and plan his future, but he doubted any task before him could ever erase the effects of his European sojourn. The ravages of war, culminating in the shock that was

Dachau, had shaken the priest. He needed to find something to counter those experiences, tasks that would rejuvenate him and restore his faith in humanity.

FATHER SAMPSON traveled a roundabout path back to the United States. After downing more vodka than he preferred in helping to relocate the renowned German scientist, he enjoyed a three-day leave in Paris, where he reunited with paratroopers of his old outfit. The soldiers informed the priest that they had assumed he was dead and had even held a memorial service for their chaplain. After two weeks of devouring steak, chicken, and ice cream Sampson, now thirty pounds heavier, sailed for home in late March. Final processing at Fort Snelling, Minnesota, led to a thirty-day leave to visit family, followed by another month at an army recreation center in Arkansas.

A disturbing moment in Cumberland, Maryland, when another train pulled alongside Sampson's, interrupted his elation at being home. He glanced out his window at the adjoining train and spotted a collection of German prisoners of war on the first leg of their voyage home. They had spent the war years in relatively comfortable prison camps inside the United States, eating decent dinners at tables and working under guards who were, while distant, at least not violent. Sampson had witnessed too much brutality at the hands of German guards, had gone too long without adequate food, and had sat with too many soldiers as they died to now view this without anger. He needed more time to readjust to peace before he could feel sympathy for his former adversaries.

Father Duffy also passed through multiple countries in three continents to reach home. After being released from Mukden in late August, he advanced through a succession of hospitals in China, Egypt, and Bermuda before arriving at Walter Reed General Hospital in Washington, DC. He told his superior that he could imagine nothing in his future that would equal or surpass his wartime tribulations, and he hoped to be a stronger individual because of his experiences. "I'm enjoying the rest and relaxation in the Army's finest hospital but tire very easily," he explained; with an improved diet he had regained some of his weight and strength, although he still lacked mobility because of legs weakened from beriberi. "I suspect that we are undergoing a fattening process after the lean years of Nipponese incarceration," he quipped. Father Duffy looked forward to returning to priestly duties and had even celebrated Mass and delivered a sermon the day before, but he confided to his bishop that "afterwards I was contented to lie in bed all day. And what a luxury after almost four years on the floor or ground!"[6]

Two CHAPLAINS remained in Germany after hostilities ceased. As the Berlin District chaplain, Father Edward Fitzgerald, the Normandy veteran from the Fifty-Third Troop Carrier Wing, provided religious services to U.S. troops stationed in the American and British sectors of Berlin, as well as Potsdam. He visited many areas of Germany, telling Father Steiner that "most of the cities and towns have been absolutely demolished." Of Berlin he said, "the destruction is beyond description . . . a once proud city now absolutely destroyed. The stench is truly awful."[7]

Father Fitzgerald mingled with some of the world's most powerful figures. When President Harry Truman arrived for postwar talks with British Prime Minister Winston Churchill and Soviet dictator Joseph Stalin, he attended one of Fitzgerald's Masses and afterward visited with the priest. Father Fitzgerald returned to campus early the next year.

Father Powers also ministered to troops in Berlin. He celebrated Masses and funeral services, organized religious instruction, counseled soldiers, and officiated at marriages. Witnessing the impact Father Powers had on the soldiers, many of whom beat a path to his office on Wilski Street, Powers's clerk, LeRoy Clementich, entered the Congregation of Holy Cross and became a priest. Powers continued his military work during the Korean War, when he served as a chaplain with the Seventh Infantry Division during landings on that peninsula and through its retreat in the brutal fighting at the Chosin Reservoir.

In THE Pacific, Father Henry Heintskill hoped to remain in the military on a permanent basis. When the war ended, the *Tulagi* was in San Diego undergoing overhaul and training. With the arrival of peace, he wrote to Father Steiner that "right now the work lies on the shore stations," with the men flooding back to the United States, and requested that he be allowed to remain in the navy. However, Father Steiner told Heintskill to return to Notre Dame and accept his next assignment, and, "we better let it go at that."[8]

Soon after reaching campus, Father Heintskill began tiring easily, had difficulty keeping food down, and lost weight. On October 24, 1946, two days before the football team defeated Iowa, 41–6, on its way to another undefeated season, and one year after he so nobly served his country, his congregation, and his university during the war, he succumbed to cancer. As was fitting for a priest who loved the university, Father Heintskill passed away in the Notre Dame student infirmary, located only yards from the Golden Dome.

FATHER THOMAS Hewitt also remained in the military, becoming one of the U.S. Air Force's first chaplains when it became a separate branch in 1947. He served during the Korean and Vietnam conflicts, acting mainly as an administrator rather than as a frontline chaplain.

ABOARD THE damaged *Pennsylvania*, Father Burke left Okinawa in mid-August for his journey home. After the ship received temporary repairs at Guam, she steamed into Puget Sound for further work to prepare her to take part in the July 1946 atom bomb tests at Bikini Atoll, an operation with which Burke wanted nothing to do. The torpedo attack that killed twenty sailors had shaken the chaplain, and Burke shrank from participating in perfecting a weapon that one day might inflict thousands of casualties. He wrote to Father Steiner that "this ship has been condemned to the laboratory of naval atomic experimentation" and "I have no desire to be a part of this project. I do not fear a dose of radioactivity. But I am overanxious to be discharged from this inhuman environment and return to Notre Dame."[9] The priest received his wish and served as vice president of business affairs before his death in 1957.

AFTER LABORING in the savage island combat that marked much of the Pacific fighting, Father Dupuis joined the philosophy department at the university. Years later he summarized his Pacific experiences with the marines in three sentences: "The 4th Division left Pearl Harbor in fourteen ships. When relieved of our mission we returned to Pearl Harbor in four ships. There was hardly anyone left."[10] His counterpart in the navy, Father Bridenstine, remained a chaplain until 1962, when he retired as a lieutenant general before passing away sixteen years later.

"I Know or at Least I Think I Am a Better Priest"

The chaplains returned home at different times and were welcomed in varying ways, but they felt similar emotions and experienced the same events in the postwar world as the soldiers they served. Most needed a recuperative period ranging from a few weeks to a few months, during which they began shedding the lives of the past few years and retrieving routines from before the war. Some wrestled with survivor's guilt and felt depressed or angry that they were now safe at home while so many of the young soldiers and sailors they had tended never made it back. They contended with physical ailments caused by cold and mud in Italy, blistering heat and malaria of the South Pacific, and—to a far greater extent—the horrible abuses of prison camp. They battled mental demons that they had shoved to the deeper recesses of their minds while the needs of their soldiers took precedence.

When Brother Rex returned to his family in Evansville, Indiana, his father and sisters greeted him at the train station, but his mother, ill and weakened by years of worry over her son, was conspicuously absent. Concerned about her welfare, he recalled, "We hurried home, and when I saw her, I realized the suffering she had undergone through the years. The cruelty and futility of war came home to me with all its force."[11]

Father Lawyer eventually claimed that he accomplished more as a missionary in the Philippines than he probably would have in India, but when he returned in the immediate aftermath of war he preferred to forget the last few years. However, to his frustration, others would not let him. "There is only one drawback—too much publicity," he wrote to Father Steiner shortly after his homecoming. "In a small town it's awful." He pleaded with Steiner to help him avoid being the focus of a war bond drive in which government officials planned to use his photograph and words in full-page newspaper blurbs. Lawyer had already registered his opposition by telling an official that as a religious, he first had to obtain permission from his superior, and that the Notre Dame publicity department might already have plans for him; he now hoped that Steiner could come to his aid. "If you could write me a letter telling me it is against our rule or some other reason I can get out of this mess," he wrote. "However, if you think for patriotic reasons I should accept, just say so, altho I don't like the idea."[12]

Father Steiner replied four days later, "While we want to do all we can to further any project that will assist in winning the war, we do feel that we have not as yet reached the stage when it is necessary to resort to the means you describe. It is not fitting to have a priest's picture in a full page advertisement, or plastered on bill boards." Father Steiner added, "There are many bigots in this country, and many, even good people, who are imbued with an innate prejudice against the Catholic Church. The display of the picture of a Catholic Priest might do more harm than good to the drive. All in all, it will be better for you to keep out of this kind of publicity as much as you can." He told Father Lawyer to "throw the burden on us by telling the organization that your Superior will not give you permission."[13]

The men paid a price for their labors, for the war hurled many challenges at the spiritual cores of each Notre Dame chaplain and missionary. They had worked with decent young men who, because of the war, engaged in violent acts that would, in normal situations, be labeled crimes. They had knelt beside dying soldiers as their lives drained away, struggling to lend comfort with the words of religion. They had endured beatings and atrocities during Christmas, a time normally associated with peace. They had written letters to mothers and wives, bringing word that they would never again see their loved ones. They had glimpsed horrors at Dachau and at Hiroshima, the opposites of every sermon they had preached.

Because of that, in the postwar world at least one priest struggled with alcohol, while others failed to address their emotions. According to his Holy Cross friends, while Brother Rex became more compassionate and caring after the war, the captive years exacted a toll. His memories of years of excruciating physical and mental abuse, against which he often felt useless, led to a postwar breakdown. "Rex paid a big price to become a deeply compassionate man,"[14] said Brother Raymond Papenfuss, C.S.C., in his 2008 eulogy for his friend.

Despite some of the drawbacks, the chaplains contended that the war service benefited them in surprising ways. Brother Rex claimed that he better understood his strengths and weaknesses from his years in the Philippines. He judged some of his actions in camp as noble and others as lacking, but concluded that if he had the grit to survive the war, he could summon similar strength when faced with future challenges. "I learned plenty about myself: my strengths and my weaknesses. I learned, too, there are good and bad people everywhere, even among prisoners. Some are very greedy; others, selfless to the end, thinking only of others—parents sacrificing what little food they had for their children, which finally resulted in their own death from starvation."[15] He enjoyed many Christmases after the war, but none meant more to him than the one he spent in Los Baños. Rex concluded that he could not witness everything he saw during the war without trying to be a better person.

Father McKee agreed. "Thank God and the Blessed Virgin that the nightmare of Los Baños is finished and dead," he wrote shortly after being liberated. "However it has left impressions that will never die." He explained to a fellow priest that the years in confinement proved to be a second novitiate for him, another regimen of intense training "teaching us realistically the meaning of detachment from earthly possessions, poverty, charity, dependence on Divine Providence. We saw human nature in the raw—exposed to storms that brought out the best and worst in a man. We lived in the atmosphere of downright deliberate selfishness, and sublime Christ-like generosity."[16]

After being wrenched from familiar surroundings and witnessing war's disruptive nature, the Notre Dame chaplains appreciated matters and people that before the war they might have taken for granted. After enduring almost four years of captivity, where their every move was watched and basic needs were denied, Sisters Olivette and Caecilius gained a deeper appreciation of the benefits of living in a free country. "We had learned to see our country in a new and more glorious light," they wrote. "We had to lose the security of her strong protecting arm to appraise her might. We had to experience captivity in the power of the enemy to know how precious are the four freedoms."[17]

Already accustomed to sacrificing material goods, the group learned during their years in confinement that they required little beyond their faith and families. Sister Caecilius wrote to her grandmother that she had lost practically everything since leaving the United States in November 1941 and now have "the bare necessities," but that the ordeal benefited them. "It has been a good lesson in detachment if we only profit by it for the future." Sister Olivette claimed, "I wouldn't trade these years for anything—the experience spiritually and otherwise I thank God for," and said that while they witnessed "many stories of suffering and hardship—most of it on the dark side," she preferred to focus on those actions which showed "the buoyancy of the human spirit." Even as late as 1999, when Sister Olivette was in her nineties, she said of those war years, "I had always wanted to be a missionary, and it was a wonderful missionary experience."[18]

They better understood that even under the worst conditions, they could still affect people by bringing the word of God into their lives. War had thwarted the missionaries' plans to work in India, but they found that amid the deprivations of a prison camp they fulfilled to a higher degree that calling which had attracted them to the religious life. The Japanese held power of life and death over them, but in their devotion to God the six religious brought solace to people trapped in a storm of cruelty.

Despite the challenges, Father Barry and most of his Notre Dame compatriots emerged as stronger individuals. Their deep faith had bolstered them. A faith that strong—one that enabled some chaplains to claim that their wartime Christmases were the happiest of their lives— was a faith one could lean on during future tribulations.

Father Sampson claimed that every Christmas since his incarceration took on a deeper meaning, and that crying babies interrupting a church service now hardly mattered. Father Barry could no longer empathize with complaints about stiff necks or atrocious restaurant service, for they could not come close to approximating the daily miseries his boys lived with in Sicily and Italy.

All would agree with Father Lawyer. Upon returning to the university in the spring of 1945, he claimed, "I haven't regretted my experiences for the past years. I know that I am a better cook, housekeeper, gardener from all the struggles of the past three years; and I know or at least I think I am a better priest."[19]

"He Never Spoke with Bitterness"

In time Father Duffy readjusted, but he was a different man. He looked forward to postwar service, but prison camp had changed his outlook, and its physical consequences hampered his ability to manage matters on a grander scale. As "the crushed vertebrae continue to impair my walking and cause a certain amount of pain," he explained to Bishop Alter, he asked to be considered "for a small parish."[20]

In January 1947 Father Duffy left Walter Reed Hospital to take up residence in his new home, Our Lady of Lourdes Parish in New London, a town of a few thousand located in central Ohio, twenty-five miles south of Lake Erie. He brought with him the American flag he had hidden around his waist in the Philippines, and once settled, he had installed behind the altar a circular stained-glass window depicting American soldiers at Bataan. His work as pastor soon made Father Duffy one of New London's most beloved individuals, and his endeavors as the American Legion's national chaplain and a former Philippine prisoner of war made him a popular figure on the lecture circuit.

His talks heralded the courage of the soldiers during the desperate 1942 months in Bataan and emphasized the nobility of individuals he had encountered in prison camp. Gone were any traces of bitterness or desire for vengeance. "One of the remarkable things about Father Duffy," said Bishop Alter, "was that, after his return to the Diocese following the end of the war, he never spoke with bitterness or manifest resentment of the brutal treatment which he had received from the Japanese following his capture as a prisoner-of-war. He often spoke in public but without recriminations."[21]

A reporter who attended one of his talks left favorably impressed by a man who had every right to be angry. Instead, according to reporter J. K. Schmidt, Duffy "is one who has lived through war's sharpest agonies, has seen man at his bestial worst and yet has lost none of his faith in God's mercy." When a crowd member asked Father Duffy how he endured the beatings and every other horror of prison camp, the priest answered, "I surely could not have stood it if I had not been buoyed up by my faith. Weakened as I was, I kept going only through God's help. I am sure."[22]

Father Duffy reunited with Ben Steele, the inmate whose drawings of life inside a prison camp Father Duffy had concealed in his Mass kit. Though the original drawings were lost when the *Oryoku Maru* sank, Steele meticulously recreated as many as possible. For a time the two considered collaborating on a book, with Steele's gripping sketches supplementing Duffy's text, but the project never materialized.

In February 1958 Father Duffy learned that he had cancer of the vertebrae. The next month he submitted his resignation in order to battle the illness and announced plans to move to California for its warmer climes. Citizens of New London, in conjunction with the local

American Legion post, organized a Father Duffy fund drive to culminate on Memorial Day with a program honoring the former pastor. Former military associates sent their expressions of support, and a letter from Douglas MacArthur boosted his spirits: "I have just learned with deep regret of your illness and send you this message of sincere hope that you will soon recover and be your old self again. I recall so vividly your devoted service in the last war."[23]

Father Duffy passed away on June 4, 1958, at Letterman Army Hospital in San Francisco, three weeks before his fifty-ninth birthday. The cost exacted by the many beatings and bayonet thrusts, combined with the ravages of cancer, took a toll the priest could not vanquish. As he had done for Father Carberry and many others during the war, a military chaplain stood at Duffy's side as he expired.

In the eulogy delivered at the funeral Mass in New London, Bishop George J. Rehring gave high praise to the Notre Dame graduate who had nobly served the military and the Diocese of Toledo. "Never was there a time in the extraordinary career of Father Duffy when he reached a greater height than in the weeks immediately preceding his death," said the bishop. He faced the end calmly, and "no deed of valor performed by him equaled the magnitude of his courage in face of incurable disease." Bishop Rehring noted that despite "the pain from the wounds inflicted upon him at Bataan which were never entirely healed,"[24] he never complained. Fittingly, Father Duffy was buried at the Presidio National Cemetery along San Francisco Bay, surrounded by his fellow military who had also sacrificed for their country.

Father Carberry never made it home, but his deeds have not been forgotten. In a July 1945 letter to Carberry's family, the chief of chaplains, Brigadier General Luther D. Miller, wrote, "It will be comforting to you and your loved ones to know that the men who have returned from the Philippine Prison Camps tell us that the men who Chaplain Carberry so faithfully served, hold him in the highest esteem and respect because of his work and his example as a Priest of God. His loyal sacrificial devotion to his Country and to his Church, especially during the long months that he was detained by the enemy, will be remembered by all who knew him." In a letter written the same day, Archbishop Edward D. Howard of the Archdiocese of Portland, Oregon, added that everyone loved Carberry: he "had a heart of gold and he counted no sacrifice too great when it was a question of ministering to the needs of others. His memory should be an inspiration for all of us."[25]

That memory continues to the present at St. Paul Catholic Church in Silverton, Oregon, a parish Carberry served from 1938 to 1940. On its website, the parish proudly lists his accomplishments, explains his time in the Philippines and his death, and praises Carberry for "his military service and sacrifice."[26] The memories of the priest who passed on a chance to escape from Davao, and perished as a result, remain vibrant.

"Father Sampson Turned Death, to Blessed Victory"

Father Sampson started his postwar life in a small parish as well, but after one year he returned to the chaplaincy when the army issued a call for additional priests and ministers to fill a shortage of chaplains. When his bishop in Iowa first suggested Sampson leave his parish for the military, Sampson told him he was quite happy with his parishioners. "Well, you'll be leaving in about a month," said the bishop. When Sampson tried to object, the bishop cut him short with, "You may now kiss my ring."[27]

By the time of his retirement from the army as a brigadier general twenty-five years later, Sampson had served in a variety of posts, including a sojourn overseas during the Korean War, three years in Germany, and as chief of chaplains in 1967. Each Christmas during the 1960s he visited the soldiers fighting in Vietnam. He followed his military life with one year as pastor in another Iowa church and two years as president of the United Service Organization before returning to campus at the request of his longtime friend, Father Hesburgh, then the university's president. For four years Sampson directed Notre Dame's Reserve Officers' Training Corps programs.

He loved the military, and when he heard the frequent question as to how he reconciled the two worlds—one devoted to peace and the other to war—he had a ready response. "I have been asked how I can wear the uniform which symbolizes war and also wear the cross upon it symbolizing peace," said Sampson. He replied that the mission of both is the same. "It is very easy for me to tell them that, by law and statute, the mission of the military of the United States is, first, to preserve peace. Second, to provide for the security of our country, its borders and internal security. And third, to implement national policy as it pertains to peace treaties with friendly nations which of themselves cannot repel the aggression of avaricious neighbors. I see nothing in this mission that does not appeal to the highest ideals of any man—regardless of his religion." Sampson agreed with those who claimed that had he not been a priest, he would have been a soldier, "because they are both called to the identical things—that is—the preservation of peace, the establishment of justice when it has been lost, and the providing of security with protection for the weak and the innocent."[28]

Father Sampson passed away from cancer in January 1996. Upon learning of Sampson's death, Peter S. Griffin, a Vietnam-era paratrooper who knew the chaplain, wrote a poem titled "Paratrooper Padre," which he dedicated "In loving memory" to Father Sampson. The fifteen verses summarize how the men with whom Father Sampson headed into battle felt about their chaplain. Three verses in particular convey their love and admiration.

> Father Francis L. Sampson, a man of the cloth,
> The PARATROOPER PADRE, his mission, not a soul lost . . . !
> An elite soldier, who jumped from the sky,
> A faithful companion, for ones who might die. . . .
>
> This is the greatest gift, Paratrooper Padres can give,
> The keys to Heaven, is for the forgiven . . . !
> He patched their bodies, to make them whole,
> He risked his life, to save their souls . . . !
>
> Bringing aid and comfort, to soldiers in need,
> The sacred Last Rights [sic], the blessed last deed . . . .
> To many dying troopers, he put their minds at ease,
> Father Sampson turned death, to blessed victory . . . ![29]

"It's Because of You That I'm Going Home"

After leaving the army, Father Barry held a variety of posts at Notre Dame. He loved his duties as a hall rector and jumped at the request to serve as the football team's chaplain because in those capacities he closely interacted with the students and athletes, a civilian version of his military "boys." On the other hand, he did not enjoy his brief stint as prefect of discipline, which required him to punish students who committed infractions. He joked that the university "relieved" him of that post because he failed to expel a single student, but the truth was that, as he did with the 157th Regiment, he preferred to offer counsel and a sympathetic ear instead of administering discipline.

In 1963 he left the university to serve as chaplain and religion teacher at one of the Congregation of Holy Cross's largest high schools, Archbishop Hoban High School in Akron, Ohio. Those who knew him at Hoban High, whether as a student, a fellow staff member, or a parent, claim that Barry's greatest impact in his nineteen years in Akron occurred outside the classroom, where his personal qualities, especially his quiet humor, engaging laughter, and warm greetings, attracted anyone who approached. Father William Simmons, C.S.C., who had first met Barry while a seminarian, said that while Barry certainly made an impact in the classroom, it was "a lifetime of living religious conviction taught to so many young men" that marked the priest as outstanding. People enjoyed his company, and students hoped to emulate his traits. Father William Craddick, C.S.C., assistant administrator of Holy Cross House at Notre Dame, said, "At Hoban High School in Akron, happened what happened everywhere Father Joe went: he captivated young and old by his friendliness, cheerfulness and understanding."[30]

Don Zwisler, the head football coach at the time, said that his players responded to Barry's repeated message to them, centered about his motto, "Play from your heart." He told the team, "Anything can happen as long as you play from your heart."[31] The priest had seen this proven innumerable times in Sicily, Italy, France, and Germany. Now, as teacher and team chaplain, he hoped to impart to a new generation the lessons he had culled from other boys in far more serious predicaments. Heartbreak and death had been constant companions in Europe, but in Akron he extracted some good from those years and transmitted it to a group unfamiliar with those sacrifices.

The ravages of Dachau had assailed Father Barry's conviction in the goodness of man, and for a time afterward he doubted he would regain that belief. However, first at Notre Dame and then at Hoban High School, he worked with groups of students who rejuvenated his optimism. Dachau's depravity had nearly overwhelmed him, but just as he had helped bolster his military boys when they engaged in the ugliness of combat, his civilian boys now provided a similar lift for Father Barry. They restored his faith in man and nullified the degeneracy of Dachau. In Italy and France the priest had feared that after the war, he would be unable to handle complaints he would consider inconsequential compared to the miseries of combat. If that were true, he worried, his postwar work might plummet to insignificance. By working with youth who needed him as much as his military boys had needed him, especially at Hoban High, he found the answer to his wartime qualms. Barry later claimed that except for his war experiences, his time at Hoban High was the best of his life.

In 1982 Father Barry retired from active work and spent the final three years of his life at the Holy Cross House, a residence for Holy Cross priests and brothers beside one of the lakes on Notre Dame's campus. After the whirlwind of war, Father Barry relished the quiet time he could now devote to prayer and reflection in the chapel and enjoying the spiritual biographies and inspirational tomes he had always wanted to read. Fellow residents became accustomed to Barry's constant smile, humorous anecdotes, and infectious laughter. "His laughs echoed down the corridors of Holy Cross House and in the dining room there, down to his dying day,"[32] recalled Father Craddick.

His smile broadened each football weekend, when former Hoban students and their families attending the game stopped at Holy Cross House to visit their former chaplain. When the Akron high school constructed a sparkling new basketball gymnasium, they named it Barry Gymnasium and mounted a photograph of Father Barry to honor the priest.

On September 25, 1985, at the age of eighty-two, Father Barry died, four days after his beloved Irish squad, under Coach Gerry Faust, defeated Michigan State, 27–10, at Notre Dame Stadium. Two days later Hoban High School held a moment of silence at its football field before the game between Hoban and Walsh High School, a touch that would have pleased the affable priest, who had a lifelong connection with sports and with "his boys," in and out of the military.

In his eulogy for Father Barry, Father Craddick related the highlights of Father Barry's life, including six decades in which the priest exerted a profound impact on young men battling the demons and dangers of war and struggling to find their way in life. He ended with a sentence that summarized the main impact the small priest with a larger-than-life heart had on everyone with whom he came into contact. "I think God gave Joe Barry to us to encourage us to see the lighter aspects of life and to laugh over them, and in doing so to make life worth living for oneself and for others."[33]

Today, alongside many of the Notre Dame chaplains who so honorably served their nation during World War II, Father Barry rests in the cemetery located not far from the Grotto. It is fitting that he and other chaplains completed their earthly lives on campus, where their careers started, for it was the work they performed for their university, and the memories of Notre Dame they held dear, from training camp to battlefield, that motivated them to perform to their highest standards. In their tenures as chaplains, laboring among young men in the cauldron of battle, they best exemplified the motto adorning the Church of the Sacred Heart, "God, Country, Notre Dame."

SHORTLY AFTER the war ended, a sergeant about to leave the service and return to his family paid one final visit to his chaplain. During their talk he said, "You know, it's because of you that I'm going home. I'd a never had the guts to get through those three years alone, without you." The chaplain protested, saying it was the man's faith combined with good fortune that brought him out whole, but the sergeant would not be swayed. "You made me feel relaxed—like there was somebody looking after me all the time."[34]

In their own ways, each Notre Dame missionary and priest at war exerted a similar influence on the people they encountered. Some, like Father Barry or Father Sampson, delivered it with the words whispered to scared boys amid bursting enemy shells and deafening noise. Others, like Fathers Duffy and Carberry, and Brother Rex and Sister Olivette, provided it with their examples of nobility among the squalor and misery of prison camp. They bolstered fragile spirits with their actions and illuminated a path out of fear and violence with their deep faith. They may not have saved lives with the arsenals of warfare, as did soldiers parachuting into France or charging Japanese machine-gun nests, but they rescued hopes and futures with the weapons of religion.

APPENDIX

Notre Dame Chaplains and Religious in World War II

The Twenty-Nine Chaplains from Notre Dame
European Theater

Rev. Joseph D. Barry, C.S.C.
Branch of Service: U.S. Army, Forty-Fifth Infantry
Division
Age on December 7, 1941: 39
When Enlisted: 1941
Where Stationed: Sicily, Italy, France, Germany, Dachau

Rev. Edward R. Fitzgerald, C.S.C.
Branch of Service: U.S. Army Air Corps, Fifty-Third Troop
Carrier Wing
Age on December 7, 1941: 38
When Enlisted: 1941
Where Stationed: England, Normandy, Southern France

Rev. Thomas P. Jones, C.S.C.
Branch of Service: U.S. Army, 315th General Hospital
Battalion
Age on December 7, 1941: 33
When Enlisted: 1944
Where Stationed: England

Rev. John McGee, C.S.C.
Branch of Service: Canadian Army
Age on December 7, 1941: 27
When Enlisted: 1942
Where Stationed: Labrador, England, France, Belgium

Rev. Vincent Mooney, C.S.C.
Branch of Service: U.S. Army, Ninth Armored Division
Age on December 7, 1941: 49
When Enlisted: 1942
Where Stationed: England, Luxembourg, Bastogne,
Germany

Rev. Edmund J. Murray, C.S.C.
Branch of Service: U.S. Army, 104th Infantry Division
Age on December 7, 1941: 34
When Enlisted: 1942
Where Stationed: Northern France, Rhineland, Central
Europe

Rev. Maurice E. Powers, C.S.C.
Branch of Service: U.S. Army, 101st Mechanized Cavalry
Age on December 7, 1941: 36
When Enlisted: 1943
Where Stationed: England, France, Germany

Rev. Francis L. Sampson, Diocesan Priest
Branch of Service: U.S. Army, 101st Airborne Division
Age on December 7, 1941: 29
When Enlisted: 1942
Where Stationed: England, Normandy, Holland,
Belgium, Stalag II-A Prison Camp

Rev. Robert Waide, C.S.C.
Branch of Service: Canadian Army
Age on December 7, 1941: 36
When Enlisted: 1942
Where Stationed: Canada, England, Italy

Rev. George Welsh, C.S.C.
Branch of Service: U.S. Army
Age on December 7, 1941: 36
When Enlisted: 1941
Where Stationed: Military hospitals in St. Lucia,
Caribbean, and France

Pacific Theater

Rev. Francis J. Boland, C.S.C.
Branch of Service: U.S. Navy, U.S.S. *Highlands* (APA-119)
Age on December 7, 1941: 45
When Enlisted: 1943
Where Stationed: France, Iwo Jima, Okinawa

Rev. Francis D. Bridenstine, C.S.C.
Branch of Service: U.S. Army, Seventh Infantry Division
Age on December 7, 1941: 32
When Enlisted: 1942
Where Stationed: Attu, Kiska, Leyte, Okinawa

Rev. John J. Burke, C.S.C.
Branch of Service: U.S. Navy, U.S.S. *Pennsylvania* (BB-38)
Age on December 7, 1941: 37
When Enlisted: 1944
Where Stationed: Saipan, Okinawa

Rev. Richard E. Carberry, Diocesan Priest
Branch of Service: U.S. Army, Forty-Fifth Combat Team
Age on December 7, 1941: 36
When Enlisted: 1936
Where Stationed: Philippines, Bataan, POW camps,
Hell Ships

Rev. Joseph Corcoran, C.S.C.
Branch of Service: U.S. Army, Seventh Infantry Division
Age on December 7, 1941: 34
When Enlisted: 1942
Where Stationed: Attu, Kwajalein, Leyte, Okinawa

Rev. John E. Duffy, Diocesan Priest
Branch of Service: U.S. Army, Northern Luzon Force;
First Philippine Corps
Age on December 7, 1941: 42
When Enlisted: 1933
Where Stationed: Philippines, Bilibid Prison Camp,
Hell Ships, Omuta 17 Prison Camp

Rev. Patrick R. Duffy, C.S.C.
Branch of Service: U.S. Navy
Age on December 7, 1941: 33
When Enlisted: 1942
Where Stationed: Base and repair facilities at Nouméa,
New Caledonia, and Emirau

Rev. John M. Dupuis, C.S.C.
Branch of Service: U.S. Marines, Fourth Marine Division
Age on December 7, 1941: 33
When Enlisted: 1943
Where Stationed: Roi-Namur, Saipan, Tinian, Iwo Jima

Rev. Gerald Fitzgerald, C.S.C.
Branch of Service: U.S. Army Air Corps
Age on December 7, 1941: 47
When Enlisted: 1943
Where Stationed: Military Ordinariate, Pacific

Rev. John J. Harrington, C.S.C.
Branch of Service: U.S. Army Air Corps, Fifty-First
Fighter Group
Age on December 7, 1941: 35
When Enlisted: 1942
Where Stationed: Assam, India

Rev. Henry Heintskill, C.S.C.
Branch of Service: U.S. Navy, U.S.S. *Tulagi* (CVE-72)
Age on December 7, 1941: 28
When Enlisted: 1943
Where Stationed: Southern France, Lingayen Gulf,
Iwo Jima, Okinawa

Rev. Thomas E. Hewitt, C.S.C.
Branch of Service: U.S. Army, 125th Infantry Division
Age on December 7, 1941: 30
When Enlisted: 1942
Where Stationed: New Caledonia, Philippines, Tokyo

Rev. Norman Johnson, C.S.C.
Branch of Service: U.S. Navy, Fourth Cargo Combat Group
Age on December 7, 1941: 36
When Enlisted: 1943
Where Stationed: China, Burma, India

Rev. Joseph Kmiecik, C.S.C.
Branch of Service: U.S. Army, Eleventh Air Force
Age on December 7, 1941: 36
When Enlisted: 1942
Where Stationed: Attu, Kiska

Rev. James E. Norton, C.S.C.
Branch of Service: U.S. Marines, Marine Aircraft Group
Forty-Five
Age on December 7, 1941: 35
When Enlisted: 1943
Where Stationed: Ulithi and other Pacific island air bases

North America

Rev. John T. Biger, C.S.C.
Branch of Service: Royal Canadian Air Force
Age on December 7, 1941: 31
When Enlisted: 1943
Where Stationed: Canada

Rev. Clement E. Kane, C.S.C.
Branch of Service: U.S. Army
Age on December 7, 1941: 41
When Enlisted: 1943
Where Stationed: Stateside military hospitals

Rev. John F. O'Hara, C.S.C.
Branch of Service: Military Ordinariate
Age on December 7, 1941: 53
When Enlisted: Appointed December 1939
Where Stationed: New York City

Rev. Robert W. Woodward, C.S.C.
Branch of Service: U.S. Army Eastern Command
Age on December 7, 1941: 35
When Enlisted: 1941
Where Stationed: Eastern U.S. defense, including
Bermuda, Cuba, Bahamas

The Six Notre Dame Religious

The six were on their way to the Holy Cross Mission in Dhaka, India, when they were detained in Manila in December 1941. They spent the remainder of the war incarcerated in the Manila area, culminating in confinement to the Los Baños Internment Camp, from which they were liberated in February 1945. The six were:

Top row:
Sister Mary Caecilius, C.S.C., age 25 on December 7, 1941
Brother Rex Hennel, C.S.C., age 22 on December 7, 1941
Brother Theodore Kapes, C.S.C., age 40 on December 7, 1941

Bottom row:
Father Jerome Lawyer, C.S.C., age 29 on December 7, 1941
Father Robert McKee, C.S.C., age 29 on December 7, 1912
Sister Mary Olivette Whelan, C.S.C., age 34 on December 7, 1941

Photographs contained in the appendix are courtesy of the Holy Cross Archives, University of Notre Dame; University of Notre Dame Archives, Notre Dame, Indiana; Army Chaplain Corps Museum, Fort Jackson, South Carolina; and Archives, Congregation of the Sisters of the Holy Cross, Notre Dame, Indiana.

NOTES

Prologue

1. Chaplain Francis L. Sampson, *Look Out Below!* (Sweetwater, TN: 101st Airborne Division Association, 1989), 58.

2. Letter from Rev. Joseph D. Barry, C.S.C., to Rev. Thomas Steiner, C.S.C., November 1943, in the Rev. Thomas A. Steiner Collection, Holy Cross Archives, University of Notre Dame, Folder No. 11:05 (hereafter Steiner Collection, letters cited as Barry to recipient, date, Folder No. 11:05).

3. Letter from Rev. Thomas A. Steiner, C.S.C., to the Reverend Francis J. Boland, December 30, 1944, in the Steiner Collection, Folder No. 11:06 (hereafter cited as Steiner to recipient, date, Folder No. 11:06).

4. Hansel H. Tower, *Fighting the Devil with the Marines* (Philadelphia: Dorrance & Company, 1945), vii.

ONE. "Our First Baptism of Blood"

1. Theodore M. Hesburgh, C.S.C., with Jerry Reedy. *God, Country, Notre Dame* (New York: Doubleday, 1990), 15.

2. "A 45th Fighter: Father Joseph Barry, C.S.C.," n.d., in the *45th Division News*.

3. Father John E. Duffy, *Philippine Memoir*, 9: these reminiscences were dictated to his niece, Dorothy Vogel, following his return from prison camp to the United States and are housed in the Father John E. Duffy Collection, Diocese of Toledo, Ohio Archives (hereafter cited as Duffy Collection).

4. William Nolan, interview with author, October 3, 1991.

5. Duffy, *Philippine Memoir*, 6, 32.

6. Father Jerome Lawyer, C.S.C., "A C.S.C. Vocation Story," *Holy Cross in the Rose Garden*, January 28, 1995, in "World War II Interned C.S.C.'s, 1941–1945," Holy Cross Archives, University of Notre Dame.

7. Letter from Sister Olivette to Mother M. Vincentia, Superior General, November 15, 1941, in "Internment in Manila 1941–1945," Archives, Congregation of the Sisters of the Holy Cross, Notre Dame, IN (hereafter cited as Letter from Sister Olivette to recipient, date, "Internment in Manila 1941–1945"); Reverend Robert McKee, C.S.C. "Holy Cross P.O.W.'s in the Philippines—1941–1945," personal reminiscences, 1985, p. 2, in "World War II Interned C.S.C.'s, 1941–1945," Holy Cross Archives, University of Notre Dame (hereafter cited as McKee, "Holy Cross P.O.W.'s in the Philippines").

8. Sister Mary Olivette, "Account of the First Days of the War in 1941," in "Internment in Manila 1941–1945," Archives, Congregation of the Sisters of the Holy Cross, Notre Dame, IN (hereafter cited as Olivette, "Account of the First Days of the War in 1941").

9. Sisters M. Olivette and M. Caecilius, C.S.C. "Round Trip to the Philippines," in *Fruits of the Tree: Sesquicentennial Chronicles, Sisters of the Holy Cross* (Notre Dame, IN: Ave Maria Press, 1991), 1:7.

10. Brother Rex Hennel, C.S.C., *Our Expedition to Manila* (Privately published memoir, June 13, 1952), 10.

11. Duffy, *Philippine Memoir*, 29.

12. John Toland, *But Not in Shame* (New York: Random House, 1961), 45–46.

13. Duffy, *Philippine Memoir*, 43.

14. Duffy, *Philippine Memoir*, 44.

15. McKee, "Holy Cross P.O.W.'s in the Philippines," 4.

16. Letter from Sister Olivette to "Dear Sisters," February 22, 1942; and Sister Mary Olivette, "My Most Memorable Experience as a Nun," *Catholic News*, November 23, 1957; both in "Internment in Manila 1941–1945."

17. Olivette, "Account of the First Days of the War in 1941."

18. Olivette, "Account of the First Days of the War in 1941."

19. Letter from Sister Olivette to "Dear Sisters," February 22, 1942, in "Internment in Manila 1941–1945."

20. McKee, "Holy Cross P.O.W.'s in the Philippines," 4.

21. Olivette, "Account of the First Days of the War in 1941."

22. Olivette, "Account of the First Days of the War in 1941."

23. Duffy, *Philippine Memoir*, 50.

24. "Greetings Latest Word from Chaplain Duffy," newspaper article in "CSC Chaplains in World War II," UDIS 39/24, University of Notre Dame Archives, Notre Dame, IN.

25. Telegram from Sisters Olivette and Caecilius to Saint Mary's, December 22, 1941; and telegram from Sister Caecilius to Mrs. William J. Roth, December 22, 1941, both in "Internment in Manila 1941–1945."

26. Hennel, *Our Expedition to Manila*, 13–15.

27. Sister Mary Olivette, *Diary, 1941–1945*, January 2, 1942, in "Internment in Manila 1941–1945."

28. Hennel, *Our Expedition to Manila*, 16–19.

29. McKee, "Holy Cross P.O.W.'s in the Philippines," 5.

30. Olivette and Caecilius, "Round Trip to the Philippines," 14–15.

31. McKee, "Holy Cross P.O.W.'s in the Philippines," 5.

32. American Legion Questionnaire filled out by Father Duffy after the war, in the Duffy Collection, "Duffy Miscellaneous" file (hereafter cited as Father Duffy American Legion Questionnaire).

33. "Tells About Philippines at War's Outbreak," undated newspaper article in the Duffy Collection, "Duffy Photo Album"; John Costello, *The Pacific War* (New York: Rawson, Wade, 1981), 186.

34. Christopher Cross, *Soldiers of God* (New York: E. P. Dutton, 1945), 35.

35. "Chaplains Say Mass in Bataan to Rumble of Big Guns; Priests Operate First Aid Stations Under Fire," United Press article appearing in the *World Telegram*, in the Duffy Collection, "Duffy Correspondence."

36. Melville Jacoby, "Chaplains in Bataan," *Time*, February 23, 1942.

37. John Hersey, *Men on Bataan* (New York: Alfred A. Knopf, 1942), 177–78.

38. Captain Tom Gerrity, "Bataan Diary," *Cleveland Plain Dealer*, April 13, 1942, in "Duffy Photo Album."

39. Nolan interview.

40. Letter from Richard Carberry to "Bid & All," February 16, 1942, in Richard Carberry Collection, J. A. O'Brien, "Family History; Family and Friends, 1872–2004," a collection of material about Richard Carberry gathered for family.

41. "Chaplain Carberry Wins Citations for Bravery in Bataan," *Rockford (IL) Observer*, July 5, 1942.

42. Olivette and Caecilius, "Round Trip to the Philippines," 17; Olivette, "My Most Memorable Experience as a Nun," in "Internment in Manila 1941–1945."

43. Costello, *Pacific War*, 213.

44. Letter from Rev. John Duffy to Most Rev. Karl J. Alter, D.D., March 17, 1942, in the Duffy Collection, "Duffy Correspondence."

45. Father Duffy American Legion Questionnaire.

46. Letter from Duffy to Alter, September 14, 1945; Talks Given at the 1948 Convention of Disabled American Veterans, New York City, August 16–20, 1948, in the Duffy Collection, "Duffy Files #1."

47. Talks Given at the 1948 Convention of Disabled American Veterans; J. K. Schmidt, "Priest, Now New London Pastor, Recalls Horrors of Death March," *Cleveland Plain Dealer*, July 27, 1947.

48. Olivette and Caecilius, "Round Trip to the Philippines," 17; Nolan interview.

49. McKee, "Holy Cross P.O.W.'s in the Philippines," 6.

50. "Reports of Father John E. Duffy Since the Fall of Batan [*sic*], April 1942 to April 1946," 1, undated postwar report written by Father John Duffy, U.S. Army Chaplain Corps Museum, Fort Jackson, SC (hereafter cited as "Duffy Reports").

51. Nolan interview.

52. Billy Keith, *Days of Anguish, Days of Hope* (Garden City, NY: Doubleday, 1972), 60.

53. Father Duffy American Legion Questionnaire.

54. Schmidt, "Priest, Now New London Pastor, Recalls Horrors of Death March."

55. Nolan interview.

56. Keith, *Days of Anguish, Days of Hope*, 65.

57. Keith, *Days of Anguish, Days of Hope*, 67.

58. Nolan interview.

59. Toland, *But Not in Shame*, 346.

60. Olivette, "My Most Memorable Experience as a Nun," in "Internment in Manila 1941–1945."

TWO. **"The Chaplain Is the Servant of God for All"**

1. Cross, *Soldiers of God*, 137.

2. Roy J. Honeywell, *Chaplains of the United States Army* (Washington, D.C.: Office of the Chief of Chaplains, Department of the Army, 1958), 103.

3. Cross, *Soldiers of God*, 137.

4. Letter from John F. O'Hara, C.S.C., to the Right Rev. Abbots, the Very Rev. Provincials, and Other Higher Superiors of the Religious Orders of Priests in the United States, July 15, 1940, in the Steiner Collection, Folder No. 11:01, "Military Ordinariate 1940–1942" (hereafter cited as O'Hara to recipient, date, Folder No. 11:01).

5. Letter from O'Hara to Steiner, November 28, 1941, Folder No. 11:01.

6. Letter from Rev. Thomas A. Steiner, C.S.C., to the Reverend Edward Fitzgerald, December 23, 1941, in the Steiner Collection, Folder No. 11:09 (hereafter cited as Steiner to recipient, date, Folder No. 11:09).

7. Letter from Reverend Gerald M. Fitzgerald, C.S.C., to Rev. Thomas Steiner, C.S.C., June 25, 1943, in the Steiner Collection, Folder No. 11:10

(hereafter cited as Fitzgerald to recipient, date, Folder No. 11:10); letter from Rev. John Biger, C.S.C., to Rev. Thomas Steiner, C.S.C., August 17, 1942, in the Steiner Collection, Folder No. 11:06 (hereafter cited as Biger to recipient, date, Folder No. 11:06); letter from Rev. Henry Heintskill, C.S.C., to Rev. Thomas Steiner, C.S.C., August 4, 1942, in the Steiner Collection, Folder No. 12:01 (hereafter cited as Heintskill to recipient, date, Folder No. 12:01).

8. Letter from Daniel M. Gleason, C.S.C., to Reverend Thomas A. Steiner, C.S.C., December 30, 1944, in the Steiner Collection, Folder No. 11:04: "Military Ordinariate 1941–1949."

9. Barry to Steiner, October 16, 1942, Folder No. 11:05; letter from Rev. John J. Burke, C.S.C., to Rev. Thomas Steiner, C.S.C., June 6, 1944, in the Steiner Collection, Folder No. 11:07 (hereafter cited as Burke to recipient, date, Folder No. 11:07).

10. Letter from Rev. Joseph Corcoran, C.S.C., to Rev. Thomas Steiner, C.S.C., September 7, 1942, in the Steiner Collection, Folder No. 11:07 (hereafter cited as Corcoran to recipient, date, Folder No. 11:07).

11. Letter from Heintskill to Steiner, March 31, 1943; letter from Steiner, to Heintskill, April 5, 1943, both in Folder No. 12:01.

12. Letter from Rev. Joseph D. Barry, C.S.C., to Father Hope, February 1944; letter from Barry to Steiner, October 16, 1942, both in Folder No. 11:05.

13. Letter from Barry to Steiner, May 12, 1941, Folder No. 11:05.

14. Letter from Barry to Steiner, May 12, 1941, Folder No. 11:05.

15. Letter from Barry to Steiner, May 12, 1941, Folder No. 11:05.

16. Letter from Barry to Steiner, May 12, 1941, Folder No. 11:05.

17. Letter from Barry to Steiner, May 12, 1941, Folder No. 11:05.

18. Letter from Barry to Steiner, September 15, 1941, Folder No. 11:05.

19. Letter from Barry to Hope, February 1944, Folder No. 11:05.

20. Letter from Barry to Steiner, September 15, 1941, Folder No. 11:05.

21. Letter from Barry to Steiner, September 15, 1941, Folder No. 11:05.

22. Letter from Rev. Joseph Barry, C.S.C., to Bishop John O'Hara, C.S.C., January 2, 1944, "Joseph Barry," COHA 9/80, University of Notre Dame Archives.

23. Emajean Jordan Buechner, *Sparks* (Metairie, LA: Thunderbird Press, 1991), 59.

24. Sampson, *Look Out Below!*, 3.

25. Sampson, *Look Out Below!*, 6.

26. Sampson, *Look Out Below!*, 8, 11–15.

27. Sampson, *Look Out Below!*, 18–20, 26.

28. Letter from Heintskill to Steiner, April 30, 1943, Folder No. 12:01.

29. Letter from Heintskill to Steiner, October 16, 1943; letter from Heintskill to Steiner, June 30, 1943; letter from Heintskill to Steiner, September 15, 1943; all in Folder No. 12:01.

30. Letter from Barry to Steiner, September 4, 1942, Folder No. 11:05.

31. Lyle W. Dorsett, *Serving God and Country: U.S. Military Chaplains in World War II* (New York: Berkley Caliber, 2012), 35.

32. Letter from Corcoran to Steiner, September 12, 1942, Folder No. 11:07.

33. Letter from Rev. Thomas E. Hewitt, C.S.C., to Rev. Thomas Steiner, C.S.C., October 11, 1942, in the Steiner Collection, Folder No. 12:02 (hereafter cited as Hewitt to recipient, date, Folder No. 12:02).

34. Letter from Heintskill to Steiner, March 31, 1943, Folder No. 12:01.

35. Letter from Heintskill to Steiner, May 15, 1943; letter from Steiner, to Heintskill, May 25, 1943, both in Folder No. 12:01.

36. Robert Sherrod, *Tarawa* (New York: Duell, Sloan and Pearce, 1944), 45.

37. Karl Wuest, *They Told It to the Chaplain* (New York: Vantage, 1953), 17.

38. Letter from Fitzgerald to Steiner, September 15, 1941, Folder No. 11:09.

39. Letter from Barry to Steiner, October 16, 1942; letter from Steiner to Barry, October 4, 1941, both in Folder No. 11:05.

40. Letter from William R. Arnold, Chief of Chaplains, to Chaplain Maurice E. Powers, C.S.C., September 28, 1943, found in "Reverend Maurice Powers, World War II Chaplaincy, 1941–1945," Holy Cross Archives, University of Notre Dame.

41. Letter from Hewitt to Steiner, November 26, 1942, Folder No. 12:02.

42. Kenneth Stemmons, interview with author, March 2, 2015.

43. Sergeant Don Robinson, *News of the 45th* (New York: Grosset & Dunlap, 1944), 47.

44. Letter from Steiner to Barry, May 18, 1942, Folder No. 11:05.

45. Letter from Barry to Steiner, September 4, 1942, Folder No. 11:05.

46. Letter from Barry to Hope, February 1944, Folder No. 11:05.

47. Quoted in Buechner, *Sparks*, 62.

48. Letter from Barry to Steiner, September 4, 1942, Folder No. 11:05.

THREE. **"Surely War Is a Dirty Game"**

1. Letter from O'Hara to the Right Rev. Abbots, the Very Rev. Provincials, and Other Higher Superiors of the Religious Orders of Priests in the United States, June 25, 1942, Folder No. 11:01.

2. Letter from O'Hara to the Right Rev. Abbots, the Very Rev. Provincials and other Higher Superiors of the Religious Orders of Priests in the United States, January 14, 1943, Folder No. 11:02 (hereafter cited as Letter from O'Hara to recipient, date, Folder No. 11:02).

3. Letter from Reverend Thomas Steiner, C.S.C., to Reverend Bernard E. Ransing, C.S.C., July 28, 1942, in the Steiner Collection, Folder No. 11:04, "Military Ordinariate 1941–1949."

4. "Duffy Reports," 1.

5. Father John E. Duffy, "Bishop Finneman," typewritten remembrance, January 12, 1958, in the Duffy Collection, "Duffy Files #1."

6. War Crimes Office, Judge Advocate General's Office, File #40-1865, October 26, 1945, Testimony of Father John E. Duffy at Walter Reed General Hospital, in the Duffy Collection, "Duffy Files #1."

7. Father Duffy American Legion Questionnaire.

8. "Duffy Reports," 8.

9. Ray C. Hunt and Bernard Norling, *Behind Japanese Lines: An American Guerrilla in the Philippines* (Lexington: University Press of Kentucky, 1986), 55.

10. Dan Murr, *But Deliver Us From Evil* (Jacksonville, FL: Stanton & Samuel, 2007), 84.

11. Letter from Father John Duffy to Most Rev. Karl J. Alter, D.D., September 14, 1945, in the Duffy Collection, "Primary Sources Folder."

12. Telegram to the Carberry family from the Adjutant General, February 23, 1942, found in O'Brien, "Family History; Family and Friends, 1872–2004."

13. Father Carberry to "Dear Sis," April 23, 1942, found in O'Brien, "Family History; Family and Friends, 1872–2004."

14. Letter from Sister M. Immaculata, R.S.M., to Father Richard Carberry, January 28, 1946, found in O'Brien, "Family History; Family and Friends, 1872–2004."

15. Letter from Steiner to Fitzgerald, January 5, 1942, Folder No. 11:09.

16. Letter from O'Hara to Mother M. Vincentia, C.S.C., Mother General, Holy Cross, Indiana, May 22, 1942, Folder No. 11:01.

17. Olivette and Caecilius, "Round Trip to the Philippines," 18, 20.

18. Hennel, *Our Expedition to Manila*, 25.

19. Letter from Brother Rex Hennel to his parents, September 14, 1943, in the Steiner Collection, Folder No. 6:2, "'H' Correspondence 1943–1945."

20. Letter from John Kapes to Father Steiner, December 18, 1943, in the Steiner Collection, Folder No. 6:2, "'K' Correspondence 1943–1945."

21. Letter from Rev. John J. Harrington, C.S.C., to Rev. Thomas Steiner, C.S.C., November 26, 1943, in the Steiner Collection, Folder No. 11:10.

22. Letter from Rev. Joseph M. Kmiecik, C.S.C., to Most Reverend John F. O'Hara, C.S.C., September 30, 1943, "Kmiecik, Joseph," COHA, 9/218, University of Notre Dame Archives.

23. Letter from Rev. John McGee, C.S.C., to Rev. Thomas Steiner, C.S.C., September 20, 1943, in the Steiner Collection, Folder No. 12:02.

24. Letters from Rev. Edward Fitzgerald, C.S.C., to Rev. Thomas Steiner, C.S.C., September 9, 1942 and no date, both in Folder No. 11:09.

25. Letters from Fitzgerald to Steiner, C.S.C., June 10, 1942 and July 5, 1942, both in Folder No. 11:09.

26. Letter from Fitzgerald to Steiner, C.S.C., October 22, 1942, Folder No. 11:09.

27. Alex Kershaw, *The Liberator* (New York: Crown Books, 2012), 21.

28. Letter from Barry to Steiner, June 1943 (censor inked out the day), Folder No. 11:05.

29. Letter from Barry to Steiner, June 1943, Folder No. 11:05.

30. Reverend Joseph Barry, interview conducted by Robert Crosby, 1980, in the Rev. Joseph D. Barry Personal Files, Holy Cross Archives, University of Notre Dame (hereafter cited as Crosby interview with Barry).

31. Rev. Joseph Barry, C.S.C., letter to Bishop John O'Hara, January 2, 1944, "Barry, Joseph," COHA 9/80, University of Notre Dame Archives.

32. Francis J. Spellman, *No Greater Love* (New York: Charles Scribner's Sons, 1945), 41.

33. Stemmons interview.

34. Vinnie Stigliani, interview with author, April 27, 2015.

35. Robert L. Gushwa, *The Best and Worst of Times: The United States Army Chaplaincy 1920–1945* (Washington, DC: Office of the Chief of Chaplains, Department of the Army, 1977), 186.

36. Kershaw, *Liberator*, 22.

37. Rev. Joseph Barry, C.S.C., letter to Father J. P. Wagener, June 3, 1943, "Barry, Joseph," COHA 9/80, University of Notre Dame Archives.

38. Letter from Barry to Steiner, July 8, 1943, Folder No. 11:05.

39. Dorsett, *Serving God and Country*, 242; Gushwa, *Best and Worst of Times*, 117.

40. Jack Hallowell, et al., *Eager for Duty: History of the 157th Infantry Regiment (Rifle)* (Baton Rouge, LA: Army & Navy Publishing Company, 1946), 22.

41. Robinson, *News of the 45th*, 67.

42. Crosby interview with Barry.

43. Letter from Barry to Steiner, August 3, 1943; letter from Rev. Joseph Barry, C.S.C., to Bishop John O'Hara, January 2, 1944, "Barry, Joseph," COHA 9/80, University of Notre Dame Archives.

44. Crosby interview with Barry.

45. Hallowell, et al., *Eager for Duty*, 23.

46. Letter from Barry to O'Hara, January 2, 1944, "Barry, Joseph," COHA 9/80, University of Notre Dame Archives.

47. Isaac Caudle, interview with author, October 12, 2015.

48. Bill Barrett, "45th Record: 511 Days of Fighting," *45th Division News*, no date, but early May 1945, 2.

49. "Chaplain Barry Wins Silver Star for Bravery in Italy," *South Bend Tribune*, September 5, 1944.

50. Barrett, "45th Record: 511 Days of Fighting," 2.

51. Elwood C. Nance, *Faith of Our Fighters* (St. Louis, MO: Bethany, 1944), 129.

52. Letter from Barry to Steiner, August 3, 1943, Folder No. 11:05.

53. Letter from Reverend Joseph Barry, C.S.C., to Patricia Brehmer, December 18, 1944, Father Barry Personal Files, Holy Cross Archives, University of Notre Dame.

54. Flint Whitlock, *The Rock of Anzio* (Boulder, CO: Westview, 1998), 63.

55. Crosby interview with Barry.

56. Crosby interview with Barry.

FOUR. **"I Never Expected to Come Out of the Philippines Alive"**

1. Dorothy Cave, *God's Warrior: Father Albert Braun, OFM, 1889–1983* (Santa Fe, NM: Sunstone Press, 2011), 313.

2. Lt. Col. William E. Dyess, *The Dyess Story* (New York: G. P. Putnam's Sons, 1944), 149.

3. Father John E. Duffy, "Bishop Finneman."

4. Brother Rex Hennel, "A Letter for Associates," *The Associate of Saint Joseph*, October–December 1945, 1.

5. Brother Rex Hennel, C.S.C., "A Prisoner of War Remembers," *Brothers*, Summer 1996, in "World War II Interned C.S.C.'s, 1941–1945," Holy Cross Archives, University of Notre Dame.

6. Hennel, *Our Expedition to Manila*, 36–37.

7. Olivette, *Diary*, January 15, 1943.

8. Pearl E. Hafstrom, "Yank 'Angels' End Over Three Years of Captivity," *South Bend Tribune*, May 24, 1945; Olivette and Caecilius, "Round Trip to the Philippines," 21.

9. Letter from Mother M. Vincentia, Superior General to Mrs. Roth, February 1, 1943, in "Internment in Manila 1941–1945."

10. Telegram from Sister Olivette to Mother M. Vincentia, Superior General, February 19, 1943; letter from Mother M. Vincentia, Superior General to Mrs. Roth, February 20, 1943, both in "Internment in Manila 1941–1945."

11. Telegram from Sister Caecilius to Mrs. William J. Roth, September 12, 1943, "Internment in Manila 1941–1945."

12. Olivette, *Diary,* July 8, 1944.

13. Hennel, *Our Expedition to Manila,* 37, 40.

14. Found in http://www.catholicchant.com/salveregina.html. Accessed December 21, 2017.

15. Hennel, *Our Expedition to Manila,* 41.

16. Hennel, *Our Expedition to Manila,* 42; Olivette, *Diary,* July 9, 1944.

17. Hennel, *Our Expedition to Manila,* 44.

18. McKee, "Holy Cross P.O.W.'s in the Philippines," 9.

19. A. B. Feuer, ed., *Bilibid Diary: The Secret Notebooks of Commander Thomas Hayes, POW, the Philippines, 1942–1945* (Hamden, CT: Archon Books, 1987), 147, 157, 188.

20. Letter from Sister Caecilius to her grandmother, March 26, 1945, "Internment in Manila 1941–1945."

21. Hennel, "Letter for Associates," 3; Hennel, *Our Expedition to Manila,* 43.

22. Michael and Elizabeth M. Norman, *Tears in the Darkness* (New York: Farrar, Straus and Giroux, 2009), 275.

23. Letter from Duffy to Alter, September 14, 1945.

24. Dyess, *Dyess Story,* 160.

25. Hennel, *Our Expedition to Manila,* 48.

26. Feuer, *Bilibid Diary,* 137.

27. Lieutenant Colonel Leslie F. Zimmerman, Diary, October 9, 1942, manuscript donated to the United States Air Force Research Agency, December 1989.

28. Dorothy Still Danner, *What a Way to Spend a War* (Annapolis, MD: Naval Institute Press, 1995), 174.

29. "We Must Recognize Supremacy of God, Declares Rev. Duffy," undated newspaper article written after the war for a Bellevue, Ohio, newspaper, in the Duffy Collection, "Duffy Photo Album."

30. Feuer, *Bilibid Diary,* 161, 187.

31. Feuer, *Bilibid Diary,* 6.

32. McKee, "Holy Cross P.O.W.'s in the Philippines," 9.

33. Zimmerman, Diary, August 1942.

34. John D. Lukacs, *Escape from Davao* (New York: Simon & Schuster, 2010), 187.

35. Foster Hailey, "Escape from a Man-Made Hell," *New York Times,* April 16, 1944.

36. Letter from Abie Abraham to Father John Sherbno, 1976, in the Duffy Collection, "Duffy Files #1."

37. Letter from Ben Steele to Father John Sherbno, November 21, 1975, in the Duffy Collection, "Duffy Files #1."

38. Feuer, *Bilibid Diary*, 163–64.

39. Sister Mary Olivette, "Reflections on the Experience of Being a Japanese War Prisoner in Los Baños during World War II," July 19, 1993, in "Internment in Manila 1941–1945."

40. Los Baños Christmas 1944 Program, in "Internment in Manila 1941–1945."

41. Olivette and Caecilius, "Round Trip to the Philippines," 23.

42. Letter from Sister Mary Olivette to her family, February 24, 1945, in "Internment in Manila 1941–1945."

43. Letter from Most Reverend Karl J. Alter to Major John E. Duffy, May 25, 1943, in the Duffy Collection, "Duffy Correspondence."

44. Feuer, *Bilibid Diary*, 182.

FIVE. **"Daily Was I Shelled, Nightly Was I Bombed"**

1. Kershaw, *Liberator*, 54.

2. Bill Mauldin, *Up Front* (New York: Henry Holt, 1945), 102–3.

3. Letter from Barry to Hope, February 1944.

4. Letter from Father Joseph Barry to Jim Costin, November 18, 1943, reprinted in "Jim Costin Says," *South Bend Tribune*, no month, 1943, in the Father Barry Personal Files, Holy Cross Archives, University of Notre Dame.

5. Letter from Barry to Hope, February 1944.

6. Father Barry Monthly Chaplain Report, November 1943, Steiner Collection, Folder No. 11:05.

7. Stigliani interview.

8. Letter from Barry to Costin, November 18, 1943, Folder No. 11:05.

9. Letter from Barry to Steiner, November, 1943, Folder No. 11:05.

10. Mauldin, *Up Front*, 93–94.

11. Stemmons interview.

12. Letter from Barry to Hope, February 1944, Folder No. 11:05.

13. Letter from Barry to Steiner, November, 1943, Folder No. 11:05.

14. Letter from Barry to Hope, February 1944, Folder No. 11:05.

15. Letter from Barry to Steiner, February 14, 1944, Folder No. 11:05.

16. Letter from Barry to Hope, February 1944, Folder No. 11:05.

17. Letter from Barry to Hope, February 1944, Folder No. 11:05; Mauldin, *Up Front*, 100, 162.

18. Crosby interview with Barry.

19. Albert R. Panebianco, "Pictures," *45th Infantry Division* (2005), http://www.45thinfantrydivision.com/index12.htm. Accessed December 21, 2017.

20. Crosby interview with Barry.

21. Crosby interview with Barry.

22. Letter from Margaret Ahern to Rev. Thomas Steiner, C.S.C., May 3, 1944, Folder No. 11:05.

23. Mauldin, *Up Front*, 57.

24. Crosby interview with Barry.

25. Letter from Barry to Steiner, November, 1943; letter from Barry to Steiner, February 14, 1944: both in Folder No. 11:05; "Local Priest Modestly Returns as War Hero," *South Bend Tribune*, October 22, 1945.

26. Stigliani interview.

27. Dorothy Fremont Grant, *War Is My Parish* (Milwaukee, WI: Bruce Publishing, 1944), 23; Russell Cartwright Stroup, *Letters from the Pacific: A Combat Chaplain in World War II* (Columbia: University of Missouri Press, 2000), 144.

28. Letter from Barry to Steiner, November, 1943, Folder No. 11:05.

29. Letter from Staff Sergeant Michael J. Jaskovich to Rev. Thomas Steiner, C.S.C., October 13, 1944, Folder No. 11:05.

30. Letter from Barry to Costin, November 18, 1943; letter from Barry to Hope, February 1944, both in Folder No. 11:05.

31. Letter from Jaskovich to Steiner, October 13, 1944, Folder No. 11:05.

32. Letter from Barry to Hope, February 1944, Folder No. 11:05.

33. Letter from Barry to Costin, November 18, 1943, Folder No. 11:05.

34. Crosby interview with Barry.

35. Caudle interview.

36. Stemmons interview.

37. Letter from Steiner to Harrington, July 7, 1944, Folder No. 11:10; letter from Steiner to Fitzgerald, March 25, 1944, Folder No. 11:09.

38. Letter from Barry to Hope, February 1944, Folder No. 11:05.

39. Mauldin, *Up Front*, 24.

40. Letter from Jaskovich to Steiner, October 13, 1944, Folder No. 11:05.

41. Letter from Barry to Hope, February 1944, Folder No. 11:05.

42. Letter from Barry to Costin, November 18, 1943, Folder No. 11:05.

43. Letter from Steiner to Barry, October 15, 1943, Folder No. 11:05.

44. Letter from Barry to Steiner, November 1943, Folder No. 11:05.

45. Letter from Barry to Brehmer, July 30, 1944, Father Barry Personal Files.

46. Letter from Barry to Steiner, February 14, 1944, Folder No. 11:05.

47. Letter from Barry to Steiner, February 14, 1944, Folder No. 11:05.

48. Father William Simmons, C.S.C., "Let Us Now Praise Famous Men," *Hoban Highlights*, Summer 2001.

49. Simmons, "Let Us Now Praise Famous Men."

50. Mauldin, *Up Front*, 164, 167.

51. Letter from Jaskovich to Steiner, October 13, 1944, Folder No. 11:05.

52. Letter from Barry to Steiner, February 14, 1944, Folder No. 11:05.

53. V-Mail letter from Barry to Rev. W. P. Corcoran, C.S.C., June 4, 1944, Folder No. 11:05.

54. Letter from Barry to Steiner, February 14, 1944, Folder No. 11:05.

55. Letter from Barry to Steiner, July 25, 1944; letter from Barry to Hope, February 1944, both in Folder No. 11:05.

56. V-Mail letter from Barry to Corcoran, June 4, 1944, Folder No. 11:05.

57. Letter from Barry to Steiner, July 25, 1944; letter from Barry to Brehmer, December 18, 1944, both in Folder No. 11:05.

58. Letter from Barry to Steiner, July 25, 1944, Folder No. 11:05.

59. Grant, *War Is My Parish*, 3; Donald F. Crosby, S.J., *Battlefield Chaplains: Catholic Priests in World War II* (Lawrence: University Press of Kansas, 1994), 118–19.

60. Crosby, *Battlefield Chaplains*, 119–20.

61. Letter from Barry to Steiner, July 25, 1944, Folder No. 11:05.

62. Letter from Barry to Steiner, July 25, 1944, Folder No. 11:05.

63. Letter from Barry to Steiner, July 25, 1944; letter from Barry to Brehmer, July 30, 1944, both in Folder No. 11:05.

SIX. "Face to Face with the Realism, the Tragedy, and the Horror of the War"

1. Sampson, *Look Out Below!*, 45.

2. John S. D. Eisenhower, *General Ike: A Personal Reminiscence* (New York: Free Press, 2003), 225.

3. Sgt. Don Malarkey with Bob Welch, *Easy Company Soldier* (New York: St. Martin's Press, 2008), 69.

4. Sampson, *Look Out Below!*, 42.

5. Letter from Fitzgerald to Steiner, December 28, 1941, Folder No. 11:09.

6. Letter from Fitzgerald to Steiner, April 10, 1944, Folder No. 11:09.

7. Letter from Fitzgerald to Steiner, no date, but April or May 1944, Folder No. 11:09.

8. Alton Earl Carpenter and A. Anne Eiland, *Chappie: World War II Diary of A Combat Chaplain* (Mesa, AZ: Mead, 2007), 98.

9. Sampson, *Look Out Below!*, 47.

10. Father Edward Fitzgerald, "Highlights of My Career," Edward Fitzgerald Personal Files, Holy Cross Archives, University of Notre Dame.

11. Sampson, *Look Out Below!*, 56.

12. Dwight D. Eisenhower, *Crusade in Europe* (Garden City, NY: Doubleday, 1950), 246.

13. Walter Bedell Smith, *Eisenhower's Six Great Decisions* (New York: Longmans, Green, 1956), 55; Carlo D'Este, *Eisenhower: A Soldier's Life* (New York: Henry Holt, 2002), 1.

14. Sampson, *Look Out Below!*, xviii.

15. Alfred D. Chandler Jr., ed., *The Papers of Dwight David Eisenhower: The War Years* (Baltimore: Johns Hopkins, 1970), 3:1913.

16. Sampson, *Look Out Below!*, 58–59.

17. George E. Koskimaki, *D-Day with the Screaming Eagles* (Havertown, PA: Casemate, 2002), 60.

18. Sampson, *Look Out Below!*, 60, 63.

19. Richard Dowd, "D-Day: Two Chaplains Remember," *Visitor*, June 3, 1984, 3.

20. Sampson, *Look Out Below!*, 65–67.

21. Sampson, *Look Out Below!*, 73.

22. Sampson, *Look Out Below!*, 32–33, 73, 169.

23. Barb Fraze, "Army Chaplain Still Remembers D-Day," *Catholic Messenger*, June 14, 1984.

24. Sampson, *Look Out Below!*, 70.

25. "Home Truths," *People*, September 7, 1998, 110.

26. "Home Truths," 109.

SEVEN. **"Our Chaplains Are Becoming More Scattered Every Week"**

1. Letter from Rev. John Dupuis, C.S.C., to Rev. Thomas Steiner, C.S.C., September 30, 1943, in the Steiner Collection, Folder No. 11:08 (hereafter cited as Dupuis to recipient, date, Folder No. 11:08).

2. Letter from Steiner to Dupuis, October 15, 1943; Letter from Dupuis to Steiner, December 2, 1943, both in Folder No. 11:08.

3. Richard Wheeler, *A Special Valor: The U.S. Marines and the Pacific War* (New York: New American Library, 1983), 236.

4. Letter from Dupuis to Steiner, March 13, 1944, Folder No. 11:08.

5. Letter from Dupuis to Steiner, March 13, 1944, Folder No. 11:08.

6. Wheeler, *Special Valor*, 239.

7. Letter from Dupuis to Steiner, April 28, 1944, Folder No. 11:08.

8. Letter from Steiner to Dupuis, March 28, 1944, Folder No. 11:08.

9. Letter from Dupuis to Steiner, April 28, 1944, Folder No. 11:08.

10. Letter from Steiner to Hewitt, June 18, 1944, Folder No. 12:02.

11. Letter from Boland to Steiner, July 7, 1944, Folder No. 11:06.

12. Letters from Heintskill to Steiner, December 31, 1943; February 3, 1944; May 15, 1944; September 29, 1944, all in Folder No. 12:01.

13. Letter from Heintskill to Steiner, July 13, 1944, Folder No. 12:01.

14. Letters from Heintskill to Steiner, July 13, and August 8, 1944, both in Folder No. 12:01.

15. Letters from Heintskill to Steiner, August 8 and September 29, 1944, both in Folder No. 12:01.

16. Letter from Heintskill to Steiner, November 13, 1944, Folder No. 12:01.

17. Letters from Heintskill to Steiner, February 23 and March 8, 1944, both in Folder No. 12:01.

18. Letters from Heintskill to Steiner, March 8, July 13, August 8, and December 24, 1944, all in Folder No. 12:01.

19. Letter from Heintskill to Steiner, January 23, 1944, Folder No. 12:01.

20. Letters from Heintskill to Steiner, April 23 and December 7, 1944, both in Folder No. 12:01.

21. Letter from Rev. Francis D. Bridenstine, C.S.C., to Rev. Thomas Steiner, C.S.C., March 8, 1945, in the Steiner Collection, Folder No. 11:07 (hereafter cited as Bridenstine to recipient, date, Folder No. 11:07).

22. Letter from Dupuis to Steiner, July 19, 1944, Folder No. 11:08.

23. Letter from Dupuis to Steiner, September 27, 1944, Folder No. 11:08.

24. Letters from Corcoran to Steiner, July 10, October 5, December 11, and December 1943, all in Folder No. 11:07.

25. Letters from Hewitt to Steiner, August 27, 1943; July 14, 1944; and January 27, 1945, all in Folder No. 12:02.

26. Letters from Rev. Patrick Duffy, C.S.C., to Rev. Thomas Steiner, C.S.C., December 10, 1943; March 21, 1944; August 4, 1944; and November 9, 1944, all in the Steiner Collection, Folder No. 11:08 (hereafter cited as Duffy to recipient, date, Folder No. 11:08).

27. Letter from Ensign Charles Varnak to Rev. Thomas Steiner, C.S.C., November 25, 1944, in the Steiner Collection, Folder No. 11:08.

28. Letter from Sister Caecilius to her grandmother, March 26, 1945, "Internment in Manila 1941–1945."

29. Hennel, *Our Expedition to Manila*, 45–46.

30. Olivette, *Diary*, August 31 and September 16, 1944.

31. Danner, *What a Way to Spend a War*, 170; Olivette, *Diary*, September 21, 1944.

32. Olivette, *Diary*, October 19, 1944.

33. McKee, "Holy Cross P.O.W.'s in the Philippines," 10.

34. Olivette and Caecilius, "Round Trip to the Philippines," 23.

35. Olivette, *Diary*, October 23, 1944.

36. Hennel, *Our Expedition to Manila*, 51.

37. Letter from Bridenstine to Steiner, March 8, 1945, Folder No. 11:07.

38. Letter from Boland to Steiner, December 11, 1944, Folder No. 11:06; letter from Dupuis to Steiner, December 15, 1944, Folder No. 11:08; letter from Hewitt to Steiner, January 27, 1945, Folder No. 12:02; letter from Heintskill to Steiner, December 24, 1944, Folder No. 12:01.

39. Olivette, *Diary,* December 1, December 11, December 13, and December 21, 1944.

40. Los Baños Christmas Program, in "Internment in Manila 1941–1945."

41. Danner, *What a Way to Spend a War*, 179; Olivette and Caecilius, "Round Trip to the Philippines," 23–24.

42. Hennel, "A Prisoner of War Remembers."

43. Danner, *What a Way to Spend a War*, 179.

44. "Duffy Reports," 17.

45. E. Bartlett Kerr, *Surrender and Survival: The Experience of American POWs in the Pacific, 1941–1945* (New York: William Morrow, 1985), 202.

46. Feuer, *Bilibid Diary*, 209.

47. "Duffy Reports," 18.

48. Gregory F. Michno, *Death on the Hellships* (Annapolis, MD: Naval Institute Press, 2001), 260.

49. Donald Knox, *Death March* (New York: Harcourt Brace Jovanovich, 1981), 350.

50. Letter from Rev. John Duffy to Most Rev. Karl J. Alter, D.D., August 23, 1945, in the Duffy Collection, "Duffy Correspondence."

51. Schmidt, "Priest, Now New London Pastor, Recalls Horrors of Death March."

52. "Duffy Reports," 20.

53. Letter from Steiner to Heintskill, December 27, 1944, Folder No. 12:01.

EIGHT. **"Hope Mr. Hitler Goes Underground before Winter"**

1. Mark A. Bando, *Avenging Eagles* (Detroit, MI: Mark Bando Publishing, 2006), 171–72.

2. "The 501st Parachute Infantry Regiment: Operation Market Garden," *U.S. Airborne During World War II*, http://www.ww2-airborne.us/units/501/501.html. Accessed December 21, 2017.

3. Sampson, *Look Out Below!*, 96.

4. Sampson, *Look Out Below!*, 101–2.

5. Letter from Fitzgerald to Steiner, October 7, 1944, Folder No. 11:10.

6. Crosby, *Battlefield Chaplains*, 151.

7. Katharine Blossom Lowrie, "Veteran Remembers Battle of the Bulge," *Redondo Beach Patch*, May 28, 2012, http://patch.com/california/redondobeach /redondo-beach-veteran-survived-the-battle-of-the-budge.

8. Lowrie, "Veteran Remembers Battle of the Bulge."

9. Sampson, *Look Out Below!*, 107.

10. George E. Koskimaki, *The Battered Bastards of Bastogne* (Havertown, PA: Casemate, 2003), 146.

11. Lowrie, "Veteran Remembers Battle of the Bulge."

12. Father Francis L. Sampson, "Statement or Report of Interview of Recovered Personnel," National Archives and Records Administration, St. Louis, MO; Sampson, *Look Out Below!*, 108.

13. Sampson, *Look Out Below!*, 118, 122.

14. Mauldin, *Up Front*, 197.

15. William Lyford, e-mail to author, February 26, 2015.

16. Thomas Riordan, "Stories: World War II Memories of Tom Riordan," *45th Infantry Division* (2000), http://www.45thinfantrydivision.com/index13 .htm. Accessed December 21, 2017.

17. Father Barry's Monthly Reports to the Military Ordinariate, August 1944, Folder No. 11:05.

18. "Local Priest Modestly Returns as War Hero," *South Bend Tribune*, October 22, 1945.

19. Letter from Mr. and Mrs. Marian Ficco to Rev. Thomas Steiner, C.S.C., February 17, 1945, Folder No. 11:05.

20. Letter from Steiner to Jaskovich, December 6, 1944, Folder No. 11:05.

21. Robert Donohue, "Stories: Robert E. Donohue, Company E, 157th Infantry Regiment, 45th Division," *45th Infantry Division* (n.d.), http://www .45thinfantrydivision.com/index13.htm. Accessed December 21, 2017.

22. Letter from Barry to Brehmer, December 18, 1944, Folder No. 11:05.

23. Daniel Dougherty, interview with author, March 2, 2015.

24. Carpenter and Eiland, *Chappie*, 155.

25. Fitzgerald, "Highlights of My Career."

26. Letters from McGee to Steiner, October 23 and October 26, 1944, and January 18, 1945, all in Folder No. 12:02.

27. Letters from Biger to Steiner, March 15, 1944, both in Folder No. 11:06.

28. Letter from Steiner to Biger, November 24, 1944, Folder No. 11:06.

29. Hesburgh and Reedy, *God, Country, Notre Dame*, 40.

30. Letter from Maurice E. Powers, C.S.C., to Bureau of Chaplains, December 22, 1941; letter from Maurice E. Powers, C.S.C., to Chief of Chaplains, November 8, 1944, both in "Reverend Maurice Powers, World War II Chaplaincy, 1941–1945."

NINE. "I Had the Devil Scared Out of Me Many a Time"

1. Letter from Thomas B. Fern to his mother, December 13, 1944, in the Thomas B. and Marguerite Fern Collection.

2. Letter from Heintskill to Steiner, February 7, 1945, Folder No. 12:01.

3. Report from Lieutenant Henry A. Heintskill, C.S.C., USNR, to the Secretary of the Navy, January 10, 1946, in the Steiner Collection, Folder No. 12:01.

4. Letter from Heintskill to Steiner, February 7, 1945, Folder No. 12:01.

5. Letter from Heintskill to Steiner, April 5, 1945, Folder No. 12:01.

6. Letter from Boland to Steiner, March 21, 1945, Folder No. 11:06.

7. Letter from Boland to Steiner, March 21, 1945, Folder No. 11:06.

8. Letter from Steiner to Dupuis, April 19, 1945, Folder No. 11:08.

9. Letters from Dupuis to Steiner, April 15 and April 18, 1945, Folder No. 11:08.

10. Letter from Heintskill to Steiner, March 9, 1945, Folder No. 12:01.

11. Letter from Steiner to Dupuis, April 19, 1945, Folder No. 11:08.

12. Olivette, *Diary,* December 31, 1944.

13. Olivette, *Diary,* January 4, 1945; Hennel, *Our Expedition to Manila,* 51; letter from Father Jerome Lawyer to Rev. Thomas A. Steiner, April 25, 1945, in the Steiner Collection, Folder No. 6:2, "'L' Correspondence 1943–1945."

14. Olivette, *Diary,* January 7, 1945.

15. Olivette, *Diary,* January 13, 1945; Hennel, *Our Expedition to Manila,* 51.

16. Olivette and Caecilius, "Round Trip to the Philippines," 24–25.

17. Danner, *What a Way to Spend a War,* 190; McKee, "Holy Cross P.O.W.'s in the Philippines," 10.

18. Olivette, *Diary,* January 28 and January 31, 1945; James T. Carroll, "Sentenced to Death—Destined for Life: Catholic Religious and Japanese Occupation," *American Catholic Studies* (Fall–Winter 2002): 70; letter from Lawyer to his parents, February 24, 1945, Folder No. 6:02: "'L' Correspondence 1943–1945."

19. Olivette, *Diary,* February 8, February 17, and February 19, 1945.

20. "In Thanksgiving for Manila Rescue," *University of Notre Dame Religious Bulletin,* April 18, 1945.

21. Olivette, "My Most Memorable Experience as a Nun," in "Internment in Manila 1941–1945."

22. Linda Goetz Holmes, *Unjust Enrichment: How Japan's Companies Built Postwar Fortunes Using American POWs* (Mechanicsburg, PA: Stackpole Books, 2001), 116.

23. McKee, "Holy Cross P.O.W.'s in the Philippines," 10–11; letter from Father Robert McKee to Father Thomas Fitzpatrick, March 3, 1945, in "World

War II Interned C.S.C.'s, 1941–1945," Holy Cross Archives, University of Notre Dame; Olivette and Caecilius, "Round Trip to the Philippines," 25; Hafstrom, "Yank 'Angels' End Over Three Years of Captivity."

24. "In Thanksgiving for Manila Rescue"; Sister Olivette, taped interview, November 27, 1982, in "Internment in Manila 1941–1945."

25. Hennel, "Letter for Associates," 3.

26. Letter from Sister Mary Olivette to Mary G., February 25, 1945, in "Internment in Manila 1941–1945."

27. Danner, *What a Way to Spend a War*, 195.

28. Olivette and Caecilius, "Round Trip to the Philippines," 26.

29. Hennel, *Our Expedition to Manila*, 53.

30. Sister Olivette, taped interview, in "Internment in Manila 1941–1945"; Olivette, *Diary*, February 23, 1945.

31. Letter from Father Robert McKee to Father Thomas Fitzpatrick, March 3, 1945, "Philippine POW's," Holy Cross Archives, University of Notre Dame; Hennel, *Our Expedition to Manila*, 55.

32. Danner, *What A Way to Spend A War*, 199.

33. Letter from McKee to Fitzpatrick, March 4, 1945, "Philippine POW's."

34. Letter from McKee to Fitzpatrick, March 4, 1945, "Philippine POW's."

35. McKee, "Holy Cross P.O.W.'s in the Philippines," 12; Hennel, *Our Expedition to Manila*, 55.

36. Olivette, *Diary*, February 23, 1945; letter from Sister Mary Olivette to Mother General, February 25, 1945, in "Internment in Manila 1941–1945."

37. Olivette, *Diary*, February 24, 1945.

38. Hennel, *Our Expedition to Manila*, 56.

39. Letter from First Lieutenant John F. Finneran, ND '33, to Father Steiner, February 24, 1945, in "Letters from Servicemen F-T," UWW2 1/08, University of Notre Dame Archives.

40. Letter from Robert R. McCormick to the Rev. Thomas Steiner, February 27, 1945, in the Steiner Collection, Folder No. 7:04, "'M' Correspondence 1943–1945."

41. Francis McCarthy, "Raid Rescues 2,146 from Luzon Camp," *New York Times*, February 25, 1945; "Foe's Manila Garrison Wiped Out," *New York Times*, February 25, 1945.

42. Letter from Lawyer to his parents, February 24, 1945, Folder No. 6:02, "'L' Correspondence 1943–1945."

43. "Notre Dame Man Rescues Notre Dame Men," *University of Notre Dame Religious Bulletin*, April 10, 1945, in "Internment in Manila 1941–1945."

44. Letter from Sister Mary Olivette to her family, February 24, 1945, in "Internment in Manila 1941–1945."

45. Letter from Sister Mary Olivette to Clare, March 1, 1945; letter from Sister Mary Olivette to Marjorie, March 4, 1945, both in "Internment in Manila 1941–1945."

46. "Six N. D. Men Freed by Seventh; Lt. John Finneran, '33, Helps in Rescue at Los Banos Camp in the Philippines," *Notre Dame Alumnus*, April 1945, 12.

47. Letter from Lawyer to Steiner, no date, but February–March 1945, Folder No. 6:02, "'L' Correspondence 1943–1945."

48. Letter from Brother Theodore Kapes to the Rev. Thomas Steiner, March 9, 1945, in the Steiner Collection, Folder No. 10:02, "World War II Interned C.S.C.'s, 1941–1945."

49. Letter from Sister Mary Olivette to Mother General, February 25, 1945; letter from Mother M. Rose Elizabeth to Mrs. William J. Roth, March 24, 1945, both in "Internment in Manila 1941–1945."

50. Letters from Steiner to Fitzgerald, March 1945 and April 16, 1945, both in Folder No. 11:09.

51. Hennel, *Our Expedition to Manila*, 58–60.

52. Letter from Steiner to Hewitt, April 20, 1945, Folder No. 12:02.

53. Hennel, *Our Expedition to Manila*, 61; Ray Gregg, "Anxious Eyes of Liberated Thank 'Rescuer' Atop Dome," *South Bend Tribune*, no date discernible, 1945.

54. McKee, "Holy Cross P.O.W.'s in the Philippines," 14.

55. U.S.S. *Admiral E. W. Eberle* (AP-123) War Diary, April 9, 1945.

56. Olivette, *Diary*, April 10, 1945.

57. U.S.S. *Admiral E. W. Eberle* (AP-123) War Diary, April 23 and April 25, 1945.

58. Pauline Peyton Forney, "Holy Cross Missionaries Return from Philippines," *Holy Cross Courier*, August, 1945.

59. Hafstrom, "Yank 'Angels' End Over Three Years of Captivity."

60. Letter from Rev. John E. Duffy to Most Reverend Karl J. Alter, Mudken, Manchuria, August 23, 1945, in the Duffy Collection, "Duffy Correspondence."

61. "Duffy Reports," 21.

62. Letter from Rev. John E. Duffy to Most Reverend Karl J. Alter, September 14, 1945, in the Duffy Collection, "Primary Sources Folder."

63. War Crimes Office, Judge Advocate General's Office, File #40–1046, October 26, 1945, interview with Father John E. Duffy at Walter Reed General Hospital, in the Duffy Collection, "Duffy Files #1"; Schmidt, "Priest, Now New London Pastor, Recalls Horrors of Death March."

64. Murr, *But Deliver Us From Evil*, 111–12.

TEN. "Facing the Insanity of Himmler's Madmen"

1. Dougherty interview.

2. Letter from Barry to Brehmer, December 18, 1944, in the Father Barry Personal Files, Holy Cross Archives, University of Notre Dame.

3. Letter from O'Hara to Steiner, 6, 1943, Folder No. 11:02.

4. Letter from Maurice E. Powers, C.S.C., to "My dear friend," May 14, 1945, found in "Reverend Maurice Powers, World War II Chaplaincy, 1941–1945," Holy Cross Archives, University of Notre Dame (hereafter cited as Powers to "My dear friend").

5. Letter from Powers to "My dear friend," May 14, 1945.

6. Letter from Maurice E. Powers, C.S.C., to Maripat McCormick, May 9, 1945, in "CSC Chaplains in World War II," UDIS 39/24, University of Notre Dame Archives.

7. Letter from Powers to "My dear friend," May 14, 1945.

8. Maurice E. Powers, C.S.C., Monthly Report of Chaplains, March 1945, found in "Reverend Maurice Powers, World War II Chaplaincy, 1941–1945."

9. Letter from Powers to "My dear friend," May 14, 1945.

10. Maurice E. Powers, C.S.C., Monthly Report of Chaplains, February 1945, found in "Reverend Maurice Powers, World War II Chaplaincy, 1941–1945."

11. Melaney Welch Moisan, *Tracking the 101st Cavalry* (Keizer, OR: Wheat Field Press, 2008), 21.

12. Efficiency Report for Maurice E. Powers, C.S.C., December 31, 1944, found in "Reverend Maurice Powers, World War II Chaplaincy, 1941–1945."

13. Letter from Powers to "My dear friend," May 14, 1945.

14. Letter from Steiner to McGee, March 3, 1945, Folder No. 12:02.

15. Letter from Rev. Edmund J. Murray, C.S.C., to Father Will, "Somewhere in Germany," 9 January 1945, found in "Letters from Servicemen F-T," UWW2 1/08, University of Notre Dame Archives.

16. Harry Spiller, *Prisoners of Nazis: Accounts by American POWs in World War II* (Jefferson, NC: McFarland, 1998), 151.

17. John Toland, *The Last 100 Days* (New York: Random House, 1965), 69.

18. Spiller, *Prisoners of Nazis*, 166.

19. Toland, *Last 100 Days*, 70–71.

20. Sampson, *Look Out Below!*, 133.

21. Bill Barrett, "Sinatra Honored, Adolf Loses Out," *45th Division News*, May 13, 1945, 1.

22. "Dachau," *Time*, May 7, 1945.

23. Bill Barrett, "Dachau Gives Answer to Why We Fought," *45th Division News*, May 13, 1945, 1.

24. Dougherty interview; Dan P. Dougherty, ed., *Second Platoon*, September 1999, 1.

25. John P. Lee, "Action at the Coal Yard Wall," *Second Platoon*, April 2001, 2; Whitlock, *Rock of Anzio*, 360.

26. Crosby interview with Barry, 10; "Dachau Captured by Americans Who Kill Guards, Liberate 32,000," *New York Times*, May 1, 1945, 5.

27. Whitlock, *Rock of Anzio*, 385.

28. Barrett, "Dachau Gives Answer to Why We Fought," 3.

29. Crosby interview with Barry, 10.

30. "Dachau Captured by Americans," 1.

31. Crosby interview with Barry, 10–11.

32. Letter from Maurice E. Powers, C.S.C., to Maripat McCormick, May 9, 1945, in "CSC Chaplains in World War II," UDIS 39/24, University of Notre Dame Archives."

33. Monthly Report of Chaplains, April 1945, "Reverend Maurice Powers, World War II Chaplaincy, 1941–1945."

34. Letter from Maurice E. Powers, C.S.C., to Maripat McCormick, May 9, 1945, in "CSC Chaplains in World War II," UDIS 39/24, University of Notre Dame Archives.

35. Letter from Powers to "My dear friend," May 14, 1945.

36. Letter from Powers to "My dear friend," May 14, 1945.

37. Letter from Paul W. Cavanaugh, S. J., to J. Walter Kennedy, no date, but after the war, in "CSC Chaplains in World War II," UDIS 39/24, University of Notre Dame Archives.

38. Daniel A. Ficco, "Sneaking into A Prison Camp," *Second Platoon*, February 1999, 8.

39. Letter from Rev. Edmund J. Murray, C.S.C., to Paul R. Byrne, April 30, 1945, in "Letters from Servicemen F-T," UWW2 1/08, University of Notre Dame Archives.

40. Bronze Star citation included in letter from William T. McCarty, C.SS.R. (Military Delegate), to Very Rev. Thomas Steiner, C.S.C., April 23, 1945, in the Steiner Collection, Folder No. 11:03, "Military Ordinariate 1945–1946."

41. Sampson, *Look Out Below!*, 145.

42. Bronze Star citation found in the Chaplain Francis L. Sampson File, National Personnel Records Center, National Archives and Records Administration, St. Louis, MO.

43. David Boyce, "Veteran Was Prisoner of War in Germany," *Menlo Park (CA) Almanac*, November 21, 2001, http://www.almanacnews.com/morgue/2001/2001_11_21.salome14.html.

44. Sampson, *Look Out Below!*, 149–50.

45. Toland, *Last 100 Days*, 537.

46. Monthly Report of Chaplains, April 1945, "Reverend Maurice Powers, World War II Chaplaincy, 1941–1945."

47. Letter from Powers to "My dear friend," May 14, 1945.

48. Monthly Report of Chaplains, April 1945, "Reverend Maurice Powers, World War II Chaplaincy, 1941–1945."

49. Letter from Maurice E. Powers, C.S.C., to Maripat McCormick, May 9, 1945, in "CSC Chaplains in World War II," UDIS 39/24, University of Notre Dame Archives.

50. Letter from Powers to "My dear friend," May 14, 1945.

51. Moisan, *Tracking the 101st Cavalry*, 329–31.

52. Barrett, "45th Record: 511 Days of Fighting," 2.

53. Letter from Powers to "My dear friend," May 14, 1945.

ELEVEN. **"You Could Have Heard My Cheer in Niles"**

1. Letter from Heintskill to Steiner, April 12, 1945, Folder No. 12:01.

2. Letter from Bridenstine to Steiner, March 8, 1945, Folder No. 11:07.

3. Letter from Steiner to Heintskill, June 12, 1945, Folder No. 12:01.

4. Letter from Heintskill to Steiner, May 20, 1945, Folder No. 12:01.

5. Letter from Steiner to Heintskill, April 24, 1945, Folder No. 12:01.

6. Letter from Corcoran to Steiner, March 10, 1945, Folder No. 11:07.

7. Letter from Steiner to Corcoran, March 15, 1945, Folder No. 11:07.

8. Letter from Corcoran to Steiner, no month or day listed, but shortly after Okinawa, 1945, Folder No. 11:07.

9. Letter from Corcoran to Steiner, no month or day listed, but shortly after Okinawa, 1945, Folder No. 11:07.

10. Letter from Boland to Steiner, April 23, 1945, Folder No. 11:06.

11. Letter from Steiner to Boland, April 24, 1945, Folder No. 11:06.

12. Letter from Rev. John J. Burke to Bishop O'Hara, September 6, 1944, from National Naval Medical Center, Bethesda, MD, "Burke, John J., CSC," COHA 9/98, University of Notre Dame Archives.

13. U.S.S. *Pennsylvania* (BB-38), *Summary of War Service*, 4.

14. Letter from Burke to Steiner, May 29, 1945, Folder No. 11:07.

15. Letter from Burke to Steiner, July 12, 1945, Folder No. 11:07.

16. *The Diary of Father John J. Burke*, August 9, 1945, in the Father John J. Burke Personal Papers, Holy Cross Archives, University of Notre Dame.

17. Letter from Burke to Steiner, October 3, 1945, Folder No. 11:07.

18. Letter from Father John J. Burke C.S.C., to Margaret L. Olges, October 30, 1945, Folder No. 11:07; *Diary of Father John J. Burke*, August 12–13, 1945.

19. Letter from Burke to Steiner, August 17, 1945, Folder No. 11:07.

20. Letter from Burke to Steiner, October 3, 1945, Folder No. 11:07.

21. Letter from Burke to Steiner, August 17, 1945, Folder No. 11:07.

22. *Diary of Father John J. Burke*, August 15, 1945.

23. U.S.S. *Pennsylvania* (BB-38), *Summary of War Service*, 5–6.

24. *The Diary of Father John J. Burke*, August 27, September 9–10, 1945.

25. Letter from Boland to Steiner, August 16, 1945, Folder No. 11:06.

26. Letter from Hewitt to Steiner, September 11, 1945, Folder No. 12:02.

27. Letter from Orn Catherine Rawls to Father John J. Burke, C.S.C., September 10, 1945, "U.S.S. *Pennsylvania* Letters of Sympathy," in the Father John J. Burke Personal Papers, Holy Cross Archives, University of Notre Dame (hereafter cited as "U.S.S. *Pennsylvania* Letters of Sympathy").

28. Letter from Mrs. J. P. McGlone to Father John J. Burke, C.S.C., September 13, 1945, "U.S.S. *Pennsylvania* Letters of Sympathy."

29. Letter from Alvena Olges to Father John J. Burke, C.S.C., September 4, 1945, "U.S.S. *Pennsylvania* Letters of Sympathy."

30. Letter from Father John J. Burke, C.S.C., to Angeline Ortbals, September 12, 1945, "U.S.S. *Pennsylvania* Letters of Sympathy."

31. Letter from Father John J. Burke, C.S.C., to Paul C. Roemer, October 30, 1945, "U.S.S. *Pennsylvania* Letters of Sympathy."

32. Letter from Burke to Ortbals, September 12, 1945; letter from Burke to Olges, September 12, 1945; letter from Father John J. Burke, C.S.C., to Mr. & Mrs. Thomas F. Quealy, September 12, 1945; letter from Father John J. Burke, C.S.C., to Mr. & Mrs. Paul Christopher Roemer, August 21, 1945, all in "U.S.S. *Pennsylvania* Letters of Sympathy."

33. Letter from Burke to Ortbals, September 12, 1945, "U.S.S. *Pennsylvania* Letters of Sympathy."

34. Letter from Burke to Steiner, October 3, 1945, Folder No. 11:07.

35. Letter from Ortbals to Burke, November 18, 1945, "U.S.S. *Pennsylvania* Letters of Sympathy."

36. Letter from Mr. & Mrs. J. P. McGlone to Father John J. Burke, C.S.C., October 22, 1945; letter from Mrs. Frank Daniels to Father John J. Burke, C.S.C., no date given, 1945, both in "U.S.S. *Pennsylvania* Letters of Sympathy."

TWELVE. "I Have Seen My Share of Blood, Death, Mud, Hunger and Cold"

1. Dorsett, *Serving God and Country*, 227.

2. Letter from Rev. John E. Duffy to Most Reverend Karl J. Alter, Mudken, Manchuria, August 23, 1945, in the Duffy Collection, "Duffy Correspondence."

3. Letter from Boland to Steiner, September 1, 1945, Folder No. 11:06.

4. Letter from Barry to Steiner, August 23, 1945, Folder No. 11:05; Father Barry's Monthly Reports to the Military Ordinariate, August 1945, Folder No. 11:05.

5. "Local Priest Modestly Returns as War Hero," *South Bend Tribune*, October 22, 1945.

6. Murr, *But Deliver Us From Evil*, 112; letter from Rev. John E. Duffy to Most Reverend Karl J. Alter, Mudken, Manchuria, October 15, 1945, in the Duffy Collection, "Duffy Correspondence"; letter from Rev. John E. Duffy to Most Reverend Karl J. Alter, D.D., September 14, 1945, in the Duffy Collection, "Primary Sources Folder."

7. Letters from Fitzgerald to Steiner, June 1945 and July 23, 1945, both in Folder No. 11:09.

8. Letter from Heintskill to Steiner, November 29, 1945; letter from Steiner to Heintskill, July 22, 1946, both in Folder No. 12:01.

9. Letter from Burke to Steiner, February 11, 1946, Folder No. 11:07.

10. Rev. Joseph A. Kehoe, C.S.C., "Holy Cross Military Chaplains in World War II," presented at the 1995 Conference on the History of the Congregations of Holy Cross, Holy Cross College, Notre Dame, IN, June 15–17, 1995.

11. Hennel, *Our Expedition to Manila*, 62.

12. Letter from Lawyer to Steiner, April 25, 1945, Folder No. 6:02, "'L' Correspondence 1943–1945."

13. Letter from Steiner to Lawyer, April 29, 1945, Folder No. 6:02, "'L' Correspondence 1943–1945."

14. Brother Raymond Papenfuss, C.S.C. "Eulogy for Brother Rex Hennel, C.S.C.," April 15, 2008, in the Archives, Congregation of Brothers of the Holy Cross, Holy Cross College, Notre Dame, IN.

15. Hennel, "A Prisoner of War Remembers."

16. Letter from McKee to Fitzpatrick, March 2, 1945, "Philippine POW's."

17. Olivette and Caecilius, "Round Trip to the Philippines," 27.

18. Letter from Sister Caecilius to her grandmother, March 26, 1945, "Internment in Manila 1941–1945"; letter from Sister Mary Olivette to Mary G., February 25, 1945; Olivette, "Reflections on the Experience of Being a Japanese War Prisoner," all in "Internment in Manila 1941–1945"; Anne Carey, "P.O.W. Nuns," *Catholic Heritage*, March–April 1999, 12.

19. "In Thanksgiving for Manila Rescue."

20. Letter from Rev. John E. Duffy to Most Reverend Karl J. Alter, D.D., June 12, 1946, in the Duffy Collection, "Primary Sources Folder."

21. Letter from Archbishop Karl J. Alter to Reverend John C. Sherbno, September 25, 1975, in the Duffy Collection, "Duffy Files #1."

22. Schmidt, "Priest, Now New London Pastor, Recalls Horrors of Death March."

23. Letter from Douglas MacArthur to Father John E. Duffy, February 23, 1958, *Japanese WWII POW Camp Fukuoka #17—Omuta* (2002), http://www .lindavdahl.com/Bio%20Pages/Father%20Duffy/MacArthur%20Letter.htm. Accessed December 21, 2017.

24. "Bishop Offers Mass in Carey for Fr. Duffy," no date, in the Duffy Collection, "Duffy Miscellaneous."

25. Letter from Brig. Gen. Luther D. Miller, Chief of Chaplains, to Rozella Soreghan (sister of Father Carberry), July 27, 1945; letter from Edward D. Howard, Archbishop of Portland in Oregon, to Rozella Soreghan, July 27, 1945, both found in J. A. O'Brien, "Family History; Family and Friends, 1872–2004," a collection of material about Richard Carberry gathered for family.

26. "St. Paul Parish—The First 100 Years," St. Paul Catholic Church, Silverton, OR (2017), http://stpaulsilverton.com/our-history/. Accessed December 21, 2017.

27. Dowd, "D-Day: Two Chaplains Remember," 12.

28. "The 501st Parachute Infantry Regiment: 501st Heroes," *U.S. Airborne During World War II,* http://www.ww2-airborne.us/units/501/501.html. Accessed December 21, 2017.

29. Peter S. Griffin, "Paratrooper Padre," in C. J. Magro, *Paratroopers of the 50's,* http://home.hiwaay.net/~magro/poemsww2.html. Accessed December 21, 2017. © Copyright Peter S. Griffin, *Paratroopers of the 50's*; reprinted with permission.

30. Simmons, "Let Us Now Praise Famous Men"; Father William Craddick, eulogy delivered for Father Joseph Barry, quoted in "Stories: Rev. Joseph C. Barry, CSC," at *45th Infantry Division* (2005), http://www.45th infantrydivision.com/index13.htm. Accessed December 21, 2017 (hereafter cited as Craddick eulogy).

31. "The Rev. Joseph Barry, Chaplain at Hoban High School 19 Years," *Akron Beacon Journal,* no date, in the Father Barry Personal Files, Holy Cross Archives, University of Notre Dame.

32. Craddick eulogy.

33. Craddick eulogy.

34. Cross, *Soldiers of God,* 182.

BIBLIOGRAPHY

COLLECTIONS

Holy Cross Archives, University of Notre Dame

A treasure of information, photographs, and correspondence rests in this indispensable archive. Files on each chaplain supplement the fascinating correspondence contained in the Rev. Thomas A. Steiner Collection. I happily spent days in the archives, scanning and reading the gripping letters that connected the chaplains with their superior back at Notre Dame. Some letters from the battle zones, such as those of Father Barry and Father Dupuis, move the reader with their insight into events and the soldiers, marines, or sailors they served. Especially helpful were:

Rev. Joseph D. Barry Personal Files
Father John J. Burke Personal Papers
Rev. Edward Fitzgerald Personal Files
Father Joseph M. Kmiecik, "Memoirs"
Rev. Robert McKee, "Holy Cross P.O.W.'s in the Philippines—1941–1945"
"Philippine POW's"
"Reverend Maurice Powers, World War II Chaplaincy, 1941–1945"
Rev. Thomas A. Steiner Collection
"World War II Interned C.S.C.'s, 1941–1945"

*Archives, Congregation of Brothers of the Holy Cross, Holy Cross College,
Notre Dame, Indiana*

This archive holds the records for the two Holy Cross brothers incarcerated by the Japanese. Especially helpful were:

Hennel, Brother Rex, C.S.C. *Our Expedition to Manila.* Privately published memoir, June 13, 1952.

Papenfuss, Brother Raymond, C.S.C. "Eulogy for Brother Rex Hennel, C.S.C." April 15, 2008.

Archives, Congregation of the Sisters of the Holy Cross, Notre Dame, Indiana

This archive holds the records of the two nuns incarcerated by the Japanese during the war. Most helpful were:

"Internment in Manila 1941–1945"

"Round Trip to the Philippines" (draft)

Olivette, Sister Mary. *Diary, 1941–1945*

———. "Reflections on the Experience of Being a Japanese War Prisoner in Los Baños during World War II" (found in "Internment in Manila 1941–1945")

University of Notre Dame Archives, Notre Dame, Indiana

The John F. O'Hara Collection contains correspondence with many of the chaplains, and files on and photographs of most of the chaplains are stored here. Especially pertinent were:

COHA 9/80: "Joseph Barry"

UDIS 39/24: "CSC Chaplains in World War II"

UDIS 133/13: "Barry, Rev. Joseph"

UWW2 1/08: "Letters from Servicemen F-T"

National Personnel Records Center, National Archives and Records Administration, St. Louis, MO:

This record center houses the official military files for army chaplains. Most helpful were:

Chaplain Joseph D. Barry File

Chaplain Richard E. Carberry File

Chaplain John E. Duffy File

Chaplain Francis L. Sampson File

U.S. Army Chaplain Corps Museum, Fort Jackson, South Carolina

This research center has files on many World War II chaplains, including information on Father Barry, Father Carberry, and helpful documents including:

"Reports of Father John E. Duffy Since the Fall of Batan [*sic*], April 1942 to April 1946."

J. A. O'Brien. "Family History; Family and Friends, 1872–2004." I was fortunate to locate this collection of writings about, letters to and from, and photographs of Father Carberry, as information on him had been difficult to find.

Father John E. Duffy Collection, Diocese of Toledo, Ohio Archives

This vast collection of the priest's voluminous writing and letters contains much of value about Father Duffy. Especially helpful were:
"Bishop Finneman"
"Duffy Correspondence"
"Duffy Files #1"
"Duffy Photo Album"
"Duffy Miscellaneous"
Philippine Memoir
"Primary Sources Folder"

INTERVIEWS

All interviews are with author unless otherwise noted.
"Reminiscences of Hanson Weightman Baldwin, U.S. Navy (Ret.)." Interviewed by John T. Mason. U.S. Naval Institute, Annapolis, MD, 1976.
Isaac Caudle, October 12, 2015: served with Father Barry
Rev. LeRoy Clementich, October 12, 2012: army clerk for Father Powers
Daniel Dougherty, March 2, 2015: served with Father Barry
Rev. Theodore Hesburgh, September 27, 2013: University of Notre Dame president who knew most of the chaplains
William Lyford, e-mail to author, February 26, 2015: served with Father Barry
Preston Niland, November 18, 2015: relative of Fritz Niland, whose brothers were killed or missing in action before Father Sampson helped arrange for his transfer from Normandy to the United States
William Nolan, October 3, 1991: on the Death March with Father Duffy
Ben Steele, June 9, 2015: in prison camp with Father John Duffy
Kenneth Stemmons, March 2, 2015: served with Father Barry
Vinnie Stigliani, April 27, 2015: served with Father Barry

BOOKS

Abraham, Abie. *Ghost of Bataan Speaks*. New York: Vantage, 1971.
Bando, Mark A. *Avenging Eagles*. Detroit, MI: Mark Bando Publishing, 2006.

Bergen, Doris L., ed. *The Sword of the Lord: Military Chaplains from the First to the Twenty-First Century.* Notre Dame, IN: University of Notre Dame Press, 2004.

Brereton, Lewis H. *The Brereton Diaries.* New York: William Morrow, 1946.

Buechner, Emajean Jordan. *Sparks.* Metairie, LA: Thunderbird Press, 1991.

Carlson, Lewis H. *We Were Each Other's Prisoners: An Oral History of World War II American and German Prisoners of War.* New York: Basic Books, 1997.

Carpenter, Alton Earl, and A. Anne Eiland. *Chappie: World War II Diary of a Combat Chaplain.* Mesa, AZ: Mead, 2007.

Cave, Dorothy. *God's Warrior: Father Albert Braun, OFM, 1889–1983.* Santa Fe, NM: Sunstone, 2011.

Chandler, Alfred D., Jr., ed. *The Papers of Dwight David Eisenhower: The War Years.* 5 vols. Baltimore, MD: Johns Hopkins, 1970.

Claypool, Captain James V. *God on a Battlewagon.* Philadelphia, PA: John C. Winston, 1944.

Cogan, Sister Mary de Paul. *Sisters of Maryknoll.* New York: Charles Scribner's Sons, 1947.

Costello, John. *The Pacific War.* New York: Rawson, Wade, 1981.

Crosby, Donald F., S.J. *Battlefield Chaplains: Catholic Priests in World War II.* Lawrence: University Press of Kansas, 1994.

Cross, Christopher. *Soldiers of God.* New York: E. P. Dutton, 1945.

Danner, Dorothy Still. *What a Way to Spend a War.* Annapolis, MD: Naval Institute Press, 1995.

Davies, Robert B. *Baldwin of the* Times. Annapolis, MD: Naval Institute Press, 2011.

DePastino, Todd. *Bill Mauldin: A Life Up Front.* New York: W. W. Norton, 2008.

D'Este, Carlo D. *Eisenhower: A Soldier's Life.* New York: Henry Holt, 2002.

———. *Patton: A Genius for War.* New York: HarperCollins, 1995.

Donnelly, Monsignor Thomas J. *"Hey Padre."* New York: 77th Division Association, 1986.

Dorsett, Lyle W. *Serving God and Country: U.S. Military Chaplains in World War II.* New York: Berkley Caliber, 2012.

Dyess, Lt. Col. William E. *The Dyess Story.* New York: G. P. Putnam's Sons, 1944.

Eisenhower, Dwight D. *Crusade in Europe.* Garden City, NY: Doubleday, 1950.

Eisenhower, John S. D. *General Ike: A Personal Reminiscence.* New York: Free Press, 2003.

Feuer, A. B., ed. *Bilibid Diary: The Secret Notebooks of Commander Thomas Hayes, POW, the Philippines, 1942–1945.* Hamden, CT: Archon Books, 1987.

Flanagan, Lt. Gen. E. M., Jr. *Angels at Dawn.* Novato, CA: Presidio Press, 1999.

Franklin, Maj. Steven C. *Blackjacks at War: WWII & the 53rd Troop Carrier Squadron*. Maxwell Air Force Base, AL: Air Command and Staff College, Air University, 2002.

Grant, Dorothy Fremont. *War Is My Parish*. Milwaukee, WI: Bruce Publishing, 1944.

Gushwa, Robert L. *The Best and Worst of Times: The United States Army Chaplaincy 1920–1945*. Washington, DC: Office of the Chief of Chaplains, Department of the Army, 1977.

Hallowell, Jack, et al. *Eager for Duty: History of the 157th Infantry Regiment (Rifle)*. Baton Rouge, LA: Army & Navy Publishing, 1946.

Hersey, John. *Men on Bataan*. New York: Alfred A. Knopf, 1942.

Hesburgh, Theodore M., C.S.C., with Jerry Reedy. *God, Country, Notre Dame*. New York: Doubleday, 1990.

Holmes, Linda Goetz. *Unjust Enrichment: How Japan's Companies Built Postwar Fortunes Using American POWs*. Mechanicsburg, PA: Stackpole, 2001.

Honeywell, Roy J. *Chaplains of the United States Army*. Washington, DC: Office of the Chief of Chaplains, Department of the Army, 1958.

Hunt, Ray C., and Bernard Norling. *Behind Japanese Lines: An American Guerrilla in the Philippines*. Lexington: University Press of Kentucky, 1986.

Keith, Billy. *Days of Anguish, Days of Hope*. Garden City, NY: Doubleday, 1972.

Kerr, E. Bartlett. *Surrender and Survival: The Experience of American POWs in the Pacific, 1941–1945*. New York: William Morrow, 1985.

Kershaw, Alex. *The Liberator*. New York: Crown, 2012.

Knox, Donald. *Death March*. New York: Harcourt Brace Jovanovich, 1981.

Koskimaki, George E. *The Battered Bastards of Bastogne*. Havertown, PA: Casemate, 2003.

———. *D-Day with the Screaming Eagles*. Havertown, PA: Casemate, 2002.

———. *Hell's Highway*. Havertown, PA: Casemate, 2003.

Lukacs, John D. *Escape from Davao*. New York: Simon & Schuster, 2010.

Maguire, Fleet Chaplain William A. *The Captain Wears a Cross*. New York: Macmillan, 1943.

———. *Rig for Church*. New York: Macmillan, 1942.

Malarkey, Sgt. Don, with Bob Welch. *Easy Company Soldier*. New York: St. Martin's, 2008.

Mauldin, Bill. *Up Front*. New York: Henry Holt, 1945.

McAvoy, Thomas T., C.S.C. *Father O'Hara of Notre Dame*. Notre Dame, IN: University of Notre Dame Press, 1967.

McCoy, Cmdr. Melvyn H., and Lt. Col. S. M. Mellnik. *Ten Escape from Tojo*. New York: Farrar & Rinehart, 1944.

McMillan, George, C. Peter Zurlinden Jr., Alvin M. Josephy Jr., David Dempsey, Keyes Beech, and Herman Kogan. *Uncommon Valor: Marine Divisions in Action*. Nashville, TN: Battery, 1986.

Michno, Gregory F. *Death on the Hellships*. Annapolis, MD: Naval Institute Press, 2001.

Moisan, Melaney Welch. *Tracking the 101st Cavalry*. Keizer, OR: Wheat Field Press, 2008.

Morton, Louis. *United States Army in World War II: The War in the Pacific, the Fall of the Philippines*. Washington, DC: Center of Military History, 1989.

Murr, Dan. *But Deliver Us From Evil*. Jacksonville, FL: Stanton & Samuel, 2007.

Nance, Elwood C. *Faith of Our Fighters*. St. Louis, MO: Bethany, 1944.

Norman, Elizabeth M. *We Band of Angels: The Untold Story of American Nurses Trapped on Bataan by the Japanese*. New York: Random House, 1999.

Norman, Michael, and Elizabeth M. *Tears in the Darkness*. New York: Farrar, Straus and Giroux, 2009.

Norton-Taylor, Duncan. *With My Heart in My Mouth*. New York: Coward-McCann, 1944.

Olivette, Sister M., and Sister M. Caecilius, C.S.C. "Round Trip to the Philippines." In *Fruits of the Tree: Sesquicentennial Chronicles, Sisters of the Holy Cross*, 1:7–27. Notre Dame, IN: Ave Maria Press, 1991.

Robinson, Sergeant Don. *News of the 45th*. New York: Grosset & Dunlap, 1944.

Sampson, Chaplain Francis L. *Look Out Below!* Sweetwater, TN: 101st Airborne Division Association, 1989.

Schneider, Msgr. Alfred A., with Kaye Sizer and James L. Alt. *My Brother's Keeper*. Green Bay, WI: Alt Publishing, 1981.

Schultz, Duane. *Hero of Bataan: The Story of General Jonathan M. Wainwright*. New York: St. Martin's, 1981.

Sherrod, Robert. *Tarawa*. New York: Duell, Sloan and Pearce, 1944.

Smith, Walter Bedell. *Eisenhower's Six Great Decisions*. New York: Longmans, Green, 1956.

Spector, Ronald H. *Eagle Against the Sun*. New York: Free Press, 1985.

Spellman, Francis J. *No Greater Love*. New York: Charles Scribner's Sons, 1945.

Spiller, Harry. *Prisoners of Nazis: Accounts by American POWs in World War II*. Jefferson, NC: McFarland, 1998.

Stroup, Russell Cartwright. *Letters from the Pacific: A Combat Chaplain in World War II*. Columbia: University of Missouri Press, 2000.

Taggart, Chaplain William C., and Christopher Cross. *My Fighting Congregation*. Garden City, NY: Doubleday, Doran, 1943.

Toland, John. *But Not in Shame*. New York: Random House, 1961.

———. *The Last 100 Days*. New York: Random House, 1965.

Tower, Hansel H. *Fighting the Devil with the Marines*. Philadelphia, PA: Dorrance, 1945.

U.S. Army. *Ever First!: The 53rd Troop Carrier Wing*. Orientation Branch, Information and Education Division, European Theater of Operations.

Paris: printed by Desfosses-Neogravure, 1945. http://www.lonesentry.com
/gi_stories_booklets/53rdtroopcarrier/. Accessed December 26, 2017.

U.S.S. *Admiral E. W. Eberle* (AP-123) War Diary, April–May 1945. National
Archives. Accessed at www.fold3.com.

U.S.S. *Pennsylvania* (BB-38) *Summary of War Service*. National Archives. Accessed at www.fold3.com.

Wainwright, General Jonathan M. *General Wainwright's Story*. Edited by Robert Considine. Garden City, NY: Doubleday, 1946.

Weinstein, Alfred A. *Barbed-Wire Surgeon*. Atlanta, GA: Deeds, 1975.

Whitlock, Flint. *The Rock of Anzio*. Boulder, CO: Westview, 1998.

Wheeler, Richard. *A Special Valor: The U.S. Marines and the Pacific War*. New
York: New American Library, 1983.

Willard, W. Wyeth. *The Leathernecks Come Through*. New York: Fleming
H. Revell, 1944.

Wuest, Karl. *They Told It to the Chaplain*. New York: Vantage, 1953.

Zimmerman, Leslie F. Diary. Unpublished manuscript. United States Air
Force Research Agency, donated December 1989.

ARTICLES

"A 45th Fighter: Father Joseph Barry, C.S.C." *45th Division News*, n.d.

"The 501st Parachute Infantry Regiment." *U.S. Airborne During World War II.*
http://www.ww2-airborne.us/units/501/501.html. Accessed December 21,
2017.

Barrett, Bill. "45th Record: 511 Days of Fighting." *45th Division News*, n.d.
(early May 1945), 2.

———. "Dachau Gives Answer to Why We Fought." *45th Division News*,
May 13, 1945.

———. "Sinatra Honored, Adolf Loses Out." *45th Division News*, May 13,
1945, 1.

Boyce, David. "Veteran Was Prisoner of War in Germany." *Menlo Park (CA)
Almanac*, November 21, 2001. http://www.almanacnews.com/morgue
/2001/2001_11_21.salome14.html.

"Capt. Joseph D. Barry Awarded Silver Star." *Syracuse Herald-Journal*, August 30, 1944.

Carey, Anne. "P.O.W. Nuns." *Catholic Heritage*, March–April 1999, 12–14.

Carroll, James T. "Sentenced to Death—Destined for Life: Catholic Religious
and Japanese Occupation." *American Catholic Studies* (Fall–Winter 2002):
57–73.

"Chaplain Barry Wins Silver Star for Bravery in Italy." *South Bend Tribune*,
September 5, 1944.

"Chaplain Carberry Wins Citations for Bravery in Bataan." *Rockford (IL) Observer*, July 5, 1942.

Craddick, Fr. William. Eulogy for Father Joseph Barry. Quoted in "Stories: Rev. Joseph C. Barry, CSC," at *45th Infantry Division* (2005), http://www.45thinfantrydivision.com/index13.htm. Accessed December 21, 2017.

"Congress Shocked by Report on German Horror Camps." *Washington Post*, May 16, 1945, 4.

"Dachau Captured by Americans Who Kill Guards, Liberate 32,000." *New York Times*, May 1, 1945, 1, 5.

Donohue, Robert. "Stories: Robert E. Donohue, Company E, 157th Infantry Regiment, 45th Division." *45th Infantry Division* (n.d.). http://www.45thinfantrydivision.com/index13.htm. Accessed December 21, 2017.

Dougherty, Dan P., ed. *Second Platoon*. September 1999, 1.

"D-Day Remembered by Two Hoosiers." *Elkhart (IN) Truth*, June 5, 1984.

Dowd, Richard. "D-Day: Two Chaplains Remember." *Visitor*, June 3, 1984, 3, 12.

"Famous Army Chaplain Returns to Notre Dame." *Register* (Duluth, MN), January 26, 1947.

"Father Barry Will Join Army on Saturday." *South Bend Tribune*, April 1, 1941.

"Father Duffy of Bataan." *New York Times*, February 8, 1942.

Ficco, Daniel A. "Sneaking into a Prison Camp." *Second Platoon*, February 1999, 8.

"Foe's Manila Garrison Wiped Out." *New York Times*, February 25, 1945.

Forney, Pauline Peyton. "Holy Cross Missionaries Return from Philippines." *Holy Cross Courier*, August 1945.

Fraze, Barb. "Army Chaplain Still Remembers D-Day." *Catholic Messenger*, June 14, 1984.

"Frontline Padre." *Michigan Catholic*, February 13, 1947.

Gregg, Ray. "Anxious Eyes of Liberated Thank 'Rescuer' Atop Dome." *South Bend Tribune*, n.d., 1945.

Griffin, Father Robert F., C.S.C. "Remembering the Past: Monsignor the General." *Visitor*, March 1, 1987.

Griffin, Peter S. "Paratrooper Padre." Reprinted at C. J. Magro, *Paratroopers of the 50's*. http://home.hiwaay.net/~magro/poemsww2.html.

Hafstrom, Pearl E. "Yank 'Angels' End over Three Years of Captivity." *South Bend Tribune*, May 24, 1945.

Hailey, Foster. "Escape from a Man-Made Hell." *New York Times*, April 16, 1944.

Hennel, Brother Rex, C.S.C. "A Letter for Associates." *Associate of Saint Joseph*, October–December 1945.

"Home Truths." *People*, September 7, 1998.

"In Thanksgiving for Manila Rescue." *University of Notre Dame Religious Bulletin*, April 18, 1945.

Jacoby, Melville. "Chaplains in Bataan," *Time*, February 23, 1942, 54.

Jones, George E. "Hungry Prisoners Soon Fed in Luzon." *New York Times*, February 26, 1945.

Kehoe, Rev. Joseph A., C.S.C. "Holy Cross Military Chaplains in World War II." Presented at the 1995 Conference on the History of the Congregations of Holy Cross, Holy Cross College, Notre Dame, Indiana, June 15–17, 1995.

Kennedy, Edward. "Allis Seek Junction, Start Drive on Cassino." *Washington Post*, February 10, 1944, 1–2.

———. "Battle of Italy Settles Down to Apparent Stalemate." *Washington Post*, January 31, 1944, 1–2.

———. "Yanks Gain 2 Miles Near Beachhead, Stalled at Cassino." *Washington Post*, February 21, 1944, 1, 6.

Lee, John P. "Action at the Coal Yard Wall." *Second Platoon*, April 2001, 2.

"Local Priest Modestly Returns as War Hero." *South Bend Tribune*, October 22, 1945.

Loftus, Josephine. "The Rosary Wins in Manila." *Maryknoll*, July–August 1945.

Lowrie, Katharine Blossom. "Veteran Remembers Battle of the Bulge." *Redondo Beach Patch*, May 28, 2012. http://patch.com/california/redondo beach/redondo-beach-veteran-survived-the-battle-of-the-budge.

MacArthur, Douglas. Letter to Father John E. Duffy, February 23, 1958. *Japanese WWII POW Camp Fukuoka #17—Omuta* (2002). http://www.lindav dahl.com/Bio%20Pages/Father%20Duffy/MacArthur%20Letter.htm.

McCarthy, Francis. "Raid Rescues 2,146 from Luzon Camp." *New York Times*, February 25, 1945.

McCarthy, William R., M.M. "The Angels Came at Seven." Reprint of an article appearing in *Columbia*, April 1950, 3–14.

McKee, R., C.S.C. "We Were Rescued from Los Banos!" *Bengalese*, May 1945, 6–7, 21.

"Noted 'Padre' Barry Back at Notre Dame." *Chicago New World*, January 24, 1947.

"Notre Dame Man Rescues Notre Dame Men." *University of Notre Dame Religious Bulletin*, April 10, 1945.

Olson, Sidney. "Dachau," *Time*, May 7, 1945, 34.

Panebianco, Albert R. "Pictures." *45th Infantry Division* (2005). http://www .45thinfantrydivision.com/index12.htm. Accessed December 21, 2017.

"Prisoners Rescued in the Philippines." *New York Times*, February 25, 1945.

"The Rev. Joseph Barry, Chaplain at Hoban High School 19 Years." *Akron Beacon Journal*, n.d.

Riordan, Thomas. "Stories: World War II Memories of Tom Riordan." *45th Infantry Division* (2000). http://www.45thinfantrydivision.com/index13 .htm. Accessed December 21, 2017.

Schmidt, J. K. "Priest, Now New London Pastor, Recalls Horrors of Death March." *Cleveland Plain Dealer*, July 27, 1947.

Schubert, Paul. "Kwajalein and Anzio." *Washington Post*, February 14, 1944, 10.

Simmons, Father William, C.S.C. "Let Us Now Praise Famous Men." *Hoban Highlights*, Summer 2001.

Simmons, Walter. "Boy Who Fled Los Banos Camp Rejoins Father." *Chicago Tribune*, February 27, 1945.

"Six N. D. Men Freed by Seventh; Lt. John Finneran, '33, Helps in Rescue at Los Banos Camp in the Philippines." *Notre Dame Alumnus*, April 1945, 12.

Trumbull, Robert. "Dawn Strike Made." *New York Times*, August 13, 1945.

Twitchell, Tom. "C Company: So Few Came Back Alive." *Sandusky (OH) Register*, April 8, 1979.

"War Chaplain Returns to Notre Dame University." *Boston Pilot*, January 25, 1947.

INDEX

McKee, Father Robert (Holy Cross
    missionary)
  Christmas 1944 in Los Baños, 194–95
  conditions at Los Baños, 105–7, 108,
    110, 111, 112, 118–19, 170, 190–92,
    230–34
  correspondence with home, 76–77,
    103, 119, 242
  following rescue, 240–45
  home front concern for, 73–74
  impact of the war on, 312
  initial lenient treatment of, 26, 75,
    101–2
  journey to the Philippines, 14–16
  maintaining morale at Los Baños,
    118–19, 190–92, 194–95
  moved to Los Baños, 103–5
  as prisoner at the Ateneo, 26, 38, 74,
    75, 101–2
  rescued from Los Baños, 234–40
  returning home, 245–46
  starvation diet at Los Baños, 107,
    108, 110, 111, 112, 191, 232
  stranded in Manila, 19–21, 23–26, 33
  taken prisoner, 25–26, 38
McManus, Father Frank, 249
Men on Bataan (Hersey), 29
Midway, Battle of, 70, 169
military (U.S.)
  history of chaplaincy in, 40
  Native American soldiers in, 47
  need for chaplains in, 41, 67–68
  training for chaplains in, 44–47
  See also specific units
Military Ordinariate, 41, 44, 67–68, 146
Miller, Luther D., 315
missionaries (Holy Cross), 327
  Christmas 1944 in Los Baños,
    194–96
  conditions at Los Baños, 105–7, 108,
    110, 111, 112, 118–19, 170, 190–92,
    230–34
  correspondence with home, 76–77,
    102–3, 119, 242–43

following rescue, 240–45
home front concern for, 73–74, 102–3
impacts of war on, 243, 244, 312–13
initial lenient treatment of, 26, 74–76,
    101–2
journey to the Philippines, 13–16
maintaining morale in Los Baños,
    118–19, 190–92, 194–96
moved to Los Baños, 103–5
as prisoners in Manila, 26, 31, 38,
    73–77, 101–3
radios of, 31, 74, 75–76, 231
rescued from Los Baños, 234–40
returning home, 245–48
starvation diet at Los Baños, 107,
    108, 110, 111, 191, 232
stranded in Manila, 19–21, 23–26, 33,
    38
taken prisoner, 25–26, 38
Missionary Sisters of St. Dominic
    (Philippines), 69–70
Monte Cassino monastery (Italy), 125,
    126
Montgomery, Bernard Law, 86, 88–90,
    94, 202, 204
Mooney, Father Vincent, 42, 322
Moosberg prison camp (German), 272
Mori, Shigeji (Japanese camp com-
    mander), 107, 110, 113, 116–17,
    118
Moses, W. M., 296
M.S. *Gripsholm* (Swedish transport), 76
Murray, Father Edmund J., 322
  awarded the Bronze Star, 273
  in France and Belgium, 216
  in Germany, 253, 258–60, 272–73
  on home front celebrations, 260
Mussell, Paul, 259

Naha (Okinawa), 287–90
Namur Island (Marshall Islands),
    172–75
National Naval Medical Center
    (Bethesda, Maryland), 291–92

JOHN WUKOVITS is a military historian specializing in the Pacific theater of World War II. He is the author of many books, including *Tin Can Titans*, *Hell from the Heavens*, *For Crew and Country*, *One Square Mile of Hell*, and *Pacific Alamo*. He has also written numerous articles for such publications as *WWII History*, *Naval History*, and *World War II*. He lives in Michigan.